RESPECT

Bob L. VandeLinde

Trafford
PUBLISHING® www.trafford.com
North America & international
toll-free: 1 888 232 4444 (USA & Canada)
fax: 812 355 4082

CONTENTS

INTRODUCTION

When the Japanese bombed Pearl Harbor on December 7, 1941, I was a few days shy of becoming twelve-years old. I was too young to realize the true impact of America entering a war that would not end until August 14, 1945 when the Japanese surrendered unconditionally. During World War II, over sixteen million Americans served in the military; 408,306 died and another 670,846 were wounded. All of a sudden young boys from my home county, Lincoln County, West Virginia, as other counties throughout the nation, started hugging and telling their families goodbye. I had seen men like my uncle Macel VandeLinde who served with General Patton in Europe for over three years, and another uncle, Boyd McMellon who served in New Guinea, leave their homes for places unfamiliar and putting their lives on the line for freedom. All the high school and college athletes that I had such high respect for were suddenly in the service preparing to fight in a war that seemed to be a lifetime away.

During the war, I can remember everyone on the home front doing their part. We would save our old newspapers, bundle them up, and take them to Huntington. We collected scrap metal, rubber, toothpaste, metal foil from gum wrappers and cigarette packs. A melted down lawn mower could make six artillery shells; and an iron could make thirty hand grenades. They removed the green from the Lucky Strike cigarettes creating the slogan "Lucky Strike green has gone to war." My father had a large "victory" garden as did millions of other Americans. He raised cattle on the farm for meat because meat, coffee, tea, butter and cooking oil were rationed. I worked at the local drug store and was only allowed to sell cigarettes to certain customers. The generation of today, have not had to sacrifice like the people during World War II.

When these soldiers, sailors and Marines came home on furlough, I looked at them with a great deal of admiration and curiosity. In what part of the world would they serve? Would they be killed or wounded? These were some of the questions that entered my mind. In Lincoln County, there were two local newspapers. One was called the *Lincoln Democrat*, the other, the *Lincoln Republican.* Out of fascination for the men serving in the military, I began cutting out newspaper articles and keeping a scrapbook. For example, on March 10, 1943 the paper recorded, "Charles Yeager Gets Wings Today" and commissioned a second lieutenant. This wasn't such a big deal then, because other local men became pilots and officers. Little did anyone know at the time that Yeager would become an "ace" in Europe and later a national and international hero? Yeager was the first to break the sound barrier in the Bell X-1 Rocket Plane on October 14, 1947. With only a high school diploma, Yeager later became a major general.

I would see a sharply dressed soldier like Jakie Meadows, a paratrooper on leave. Jakie's trousers were bloused, which was a trait of someone serving in the airborne. His boots were highly spit-shined. He wore silver wings on his chest with pride and his hat displayed an airborne patch. I thought, this is the sharpest soldier I had ever seen. Little did I know that I would become a paratrooper myself one day? I served our country fighting the Communists in Korea in 1950-1951. I saved clippings from my neighbor and best friend, Homer "Drummer" Hager, Jr. Drummer served in the 4th Marine Division in the Pacific and was wounded three times. Each paper recorded other events such as weddings, births, those wounded or killed in action. I suppose you could say that I became obsessed with the men and women serving our country. Several county men became prisoners of war (POW). For example, three men, Okey Pack, Sherrill Brookover and James

Edwards served three and one half years in a Japanese prison camp. They were fighting in the Philippines when the American forces were forced to surrender on April 9, 1942 at Bataan. The Death March had begun. Many others from my home county were captured by the Germans. The paper also recorded the death of Maywood Edwards, a marine who was killed during the battle on Iwo Jima. These men paid dearly for our freedom. We can never repay them for their sacrifices. I wrote about these men in my last book, *"A Tribute to Lincoln County Veterans."*

In *Respect,* I am sharing the experiences of ordinary men and women, who as proud-patriotic Americans accomplished their mission. I have conducted 47 interviews, in person, by tape, written and by telephone. This has required traveling in several locations throughout Virginia and West Virginia. However, I have written about veterans as far away as Texas, Florida, Pennsylvania, Arkansas, Mississippi, North Carolina and Georgia.

Stories which you will find interesting yet troubling include an army flight nurse, Evelyn Kowalchuk who tells of a wounded soldier whose jaws were wired together, with scissors tied on a sting around his neck to cut the wire should the patient become nauseated; or Frank Kaiser, a prisoner of war in Korea for 33 months, when captured at the *Chosin Reservoir*. When asked if he ever tried to escape, Frank said, "Let's face it. We could walk out of the camp anytime we wanted to. I'm 6 feet 4 inches tall, blond hair and blue eyes…and I'm going to walk out of there where people are about 5 foot tall, black hair, slanted eyes, and dark skin." A 13 year old Dutch girl, Tina Bower, survived the Nazi occupation, living in fear for five years; or William Story, a member of *"The Force"* who was called the black devils by the Germans. Members of The Force would roam through the German lines killing or capturing the enemy.

I retired from the Woodmen of the World Life Insurance Society, Omaha, Nebraska after 38 years of service. Writing has

---

become a new passion for me. My first book was my life story written especially for my grandchildren. The title was, *What You See Is Not What You Get* because someday, they might gain some wisdom seeing the world through my eyes. In the interest of keeping family heritage alive, I wanted to share with them my days as a boy growing up in Hamlin, West Virginia. I also wanted to share with them my athletic achievements, my military life and my business career.

At the present time, I live in Moneta, Virginia (Smith Mountain Lake). One of the activities that I am involved in is being a volunteer at the D-Day Memorial located at Bedford, Virginia. I have been fortunate to interview several men for this book who are D-Day Veterans, landing on *Omaha* or *Utah Beach* on June 6, 1944. I try to do tours at the Memorial every week. This brings me a lot of pleasure, not only a means of giving back but meeting wonderful people from all over the world.

World War II veterans are dying at such a fast rate that I wanted to preserve these stories for future generations. It was my honor in November 2005 to put together a special Veterans Day Program, sponsored by the Golden Agers from the Halesford Baptist Church. The program honored several local heroes living at Smith Mountain Lake. We honored several people like Paul Suter who survived Pearl Harbor, Normandy, and the Battle of the Bulge, William Colls, a survivor of the Bataan Death march, and was a prisoner of war for 42 months. Jim Bryant, a member of the 82nd Airborne who landed in Normandy and Holland in a glider, was wounded in the Battle of the Bulge. We honored a US Army Flight Nurse, Evelyn Kowalchuk, who landed in Normandy D-Day + 3 to care for the wounded. LTC Darrell Hodges served in Afghanistan; Ray Haymaker was a P-47 pilot, and Roy Stevens was one of the original "Bedford Boys."

The thought occurred to me, if these heroes and others share with me their personal stories, this would be the basis for a new book. It would perhaps be their last chance to have their experiences told for future generations. There are many definitions for the word *hero*. The *Webster Dictionary* describes a hero in these words, "Any person, esp. a man, admired for courage, nobility, or exploits, esp. in war." The *American College Dictionary* defines hero as, "A man of distinguished valor or performance, admired for his noble qualities." The purpose of this book is to share stories about ordinary men and women who through circumstances beyond their control were put into situations that made them special. Each person rose to the occasion and preformed his or her duties with pride, dedication and loyalty to America.

When asked if I planned to write another book, my answer was always "no." I was attending a convention at Myrtle Beach, SC, in 2006 when a retired lawyer friend and a Korean veteran, James Bosler from Louisville, KY asked me if I planned to write another book. I gave him the same answer, however his encouragement triggered my ego and the thought began to haunt me. After all, at the age of 76, at that time, now age 78, I asked myself, do I have it in me to dedicate myself to another three years of traveling, interviewing and personal sacrifice to write another book?

Of course the first person that I consulted about writing this book was my wife Jean. We had been partners for 55 years, so naturally her feelings and advice are extremely important to me. Jean was not in favor of my writing another book for a couple of reasons: first, because of the amount of time that writing and research it takes. Secondly, she says that when writing my last book, I would get moody, lose my positive attitude and fun ways, as well as at times become depressed. All of these reasons are true and justified. I guess that I just have a burning desire to write about some of our forgotten heroes who have served their country honorably and with great sacrifice. Their stories need to be told and read about by our younger generation who really take freedom for granted, and as the famous saying goes, freedom is not free.

Jean knowing my passion to honor these veterans softened up a bit after I plead my case. My next avenue to approach was to pray earnestly and sincerely to my Jesus, asking Him to guide me and even give me a sign if I was doing the right thing. Then one day in a daily devotion from Dr. David Jeremiah, I received my answer. Let me share some of that devotion with you. In Psalms 90:12, the Bible says, **"So teach us to number our days that we may gain a heart of wisdom."** "Instead of 65 being presumed age for retirement, it ought to be seen as the age when a lifetime of learning is focused on new achievement. The fact is, the older we get, the more accumulated wisdom and perspective we should have to bring to bear on new goals. Age is a small part of growing old, but attitude is the largest. So instead of counting the days, make the days count." I intend to make my days count.

Having the opportunity to meet and interview the men and women for this book has been a blessing and an honor. Some have never talked about their military service even to their families until now. Their experiences have been too painful and were pushed back into their memory bank for many years. But now, we must appreciate their willingness to share, and not let their stories go untold.

SFC Bob VandeLinde. Picture taken at Tague, Korea 1951

Decorations: Purple Heart, Combat Infantry Badge, Korean Presidential Citation, Two Presidential Citations, Navy/Marine Citation, Korean Service Medal w/4 combat stars & 1 Arrow Head, Korean War Service Medal, Good Conduct Medal, United Nations Service Medal, National Defense Service Medal, Army of Occupation Medal, Airborne Wings w/2 stars, Glider Wings.

X

To the heroes in this book who served in obedience to duty.

ACKNOWLEDGMENTS

When writing a book, the author, certainly true in my particular case, needs the help, cooperation, talents and inspiration from many people. My wife, Jean, has certainly exercised her patience time and time again. She has been wonderful. Thanks Jean.

To get started it was necessary for me to purchase a new computer. Two people assisted me in researching what would be best; they helped me to order and install a new Dell computer. My special thanks to Larry Vass and Bob Jackson. Thanks for giving of your personal time, using your knowledge and computer skills to keep me straight and on track throughout this process. It wasn't easy.

I cannot adequately express my appreciation to all the wonderful men and women whom I have had the privilege to interview, and gave me permission to share their experiences. The book would not have been possible without your cooperation. I humbly say "thank you." You are truly heroes.

Jennifer L. Williams, a graphics designer for the National D-Day Memorial in Bedford, Virginia used her super talents to design the cover for *Respect*. Thanks Jennifer.

My gratitude to Colonel Richard Cairns, RET, for providing me with the information about JAG officers who served during World War II. Colonel Cairns served his country as a JAG officer in the US Army.

Special thanks to Bob Jackson who put the final touches to prepare the book for the publisher. His skills were invaluable.

ABBREVIATIONS

ARCT	Airborne Regimental Combat Team
BAR	Browning Automatic Rifle
CIB	Combat Infantry Badge
CP	command post
D-Day	the day that the battle begins
DZ	drop zone
FSSF	first special service force
G-1	personnel officer
G-2	intelligence officer
G-3	operations officer
H-Hour	the hour the battle begins
KIA	killed in action
LZ	landing zone
NPKA	North Korean People's Army
LCVP	landing craft vehicle personnel
Pfc.	private first class
ROK	Republic of Korea [South Korea]
R&R	rest and recuperation
SHAEF	Supreme Headquarters Allied Expeditionary Force
UN	United Nations
WIA	wounded in action

Personal or Tape Interviews

Cary Jarvis
Charles Boss
Don Gibson
Evelyn Kowalchuk
Felice Nappi
Frank Kaiser
Frank Tucker
George Hess
Hershel "Woody" Williams
J. Shelton Scales, Col.
Jahue Mundy
Jackie Lithgow
James DeLong
James Swanson Rigney
James Vickers
Jim Bryant
John Fowler
Marie Philippi Bower
Paul Suter
Raymond Haymaker
Richard "Dick" Still
Robert "Cal" Moore
Fred Toothman
Robert Torrence
Tommy Harbour
Warren Tuck
Wesley Dixon
William Ondo
William Story

Written and telephone Interviews

Arthur Lee
Bill Goodwin
Claude Grinslade
Bill Leonard
Eduardo Peniche
Ed Mull
Evelyn Kowalchuk
Everett Still, Capt.
Felice Nappi
Jean McCrady
John Singleton III
Luther Reems
Mary Boyles
Paul Suter
Robert Gonzales, Col.
Sedric Wirt
TOOTHMAN
Fred
Glenn
James
Melvin Lee

Bibliography

Books
The Army Nurse book
First Special Force by Robert D. Burhans
Flying Coffins over Europe, by Jim Bryant
Wikipedia, the free encyclopedia

Newspapers
Calgary Sun
Martinsville Bulletin
Montreal Standard
News & Advance Newspaper-Lynchburg
The Oregonian.
River Oaks Examiner
The Smith Mountain Eagle
Washington Post

Periodicals
African American Odyssey
CBIVA Sound Off Magazine
CVCC (Central Virginia Community College) Magazine
Friends Journal
Higgins Boats, WWII by Jerry Estraham
Koje Doby
National WWII Glider Pilots Association
Sixth Marine Division
Soldiers of the Law (JAG) by Col. Robert F. Gonzales
US Marines Special Units of WWII-Reprint

Pictures furnished by:
Tina Bower
Jim Bryant
Tommy Harbour
George Hess
Frank Kaiser
Robert Murin
Press Association
Swanson Rigney
US Air Force
US Marine Corps
Hershel "Woody" Williams

CHAPTER ONE

THE FOUR TOOTHMAN BROTHERS

JAMES STERLING TOOTHMAN was the oldest child of Glenn R. and Elsie Rees Toothman. He was born in Edwardsville, Illinois on November 3, 1915. James saw action at the battles of Coral Sea and Midway on the battleship *Yorktown*. He said, *"Around noon, Japanese dive bombers scored two hits. After the torpedo hit, about 3:30 in the afternoon and suddenly the ship's bull horn boomed out 'Abandon Ship'."There were almost 3,000 men aboard. I started swimming toward the nearest destroyer."*

This is a story of the experiences of four brothers, who from humble circumstances, became commissioned officers in three branches of the armed forces of the United States, and served in combat zones in the World's greatest war, World War II. After the war, like millions of discharged men and women, the Toothman brothers used the G.I. Bill to further their education. James became a professor at Penn State University; Fred, who had graduated as an Engineer, received his Masters Degree; Glenn, completed Law School and served as a Judge for many years; and Lee completed his education and became a dentist. Lee also served in Korea during the war.

FRED REES TOOTHMAN. Fred was born two weeks before the Armistice was signed in World War I, on October 26, 1918, in the small coal mining town of Erie, West Virginia, six miles north of Clarksburg. Fred was the captain of the football team at Victory High School in Clarksburg in 1935 when they won the state championship. He played center. In 1941, Fred graduated from West Virginia University in Morgantown with a degree in Mining Engineering.

GLENN TOOTHMAN, JR. was attending Hampden-Sydney College in Virginia on December 7, 1941. Glenn said, "Needless to say, the immediacy and shock of this event struck me with a sharp sadness. My little world of college exams and college dreams was invaded the same as the bombs that sank the battleships at that famous mid island Naval Harbor did to the nation." He joined the Marines.

MELVIN LEE TOOTHMAN was the fourth child born to Glenn and Elsie Toothman. When Lee was born, the family was living in the hamlet of Hepziban which was six miles north of Clarksburg, West Virginia. He entered the Army Air Force in the middle of his junior year in college, and eventually became a B-24 pilot and flew 26 missions over Germany as a member of the 707 Sqdn. of the 446 Bomb Group. With the urging and influence from their brother Fred Toothman, each brother wrote his own story for the benefit of the Toothman family. This is a remarkable family, all well educated and whose accomplishments are many. I visited personally with Fred in his West Virginia home. The following stories are a review of their experiences in their own words.

JAMES S. TOOTHMAN
Lieut. Comdr. USNR, Ret.

I think it will be apparent to readers of these wartime recollections that there were early home influences strengthening the character and motivation in the four young men involved. The contribution of our parents and the tone of home life instilled desirable traits guiding our lifelong behavior. Father and Mother were graduates of the Fairmont Norman College in Fairmont, West Virginia and devout Presbyterians. Our father, though raised as an only child without a related large family paternal role model, had a remarkable, even tempered commitment to his children's development of abilities and accomplishment. He had considerable musical talent, played the piano and sang semi-professionally. Our mother instilled high self-esteem and ambition. We sensed that we were the recipients of more parental attention than our playmates and classmates. Our parents were mutually supportive in all of our endeavors.

In the early years of the Depression there was no unemployment compensation, no social security and no formal government welfare program. Many counties in Northern states had a long history of operating county poor houses and county poor farms. These were refuges, along with state asylums, for the elderly, poor, and mentally or physically disabled. The care of most elderly up to this point in time was, as it has been in all agricultural societies, the responsibility of younger family members. The depression forced attention on and development of government managed safety nets such as those mentioned. About thirty years later, because of the higher costs of advances in medical technology, the government was obliged to get involved and originated Medicare for senior citizens. The excellent care it provides at a very low premium cost to the individual, partially explains why I am able to write this in good health at age 85 and my four siblings survive. My generation has experienced unprecedented improvements in the areas of human comfort, convenience and entertainment, in addition to miraculous medical advances.

Our father experienced pay cuts after 1930. For several years coal mines worked only two or three days per week. There were no checks for some pay periods. In 1941 he moved to a new position as a Federal Mine Inspector. His father, our grandfather, lost his job as superintendent of a small mine. He and our grandfather were obliged to exist on his meager salary as night watchman in the

County Court House. The impact of the depression on the family, combined with the crowding of four growing boys in one bedroom, were the primary reasons for my leaving home in July 1932. Fortunately, an opportunity had presented itself for me, the oldest fledging to leave the nest. Uncle Harold had a job opportunity for me in Washington, DC.

I was 16 years old and had yet to complete my senior year in high school. Uncle Harold had determined that I could complete high school by attending evening classes. The early months of my life in Washington went very much as expected. I lived in a second floor apartment with Aunt Anna at 14th and Harvard Streets. The possibility of my entering military service was under consideration a few years before the events precipitating US involvement in World War II. It was suggested that I try for an appointment to the Naval Academy at nearby Annapolis.

I did try, but my light high school math preparation was not equal to the rigorous competition for appointment. Meanwhile in early 1934, having previously put an application in to the civil Service Commission, I entered the white collar working ranks as a messenger in the Public Works Branch. Each fall and spring semester I was reluctantly, but dutifully, taking courses for a few credits in the George Washington University Evening Division. This was done while partying and dancing with newly found friends. There was an influx of young people from many states taking jobs in new federal agencies created by President Roosevelt to combat the serious economic distress throughout the country.

In early 1936, I passed the Navy physical exam and began a four year enlistment in the Naval Reserve as a Seaman 2nd Class. In mid-summer 1936 most members of Lieutenant Nicholson's unit (about 10 or 12) assembled at the Washington Navy Yard and went aboard the USS *Upshur*, DD 144. The Upshur was a destroyer built during World War I. My strongest recollection of this two week cruise stopping at Ponce, Puerto Rico and the US base in Guatanamo Bay Cuba, is the extreme seasickness I experienced.

With the help of Goldie Allen, sister-in-law of my Uncle Melvin Rees, I saw on a huge wall chart the newest Navy aircraft carrier, the USS *Enterprise* CV-6 was to be commissioned. Lieutenant Nicholson was helpful in getting my orders to the *Enterprise* shakedown cruise, the only reservist amid a ship's company of about 2,800 enlisted men. By the time of the cruise I had a petty officer rating of Yeoman 3rd Class.

Sleep was often interrupted by noisy flight operations directly above our hammocks. In 1937 airplanes were still rare and fascinating machines. I had only one ride in a Piper Cub plane cross country from Jamestown, New York to Alexandria, Virginia. Watching larger torpedo and dive bomber planes take off and land on a carrier deck was an exciting thrill.

To a West Virginia hillbilly, Rio de Janeiro, Brazil, was an exotic part of another world, the home of carioca dancers and Carmen Miranda on Copacabana Beach. My dentist in Washington gave me a letter of introduction to a classmate then practicing dentistry in Rio. He introduced me to his technician, a nice looking English speaking Brazilian girl about my age. She had a sister. A friend of mine and I went on a double date. My wife, Eulene, and I made a seven day visit to Rio by air in 1974.

In early 1938, I managed to get duty on the USS *Nashville*, moving from Norfolk to San Pedro, California. I would be the first Toothman in my lineage to visit California. When the *Nashville* arrived at the San Pedro Naval Base, I was discharged from active duty and to find my own way back to Washington. A major concern was finding an inexpensive way to get back across the continent to DC. I answered an ad for share expense passengers. The trip was made with a man about 30 years old driving a 1936 Ford with me and two women, a mother and teenage daughter on a share the expense basis. I definitely remember my share was $17.

During 1939 Adolf Hitler raised his saber rattling to a fever pitch. I was with eight or ten young people at a camp site on the Potomac River on that Labor Day. That was the weekend Hitler's Panzer Divisions stormed into Poland. President Roosevelt seemingly knew with certainty in early 1940, that the resources of the USA, including military would be needed to avoid German domination of all of Western Europe and Great Britain. President Roosevelt worked diligently to prepare for the inevitable.

The Navy announced several new officer training programs. I saw this as my chance to wear Navy blue with gold stripes. I barely met the requirements. I applied and was accepted for the two stage training; two weeks duty on a combat ship and three months in one of two reserve midshipman training schools. I was obliged to use my 1940 military leave for a late fall two weeks training cruise aboard the USS *Tuscaloosa*. This was the fourth combat ship on which I had received training. In early June 1941, I left my 1935 V-8 Ford Sedan in DC (don't remember where).

Public interest in, and support of, the military establishment began a steady decline after the horrors of World War I. Looking back, I'm surprised that F.D.R. was able to get Congressional approval of money to build four new aircraft carriers during the Depression—*Yorktown*, *Enterprise*, *Wasp*, and *Hornet*. Perhaps this was the result of skills he acquired as Assistant Secretary of the Navy during World War I. The success of Army General Billy Mitchell during the late 1929s, in demonstrating the effectiveness of aerial bombing of armored navy ships, was the beginning of a long and bitter dispute in the commands of the army, navy, and to a lesser extent to the marine corps, as to whether scarce money should be spent on more guns or attack aircraft.

About three weeks before graduation, our commanding officer posted a listing on the duty assignments available upon our commissioning as ensigns. I expressed my choice as "Fighter Director School" at the Norfolk Naval Air Station, and was surprised and pleased to receive orders accordingly. Separation from the FDO School came in late November 1941. I received orders to Boston and to await the *Yorktown's* arrival in the Navy Yard there. Since June 7, 1942 when the *Yorktown* sank, this coat has laid at the bottom of the Pacific without ever a single useful wearing. On December 5th I boarded the USS *Kilauea* for Norfolk where the Yorktown was for scheduled repair. The ship was off the New Jersey coast about opposite Atlantic City, when around two o'clock in the afternoon, Sunday December 7th, the chilling news was received. The Japanese were making a massive aerial attack on Pearl Harbor. We arrived at Hampton Roads after dark and anchored a couple miles from the Norfolk N.O.B. dock, where the *Yorktown* was.

I reported for duty aboard USS *Yorktown* around 8:30 AM. A little after 9 a.m., the ship's bull horn blared out, "Now hear this; a state of war now exists between the United States and Japan." About an hour later the bull horn announced, "A state of war now exists between the United States and Germany." The coincidence of my reporting aboard the *Yorktown* and the declaration of war has allowed me to claim, with tongue in cheek, that President Roosevelt waited until I was ready for combat duty to declare war. Later on the 8th, all of the 70 odd planes in the *Yorktown* air group were taxied back over the asphalt paving between the Air Station and the Operating Base and were hoisted aboard the flight deck by a crane.

Two passenger ships previously in regular service between San Francisco, Los Angeles and the Hawaiian Islands, the SS *Mariposa* and SS *Luriline*, were now troop carriers. They were loaded with US Marines destined for duty in American Samoa. All the times when we were at sea in the Pacific, we sailed in a formation with four or five destroyers and two cruisers. As the *Yorktown* cruised past the Southern edge of the Marshall Islands, a Japanese scouting plane was sighted but not pursued. We entered

Pearl Harbor on February 8, 1942 and saw for ourselves enormous ship damage. The wreckage was an awesome, sad sight to behold. All ships fully restocked with food and refueled, departed Pearl Harbor as a task force about February 10th. Symbolic of a revolutionary change in naval warfare was marked when the eight battleships in Pearl Harbor were put out of action by aerial bombs and torpedoes. The battleship was no longer a major factor in naval strategy.

It was a major stroke of pure dumb luck that all US carriers were out of sight of the Jap planes coming into Pearl Harbor. Had one or more carriers suffered the fate of the battleship's the outcome of the Battles of Coral Sea and Midway would probably have been reversed. When the *Yorktown* and *Lexington* Task Forces were dispatched to the Coral Sea 3000 miles from Hawaii, and finally, after these ships spent over three months patrolling the area, a Japanese attack force showed up in that area. It is logical to conclude that Admiral Chester Nimitz had some advance information about Japanese planes. Three weeks later the Admiral sent three carriers and many supporting ships to the Midway Island area.

The following 101 days after we left Pearl Harbor were to be the longest continuous period at sea ever experienced by Navy ships. Between our mid-February departure from Pearl Harbor and the Coral Sea engagement on May 8th, there were day after day routine aircraft morning search flights. The variety in our meal menus gradually declined. This narrative has now reached the time of the *Battle of the Coral Sea* May 8, 1942. It is written mostly from memory in the latter months of the year 2000. Only a few memorable high points are included.

THE BATTLE OF THE CORAL SEA. I will briefly summarize the few things I remember occurring on May 8, 1942 the date of the **Battle of the Coral Sea.** I was one of four ensigns rotating 4 hour watches in what was then called, Radar Plot, sharing space with Air Plot located in the island structure aft of the Navigation Bridge. I was on duty from 8:a.m to noon on May 8th. After a shore based patrol plane reported sighting the Japanese Carrier Force, the *Yorktown* launched its torpedo and dive bomber squadrons. They flew off in the direction of the Japanese force. The *Yorktown* then promptly launched about 10 fighter planes designated as the Combat Air Patrol. In accordance with long established carrier tactical procedure, the fighters climbed to an altitude of 10,000 feet circling directly over our Task Force.

That GALLANT SHIP U.S.S. YORKTOWN [CV-5]

by ROBERT CRESSMAN

About thirty minutes after the last torpedo and dive bombers flew off the ship, the radar oscilloscope operator reported, "Radar contact many bogeys", and gave the range 89 miles and bearing. Within a very few minutes the Senior Aviator leading the *Yorktown* attack group broke radio silence and reported, *"Many Jap planes headed your way."* The two air groups were passing in sight of one another. If the intercept procedure, in which I had been trained, had been followed at the time of the radar contact, I would have had prior authorization to immediately contact the Combat Air Patrol (fighter planes orbiting above us) by voice radio. The report of a large radar contact, visually confirmed by our own air group, created shipboard pandemonium, especially with the Air officer, Air Group Officer and the Captain.

The attacking planes were almost simultaneously in range of ships 5 inch AA guns. The ships began radical maneuvering to avoid torpedoes and bombs. The *Yorktown* suffered only one hit by an armor piercing 800 lb. bomb. It penetrated the edge of the flight deck, the aviation Ready Room just below the flight deck through the hangar deck and exploded in the second deck below the hanger deck. We were soon to learn that there were heavy personnel casualties from that one bomb. The two officers and 34 enlisted men were killed instantly in that compartment. At 10 o'clock that evening, I watched the burial at sea ceremony on the ship's fantail, (stern) conducted by the ship's Chaplain, and medical corpsmen. All 36 bodies wrapped in heavy canvas, were dropped into the foaming wake of the ship now headed east for the Tonga Islands.

The carrier *Lexington* also received one bomb hit. The bomb started fires in the hangar deck. This fire was fed by highly flammable aviation fuel. In late afternoon crew members began abandoning ship to be picked out of the water by their escorting destroyers and cruisers. It was about this time that the *Yorktown* force left the area, presumably headed for Pearl Harbor. In the late evening of May 8th, we learned that, with fires still raging, the USS *Lexington* had been sunk by torpedoes fired from one of its destroyer escorts. The Coral Sea Battle between carrier groups, in which each side lost one carrier, was considered a draw.

As I recall, the continuous time at sea for the *Yorktown* Task Force was recorded as 101 days. Now 58 years later, I'm not sure whether the ending date was our entry into Pearl Harbor or our stopover at Tongatabu in the Tonga Islands. There were no port facilities for a ship our size, so the *Yorktown* and escorts anchored in the bay. I went ashore with four or five other junior officers. We were fortunate to almost immediately meet the British Public Health Officer, who had been in service there for many years. It was a very primitive environment, very few wood or masonry structures. The British officer took us to one of the grass huts of a native family. We sat on grass mats while he described life in the Tonga's.

After Tonga we headed for Pearl Harbor. We, the *Yorktown* task group survived with only one bomb hit, the first aerial naval engagement in history in which opposing ships were never within gun firing range of each other. I don't think the full significance of the Battle of the Coral Sea was immediately recognized by the participants. The bomb damage on the second deck below the hanger deck would have to be repaired. The repairs would take weeks, we thought. No sooner than we were docked and connected to fuel and water replenishment hoses, than it was apparent that we would soon put back to sea. We were only at a carrier pier on Ford Island Air Station a couple of days, and then we prepared to cast off. Intelligence confirmed that a large Japanese force was heading for Midway Island, and another force was aimed at the Aleutian Islands. The aircraft carriers *Hornet* and *Enterprise*, with escorting ships, were already conducting searches along with the PBYs from Midway of a big Pacific expanse West of Midway Island and in the vicinity of Wake Island.

THE BATTLE OF MIDWAY   I was not on duty in Radar Plot on the morning of June 4, 1942. So during the **Battle of Midway** I was an unassigned free spirit roaming the ship at leisure. I remember observing aircraft fueling and I also observed landings on the flight deck and had nervous conversations with fellow junior officers who were eating in the Wardroom. Around noon, as the ship maneuvered violently, Japanese dive bombers scored two hits on the *Yorktown*. One bomb exploded near the AA guns aft of the island inflicting several fatalities and serious injuries on gun crews. The other was a delayed action bomb which dropped through the smoke stack and exploded on the way down to the fire room. It blew out the fire creating the steam that propelled the ship, so we were soon, "dead in the water". No planes could be launched and those in the air were ordered to land on the *Hornet* or *Enterprise* when their fuel ran low.

A repair crew worked quickly and expertly and the *Yorktown* started to move again in mid afternoon. When the speed was up to about 10 knots, Japanese planes were detected on the horizon. Two torpedo planes got within range of the *Yorktown* and their aim was perfect. The torpedoes exploded almost simultaneously in the portside hull and the shuddering vibration was felt in every part of the ship. The water rushed into the lower deck compartments opened by the torpedoes and the ship began to list toward the port side. Shortly after lunch I visited radar Plot while the ship was not moving. There was neither friendly nor enemy air activity being plotted.

ABANDON SHIP   After the torpedo hit, the ship listed heavily and it was very difficult to walk across the deck to the port side. It was about 3:30 in the afternoon and suddenly the ship's bull horn boomed out, "**Abandon Ship.**" I was sitting on a ladder in the island structure and immediately went up and out on the flight deck. Large diameter ropes (about 2 inches), intended for use in abandoning ship were already in place about every 20 feet along the catwalk. The catwalk was a steel walkway about four feet below the level of the flight deck the full length of the ship. I waited near the mid-ship lines until there were no more enlisted men waiting to go down the line. There were almost 3000 men aboard. I still have a vivid mental picture of hundreds of heads bobbing in the water. All of them were swimming at various speeds away from the *Yorktown* towards the two cruisers and four destroyers. I took off my shoes and left them on the catwalk. I lost my grip about 15 feet above the end of the line, so I plopped into the water with minor rope burns on both hands. Once in the water, it became of utmost importance to get in the vicinity of one of the rescue ships. I started swimming toward the nearest destroyer. It was soon evident that swimming speed would be faster without trousers. So I unloosened my belt and slipped out of them.

During the rescue operations extending over a couple of hours, there were three or four instances when the rescue ships suddenly blew their horns and quickly moved away from the men in the water. These moves were in response to reported sightings of aircraft and the uncertainty as to whether they were friend or foe. When I got alongside the USS *Anderson,* two of its crew grabbed each of my arms. Once on deck, I crawled inboard to what I think was the fire room smoke stack coming through the main deck, and leaned my back against it—a warm feeling of relief but wondering what would come next. Admiral Nimitz had sent the USS *Fulton,* a big submarine out from Pearl to the battle area. Survivors were loaded into whale boats, about 20 to 25 per trip, and moved alongside the Fulton. The water was choppy. Once aboard the Fulton, we were promptly issued new underwear, a dungaree shirt and trousers. As soon as all the *Yorktown* survivors were picked up, we headed for Pearl Harbor. From Hawaii, we landed in San Francisco, debarking in mid June.

During the next 30 days my itinerary took me from San Francisco to Washington, Pennsylvania, the new location of my parents. The loss of the *Yorktown* was not published until late in the summer. We survivors were not supposed to reveal the fate of the ship but I did confide in family and close friends. I learned of the final hours of the *Yorktown* from a visit with the officer in charge of the repair party. One of the Task Group escorting destroyers, USS *Hammann,* transported the repair party and was moored alongside the *Yorktown.* A Japanese submarine fired two torpedoes, one broke the *Hammann* in half, with substantial loss of life and several were seriously wounded as the depth charges from the destroyer exploded from water pressure as they sank. The

Yorktown was further damaged and sank the morning on June 7, 1942.

By the time I got to my parents in Washington, PA it was early July 1942. Only sister Betty remained at home. The three brothers between us were already started in their World War II military service. Brother Fred had his navy officer's commission; my brother Glenn was becoming a marine officer, and my brother Lee had been accepted for Air Force flight training.

The *USS Altamaha* was a unique new hybrid type aircraft carrier that came to be known as "baby flattops" or "Grease Spot" carriers. The advance of radar equipment was startling. At the time of the commissioning of the *Altamaha,* I was promoted to Lieutenant junior grade. I was now senior in rank, and the only one of the CIC trained ensigns with prior combat experience. The Captain was Jackson R. Tate, a man who rose from enlisted status through the ranks and was not a Naval Academy graduate. He was of the rough and ready type, heavy black beard not always close shaven, heavy smoker of Pall Mall king size cigarettes, blood shot eyes and a strong appetite for bourbon whiskey. While in Moscow, he became intimate with a Russian film star, Zoya Fyodorova. A pregnancy resulted. Zoya was sent to prison for 25 years and Tate was sent back to the states. The story didn't make headlines until about 20 years later, when the child Tate fathered also became a movie star. The daughter, Victoria, initiated a reunion with Tate in his Florida retirement home in the 1970s. She stayed in the US, and married an airline pilot.

The longest voyage and the most fascinating sightseeing of my sixty months on active duty started in Alameda, California on 16 July and ended December 21, 1943. Our primary cargo was 70 P51 fighter planes to be used in the China Burma India Theater by British and US pilots. We also transported 300 Marines to a South Pacific island. In early 1943, after we had put our squadron of 25 planes and pilots ashore in Guadalcanal, it became apparent that escort carriers were not likely to have a part in combat operations so I asked for an assignment to a fleet carrier. I received orders to the Pacific Fleet Radar Center. My fellow officers and I celebrated. Still feeling the stimulus of "O" club spirits, I failed to duck my head running through a water tight door hatch, struck the center of my scalp on the knife edge, and started bleeding profusely. Some stitches at sick bay stopped the bleeding.

I received orders for temporary duty aboard the USS *Princeton CVL*. The *Princeton* had a full complement of experienced CIC officers, so there was no need for my services. The radar plotted on the vertical plotting board using wax pencils, showed a bearing of both friendly and enemy unidentified planes. The aerial encounter on June 19, 1944, was almost immediately characterized as the "Great Marianas Turkey Shoot." Over 300 Japanese planes were put out of action that day. The US suffered a loss of only 29 aircraft, 27 air crews, and 31 shipboard fatalities from Japanese bomb hits. This has been described as the greatest air battle in history. It decimated Japan's carrier capability and forced Japan to resort to aerial suicide attacks known as *"Kamikaze,"* which is translated as *"Divine Wind."* All Japanese pilots were sworn to crash their planes, usually armed with a 500 lb. contact bomb, into the navigation bridge area of US ships.

Having completed my refresher training in CIC operation, on or about June 22, 1944, I was detached from the *Princeton* and put aboard the USS *Enterprise* for transportation back to Pearl Harbor. I had served seven years earlier on the shakedown cruise to Rio de Janeiro on the *Enterprise.* In Hawaii, I received shore duty. During the thirteen months I served at the Radar center, I was visited by two relatives passing through Pearl Harbor. One of those visitors was my brother, Marine second lieutenant Glenn Toothman, Jr., who was attached to an artillery battalion. By the time I was given the personnel job, I had been on sea duty for about 32 months.

In the summer of 1945, as the planning for the invasion of Japan began, and the surrender of Germany, there were fewer fatalities from Kamikaze attacks. It was finally agreed that the Pacific fleet would not be jeopardized if I was transferred to the Bureau of Personnel of the Navy Department in Washington, DC.

I had met Eulene Smothers at a George Washington University Alpha Delta Pi Sorority dessert party. We had several dates before

I left for Midshipmen's School. Eulene was waiting for me on the Union Station Platform. During my long months of oversea duty I had become certain that I should marry Eulene and had increased the passion in my letters accordingly. We went to dinner together in high spirits, talking of the events of intervening years. I was invited to spend the weekend at Eulene's mother's farm in Clifton, Virginia, near the present location of the Dulles Airport. I proposed to Eulene and was accepted and we began making wedding plans. We were married on September 4, 1945 in the Fairfax Episcopal Church. Eulene and I went to Cloister's Resort Hotel in Georgia for our honeymoon. I borrowed my father's almost-like-new, 1941 Plymouth sedan for the trip to Georgia.

After the surrender of Japan, a new upbeat, optimistic mood quickly appeared in people's behavior. For a little over 15 years, beginning with the stock market crash in October 1929 until the cessation of hostilities in August 1945, the USA and most of the Western World had lived under a worrisome cloud. Wartime priorities had created full employment with more and larger paychecks but a scarcity of consumer goods. Now with peace plus money and EE Bonds in the bank, there were expectations of a brighter future. Another major factor influencing post war behavior was President Roosevelt's GI Education Bill. It paid for my last two years of college and for advanced degrees for each of my better focused three brothers. By 1948 I realized I had made a mistake in not making college degree for myself a postwar priority. I began taking part-time courses at the University of Washington, and by August 1951, I had my B.S. degree in Business Administration. Later I received my Master of Business Administration degree at Temple University.

In March 1946, I transferred to the Sand Point Naval Air Station in Seattle. We were able to purchase a 1941 Chevrolet convertible in good condition. It got us to Seattle without any trouble. I separated from the Navy in October 1946 and started work with Pete Hamilton in the frozen- food brokerage business. I was offered and accepted the faculty position as Assistant Professor of Agricultural Economics Extension, beginning in early 1968. Eulene had become a highly respected teacher in an elementary school in Philadelphia. She was not enthusiastic about another move. I began teaching at Penn State in February, still working evenings on my master's thesis, and driving to Philadelphia most weekends. In July Eulene accepted a teaching position in State College. (James and Eulene had two children, a daughter, Karen and a son Rees.) Eulene retired in June 1982.

It is my conviction that the greatest privilege since the origin of mankind, is to have lived the greater part of one's life as a healthy US citizen in the last half of the 20th century. I am profoundly thankful for a long and interesting life. I give credit for my health to my genetic fore-bearers and to my wife for her steadfast beneficial influences on my life including the application of sound nutritional principles.

Although I cannot point to any notable personal accomplishments, I am thankful to have witnessed many notable events in wartime and in peacetime—beginning in my early youth. When the Nation's President and First Lady still held public receptions once a week in the East Room of the White House, my Aunt Jess took me to shake hands with President Calvin Coolidge and Mrs. Coolidge in the summer of 1925. A couple of years later, I was, thanks to having relatives in DC, an observer of the parade up Pennsylvania Avenue honoring Charles A. Lindbergh. In March 1929, I witnessed the Inaugural Parade of Herbert Hoover. I was present on Pennsylvania Avenue during the first three or four inaugurations of Franklin Delano Roosevelt. Those were early thrills leading up to widely varied experiences in the US Navy including being a participant in the three major naval engagements of World War II; The Battle of the Coral Sea, the Battle of Midway, and the Second Battle of the Philippines.

In summation, I feel that fate has been most kind to one lacking a strong sense of self direction. Most gratifying has been a long lasting marriage and a congenial relationship with the many productive, upstanding members of my extended family.

FRED REES TOOTHMAN
LIEUTENANT (JUNIOR GRADE)

I was born two weeks before the Armistice in World War I on October 26, 1918, to Glenn Roy and Elsie Rees Toothman in a small coal mining town of Erie, West Virginia, six miles north of Clarksburg. Victory High School in Clarksburg is where I captained the 1935 football team and played in the band. In 1941, I graduated from West Virginia University in Morgantown with a degree in Mining Engineering. Having been elected to Tau Beta Pi, the highest honor in engineering, I also played in the band and was head waiter in Women's Hall for three years.

While continuing my studies on a Masters Degree, Uncle Sam called me to the Navy in May 1942, as an Ensign and sent me to the Ship Repair Unit in San Diego, California. After the war, I returned to West Virginia University and completed my studies and received a Masters Degree.

My college roommate and I had just finished playing 18 holes on the small golf course in Grafton, West Virginia. It was a little after noon when I went to get back into my 1936 Ford sedan to head back to Morgantown. I immediately turned on the car radio to hear a loud voice proclaiming, *"Pearl Harbor is being bombed by a large contingent of Japanese planes."* My heart sank as my friend, Bob Earle, entered the car in the other side. We both listened to several minutes of lurid description and then looked at each other thinking the obvious thought of our own likelihood of war service in the very near future. The enormity of the destruction continued to be regaled as we drove back to West Virginia

University in Morgantown were we both engaged in post-graduate work. We speculated on how soon we would be personally involved in the war; which seemed inevitable from this newscast on Sunday, December 7, 1941. A date which President Roosevelt later said would live in infamy.

Back at school, where I lived in a small room on the second floor of a house behind the men's residence hall, I reflected on the fact that my life, which began three weeks before the end of WORLD WAR I, was about to be taken over by WORLD WAR II. I was working on a scholarship from the State to produce a study of the use of conveyers in the coal industry, for which I received a small salary and would lead to the earning of a Masters Degree in Mining Engineering. My work consisted of reading up on the history of coal mining at the school library and visiting coal mines in the State (West Virginia) and studying the use of conveyers to prepare a book based on these inspections.

An older brother, James, had been called up for active duty in the Navy. He generously offered to turn his automobile over to me to use in my field work, with the understanding that it be sold when I entered service and the money sent to him. The car, a Ford V-8 sedan, was a real thrill for me to drive. By the time of Pearl Harbor, I had almost completed two semesters of work towards my degree and had inspected about 20 different coal mines located mostly in the southern part of West Virginia, where the coal beds were of the highest quality but limited thickness.

Realizing my selective service draft number would probably be called within three months, I wrote to the Army Air Corps, the Marine Corps and the Navy, giving my qualifications. While waiting, I made a trip to the southern part of the State. On Sunday, I decided to visit my youngest brother, Lee, at Marshall College in Huntington. I had never been to that city and looked forward to some sightseeing. I was much impressed by the wide streets and many trees which were laid out in a plan by the C&O Railway.

I started dating Nadine Bailey, a girl who had been a student and resident in the girl's dormitory. Her father was a merchant in the small town of Bridgeport and also the Mayor. Nadine and I eventually married. She died of cancer in 1966.

In March, I started getting replies to my inquiries about the services. My first reply was from the Army Air Force offering me a commission. Later, I received a letter from the Marine Corps stating that I had been accepted for a commission but would be required to attend a 3 month training course at their Quantico Base before commissioned as an officer. Towards the end of the month, I received a letter from the Navy with a whole packet of orders. It stated that I would be commissioned by a local reserve naval physician, if I passed his physical exam. I was a little reluctant to follow my older brother in the Navy, but decided this offer was too good to pass up.

I decided to make the plunge. I wrote my acceptance to the navy in early April and received a large brown envelope full of papers in a couple of weeks. My orders were to report for duty at the Ship Repair Unit at the Navy base in San Diego, California. It also ordered me to report immediately to a local obstetrician, who was a Navy reserve Officer, for a physical exam. His office was packed with pregnant women. The exam took about 15 minutes, after which he asked me to raise my right hand and repeat a pledge to service. He then told me that before I reported to my post in San Diego, to eat as many bananas as I could because I was slightly under weight. He also suggested that I visit the Circus Room bar in the Coronado Hotel at the first opportunity and toast a drink to his health.

My orders stated that I would be required to buy a uniform at an approximate cost of $300. I asked my great Uncle Fred to loan me the money for the uniforms. He graciously handed over the money. I arrived in San Diego early in the morning. I arrived at the large and impressive main gate to the Navy Base. There was a

Marine guard standing at attention in front of the gate. He had a jeep pick me up, taking me to a Quonset hut with a sign on the front; "Ship Repair Unit."

I reported to the Commanding Officer who was sitting behind a huge desk and had a large bald spot showing on top of his head. He looked up and said to me, "Boy, where is your uniform?"I tried to make an excuse of ignorance when he ordered me to sit in the waiting room until he came out and he would drop me off at a uniform store. I returned to the office in a brand new khaki working uniform. They sent me to a nearby Quonset hut where I was assigned a bunk.

The unit that I was assigned to was taking World War I destroyers out of their storage anchorage and refitting them as Marine transports. This renovation required the removal of one engine room to make room for a troop compartment. I was assigned to the electrical division. There were 200 men and 50 officers in our unit alone and about five times that amount in the whole base.

Remembering my admonition from the physician in Morgantown, I went over to the beautiful Coronado Hotel to have a libation. As I approached the main entrance, I stopped and stared at a man in a straw hat with a blonde on each arm. I easily recognized Rudy Vallee, the famous actor and singer. He was obviously in high spirits strutting out of the hotel. The main bar was called the "Circus Room." I pulled up to the stool and enjoyed two Manhattan cocktails.

My mother wrote me consistently about every two weeks, and her last letter indicated that they hadn't heard from by brother (James) on the carrier, *Yorktown* for over a month and were concerned about him. I went to Chief Petty Officer in our division who was an old sea dog and seemed to know all the Navy scuttlebutt. I asked him if he knew anything about the *Yorktown*. He replied, "Haven't you heard? It was sunk in battle a little more than two weeks ago." My heart sank at this news but the Chief explained that most of the crew was saved, which encouraged me. The next letter from home confirmed that he was all right. I learned later that it was the battle of Midway and he had been rescued after several hours in the water.

After a couple of months, I received orders to report to a unit called Cub Three located at Moffet Field near Palo Alto. The huge hanger that had been used to house the dirigibles was visible several miles away. It was a base designed to be a portable navy base that could be shipped where needed in the coming advance across the Pacific Ocean. It consisted of about 30 officers and 250 enlisted men. My living quarters turned out to be a bunk in a temporary type two-story building. Our office was in a nearby Quonset hut. Our commanding officer was a crusty old regular Navy Commander who had obviously been passed over for promotion and discharged in peace time, but recalled to duty when the war broke out.

We learned that as officers that we could draw subsistence pay if we found a rental unit in the adjacent town of Palo Alto. There were eleven of us in a group and we went into town to see a real estate agency. We learned from the middle-aged lady in charge that she had a fully furnished former physician's residence for rent but was afraid we would not take good care of the house. In talking to her, we learned she had a desire to ride in a jeep. A Lt. junior grade senior officer offered to take her a ride in a jeep if she would rent us the house. We named the house Club Three. A few of us would occasionally buy our own groceries and cook dinner. Most of us also had cereal at the house for breakfast.

Later, this same lady made arrangements for all of us singles to meet a group of girls at Stanford. The last girl to arrive at the meeting had to be my date because all the other guys had paired up. She was a tall reddish blonde, well proportioned with green eyes and freckles. Her name was Doris Myers and her father owned a department store in Whittier, Calif. She had a steady boyfriend but we still had several dates.

The rainy season finally ended in the spring of '44 and we got orders to prepare to embark for action out in the Pacific Theatre. By this time the Marines and Army had secured Guadalcanal and we knew that a big offensive towards Japan was being planned. My most pleasant interlude while in California was a 2-day visit to Doris' home in Whittier. The scenic coastal trip on the Southern Pacific R.R. during the week after Christmas was awesome even in the midst of winter. Her parents were most gracious, even though it was obvious that I was not considered a serious contender for their daughter's hand.

On May 3, almost exactly one year after I entered the Navy, a train of passenger cars arrived on a siding at Moffet Field and we went aboard. Each officer was allowed to have a sea chest with personal effects and we each had a sea bag of canvas to carry toilet articles and extra clothes. After a short trip of about 20 miles, the train pulled onto a siding in San Francisco Harbor alongside two ships waiting at the dock. Most of us were herded aboard the USS *LaSalle* which I later learned was a ship built to haul bananas from South America and was converted to be a Navy troop carrier. My group, twelve junior officers were assigned to a cabin on the main deck near the stern of the ship.

Most of us who had never ever seen the ocean let alone ride on it were concerned about getting seasick. I saw lots of our men vomiting and some passed out lying on the deck. Our senior petty officers were trying to help these victims, but it was a losing job. We sailed due west for our secret destination. We never learned what it was until we arrived in the Figi Islands. The days slipped by slowly but a great experience for one like me who had never ever seen the ocean until the navy accepted my services. The food was fairly good for a few days. One day one of my fellow officers pulled out a carton of O'Henry bars, which caused my salivary glands to respond. I have never before or since seen any food that looked as good as that box of candy. I would have paid him $5 dollars for just one of the bars.

After 18 days at sea, we began to notice some of the older hands on board were building a platform and canvas tank on the main deck. We soon learned that this was preparation for initiating all of us neophytes aboard into the Order of the king Neptune when we crossed the equator. It consisted of taking off your clothes down to the skivvies running thru a puddle gauntlet, being fed a forced dose of green foul-tasting liquid and dumped into the tank filled with sea water.

Several days later, Lieut. Robinson, called me aside and said that our ship had received a radio message that a ship on our course and two days ahead of us, had been torpedoed and sunk by a Japanese submarine. Everyone was uneasy, to say the least. The food on the ship had declined in quality due to complete lack of anything fresh and spam became the main course of most meals which had been reduced to two a day for a couple of weeks. We didn't realize this fact at the time, but spam was to become our main course for the remainder of our service overseas. After 28 days at sea, we were notified that we would arrive in a cove on the Figi Islands the next day.

The gasoline drums were unloaded onto landing craft operated by a local Coast Guard outfit. They had been overseas eleven months and received our sympathy. After we reached the shore, my crew had to unload the barrels onto a truck, which then took us to a storage area where the barrels were stacked. We returned to the ship at midnight, wet, cold and glad to get into the sack. The next day we went ashore and a Seabee outfit had built a tent city for us. There was a make-shift head down over the hill about 30 yards away which was 3 holes to serve about 30 officers. Dinner call came at 5 o'clock in a large tent. It could accommodate the 30 officers and close to 150 enlisted men. The meal consisted of boiled mutton and some fresh vegetables. I got up about 0700 hours and my tent mate was missing. I dressed and walked down the road toward the mess tent. I saw what looked like large white flowers along the edge of the forest about a hundred yards away. A steward asked me if I was sick. I told him no. He explained that everybody who had eaten the mutton was suffering from diarrhea. I realized the white flowers were really white caps of sailors squatting to relieve themselves. On the way back to the tent area, a pain in my lower abdomen began to increase. A bowel movement was evident and could no longer be restrained. I took off my pants and underpants and took off for the head. Two senior officers were sitting on the outside holes. I said, "Excuse me, gentlemen" and backed onto middle hole just in time to relieve myself and it shot out like a cannon.

Another ship, the USS *Tryon,* a hospital ship with no markings arrived to pick us up. The accommodations were much better than on the LaSalle. Before we left Figi, we learned that we were going to staging at Guadalcanal for an invasion of the New Georgia group of Islands in the Solomon's. We were headed for the real war.

When we arrived at Guadalcanal and bivouacked in a temporary camp, we received our orders for the coming campaign. I was assigned to the smallest of four groups prepared to land on New Georgia on D-Day. I had been promoted to Lieut. J.G. and was assigned to Lieut. Robinson as his Executive Officer with 3 Ensigns, 1 physician and the 35 men of my former Division. This was to be the first joint Army, Navy and Marine operation of the Pacific Campaign under the overall command of Admiral Halsey.

Very few of our plans were on schedule. It was later referred to as "JANFU," Joint Army, Navy foul up. Each officer had a .45 Colt revolver but now was issued carbines. I took three clips of bullets and went out into the woods where we were to practice with the gun. After a couple of days, our unit was moved forward to the

Russell Island by boat. It was between Guadalcanal and New Georgia Islands. Lieut. Robinson advised me that I had been selected to go with a party of marines and reconnoiter the Island before the invasion. I protested but was advised that I was the only unmarried junior officer in our outfit.

Soon I met with the marine captain that I was assigned to. Instead of going with the group to look at Viru Harbor where my unit was going to land, I was going with the marines clear across the main island to find a place for the marines to come ashore, protect the back door of the Army invasion force. The main objective of the invasion was the Munda airfield already under construction by the Japanese. I was to prepare a sketch map showing the beach landing area and depth of the water, etc.

There were four different groups organized to reconnoiter the New Georgia Islands where the D-Day assaults were to take place. The date was June 11, 1943, and I had met up with the five members of the First Marine Raider Battalion who didn't seem to be much impressed with having a shave-tail Navy officer along as excess baggage. The invasion was a first by a combined US Force of Army, Navy and Marine Corp scheduled for June 30, 1943. The operation was given the code name of "Toenails," which turned out to be an appropriate description.

All 30 men who were to perform the reconnaissance expedition were milling around on the beach. Most of them were officers from the National Guard 43rd Division from New England. The major objective was the capture of a half-completed airport on Munda Point from which our heavy B-24 bombers could pound Truk, the Japanese port in the Caroline Islands. The Japanese already had in operation an airfield and base called Vila on the southern tip of Kolambangbra Island which was about 20 miles northwest of Munda.

We had been advised at the briefing that the New Zealand coast watcher who occupied these islands during the Japanese invasion estimated that there were 2,000 troops at Munda, 6,000 at Vila and another 1,000 at scattered locations. We were advised not to wear insignias because officers were always targets and we were almost certain to be tortured and killed if captured. Everyone was obviously a little nervous as we boarded the small coastal vessel which was to take us to our jumping-off point called Segi. Segi Point was the base of an Australian coast-watching officer by the name of Captain Donald Kennedy. Each of us wore Army green fatigue suits and soft fatigue caps.

Up to this point, our food had consisted of K-rations, condensed food packages in a large crackerjack-type box. Our guides turned out to be very small black men. We learned later that they were Melanesians and were much darker and smaller than the Polynesians of the Central Pacific. They had fuzzy black hair and wore only a loin cloth. We were warned that if we encountered any Japanese, our guides would disappear because they despised them due to being tortured and mistreated. We boarded 3 canoes dug out by hand from the trunk of large trees. All were fitted with crude outriggers and crude wooden seats. Two of the canoes carried three passengers each with two rowers fore and aft.

At about midnight, we approached the mouth of Viru Harbor where my unit was scheduled to land on D-Day. It was known to be held by about 150 Japanese troops. Our scouts steered the canoes well out into Blanche Channel at least a half mile from the harbor entrance. At about 0500, we came to an opening on the coastline which was obviously an abandoned native site. There remained several shacks which resembled large corn cribs, with thatched roofs. After a hearty breakfast of C-rations, we all lay down in the huts on leaves and branches to sleep. In late afternoon, we aroused ourselves and got ready for a second night out in the canoes. The natives had been cannibals at one time as testified by the presence of small mounds of skulls outside of some villages.

They had since been converted to Christianity by Methodist and Seventh-Day Baptist missionaries.

Before daylight, we arrived at another abandoned village where we scurried ashore to eat and rest. Two of our native guides went ahead of us to mark a trail for us to reach our destination on the northern coast. The lead guide stayed in front to guide us. The trail was torturous and our progress slow. After about four hours on the trail, we came to a sizable stream, which was mighty cool. When we were up to our waist in mid-stream, the sergeant with the mustache pointed to a small sandy bluff on the far side and said "Wouldn't that be a good spot for a Jap machine gun?" This remark caused me to have a spine-chilling reaction.

The next morning, two of our native guides used machetes and built a platform near the top of a very large tree nearby. When it was completed, I decided to try it out. The view was breathtaking. I could see the coast clearly about a mile away and the large island of Kolumbargora was in full view. The runway of the Japanese airfield was barely discernable in the thick jungle foliage. Early afternoon, Captain Boyd and his party returned to camp. His news from looking at the terrain along the coast was a great relief to me because the entire coast line was a series of mangrove swamps which precluded the plan of having landing craft beach there. However there was a fair-sized river outlet nearby which emptied into the sea and the Captain decided that the boats could enter the river and discharge the troops.

Captain Boyd told me to stand watch that night in the tree platform and observe any possible movements of Japanese ships, barges or planes in the area in front of us. It was beginning to get dark and the two sergeants had not returned from their mission and we were all concerned for their safety. The next morning we had just finished breakfast and the two marine sergeants came wearily striding into camp. They had almost walked into a Japanese camp the afternoon before. It was now June 17, and time for us to head back to our starting base at Segi Point.

Early the next morning, as daylight was breaking, Captain Boyd with two of his men and I, started slogging back to the southern coast over the trail we had arrived on. We finally reached the coast at about 5 o'clock hours where a native messenger was waiting for us. He could speak Pidgin English and told Captain Boyd that we would have to change our route in returning to Segi Point because Japanese patrols had been observed in the vicinity of Viru Harbor. He also told us that a new coast watcher was on his way to Rendova Island to act as an observer during the coming invasion. We met him in an abandoned coconut plantation on the east coast of Rendova. That evening we feasted on a gallon can of cooked chicken which was the last of our rations. I'm not too fond of chicken, but this tasted mighty good for a ravenous appetite.

The native guides had retrieved one of the canoes hidden from our last voyage and all four of us were soon loaded aboard and headed out across the six miles of open water. It was pitched dark now, and the moon was no longer with us. The evening of June 19, the only items on the menu were a couple of yams and coconuts produced by our guides. We baked the yams "potatoes" on the coals of a small fire. Dessert was raw coconut which wasn't too bad either.

As dusk descended on the coast, we embarked in our dug-out canoe for what proved to be a startling near encounter with the enemy. We were cruising along about 40 yards off the coast, when suddenly a large engine started up not more than 30 or 40 yards directly ahead of us. We hunched down in the canoe and turned our heads to see a large Japanese barge pass by not more than 10 yards away with the faint outline of a Japanese sailor standing in the stern singing a weird tune while piloting his vessel. We let out a big sigh of relief when the danger passed.

We arrived at the abandoned village where we were to meet the coast watcher at daybreak and a slight misty rain was falling. The natives hid our canoe. Hunger was becoming a constant distraction that was gnawing at my innards. I dreamed about the carton of O'Henry bars. When our new friend, the coast watcher, found out that we were out of rations, he graciously requested that we have supper with him. While our host was saying grace, I could hardly restrain myself from grabbing a cookie right in front of me on a plate. Our meal consisted of C-rations and a few extras. As darkness approached, we loaded back onto our canoe sufficient food supplies to see us back to Segi. We reached the eastern tip of Tetipari Island on June 22 after sailing for two nights. We crossed the thirteen miles of open water in Blanche Channel to reach our destination at Segi Point. We had been gone for 10 days and traveled about 130 miles, but the single most difficult feat of our trip lay ahead of us.

As morning approached, the first flicker of light appeared in the east. Before long, we realized that we were alone out in the open water in broad daylight and no place to hide. The natives started jabbering and pointing to the route west. We recognized an approaching aircraft. The natives quit paddling as the plane passed directly overhead at an elevation of about 3000 feet, displaying two large red meat balls on the wings. It was not until about 1100 hours that we passed by the Hele Islands and entered Panaga Bay which led to our destination.

The same afternoon when we arrived, we were summoned to a meeting with Admiral Turner's staff and the other scout parties where our findings were all reported and discussed. I rejoined my unit that evening and learned that there had been a Japanese air raid on the island during our absence which caused some damage and casualties, but mainly scared the daylights out of our group.

D-DAY FOR TOENAILS   The day after the big meeting, we received a copy of the battle plans. In it was the plan for attacking Viru Harbor where our little unit was to land on D-Day. The marine platoon at Segi was being dispatched that same evening scheduled to travel overland and attack the small garrison at Viru Harbor from the rear and wipe them out, even before our unit and troops from the 43rd National Guard Division from New England landed on the beach. Our unit consisted of 35 men I had selected with three Ensigns besides Lieut. Commander Robinson and myself. Our mission was to set up a small Navy base in Viru Harbor to augment the PT boat base which was to operate out of Viru Harbor.

On the evening of June 29, we boarded a marine transport converted from a World War I destroyer. As daylight arrived, we started to see lots of airplanes flying in all directions. I will never forget seeing a lumbering Japanese flying boat being chased by two fighters as they disappeared behind an island. Viru Harbor loomed directly ahead and we were alerted by the shrill pipe of the boatswain signaling the call to assemble at our designated landing craft already being lowered over the side of the ship. I saw a puff of smoke and splash in the water directly in front of us where a large shell had landed. The Japs were firing on us from their base.

I heard a sizzling sound directly overhead which was the next round bracketing our ship. My insides turned to concrete as fear overwhelmed me. I felt a jerking motion and realized that our ship was starting to pull away from the shore just in time to keep us from a sure hit from the next round. We learned that there was a heated discussion on the bridge of our ship. The Captain of the ship was determined to get us off in the boats immediately, but the Commander of the two-ship squadron ordered him to retreat because of the hopelessness of our landing safely due to the Jap artillery piece. The marine platoon encountered delays in traversing the jungle approach and were challenged by Jap snipers.

The marines arrived in the afternoon and wiped out the Jap base with 12 casualties.

I developed a huge fever and nausea on the trip back to Russell Island. My incarceration in the tent hospital on Russell Island lasted three days. My case was diagnosed as probable malaria, but entered on my record as "jungle fever." On the third day I hitched a ride on an LSM and returned to base. My mother had given me a daily Bible reading book when I left for service. On my first Sunday at this location, I mustered the men at 11:00 a.m. and read the daily lesson for that day which was *"Let your light so shine before men that it will glorify your Father who is in Heaven."*

Even before our D-Day assault, a contingent of Seabees had started to build a landing strip on Segi Point and before Munda airfield was captured, they had a group of Marine gull-wing fighters operating off the field.

After about two weeks, we were notified to move our camp to the southern tip of Bau Island where the PT boat base was located on the northern side. Bau Island was approximately a half-mile long, east to west. The PT base was already in operation on the western end of the island. This was the outfit that John Kennedy was attached to, but we were unaware of his presence. Our camp consisted of about ten tent platforms erected by a Seabee outfit for our enlisted men. The officers had a separate galley tent and four tents for sleeping. Our boat pool consisted of one light tank landing craft and three smaller personnel landing craft. A two-hole privy was set up behind the camp for officers and a four-hole for the 34 enlisted men. I was in charge of overseeing the camp.

During the first two months at our new location, we got used to at least one air-raid alert every evening. A giant red flare from the Munda air base was the signal for an alert. We learned from the mainland that we had night fighter planes to confront the Japanese raiders. That night we peaked out of our shelter to see the Jap plane turn into a ball of fire. A few times the Jap plane would only carry empty fuel drums instead of bombs and when dropped they made an eerie sound. One night we were alerted to the sound of big guns and brilliant flashes in the night sky coming from the north part of Munda airfield. The next day, we learned that our Navy had fought an engagement with a Japanese task force and a senior officer would visit our camp. He proved to be Professor Morrison, a Harvard history teacher commissioned by orders of President Roosevelt to write a history of the US Navy in World War II.

Orders arrived for me to fly with air transport authority IV to report to the Naval Academy on July 1, 1944. I flew in a Navy C-47 transport plane to Guadalcanal. The flight to Guadalcanal was uneventful. After a good nights sleep at Hotel DeGink, (a Quonset hut but consisting of a single iron bunk), we boarded another C-47 destined for Esperito. I was advised that I would ship out the next day on a Pan American flying boat. I spent the day looking up old friends from the Cub Three outfit. My orders changed and I was sent out the next day on a PB2Y navy seaplane. We took off for Hawaii, landing in the harbor at Pearl. The next day I left for San Francisco.

While overseas, I kept up a steady correspondence with all my girlfriends, except Doris Meyers who wrote me a Dear John letter to let me know she had married Joseph Pew, IV, an heir to the Sun Oil Company fortune. When I got to Chicago, I took a train to Madison where Pat Salter was expecting me. Her family was most kind and showed me around the city. My parents had moved to Pittsburg. I made arrangements with Pat to come to Pittsburg and visit my family on the following weekend. Pat's visit was not very satisfactory. She had to sleep with my sister, Betty; and my family had already decided that I was going to marry Nadine Bailey. I borrowed the family car and made a trip south to visit my old haunts at the University. Nadine was glad to see me, but it soon became obvious that she expected me to pop the big question, which I wasn't prepared for. When I left her, it was obvious that she was much disappointed by my lack of commitment.

I took the B&O to Washington and the street car to Annapolis for my class in Aero-logy. The class consisted of about 45 officers. The regimen was strict and tough. Our math teacher was a 26 year old PhD from Yale University. Half way through the class in January 1945, we started a laboratory class where each of us had a drawing desk and drew daily weather maps and our own forecast of the weather for the next day.

I had spent a week at home for Christmas and asked Nadine to marry me. I had decided that the war was going to last a year and possible two, and I was facing another tour of battle duty in the Pacific. I decided she was my best bet for a companion and was determined to have a go at married life before I would probably see combat again. We were scheduled to get a spring break in March and we decided to get married in her Methodist church in Bridgeport, West Virginia where she lived. The wedding went off on schedule on March 10, 1945. All of my local family attended. The reception was held at her parents' house about five blocks from the Methodist Church. I told Nadine that we would spend our wedding night in the Statler Hotel in Washington. I found out that she told everyone where we would be so I changed our reservation to the Sheraton Hotel to surprise her. I rented a small basement apartment near the Main Circle in downtown Annapolis where we started housekeeping. The wedding presents we received were mostly of cloth and pottery. My parents had found a set of silverware in different patters at a second-hand store. I found a new bicycle which I rode to school on. During the month of June, we were anticipating the final exam we would have to take before the class ended on July 1. The Results of the exam were a complete surprise to me in learning that I was among the three top finishers. I then received orders to report to the Navy command in Guam which I assumed would result in being assigned to a ship or unit destined for the invasion of Japan.

Nadine insisted on accompanying me on the train trip to the West Coast. The trip was a bad experience. It took three days and two nights to make the trip. The day we landed in San Francisco, the news broke about the atomic bomb drop on Japan. I felt some relief that my service in the possible invasion of Japan would be a lot less gruesome than anticipated. The voyage to Hawaii took three days during which we learned about the second bomb and the capitulation of Japan. My future took a sudden turn for clear sailing and getting out of the Navy and back to real life in the home State of West Virginia. When I got back to West Virginia, I stayed a month with Nadine at her parents' home waiting for the second semester at WVU to finish my Masters Degree requirements. I completed my degree and graduated with a MSEM in June 1946. I accepted a job with the C&O Railway in Huntington, West Virginia.

Fred and wife Velma Smith Neale Toothman

My first wife, Nadine Bailey, died of cancer in 1966. I married Velma Smith Neale in 1973. After retirement, I embarked on a career of writing and publishing books under the name of Vandalia Company. I have authored five books. Fred and Velma live in Barboursville, West Virginia.

GLENN TOOTHMAN, JR.
MAJOR- US MARINE CORPS

On December 7, 1941, I was at Hampden-Sydney College in Virginia. Needless to say, the immediacy and shock of this event struck me with a sharp sadness. My little world of college exams and college dreams was invaded in the same way as the bombs that sank the battleships at that famous mid island Naval Harbor did to the nation.

I had transferred to enroll at Hampden-Sydney after completing two years at Potomac College, a two-year college. My attendance at both was dependent on a football and basketball scholarship—each coupled with table-waiting duties. I started my higher education with a pre-law major and finished it with that major and a minor in English. Although I found Hampden-Sydney's academic schedule to be so rigid that I had to start there by taking first year courses—Bible, Algebra & Trigonometry and Greek. My grades were respectable and I was on track to graduate with honors. So it was Pearl Harbor that changed my educational dreams from the academic to the military as graduation approached. I did not remain on campus for the graduation ceremony and saw a few of my classmates already called into military service.

When I surveyed my military options I found the only preferred choice available was the United States Marine Corps because of my marriage on April 3, 1942 to my longtime sweetheart, Katherine Throckmorton who was by then a teacher at

Waynesburg High School. Katherine and I moved to Holbrook, Pa. and lived with her parents while I started my enlistment in the Marine Corps Officer Program. According, I promptly went to the recruiting offices in downtown Pittsburgh. I expected my acceptance to be a breeze but little did I know about the prospective problems when the medical exam was administered. I flunked that due to an excessive blood pressure reading. This not only threw my enlistment off track, it made me feel my health was in jeopardy.

I returned home determined to find out how I could overcome this obviously serious setback and I got an appointment with a reliable Waynesburg doctor. He quickly admitted me to the local hospital for study and treatment and brought into the effort his partner, a well known surgeon. After a Sunday visitation by my wife and parents and without any knowledge of his plans told to me, the doctor told them he was going to schedule me for a thyroid operation the next day. They collectively put that on hold and got me released from the hospital to get a second opinion. We determined that the best place to get that was at the Cleveland Clinic and arranged to go there the following week. Katherine then drove me up to the clinic for a thorough observation and examination. After several days, I was advised that there was no reason for any operation and suggested only rest and relaxation.

During that time, I felt good and decided that I would live a somewhat normal life. I got a job at Jessop Steel at Washington, Pa. working on the maintenance gang. After working there three or four months, I returned to the Recruiting Office for additional medical examinations. After two or three exams over a period of two months, I was finally sworn in the Officer's Program and was ordered for report on November 3, 1942.

Next, I received my train ticket to Boot Camp in Carolina and orders to that location. The Pittsburgh train station was a somber parting place for Katherine, my parents and me. With good-bye's all around, I boarded the train heading into a strange new world, no part of it known to me, a training ground where men learn to kill or be killed. The roughest part of my life to that time had been on the football field were the combat was physically severe at times, but always far short of deadly.

The train was carrying many recruits in civilian clothes bound for the same destination. Not knowing what I would need, I got on board with a minimum amount of baggage. The train made several stops along the way, the most notable being in DC, but otherwise stayed on its fifteen-hour course to Beauford, South Carolina. It was late night when we arrived and there was a convoy of big Marine trucks known as cattle trucks ready to take us to Paris Island, Boot Camp East. I had some realization of the horrors of the Marine Boot Camp, for its reputation had long and well preceded my arrival.

Reveille came early and we were roused out of our slumbers quite rudely getting prepared for the rigors of the day, which consisted in part of the issuance of leather boots, Marine dungarees and dog tags, which was our common dress code for the duration. The next ritual was a two minute shaving off our hair. Then we were lined up in rough formation for the reading of our status. Our Sergeant told us that we were there entirely at his beck and call, that he was our God and Master; that we were without rights or escape. After explaining that we forget about civilian rights and privileges, we were led into the lines for breakfast consisting of a standard diet of meat gravy on toast. Finally finishing a long day of indoctrination, we were allowed to bed down to dream about what the fates had dictated for us.

Close order drill was the main theme of boot camp. That and long forced marches were the standard means to test the physical stamina of the troops, especially their endurance ability. Day after day, and night after night, always with the loud verbal admonitions of our Platoon Sgt., we were put to the test of our manhood and our patriotism. The main interruptions to this mass means of building discipline were mail call and meals, which we received as blessed events. Getting a letter from home was sure to be a morale builder but the meals were stereotyped and quite tasteless, were still reminders that we were alive and had taste buds to prove it.

Of course, the relief of our body functions was accommodated by the availability of a toilet called a latrine, one unit to a section. Visits there had to be made only as you could between the scheduled programs. I recall on one of my visits, and I found scrubbing the floor on the latrine duty the budding movie star, McDonald Carey, who after the war became a major actor in soap operas!

Close order with our standard issue Garand Rifles was a prominent part of our drill sections. Frequent classes and demonstrations on the rifle were used to emphasize that eventually combat was the aim and purpose of all this intensive training. We learned how to take the rifle completely apart, clean and oil it, and reassemble it, and on punitive occasions, sleep with it.

Visiting the boon-docks, the ragged land areas outside the bounds of the camp, was a special ritual with long day marches as well as overnight trips with bed rolls and backpacks, ammunition belts and full combat dress. All of this training was done in preparation for a week at the final end of our stay in Boot Camp when we were trucked out to an isolated location called the Rifle Range for a week of rifle firing and testing. It was arranged for approximately 25 shooters at a time with parapets located approximately 300 yards in the distance, behind which were target operators who held up the targets when the command to fire was given. Obviously this was a critical part of the training, going to the heart of what our lives were being dedicated to. I was a total neophyte to all types of guns and gunnery except the BB gun and was initially intimidated by this part of the course. To fail the test at the Range was practically tantamount to failing Boot Camp and being discharged from the Corps, or in the alternative, being assigned to the Cooks and Band-Aids segment of the service.

However, I must say that I soon got to like this part of the training and when it came my turn to fire the live ammunition for the many set number of rounds from the several positions-standing, sitting, and lying, I brought myself to a determination that I would succeed. In this skill test there were two standards of success: attaining the rank of "Expert" (the top award), or "Sharpshooter", the runner-up award. I came through this test proud to have earned the "Sharpshooter" Award—proving myself to have earned the title of Private Marine. With eight weeks of Boot Camp, which was both physically and mentally difficult, it finally and thankfully came to an end. I must say it taught me much about what was intended for one to be a Marine and did much to measure ourselves as to what it took to measure up to that standard. To say the least, I came through the experiences deciding that *I belonged*.

Next our training regimen took us to an assignment to Quantico, the historic and time honored permanent Marine Corps, approximately 50 miles south of DC for Officer' Training. Our dress there changed from Marine green dungarees to green and khaki colored uniforms. The training there was an elevated schedule of classrooms; some close order drills and an education in what it took to be an officer in the Corps. This course was intended to make one feel as though he was a human being, but was also coupled with a solid sense of command responsibilities with Marine traditions.

We were billeted in the permanent, brick built structures, much like dormitories on our college campus. And the educational portion of the course was located in similarly styled classroom buildings. As one might expect, these were about combat units, their employment, and the combinations and purpose of their objectives. It also included the ability to use a whole range of the different guns and armaments used by the Corps in combat. As to the personal accommodations on the base, they were much improved with better meals, a large PX, on base movies, and occasional entertainment programs.

One part of the course I well remember was located on the small arms firing range. Unlike the boot camp rifle range, this range was constructed for firing a handheld pistol at a distance of approximately 30-50 feet. The only weapon here used was the Colt 45 caliber pistol. I recall this test because of my abject failure to be able to fire it accurately. My shots were scattered all over the target, some of them missing it completely. Fortunately, we were not graded on this test and I am not sure it was ever entered on our records.

There were two incidents here that stand out in my mind. One was when a drill sergeant singled me out of the whole battalion on the drill field because he mistakenly thought I had been talking in the ranks and ordered me to step out and shout the drills for the whole battalion. The incident tested my nervous system and self-confidence, but I got through it all right. The other incident was on a weekend at the base hospitality center, I witnessed Tyrone Power with his girlfriend coming out of the PX in full Marine Corps dress. He looked much shorter than he did in the movies.

Glenn and his parents   Glenn & Katherine

RESPECT

Since we had free weekends, Katherine came there for visits. On occasions, we went to DC and attended the New York Avenue Presbyterian Church service to hear Rev. Peter Marshall deliver the sermon. He was a spellbinding speaker who later became well liked as Chaplain of the US Senate. We became acquainted with him while attending Potomac State. His father-in-law, the regular minister at the Presbyterian Church in Keyser, invited him to come there to hold a week's evangelic service with Peter, preaching a sermon each night. He was a truly fine, engaging speaker. He was one of the two of the finest orators I encountered in my life, the other being Dr. Francis Pendleton Gaines, President of Washington and Lee University when I attended Law School.

Needless to say, these weekend visits and the new found freedom allowed in this training course did much to enhance my devotion to the corps. However, I had quite a shock after several months. While in a class session, I got a summons delivered personally by an M.P. to go with him to the Base Hospital. I had no knowledge of the reason, but I did suspect that it had something to do with my previous high blood pressure problems. This proved to be true. There a medical doctor holding the rank of Captain conducted the examination and tests. He was an older man who showed a personal concern for each problem. In truth, he was to determine if I remained a marine or would be summarily discharged. Over several days, he tested me personally allowing me each time to be set at ease. After several readings that were administered by the Captain M.D. personally, he gave me clearance to remain in the program. What still haunts me, in the light of the advance of medical cures over the years that, at no time was I ever given any medicine to lower my blood pressure.

In due time, a full scaled graduation was held, patterned after the scholastic example with a speaker and music, but no caps and gowns. There was the automatic pinning of 2nd Lieutenant's bars on our uniforms. In this ceremony, I took my leave of the

Candidates Program in my well tailored marine officer's uniform, thinking myself, probably wrongly, that now I was every inch a marine combat soldier.

Other than obtaining our Officer's Bars, a more lasting effect of our graduation at Quantico was that the orders to the type of service and units were then cut. Every graduate then found out when and where he would serve. These orders were cut without any regard for choice or preference and by a mysterious method never explained. Surprisingly, I was ordered to heavy artillery school at Camp LeJeune, at New River, North Carolina. The majority of men were immediately assigned to combat divisions, those now in existence and those being formed. Others were ordered into Medics, Shipboard duty, transportation, guard and MP duty and all the other needs of building a fighting Corps.

Consequently, with my orders in hand for my next duty station and wearing the newly tailored uniform, I went home to Waynesburg and Holbrook on a 10 day leave to bask in the glow of being a full-fledged marine. I soon found that the small county was known for its high number of enlistees and draftees, with a small number of those detested draft dodgers. But it was a short-lived experience and I was soon aboard a B & O train out of Union Station in Pittsburg to my next duty station and its special training.

Camp LeJeune was a newly constructed sprawling base built with mortar and bricks, able to accommodate many of the various types of training and planning. I found the living quarters, the mess halls, and the overall setting, to be both spacious and comfortable, located on the edge of the Atlantic Ocean. I found this to be ideal for gunnery training using our allotted complement of Long Toms, which when solidly set, could easily hit targets with 100 lb. rounds a distance of 25 miles. The early part of our training was exclusively centered in the classrooms. We learned everything there was to know about the Long Toms.

The next phase was more like a concentrated course in math or at least that part of the subject that emphasized surveying, since for the guns to be correctly fired, they had to be set on the correct azimuth and distance for successful accomplishment of its long range missions. With my father being a professional surveyor, he sometimes used me in the coalmines for his sightings, so I felt that I was now following in his prestigious footsteps.

While we were enjoying the quiet and balmy beauty of the North Carolina beaches it must be remembered that on the orders of General Howling "Mad" Smith, a unit under the command of General Archie Vandergrift, the 1st Marine Division, had been ordered to land and take the isolated island of Guadalcanal, which it did in fierce hand to hand combat in dense jungles infested with yellow fever and against a full complement of well armed banzai Japanese soldiers well dug in. The newspaper accounts daily reported the tenuous and deadly struggle involved in the first battle of World War II, leaving many bodies and crosses planted there. The final outcome was for a long time in serious question. All the while our sympathy and admiration went out to the battle tested marines who were already writing the story of the Pacific War in their blood and remarkable courage.

The last week of Artillery School was in effect the final exam. The test involved how quickly the crews could orient, load and fire at the assigned target. As I recall, we came through these test firings probably not with flying colors, nor with precision skills, but at least with passable evidence of our recently learned skills. When these tests were over, we were ordered to completely clean our guns, which meant swabbing the bores mainly but also every part of the metal giant. After the cleaning was completed, the guns were secured and towed back to their storage area.

They used heavy artillery in the past in the Corps over and above the wide assortment of small arms, like machine gun, the BAR, the MI Rifle, hand grenades, etc., which later in World War

I grew to include the 77mm canons. By the start of World War II, these came to include the small caliber mortars, the 105 mm guns and still later the 90 mm antitank guns. It was no secret that the Long Tom was being added to the corps firepower for use in the invasion of larger land areas beyond the island hopping campaign now ongoing.

The new unit added to the Marine Corps was to be known as corps artillery, 5th Amphibious Corps. It was at that time that the graduates of the training course at Camp LeJeune received their assignments. My assignment was to Battery A 10th Battalion, Corps Artillery, 5th Amphibious Corp. The Battalion was made up of 3 batteries with firing crews, support troops and equipment sufficient to employ the Long Toms when and where needed. I found out that my Battalion in the newly formed Corp was headed by a veteran Marine, alcohol-soaked Major of the old school, who commanded the 10th Battalion. After getting acquainted with our fellow officers and men, our next assignment was for the whole Battalion to load the freight and troop trains to head off the marine base at San Diego, California. Here we spent the next week on shore loading a transport ship, which soon lifted anchor for Hawaii.

We landed first at the island of Maui, but after building our own tent camp, we were ordered out—over to Camp Tarawa, in the Camp of the 2nd Marine Division where it was stationed on its return from the bloody battle of Tarawa. As you may know, it was brought back here from the ravages of the bloodiest battle of the Pacific so far. Here the Division was being restored in manpower and training and told it would be shortly headed for the assault on Saipan.

Our artillery battalion was totally under a separate command from the division. We continued our training, taking our guns to a firing sight, with the considerable firing of many rounds on the lava beds below the venerable twin volcanic Mountains, Mona Loa and Mona Kei. The camp itself was built on the edge of the lava bed at a high altitude some 15,000 feet above sea level. It was generally cold and often windy and rainy.

The first thing in my memory that stands out took place after some months training on the lava bed. I received a message that my brother, James, and two other officer friends, were at the Hilo airport, having arrived there by plane. My brother was, indeed, a Naval Officer who, while serving on the Aircraft Carrier *Yorktown* in the ferocious battle of Midway, was one of the many heroes of that experience and was one of the many who were plucked out of the water when the *Yorktown* sunk, to live for other naval experiences. After the rescue James was ordered back to Naval Headquarters at Pearl Harbor and assigned there to serve in personnel matters. It was through that sensitive service that he had been able to locate me on the windswept barren island of Hawaii.

James was able to get time and air transportation to make the visit. What was more notable about it, more than just the complete surprise, was that it was the day before Christmas in the year 1944. Upon receiving this message, I hurriedly boarded my trusty jeep and headed to Hilo, the main town that was 60 miles away on the other side of the island. We had an inexplicably fine visit that Christmas Eve and it continued through to the next day until they had to return to Pearl Harbor. What a coincidence that was, miles away from our homes, both in different branches of service and bound by the blood of our birth, that we had the privilege of being together in the middle of a World War.

One of the most moving experiences of my life occurred late in our stay in Camp Tirana. That was the day the whole newly rested and reinvigorated 2nd Marine Division was ordered to go by truck convoy to the port of Hilo for loading and heading for the upcoming assault on *Saipan*. As I saw the youthful, always smiling faces of the endless caravan of marines and their equipment, I could not help but feel a deep sympathy for all involved in that

Division of more than 20,000 men, fresh from one bloody fight and now heading for another. In truth, my sympathy was soon overwhelmed by a deep respect for their obvious show of courage. This much I did know, an artillery marine was sheltered in a harbor that was much safer than the life of the combat infantryman.

From the safe harbor in Hawaii, our Battalion, the 10th Corps Artillery, 5th Amphibious Corps, was loaded and shipped to Guam. To this end, our shipboard journey was ordered to make port in Guam. The whole Battalion was loaded in mass, personnel, gear, guns and all. The journey by sea took approximately 10 days. We did little training at this time and did nothing more than mark time for several months. Marines played penny ante poker, some, like myself, played chess, while others rested and wrote letters home. Battery B was ordered into combat action, assigned to the Army-Navy landing forces for a long awaited attack on the Philippines in the Island of *Leyte*. The combined troops and support forces were under the command of the renowned General Douglas MacArthur who had been rescued from the battle of Bataan in the Philippines when it was overrun by the Japs. In the Marine Corps, he was known as "Dug out Doug" and was not a favorite of the marines.

An interesting situation involving the orders for one of our Batteries to be made as part of the Leyte Assault Forces was that I was singled out and ordered to accompany Battery B as an Observer. I never understood the reason or high level thinking for that, but I reconciled myself by the thought that after all of my training, I was going to be a part of actual combat.

As "D" Day approached for the attack, all of the Battery B and its complement of Long Toms (4) were loaded aboard a large landing boat, and then joined the Armada of ships and men who made up the gigantic force that was composed to invade and secure the Philippines. The landing was preceded by a heavy naval ship bombardment of the landing area. This was completed without much return fire and the landing boats made ready to storm ashore.

Ahead of them, however, was General MacArthur, triumphantly with a contingent of fellow officers seen wading ashore. This was in celebration of the General's famous statement after being rescued from Bataan, *"I shall return!"* As it was to be expected, our landing craft did not go ashore until D plus 5 days and was done and accomplished without any resistance

By that time, the invading troops had fought their way into the island 6 to 10 miles deep. So when we landed the heavy trucks, we pulled the Long Toms to an initial location some 3 or 4 miles inland. As an observer, presumably to learn firsthand about the difficulties and problems of using the guns in actual combat, I had no duties with the putting the guns in place or firing, but Battery B were soon made to start firing. The targets identified for them were made by spotter planes flying over the front lines.

Soldiers placing sandbags on the island of Leyte

After being with Battery B for about 15 days, I got a real shock. While in the field, I was visited by the battery adjutant delivering personal orders for me to go to battalion headquarters for arrangements to fly in a military plane back to Guam. As always, in the military, you do what you are told to do without hesitation or question. I boarded a C25 Transport plane and with me were several other passengers who were high-ranking officers in the Philippine Army in exile.

Coming back to Guam was like a homecoming to me. It was a reunion with my marine mates, a time to catch up with my mail, and most of all, a time to tell anyone who would listen about my so-called "combat experience." I came back to the schedule that existed before my departure—some training, some relaxation and a lot of speculation. It should be no secret that the Pacific War was in its final stages. Leyte, the front door to the Japanese homelands was now secure and we could realize that the final assault soon to be enacted would take place against the Japanese southern island of Kyushu. We could watch and wait. Already the war in Europe had been concluded when the massive armies of the Americans, English forces converged on Berlin with the highly motivated Russian army coming in from the East. The total effect of the combined forces of the three armies put forever the mocking, hateful voice of Hitler into an eternal stillness.

But through world news turning to the Pacific—by radio and some newspapers, we learned of the dramatic events that were rapidly unfolding. Heavy Air Force attacks that led to the ultimate dropping of the atomic bomb on Hiroshima and Nagasaki, totally removed their existence from the face of the earth. This was the year 1945, after Harry Truman had succeeded to the Presidency on the death of Franklin Roosevelt. While world pundits are still debating the wisdom of Truman's ordering the use of the atomic bomb, make no mistake, out in the field and among the troops, there was nothing but jubilation and celebration for its use.

What was the immediate result of the use of the atomic bomb, the ultimate destructive device? That question is not hard to answer. What it did for me was, for all practical purposes, put in motion my release from the Marine Corps and let me get on with the rest of my life. The word came down from Marine Headquarters that it had devised a system for determining the order of release from the service for all marines. The heart of that system was to assign points for one's time of service overseas. By 1945 I had been two years overseas. I believed that I would be heading home in the first echelon. Following the system, in short order I received my orders for transportation by air back to the mainland from Guam and then home.

I flew in a Marine B 25 to Camp Pendleton. I was quickly informed that the required uniform of the day was the Marine Corps green and that I would be restricted to the base until I could comply. Since I didn't have the money to buy another uniform, or the inclination, I called Katherine to mail my uniform to me fast. I had the inward joy of going home. Katherine, a teacher at Waynesburg during my time in the service, met me at Union Station in Pittsburgh.

I received my full honorable discharge from active duty and into the Marine Reserves. By then I held the rank of captain, and later, after 2 years in the Reserves, I received the rank of major. The Marine Corps has left a lasting mark on my mind and personality. It made me appreciate the worth and meaning of discipline, the need for the constant devotion to liberty and an appreciation of the many of my fellow citizens who interrupted their lives and their plans to go the last mile to continue America, the land of the free and the home of the brave.

In the course of my years of service, I made many friends who were good marines who brought to the corps strong individual character much of it formed before entering the service. Two men I remember were "Greasy" Greaves and "Hi" Raisin, both attorneys from New York City. The Marine Corps trademark *"Semper Fidelis"* meaning Always Faithful, has much to do with the esprit de corps of the body of the men and now women who come under its spell. While I have never worn its' banner on my sleeves, I have never been ashamed to sing its praises when asked.

The Veterans of World War I came home to victory parades and universal adulation, but once that was over there was nothing left to help them bridge the gap between war service and a normal well adjusted life as a civilian. Not so with the millions of Veterans of World War II. Due to a generous and meaningful display of gratitude, President Harry Truman and Congress forthwith established by official action the GI Bill of rights. Among them was the most important provision of payment for any and all types of academic and trade school education for each and every World War II Veteran with no exception. This benefit felt like money from heaven and following my earlier dream and desire to become a lawyer, I set about to enroll in an accredited law school. I decided to cast my academic lot with Washington & Lee, that historic institution. Washington & Lee Campus joins VMI Military Academy, a prestigious school in itself where my fellow West Virginian who was born in Harrison County, who after years of teaching at VMI, became a monumental legend for his service in the Confederate War. That was Confederate General Thomas Jonathan (Stonewall) Jackson.

I commenced a career as a lawyer, practicing law in Waynesburg, Pa. In due time I taught law and government at Waynesburg College and served two terms as District Attorney of Greene County and two terms as the common Pleas Court Judge. After I retired, I wrote and self-published several paperback books of my political convictions, some in fiction and two books of poetry.

Judge Toothman was born August 9, 1920 and died on November 18, 2001. He wrote the following article in conclusion to writing about his experiences. *"I agree with Tom Brokow's view of the World War II Veterans ranking them militarily as the World's greatest generation by their unbounded show of courage and devotion to duty over a period in time they brought to destruction three evil Empires—Germany, Japan, and Italy, and further held at bay a Russian Communist regime bent on taking over the world. It didn't take a TV announcer like Brokow to identify the importance of the World War Veteran. It appears to me that he realized it would be a good horse to ride and might even come to including him by literary proxy as one of that distinguished generation."*

MELVIN LEE TOOTHMAN
ARMY AIR FORCE

(L to R: Stinnant, Falloner, and Lee Toothman)

I was the fourth child born to Glenn and Elsie Toothman living in the hamlet of Hepziban which is six miles north of Clarksburg, West Virginia. My parents met while attending Fairmont Norman College and my father subsequently became a mining engineer. The family was completed when my sister, Betty Jane (Halversen) was born in 1924. I was little more than an average student through High School, however playing on the family name I was elected class president my freshman and senior years. Being undersized I was not successful at football after trying for two years. My other interests were airplane modeling and dramatics.

I entered Marshall College (now University) in Huntington, West Virginia in 1940 supported in part by a speech scholarship and further by working in the school cafeteria. Again my extra curricular activity included dramatics in which I was given parts in several school plays.

I entered the Army Air Force in the middle of my junior year at Marshall to eventually become a B-24 pilot. I flew 26 missions over Germany as a member of the 707 Sqdn. of the 446 Bomb Group, Eighth Air Force. After returning to civilian life I entered Dental School at the University of Pittsburg and upon graduation in 1950, I joined the Army Dental Corps and was subsequently sent to Korea to serve with the Third Infantry Division. Upon return to the United States I married Shirley Snyder and continued to serve Aberdeen Proving Ground for one year.

I was just about to end my Sunday lunch service at Marshall College school cafeteria in Huntington, West Virginia, when someone came bursting in with the announcement that the Japanese had just bombed our military base at Pearl Harbor in Hawaii. No details were given, just that it had happened. As soon as our shift was finished, a group of us ran across campus to our dorm which had a large radio in the lobby. Confirmation was immediate and details as they became known were given. Every man in that room knew that his life's dream would soon be altered. Our parents had moved to Washington, Pennsylvania, where our father was assigned. He had accepted a position with the Federal Bureau of Mines as a mine inspector. I proceeded home for the Christmas holiday and returned to Marshall for the completion of my second year.

Having not been called in the draft and knowing it was inevitable my plan was to enlist in the Army Air Corps that summer. My interest in airplanes began very early in life and was greatly intensified when I was in the fifth grade. While serving as an official for the Annual Mine Safety Meet of West Virginia (held at Jackson's Mill—birthplace of Stonewall Jackson), our father was given a complimentary pass for a ride on a Ford tri-motor airplane operating from the nearby field. His duties precluded him from going, so he gave the ticket to me. I remember every detail of that ride as if it were yesterday. It wasn't a very long ride. We just circled the town of Weston and returned; but in terms of making an impression, it might just as well have been transcontinental. Also at this time, I was an avid airplane modeler.

The reality of war came a little closer that summer when our older brother James became a survivor of the sinking of the aircraft carrier *Yorktown*. He came home shortly thereafter, but was soon sent back in the melee having been assigned to a new much smaller carrier.

I reported to the old post office building in midtown Pittsburg for my first experience of an army physical. At the end of the process, we faced a major who had a file of papers. He had several large stamps on his desk. He asked me if I was enrolled in school and planned to continue. When I answered in the affirmative, he took one of his large stamps and slammed it on my file—it read "educational deferral until June '44." I worked that summer on an engineering survey crew based in Cannonsburg.

College resumed in the fall and it was obvious that the male population was thinning rapidly. My call came when I was just ready to start the second semester. I was ordered to report to Fort Benjamin Harrison in Indiana. After getting a refund of twenty-six dollars for lab fees from the school, which I needed for bus fare, I proceeded to Benjamin Harrison arriving in a snowstorm. After one night there, we were loaded on a sixteen-car troop train headed south. The baggage car was outfitted with a stove and three large barrels—one contained canned peaches, one was a stew, and the final one was Kool-Aid. We arrived at Miami on the third day. My new home was the Anglers Hotel on South Beach. The hotels had been stripped of all regular furniture and GI cots were installed. This would be our home for army basic training. We were issued uniforms, haircuts, more physicals, and daily marching up and down the streets across golf courses.

Add to this close order drill, physical training, cross-town runs, and shots-ad-nauseam. Large comfortable movie houses were used for lectures and the now famous GI films. One day we were issued a broomstick and marched to the beach for a new drill with our newly issued equipment.

At the end of March, another troop train took us to a destination unknown. We arrived at Allegheny College, a highly regarded liberal arts school in Meadville, Pennsylvania, again arriving in a snow storm. We attended classes which were condensed versions of regular college courses. Those of us with previous college experience were sent by troop train to a miserable place in South Nashville, Tennessee to be classified. We would be cast either as a pilot, navigator, bombardier, or gunner. Pilot candidates were then designated Aviation Cadets and sent to Maxwell Field in Montgomery, Alabama. The next time we saw a very tightly supervised routine of physical training-marching, class work related to aviation. Our class was 44D, meaning we should graduate in the fourth month of 1944.

The next move for some of us was to a neat little airfield in Lafayette, Louisiana, for what was called Primary Flight Training, which was our first real exposure to an airplane—in this case, a Ryan PT23 open cockpit monoplane with a radial 200HP engine. This school was operated by civilians. Flying there was fun, but with the dark side being the realization that you could be terminated, "washed out," very quickly after which you would be dispatched to gunnery school. My instructor was Herman Meltzer of Pittsburg, an accomplished pilot and a no-nonsense teacher. After some eleven hours of instruction, I knew I was set to solo.

We proceeded this day to a newly mowed hayfield a few miles north of our base. After a couple of landings under Mr. Meltzer's supervision, he taxied the plane over to the fence and told me, rather gruffly, that he wanted out and if I wanted to solo it was my option but he had his doubts—an act I'm sure designed to make me mad enough to show him what I could do. I still remember that flight totally. In the air I was elated but, I must admit, lonely. On the downwind leg, I sang "There'll be a Hot Time in the Old Town Tonight." Upon landing, I taxied over to pick up my tormentor, who, by this time was smiling. This was known as the Maytag ride for this had the possibility of washing you out of the program. Gradually our ranks began to thin somewhat.

Looking back on my total flying experience, this plane was the most fun. My favorite solo activities were doing spins, pylons, and loops. Well into the program, feeling confident of passing this phase, my friend Bill Todd and I conspired to meet in our planes several miles northwest of the field for the purpose of showing off for each other. I climbed to 6,000 feet and decided to show off my spin technique. Upon recovery, I flew back to the oil tanks, but my friend was nowhere to be found. Later, at supper, he explained that he lost sight of me thinking that I had spun in and he didn't want to be caught in that area. What we were up to would have been a sure cause for a wash out...especially if you killed yourself.

The next phase of training, most of us proceeded to a small Army airfield at Walnut Ridge, Arkansas. Here the flying phase was done in a single engine all metal monoplanes with the designation BT13, known as the Vultee Vibrator. It had a larger engine, more instrumentation, and a greenhouse siding cover over both cockpits. Our instructors were regular Army officers. We were also introduced to night flying and after being checked out, we were ready for "big night"--- which consisted of sending about sixteen planes to an auxiliary field ten miles away. My instructor was an excellent stunt flier. The next phase of training for Walnut

Ridge graduates would normally be Blytheville, Arkansas, about eighty miles ease and very close to the Mississippi River.

Two basic graduates from each school in the Southeast Training Command were selected to go to Stewart Field in Newburg, New York. A friend, Sweeney from Scranton, Pennsylvania, and I were selected for what reason we never knew. It turned out that facilities set up there to train West Point cadets were being unused, so seventy of us arrived known as GI Cadets. Each set up introduced new things, such as a second engine to keep track of, flaps to be used on landing along with a host of other things. I did well. It was fun.

While at Stewart Field, we had a day at the Academy and an opportunity to get into the big city. While walking the streets of Manhattan, I ran into a former candidate who had washed out early in the program for physical reasons and was now in civilian clothes. I requested the B-25, the plane Doolittle's Raiders flew from the *Hornet*. We graduated and became full-fledged Army Lieutenants with our first increase in pay and sent to Maxwell Field in Montgomery, Alabama for B-24 Transition School. After three months of flight training, ground school, and Link Trainer, we were declared ready to move on.

We moved on to Boise, Idaho, where the commanding officer was Colonel "Killer" Kane of Polesti fame. We were assigned our crew members and flying soon began. We all got to practice our new trade, i.e., gunners gunning, navigators navigating, bombardiers bombing, as well as the engineers monitoring all the plane's systems. We departed Boise in early December and spent a few days at a large base in Lincoln, Nebraska for a final briefing about what was in our future and that was the European Theater of Operations—that could only mean the 15th Air Force based in Italy or the Eighth Air Force based in England. It was common to tease the Fifteenth Air Force friends that the reason for their lesser assignment was that they had failed their screen test. After all, we had Clark Gable and Jimmy Stewart. One day in a large theater building it was announced that our next speaker would be sergeant Billy Wells. Out on the stage stepped the same Billy Wells that I had served with in the Marshall College cafeteria. Billy recounted a remarkable story of being the engineer on a B-17 shot down deep in Germany. He had contacted the underground in Holland, moved into France and eventually across the Pyrenees into Spain then back to England and the States.

Our next stop was Camp Miles Standish, south of Boston which served as a holding pen for shipment to England. We didn't wait long and were soon aboard the SS *Mt. Vernon.* The ship was jammed full with 500 flying officers housed on the top deck. We landed at Liverpool, dispatched to Stone in the center of England. Then we were assigned to our combat group. This was the last time I saw my friend Donald Wood of St. Louis. We found out about six weeks later that he had been assigned to a B-17 base and was killed in a formation flying accident.

Our base was two miles outside the small town of Bungey, just fifteen miles from the channel coast. The days were short and it was quickly becoming very cold. Europe was experiencing the coldest winter in seventy years. It was now mid December. There was no heat. I remember sleeping on a bunk of straw mats fully clothed with the two allotted blankets plus topcoat. I was given an orientation and check-out ride and thereafter assigned to fly as co-pilot.

Next, we took off, the formation formed up, and we departed for Germany. The battle-hardened pilot never offered to let the rookie fly formation, so he did all the flying. When we hit the initial point and started the bomb run, we all donned flack vests and helmets. I noticed a black cloud up ahead and thought that unusual in an otherwise clear sky. As we drew nearer, it was plain that the sky was full of flack and these gunners had our altitude perfectly. I became transfixed, certain that we would never make it out safely. Finally, with bombs away, the co-pilot is supposed to swing into action and change all the power settings on the engines. The pilot finally whacked me on the shoulder to bring me out of my stupor and get the job done. When we got home, there were holes in the plane and I became awakened to the facts of life. If this was an easy mission, it would be a long tour indeed.

The weather grounded us for several days. We learned that in Belgium our ground troops were dealing with a severe problem later to be known as the *Battle of the Bulge*. At the time we were needed most, we could not move because ceiling and visibility were very poor. Gradually we were able to fly again and the missions were beginning to chalk up. The tour for a crew that began with twenty-five missions was now moved up to thirty-five and before the war ended would move on to fifty-five as the minimum number to rate a trip home.

A typical mission would involve having yourself and crew posted as being up to fly the next day and awakened anywhere from two to five in the morning. There was breakfast and then a walk to the operations center for a general briefing followed ten minutes later with a specific briefing for navigators, bombardiers, and pilots. As we ate breakfast, you could hear the planes all over the base being warmed up by the ground crews, loaded with today's type of bombs and finally gas tanks topped off to the maximum 2,700 gallons. So with all that gas, which weighed 16,200 pounds, 5,000 to 6,000 pounds of bombs, thousands of rounds of 50 caliber ammunition, nine crew members, body armor, and a host of other paraphernalia, we had a total weight in excess of 63,000 pounds.

After the initial briefing and now knowing the target, I usually used the ten minutes between briefings to visit an open pit privy located nearby. The missions were so precisely planned that you had time to be in your plane, a time to start engines, a time to taxi out to your proper place. The takeoff was signaled by a green light from the tower. Usually it would be totally dark but three hundred feet from the end of the runway a search light beam crossed the runway. If you went through that beam, you had no alternative but to pull the plane off. Our lead plane, up to this time would have been *Fearless Freddie*. It wasn't until the tenth mission that we were assigned *Queenie*, a relative new "J" model that did much to relieve stress.

We would start climbing in order to reach the desired altitude of around twenty-three thousand feet, which usually put us over Holland which was still in enemy hands. We would Cross the strip of land that was the western border of Holland before coming to the Zider Zee. Then we would face our first flack. The Germans had 88mm guns mounted on railroad flat cars and these gunners were Hitler's very best. It was always cat and mouse, hoping we would avoid these guys, but it didn't happen that way. One morning they picked off a plane in a squadron to our right with a single burst. Most of Holland was occupied until late March, so ground fire was possible in a number of places. Once we were aligned on a target, much attention was given to closed formation.

Only the lead plane had a bombardier, everyone else toggled their bombs just as the leader released a smoke bomb.

The landing procedure was that each squadron, usually twelve planes, took turns flying down the runway at five hundred feet then peeling off in a circle to land. This system got each plane down at intervals of thirty seconds or less. Since the B-24 had a tripod gear, we could taxi quite fast. Once down and log book and other write-ups completed, we were picked up by trucks and taken back to operations for debriefing. By then it was suppertime. The average mission was six to eight hours long.

A particular mission in mid-March was one that gave our group notoriety of sorts. At briefing, we were told that our commanding officer, Colonel Crawford, a John Wayne Texan type, would be policing the bomber stream in an English Mosquito (a very fast twin engine molded plywood plane). On this particular day, we got our first look at Germany's newest air weapon, airplanes without propellers. We were deep inside Germany, well beyond the combat line, but still had not reached our target. Everyone was awed to see a plane so fast that even our P-52s were left in the dust. I had a front seat to a most amazing event. Suddenly there appeared the Mosquito about a mile to our left, just beginning a fighter approach to our very group. Guns from our squadron opened up and I could clearly see the tracers going into our little friend. It soon faltered, went over on one wing and into a spin, trailing white smoke. It disappeared in a cloud layer and it appeared that both men were doomed. However, a few weeks after the war was over, Colonel Crawford showed up at our base. He was a much changed person. He had lost forty pounds and though he had broken his shoulder in the jump, both survived only to be held as prisoners at a German airbase that was often being bombed and strafed almost daily.

Our mission was also the last for the 8th Air Force. This trip took us well past Munich to Salzburg, Austria, where we bombed railroad marshaling yards. This was truly a "milk run" because there was no enemy opposition of any kind. The date was April 24, 1945. It amazes me now that while all of this activity was going on in my life and equally with my three brothers, that I failed to appreciate the supreme stress for our parents that having four sons overseas at the same time must have produced. Possibly part of the reason could be explained by the fact that almost everybody was living with the same circumstances.

Believe me, after becoming a parent, I have thought about it many, many times and now deeply regret that I was not as sensitive to their plight as I should have been. There must have been a lot of praying since we all made it home safely. I think now of the biblical story of the prodigal son whose father looked for his return daily despite that fact that he had literally turned his back on his family an dishonored them. Even under these circumstances, he was welcomed home with open arms. Combat was tough; home-front duty could be even tougher. When the war ended we had been credited with twenty-six missions and no credit for times recalled over the channel or for coming across the North Sea from Denmark on three engines. With the end of hostilities, we did some training flying and some pleasure flying but no more dreaded formation stuff. One interesting trip was one in which we took about twenty ground personnel into Germany to fly up the Ruhr Valley to view the bombing devastation, most of which in this area had been done by the British Air Force.

Our planes were prepared for the long flight home, and we would fly with a squadron operations officer by the name of Captain Henry Gardnier. We had nineteen people aboard with their luggage. Our first stop was the Valley of Wales. From Wales to the Azores, to Newfoundland, and the final leg into New England, landing at Bangor, Maine. Our destination was Connecticut and all departed for thirty days of leave, then to report to a base in Sioux

Falls, South Dakota. We were to be retained on B-29s and sent to the Pacific. While there, the atomic bombs were dropped on Japan.

A group of us were sent to Long Beach, California for no particular purpose. Long Beach was a joy with few duties and many opportunities to explore. We enjoyed the beach and I remember spending one weekend at Arrowhead Lake, a beautiful spot in the mountains northeast of Bakersfield. While there, I had an overnight visit from my brother Glenn who had just returned from the Pacific and was now stationed at Camp Pendleton about twenty-five miles south. I had drawn Officer of the Day duties, so he got to go with me in my Jeep to monitor fuel truck dumping and other duties. Eventually I was dispatched to Andrews Field in Washington to be discharged. Uncle Harold, then a Lieutenant Colonel in the finance section of the Army stationed at the Pentagon, gave me a tour of the Pentagon where I saw general "Vinegar Joe" Stillwell newly returned from the China Burma India Theater.

It has taken years to gain perspective about the momentous events that made up the history of our country's participation in World War II. The individual participant is involved in such a small part that it is difficult to gain a comprehensive picture. For example, I know now that I have been involved in bombing missions involving close to two thousand bombers and one thousand fighters—which means that if the leader of this parade were coming across Atlanta, tail end Charlie would be just clearing Memphis.

When we look at Germany, its size, its limited resources, we have to be impressed by their cohesion in carrying out the most horrific slaughter of humanity the world has ever known. What our country did after Pearl Harbor's wake-up call is equally or even more striking. Consider the 8th Air Force. We were never stood down because of a fuel shortage and we never went hungry. The 8th Air Force suffered a higher casualty rate than any other branch of service and that was particularly true of the early period of 1943-1944. We had never seen a conventional enemy fighter. We saw plenty of flack, but at times poorly executed.

Back in Pittsburg, I had decided by that time to try to be admitted to Pitt Dental School. Only the secretary was there when I visited during the Christmas holiday. She encouraged me to register. She said "How is your brother George?" Another Toothman had graduated two years earlier. After filling in some needed requirements at Marshall, I started in dental school in September 1946 with an expected graduation time of June 1950. My senior year, Betty had married and I was the only one at home, now in Mt. Lebanon.

In the fall of our senior year, George Campbell asked me to go to the Delta Zeta house to a sorority tea dance. I refused but George was persistent. I had dated many girls but cupid's arrows had never come my way until that night. There standing behind the piano was a lovely creature. I introduced myself and I think we danced, but my motive soon became getting a date with her as soon as there was an opening in her busy schedule. Her name was Shirley Snyder and her phone number was Dorseyville 72. Sometime in the spring I proposed and she accepted. We were both soon to be graduated. My GI Bill benefits were to expire in my senior year, so during the summer I signed up in an Army program that offered a commission and paid for my last year of schooling in exchange for two more years of active duty service. I was scheduled to be assigned to Fort Eustis, Virginia. Shirley and I had planned to be married in October. Shirley got a job teaching fifth grade in Millvale, Pennsylvania public school and I proceeded to Fort Eustis. Just a few days after graduation, the North Koreans crossed the agreed upon partition of that country known as the 38th Parallel. Troops totally unprepared for war were dispatched from Japan.

It was clearly an unbelievable foreign policy blunder for the Truman administration. Truman's Secretary of State Dean Atchinson, in a major foreign policy speech, stated that our general sphere of protection *did not include Korea.* That statement, made approximately six months before the North Korea invasion was clearly an open invitation for the Russian and Chinese supported North Koreans to make their move. Such a lapse is beyond criminal since it resulted in fifty-four thousand American and United Nations casualties and perhaps millions of others.

After being at Fort Eustis for six weeks, another dentist and I received orders to proceed to Fort Benning, Georgia for assignment to the Third Infantry Division who were packed and ready to board trains that morning for San Francisco, headed for Korea. We received permission to take our new automobiles back to our homes and promised to fly to San Francisco. This was indeed a sad time for Shirley and me. After leaving the Pontiac hardtop with my parents, Shirley saw me off at the airport. I was soon aboard a troop ship headed for Korea. As we crossed the Pacific (twelve days), the war news was increasingly grim. The North Koreans were within thirty-five miles of Pusan, the south's southernmost city. The Third Division was not combat ready. We were sent to a remote area in southern Japan to an area in the mountains that had been an American prisoner of war camp during World War II.

About this time we received two thousand young Korean men who had literally been rounded up on the streets of several South Korean cities. They were to become filler and service troops for the Division. The language barrier was enormous. Our medical detachment was fortunate in receiving a young Christian theology student named Min Jusick. He was an exceptional young man, very bright, personable, and eager to learn.

Our camp at Beppu, Japan was a first class mud hole. After six weeks there, we packed up and headed for Korea. By this time general MacArthur had made his now famous end run by landing at Inchon, proceeding to Seoul, then north across the 38th Parallel and on toward the Yalu River. We landed on the east coast of North Korea in the city of Wonson and set up camp. Within a couple of days it was Thanksgiving (1950). The news was all rosy and MacArthur was predicting we would be home by Christmas. We had hardly finished our Thanksgiving feast when we got the word that our troops up at the border were under attack by swarms of Chinese soldiers. There were reports of thousands of North Korean soldiers in the mountains west of us. A South Korean infantry with a battery of our light field artillery was sent on patrol. I was selected to be the medical officer for the artillery unit. We advanced westward ten miles or more without event.

(Dentistry under ideal conditions with Lee Toothman)

We dug foxholes in a cabbage field, but the night was peaceful though very cold. After a couple of days, they returned after not being able to provoke a fight. The entire Division was again soon on the move. We arrived at the port city of Hungnam and set up camp. Our infantry set up a perimeter defense while the marines were brought to the port. When this operation was complete, the Navy Seals blew up the harbor. It was now Christmas Eve and we were soon on our way to Pusan. The roads and railways were jammed with many thousands of refugees pouring into the south. We got about halfway up the South Korean part of the peninsula when we made contact with the enemy. By this time, I was rotated between the 39h and the 10th field artillery battalions both using 105mm guns. Part of the time I was Battalion Dentist and part of the time I served as the Battalion Physician

.(Generals MacArthur and Ridgeway-taken by Lee Toothman)

The Chinese obviously had no consideration for the lives of their own soldiers because they poured in thousands upon thousands of infantry troops against us. General MacArthur visited our Division in February. I took a picture standing by his jeep with General Ridgeway in the back of the jeep. MacArthur's replacement was General Matthew Ridgeway of World War II airborne fame. (Ridgeway was age 49 when he commanded the 82nd Airborne. They parachuted into Normandy on June 6, 1944). We eventually reached the Han River just south of the capitol city of Seoul. All the bridges had long been destroyed, but the engineers soon solved that problem.

I left Korea in September as the first dentist to be rotated in the 3rd Division. The war dragged on until 1953 when a peace agreement was finally signed with the boundaries at about the same place they were when I left. My only break during this year was a visit to the hospital ship *Hope* as a patient. While sharpening an axe one evening, I got a piece of steel in my right eye. My medics took me to a nearby Mash hospital where a young ophthalmologist attempted to remove the sliver, but to no avail. At the ship Hope, the doctor concluded that the silver evidently had come out during the flight to Pusan. A small Army transport ship took us from Inchon to Sasebo, Japan

When I arrived in Seattle, I got a special dockside reception from my brother James and his family complete with "Welcome Uncle Lee" signs. After arriving at Pittsburg and being greeted by my folks, I was on my way in the Pontiac Catalina to Florida where my bride-to-be was with her parents. We had a great time together while making plans for our wedding and new life together.

The wedding took place in the first Methodist Church in downtown Fort Lauderdale by a wonderful pastor, Dr. John Hangar, on a Saturday afternoon with about a half dozen guests which included Aunt Harriet and Uncle Frank from Coral Gables. After a brief honeymoon in Miami Beach, we departed for my new assignment at Aberdeen Proving Grounds, Maryland.

We stopped in Pittsburg for a couple of days then on to Baltimore where we found an apartment in a housing development on the north side of the city near the Martin Bomber factory. Within two weeks, Shirley had a job teaching fourth and sixth graders in Victory Ville School and thus began a wonderful 50 years together. We now skip ahead to see what this marriage has produced in fifty years. There are now three grown children, Mark, Pamela, and Amy. They have blessed us with eight grandchildren.

CHAPTER TWO

PEARL HARBOR

December 7, 1941, a date which will live in infamy...
No matter how long it may take us to overcome this premeditated
invasion, the American people, in their righteous might
will win through to absolute victory.
                    President Franklin D. Roosevelt

In 1933, Adolph Hitler became the chancellor of Germany. That same year, the first concentration camp opened outside Berlin. With the Enabling Act giving Hitler dictatorial powers, the wheels were set in motion for the impending war between the Axis (Germany, Italy and Japan) and the allied nations (the United States, Australia and the majority of the remaining European countries). In 1936, Germany's invasion of the Rhineland set up the plan for Hitler to conquer all of Europe. A declaration of war from England followed Hitler's invasion of Poland on September 1, 1939. Hitler deceived the German people to justify this attack by telling them that Poland had not accepted the peace agreements that were offered; and that they had persecuted the German people who were living in Poland. Germany had submitted a plan to Poland. When the ambassador tried to file this report with Warsaw, he was unable to because the communication lines had been cut. When the Germans did not receive a reply, they used this to invade Poland. Great Britain and France had an alliance with Poland. They were forced to declare war on Germany. As one writer put it, "the holocaust of the world was under way." The Polish army was brave however the German weapons and planes were too much for their small, under-equipped army. The Polish cities began to fall one by one. On September 23rd, the Germans announced that it was over. Poland had surrendered. The Capitol, Warsaw did not surrender until four days later.

In a broadcast to the world from No. 10 Downing Street at 11:15 A.M. Sunday, September 3, 1939, Prime Minister Neville Chamberlain said: *"This morning the British Ambassador in Berlin handed the German government a final note stating that unless we heard from them by eleven o'clock that they were prepared at once to withdraw their troops from Poland a state of war would exist between us. I have to tell you now that no such undertaking has been received and that consequently this country is at war with Germany...Now may God bless you all. May he defend the right! It is the evil things that we shall be fighting against–brute force, bad faith, injustice, oppression and persecution–and against them I am certain that the right will prevail."* [Quote from Acme News pictures, Inc.]

In May 1940, Hitler sent troops across the borders of Belgium, Holland and Luxembourg. Hitler's troops continued the attack and were caught unprepared on December 4, when the Soviets launched a counteroffensive. Then after the Japanese attacked Pearl Harbor, Germany declared war on the United States.

It is well known that the United States entered the war after the Japanese attacked Pearl Harbor on December 7, 1941. The Japanese Aircraft carrier *Akagi* was moving toward Hawaii about 5:50 in the morning. There were 183 fighters and torpedo planes that took off from six aircraft carriers under the command of Captain Fuchido. The number of military and civilian deaths reported was 2,403. The United States suffered great losses during this surprise attack. Twenty-one US Navy ships were sunk and destroyed with a loss of 185 planes. The *Arizona's* death toll was the greatest with 1,170 crew members killed during this attack.

HONOLULU STAR-BULLETIN 1ST EXTRA
Honolulu, Territory of Hawaii, USA. Sunday, December 7, 1941 (Price five cents)

WAR! OAHU BOMBED BY JAPANESE PLANES.

Six known dead, 21 injured, at Emergency Hospital
Attack Made on Island's Defense Areas. By United Press

WASHINGTON, Dec. 7.-*Text of a White house announcement detailing the attack on the Hawaiian Island's is: "The Japanese attacked Pearl Harbor from the air and all naval and military activities on the island of Oahu, principal American base in the Hawaiian islands."*

Oahu was attacked at 7:35 this morning by Japanese planes. The Rising Sun, emblem of Japan, was seen on plane wing tips. Wave after wave of bombers streamed through the clouded morning sky from the southwest and flung their missiles on a city resting in peaceful Sabbath calm.

According to an unconfirmed report received at the governor's office, the Japanese force that attacked Oahu reached island waters aboard two small airplane carriers. It was also reported to the governor's office that an attempt had been made to bomb the USS Lexington, or it had been bombed.

CITY IN UPROAR   Within 10 minutes the city was in an uproar. As bombs fell in many parts of the city, and in defense areas the defenders of the islands went into quick action. Army intelligence officers at Ft. Shafter announced officially shortly after 9 a.m. the fact of the bombardment by an enemy but long previous army and navy had taken immediate measures in defense.

"Oahu is under a sporadic air raid," the announcement said.

CIVILIANS ORDERED OFF STREETS   The army has ordered that all civilians stay off the streets and highways and not use telephones. Evidence that the Japanese attack has registered some hits was shown by three billowing

RESPECT

75

pillars of smoke in the Pearl Harbor and Hickam field area. All navy personnel and civilian defense workers, with the exception of women, have been ordered to duty at Pearl Harbor. The Pearl Harbor highway was immediately a mass of racing cars.

A trickling stream of injured people began pouring into the city emergency hospital a few minutes after the bombardment started. Thousands of telephone calls almost swamped the Mutual Telephone Co., which put extra operators on duty. At the Star-Bulletin office the phone calls deluged the single operator and it was impossible for this newspaper, for sometime, to handle the flood of calls. Here an emergency operator was called

HOUR OF ATTACK-7:55 A.M.   **An official army report from department headquarters, made public shortly before 11, is that the first attack was at 7:55 a.m. Witnesses said that they saw at least 50 airplanes over Pearl Harbor. The attack centered in the Pearl Harbor. Army authorities said: "The rising sun was seen on the wing tips of the airplanes." Although martial law has not been declared officially, the city of Honolulu was operating under M-Day conditions.**

It is reliably reported that enemy objectives under attack were Wheeler field, Hickam field, Kaneohe Bay and naval air station and Pearl Harbor. Some enemy planes were reported shot down. The body of the pilot was seen in a plane burning.

ANTIAIRCRAFT GUNS IN ACTION   **First indication of the raid came shortly before 8 this morning when antiaircraft guns around Pearl Harbor began sending up a thunderous barrage. At the same time a vast cloud of black smoke arose from the naval base and also from Hickam field where flames could be seen.**

BOMB NEAR GOVERNOR'S MANSION   **Shortly before 9:30 a bomb fell near Washington Place, the residence of the governor. Governor Poindexter and Secretary Charles M. Hite were there. It was reported that the bomb killed an unidentified Chinese man across the street in front of the Schuman Carriage Co. where windows were broken. C.E. Daniels, a welder, found a fragment of shell or bomb at South and Queen Sts. which he brought into the City Hall. This fragment weighed about a pound.**

At 10:05 a.m. today Governor Poindexter telephoned to The Star-Bulletin announcing he has declared a state of emergency for the entire territory. He announced that Edouard L. Doty, executive secretary of the

major disaster council has been appointed director under the M-Day law's provisions. Governor Poindexter urged all residents of Honolulu to remain off the street, and the people of the territory to remain calm.

Mr. Doty reported that all major disaster council wardens and medical units were on duty within a half hour of the time the alarm was given. Workers employed at Pearl Harbor were ordered at 10:10 a.m. not to report at Pearl Harbor. The mayor's major disaster council was to meet at the city hall at about 10:30 this morning. At least two Japanese planes were reported at Hawaiian department headquarters to have been shot down.

HUNDREDS SEE CITY BOMBED Hundreds of Honolulians who hurried to the top of Punchbowl soon after bombs began to fall, saw spread out before them the whole panorama of surprise attack and defense. Far off over Pearl Harbor the white sky was polka-dotted with anti-aircraft smoke. Rolling away from the navy base were billowing clouds of ugly black smoke. Sometimes a burst of flame reddened the black sources of the smoke

CAPTAIN EVERETT HALE STILL

One of the United States Naval Officers on duty that day was **Captain Everett Hale Still**. Captain Still was born in Blacksville, South Carolina on November 15, 1902, the son of James J. and Ella Able Still. Still was appointed to the US Naval Academy by US Senator James F. Byrnes, graduating in 1926. The majority of Captain Still's naval career was spent in sea duty primarily in engineering officer billets on destroyers, qualifying him as one of the first officers in the Navy selected for the Engineering Duty Officer (EDO) specialty.

At the time of the attack on Pearl Harbor, Captain Still lived in Hawaii along with his wife Grayce Boteler Still and two children. His son, Richard Lee was 13 years old; his daughter, Jacqueline was age six at the time. Following are some of the children's reflections on December 7th and the difficult days ahead for their family.

Jacqueline (Jackie) Still Lithgow now lives at Smith Mountain Lake, Virginia. She is retired from a 30 year career in public education. Jackie said, "December 7, 1941 was a day I will long remember." Her brother Richard is an Assistant Professor of Business Law Emeritus at Mississippi State University. It was a quiet Sunday morning and the family were getting dressed to attend Sunday school and were listening to the radio. Richard was outside near Diamond Head when a number of airplanes started down "battle row." He thought a war movie was being made. There was an urgent message being broadcast asking everyone to stay under cover. Pearl Harbor was under attack. Jackie was in the first grade, the schools were closed. In fact, she and Richard were not able to attend school again until they returned to the United States. This was a very stressful and difficult time for the Still family and all other military families living in Hawaii. During the Japanese bombing Jackie said, "Looking out our picture window, we would lay on the floor of our living room, watching the Japanese planes come up and rise over our house so low that we could see the pilots smiling in the cockpits. I'll never lose that mental image. Our lives became fearful as we put up dark curtains on windows so lights couldn't be seen at night." The MPs patrolled their neighborhood on a regular basis. Fear was common. The family did not know the fate of their loved one, Captain Still. They had not received any word and did not know if he was alive or dead.

The family stayed in Hawaii for several days before space was available to evacuate them. Most of their personal possessions were left in Hawaii. All of Jackie's toys and handmade wood furniture for her playroom were left behind. These items were cherished by a little six year old girl. After returning to the States, her mother, at her own expense, had to buy furniture and all the things needed to furnish a house. The Navy did not pay for any of this.

A special convoy with over 100 ships was provided for the families to leave Hawaii and return to America. The weather was not cooperating very much. It was very foggy. They sailed on the USS *Henderson* from Pearl Harbor on January 11th. The waters were covered with oil, fires were still burning, and body parts were in evidence. Richard said, "We manned the rails and a complete silence took place. This is a sight I have never forgotten. During our ten day zigzag trip to San Francisco, we were attacked by a Japanese submarine on the horizon, which, I believe was sunk by our escorting destroyers." The fate of their Naval Officer father was still unknown. Later they learned that Captain Still was a hospital patient and being sent to Norfolk, Virginia. Mrs. Still was about 30 years old at the time. She bought an old automobile and along with Jackie and Richard started driving across country. The children were left with an aunt and uncle in Annapolis while Mrs. Still went to Norfolk to be with her husband. The children lived with their relatives for three years but were able to travel to Norfolk on occasions to visit their parents.

At the time of the attack on Pearl Harbor, Captain Still was the Flag Officer of a squadron of destroyers. His job was running the Japanese mini subs aground. Due to absolute exhaustion, Captain Still had a heart attack. Richard said, "At the time of the attack, dad was bringing his squadron of four destroyers through the submarine nets at Pearl City (the destroyer base). He spent the next week running Japanese midget submarines aground. He had a number of '90 day wonders' as newly commissioned ensigns attached to the squadrons. He had to replace them with Chief Petty Officers in command due to the lack of training and inexperience of the newly commissioned ensigns. Dad remained on the bridge of his flagship during the week following the attack with very little sleep, eventually collapsing from exhaustion and what proved to be his third heart attack during his naval career.

Prior to World War II, the Captain served on the USS. *Salt Lake City* cited for exemplary service to the city of Long Beach, California, during the 1933 earthquake. Other assignments included Assistant Engineering Officer of Destroyer Squadron Three and Engineering Officer Destroyer Squadron Twenty under the command of former Chief of Naval Operations, Admiral Arleigh Burke. He became Chief Engineering Officer of the USS *San Francisco* of the Battle of Salvo Island fame in 1940, from which he, as a Lt. Cmdr., assumed command of a squadron of four destroyers (Flag ship–USS. *Hopkins*) which engaged Japanese midget submarines at the time of the attack on Pearl Harbor. His World War II service included duty aboard the USS *Arkansas* (North Africa campaign), as Chief Engineering Officer. He was responsible for fitting out the USS *Birmingham* when serving as Engineering Officer in the Sicily Campaign.

Still was placed on the retirement list as a Captain on April 1, 1947, as a result of physical disabilities acquired during his naval service (three separate heart attacks). Captain Still died on February 20, 1948 from a coronary thrombosis in Arlington, Virginia. At the time of his death, his son, Richard was a midshipman at the US Naval Academy.

Jackie said, "Yes, families carry their burdens too, and these memories linger for a lifetime. In spite of it all, our family is very proud of those who have served: My dad, navy-Pearl Harbor; my brother, marines, Korean War; my first husband, army, Vietnam; my second husband army-Korea; my step father, navy, WWII; my uncle, army, World War II. All of these are heroes to us and now rest in Arlington Cemetery, except for my brother and second husband who are still alive." Jackie's brother, Richard, was a young marine lieutenant serving in Korea.

RICHARD L. "DICK" STILL   (Prisoner of War-Korea)

The author met with Richard and Mrs. Still at the home of his sister and brother-in-law, Jackie and Gene Lithgow at Smith Mountain Lake on Sunday, March 18, 2007. Following a delicious dinner, we spent about four hours together discussing Dick's military service and his suffering as a POW (Prisoner of War). Dick was a highly intelligent person, very talkative, humorous and willing to share his experiences.

Richard was appointed to the US Naval Academy in 1946 and was commissioned 2nd Lieutenant on June 2, 1950, 23 days before the North Koreans invaded South Korea. Richard was captured while on a mission over enemy territory in December 1951. He was put in solitary confinement for helping others escape from prison camp. He was tortured and even tried to escape himself through the sanitary system. Richard was the last American prisoner released in September 1953. He was six feet tall and only weighed 90 pounds when released by North Korea. This is Richard's account of the events that took place prior to and during his two years as a prisoner of war in North Korea. He was interviewed by Chaplain (Colonel) Dave Peterson, Retired. "Dick" Still was featured as the Veteran of the year in 2003 by the MNA Chaplain Ministries in Lawrenceville, Georgia. This is Peterson's account with comments by the author.

Midshipman at the Naval

In September of 1951, as a second lieutenant in the Marine Corps, Richard left Fort Thomas, KY, under individual orders to rejoin his outfit, the 1st 90MM AA (Anti-Aircraft) Gun Battalion in Korea. His wife and two-month-old daughter, Sally, remained with his wife's parents. Sally was born June 25, 1951, the one year anniversary of the Korean War. Dick attended the Army's AA and GM school at Fort Bliss, TX, on temporary duty. During his schooling, his outfit was deployed to Pusan, Korea, where 85% of the war supplies entered for conducting the war. The battalion was attached to the 1st MAW (Marine Air Wing) at K-3 (Pohang), located at Pusan, due to the threat of possible Chinese aircraft attack from bases around Shanghai, about 500 miles from Pusan across the Yellow Sea.

Beginning in the fall of 1951, the 1st MAW began to experience heavy aircraft loss from enemy anti-aircraft fire. Richard's commanding officer, Colonel Charles W. May, became an advisor to the 1st MAW on AA avoidance tactics. Since Richard had recently completed AA and GM school at Fort Bliss, he was directed to accompany Colonel May for conferences with Major General Christian Schlit, Commanding General 1st MAW, at his quarters in Pohang. At the conclusion of their meeting, it was agreed that Richard would fly twelve missions to selected targets where losses had been experienced. General Schlit ordered him to report back to him personally after completion of his missions with his observations and recommendations. Due to his subsequent capture, he was unable to comply until released two years later. Richard obeyed that order and reported to Lieutenant General Schlit, Assistant Commandant of the Marine Corps for Air at Marine Corps Headquarters, Arlington, VA, in the fall of 1953.

Colonel May made the first flight on December 21, 1951, to assist Richard in developing a reporting methodology for subsequent flights. They were piloted by Lieutenant Colonel William Gay Thrash, Assistant Operations Officer, 1st MAW, who subsequently retired as a Lieutenant General, Commanding General Marine Corps Schools at Quantico, Virginia. Unfortunately, they did not have the benefit of pre-strike photo reconnaissance, since all photo squadrons were under the control of the 5th Air Force headquarters in Seoul. They flew in a converted TBM, the only plane at 1st MAW capable of carrying two observers in addition to the pilot. The plane had been modified by replacing the gunner's turret with a passenger cockpit directly behind the pilot. Richard was in the lower level radio compartment with aerial maps of the target area. The plane was normally used by 1st MAW for administrative purposes. After a pre-dawn briefing, they stated, "If anybody has to evacuate the passenger cockpit, there will be no way, since the access door is not functioning." Tragically, that proved to be the case when they were hit over the target.

They were part of a large strike force with their target being Sunchon, a major rail marshalling yard and ammunition storage area located about 90 miles northeast of Pyongyang. The strike force consisted of a large number of Marine AD dive- bombers, a number of F9 Panther jets, some WWII Corsairs, Air Force F84's and F86's flying top cover. Between 90 and 100 aircraft took part in this strike

The plane Richard was in made three passes as the last plane in the strike formation. Each pass began between 7,000 and 8,000 feet from north to south longitudinally under extremely heavy AA fire. The flak bursts were so heavy as to make visibility extremely difficult and hence, made mapping and firing location, at best, guesswork. On the third pass, they became the last plane in the area, drawing fire from all AA units. The attacking aircraft, having dropped all bombs, rapidly disappeared to the south. They were hit repeatedly at 7,000 feet. Shortly after Colonel Thrash gave the order to "bail out," they lost all communication. The cockpits began to fill with burning oil as flames and smoke broke out. At this point Richard said that he was calmed by what seemed to be a voice saying, "Fear not, for I am with you always," and he even observed a silhouette of the Lord

Colonel Thrash had placed the plane in a shallow dive and, as Richard sought to exit the radio compartment, he heard Colonel May, who appeared to be badly wounded (blood covering the canopy). Richard tried to force open his cockpit while keeping his balance on the wing and holding on with one hand to the radio compartment opening. Colonel May's cockpit was completely jammed, as the crew chief had stated. Then the flames spread to the wing and

Richard slipped off the wing as a result of hot oil, rear end first and tumbling. With no training in parachuting, he delayed pulling the ripcord so as to fall free of the aircraft. The color blobs became distinct, as did the mountain top trees. Richard pulled his ripcord, the chute jerked him upward, and when he hit the ground he was knocked unconscious. The enemy later said they thought he was a bomb, so he estimated that he pulled his ripcord less than 500 feet.

After a passage of time, he regained consciousness. Two groups of troops were climbing from opposite sides of the ridge located between two mountains on which he landed. He subsequently learned that one group was Chinese and the other North Korean. Still in a daze (concussion), he fired at both groups with his 45 cal. Pistol until he ran out of ammunition. He then stripped the pistol, burying the firing pin and spring. Fortunately, the Chinese reached him first, since aviators taken prisoner by the North Koreans were often executed on the spot. Snow began to fall and the North Korean winter set in. Colonel Thrash and Richard were eventually taken to the outskirts of Pyongyang. During the six weeks in Pyongyang, they were subjected to intensive interrogation including several days at the infamous Pak's Palace (Colonel Pak was a North Korean Colonel educated at Oxford, England). A number of corpses were stacked outside the compound awaiting the spring thaws. Thrash was second team All American end at Georgia Tech. He is age 90 and retired as a Lt. General.

In February, during the coldest night of the winter (60 degrees below zero), they were taken north in an open truck, strafed by B25 en route. He was kept in solitary confinement, separated from Colonel Thrash, for a number of days outside of Camp #2, Ping Chung-Ni, North Korea. It was reassuring to see POW's (Prisoners of War) in the main camp exercising and carrying out work details. Two months of captivity had certainly created fears, so that the presence of POW's (some captured in the winter of 1950) gave Richard hope, although they trusted no one.

In the room next to where Richard was being held was a commanding officer of the British Gloucester Battalion named Colonel Carn. The battalion was virtually wiped out in the spring of 1951 at the Battle of the Imjin River, on the outskirts of Seoul. He received the Victoria Cross as a result of that battalion's valiant efforts. Colonel Carn was kept in solitary confinement during his entire period of captivity. Richard talked with Colonel Carn through a hole at the floor between the two rooms in which they were held. Richard expressed his regrets at the death of King George, which stunned the Colonel since he had not heard previously of his passing. He instructed Richard to notify Major Weller, Executive Officer of the battalion, when he was taken to the main compound. Richard informed Weller who immediately directed the Sergeant Major to "fall out the battalion." The battalion consisted of 30 to 40 British soldiers in tattered clothing; some were amputees, all in miserable shape. From a bank in the compound, Richard watched this group fall in and the Sergeant Major proceed to announce the death of the king. This was followed by the singing of "God Save the Queen." This ragtag group of survivors to Richard became ten feet tall. The spirit manifested was really indescribable and remains with him until this day.

During Richard's first days in the compound, he was to hear of the example set by a Catholic chaplain, Father Capon, who had died the night before he arrived. The chaplain's service to his fellow POW's during his captivity, including his last days, was such a source of strength to this young and frightened 2nd Lieutenant, so that he believed then, and continued to believe, that the man who meant the most to him was a man he had never met—Father Capon. During the days immediately preceding his death, Father Capon, himself a victim of acute dysentery, crawled on his hands and knees collecting the soiled underwear of a number of POWs lying in their own filth. He crawled to an icy creek bordering the compound, washing by hand with crude soap the underwear, drying and returning it to those too ill to care for themselves. A sacrifice of this magnitude was even more incomprehensible when one realized that most POW's had been reduced to almost animalistic state. As he lay dying, Father Capon vested certain priestly powers to a rough and crude talking Army 2nd Lieutenant, Ralph Nardella. Ralph never missed a Catholic mass day, spending many days in solitary confinement as a result of ignoring Chinese orders.

Four chaplains had died in captivity prior to Richard reaching Camp 2. The only survivor was the chaplain of the British Gloucester battalion, Reverend Sam Davies. He delighted in their description of Lil' Abner characters and was quickly nicknamed "Marrying Sam," after one of the Lil' Abner characters. Sam had that unique understated British wit and marvelous stoicism in the face of Chinese persecution. The chaplains all had it rough (high death rate), as the Chinese were determined to destroy any vestiges of Christianity. Hence, all religious services were banned.

Ignoring the banned order, they held a Christmas Day service in 1952, conducted by Reverend Sam. It will be forever an inspirational memory. In December 1952, the truce talks at Panmunjom had broken off and, understandably, morale had sunk to an all-time low. It sure seemed as if they would never be released. Gifted POWs had spent weeks carving a beautiful manger scene, complete with stuffed animals using cotton from quilted Chinese uniforms. The service was held at dawn in what had been a library or assembly room of a school during the Japanese occupation. As the sun rose over the towering mountains to the south, the room became bathed in a rosy glow, due to the presence of vivid red drapes (Communist color). The library had huge poster pictures of Mao Tse Tung, Chou En Lai, Stalin, etc. What an incongruous scene for the celebration of the birth of Christ.

Suddenly into the room burst an English-speaking Chinese officer and a platoon of burp-gun armed Chinese soldiers. The officer commanded the men to "disperse-all religious services are forbidden." Sam continued the service without pause and to a man everyone ignored the troops who, upon command, had raised their weapons. The order to fire was given, ignored by the soldiers, infuriating their loss of face commander. Slowly, the soldier in charge of the troops removed his cap, followed by the rest of the detachment causing the officer in charge to storm out in a rage. That evening, in sub-zero temperatures, as several men walked around, the compound had never seen the stars so bright. The memory of that service gave the men hope where there had been none.

Shortly after the Christmas service, in a state of depression, Richard had planned to escape, however, it was thwarted due to an informer. He spent, in the middle of the winter, about a month in solitary confinement in a hole so small that it was impossible to lie down to sleep. The floor of the hole was either muddy or frozen, since the temperatures were sub-zero. He was fed by a pan on the end of a long pole through an opening at ground level. Through this hole he could obtain a limited view when a guard wasn't present. He was permitted to go to the "head" once a day when the guard felt like it—otherwise he had to endure in his own filth. It was at this point that Richard's morale sunk to its lowest ebb with suicidal thoughts. He came close to experiencing "give-up-itis," which was the cause of death of many POW's.

One afternoon as the sun was setting an elderly Korean with a long scraggly beard appeared at the opening and pushed a coarsely wrapped package into the hole, saying in English only the words, "Me Christian."The package contained a bar of lard soap, Korean leaf tobacco with coarse cigarette paper, and several pieces of Chinese candy. Had he been seen by the guard, he would have been shot and killed on the spot. For someone to risk his life for someone he didn't even know, at the time, seemed to be truly God's miracle. Richard believed that the Presbyterian missionaries had at some point led this old Korean Papa San to the Lord. Richard said, "It gave me the lift I needed, snapping me out of my depression and suicidal thought's which never reoccurred.

The torture that Richard had to endure came in different forms. Much was mental. For example, he would write letters home. The Chinese guard would call him out and tear the letters up in front of him. Once the guards had him remove all his clothes and stand out in the cold for eight or nine hours. He would have frost bite all over his body but still did not break. Another method of torture was germ warfare. The prisoners took material and made a fake man in an Air Force uniform and hung it over the guard house. The Chinese guards said it was proof of germ warfare.

Many of the prisoners in the '50s died of exposure. They were captured in the summer and winter clothes were not available. Food was very limited. They were given cracked corn, some form of a turnip, sometimes sugar and soy beans and rice. He was asked what was his motivation was for wanting to live. Richard replied, "My exposure to church, proud to have graduated from the US Naval Academy and pride in the Marine Corps."

The next day, using an aluminum pot that he ate with, he carved a crude cross on the wall of the hole. The following morning, only the cross was illuminated as rays of sunshine entered through the hole. It was not until he was repatriated in September of 1953 and returned to the United States that he learned that Pyongyang University had been founded by Presbyterian missionaries at the turn of the 20th century. Richard said, "Truly, God works in mysterious and wonderful ways." When Richard was a young boy growing up, he attended a Baptist church and participated in the youth group called the Royal Ambassadors or (RA's). During this program they were required to memorize Bible verses each week. Richard said that while in solitary, the scriptures that he learned as a boy came back to him

Regardless of what circumstance a prisoner might find themselves in, there is always something to laugh about. Laughter was important. Richard relates an incident where some prisoner stole a bell. The Chinese guards were very upset. The POW's told the Chinese that they would elect a sheriff who in turn find the bell and return the bell to them. The men started making speeches and their platform was if elected how they would find the bell. The guards wanted to know from time to time if they had elected a sheriff. The men told the guards that there was a "challenge." The guards wanted to know what a challenge was. They were told that someone had challenged the vote and that the vote may not be legal. This procedure was used to delay any decision or punishment from the guards. Finally in disgust, the guards gave up.

Negotiations were under way for a cease fire. The first meeting was suggested to be near Kaesong by General Ridgway. This was agreed on for July 8, 1953. During this meeting, it was agreed that the meeting with the main negotiators would be held on July 10 in Kaesong, which was about six miles northeast of Panmunjom. The meetings were held in a metal building. The POW's were moved on a regular basis toward the end of the war to avoid being checked by the International Red Cross. It is interesting to note that Richard Still was never listed on a Prisoner of War list. His name came out on a cigarette wrapper just before he was released. Prior to the Armistice being signed on July 27, 1953, the Chinese gave Richard a letter from home. The letter included a picture of his daughter that was taken when she was two weeks old. She would now be two years old.

The war that started on June 25, 1950 when the North Korean army invaded South Korea ended when the armistice was signed but no peace agreement has ever been signed. The total US casualties: 33,651 battle deaths, 103,284 WIA; 7,140 POW's of which 51% died while in a prison camp. The U.N. delegation was: Maj. General Laurence C. Craigie, Maj. General Paik Sun Yup (South Korean), Vice Admiral C. Turner Joy, Maj. General Henry I. Hodes and Rear Admiral Arleigh A. Burke. The North Koreans were not only tough and well experienced, but also very difficult to deal with. Finally on July 25th, after many meetings, with the communist walking out at times, they agreed on an agenda. They were down to only five items to discuss and try to come to some kind of agreement.

...Fixing a military demarcation line so as to establish a DMZ.

...Agreeing on a ceasefire and armistice in Korea.

...Agreeing on arrangements relating to prisoners of war.

They met again on July 26 to discuss these items. The negotiations finally broke off on August 22, 1953. The shooting stopped but a peace agreement was never reached or signed.

Slowly, the days passed and Chaplain Sam continued to minister to the prisoners, unfazed by Chinese harassment. In the late spring, "Little Switch" took place for the seriously injured and "Big Switch" began in late August, extending into September as the cease fire held. The day of Richard's release dawned crisp without a cloud in the sky. As the convoy came down a ridgeline, they saw an American flag snapping briskly in a strong wind. Words are inadequate to describe their choked up emotions. After a few tense moments, the exchange took place and Richard was greeted by Major General Randolph McPate, Commanding general 1st Marine Division, who subsequently became the Commandant of the Marine Corps, who saluted Richard with the words, "*Welcome to freedom, Captain.*" Off in the distance, a large crowd of reporters and cameraman were gathered, but to the authorities' great credit, booths had been prepared out of onlookers' sight, with chaplains of each religious faith present offering them the opportunity to give thanks to their individual God, should they desire to do so.

Richard was in the last truck of POWs to be released. It was a cool day in September. It was a tense moment with Chinese soldiers on one side with Burp guns and US Marines on the other side. The interrogator was a person that everyone disliked. One of Richard's friends, Jerry Fink, slugged the interrogator and broke his jaw. The sound seemed to echo like a rifle shot. The convoy stopped for a short time. The tension increased between the two sides. After a short time, the trucks started moving slowly again.

(Captain Richard Still meeting President Johnson)

Richard said, "It happened that I came across with two Sergeants, both old

Moments after release from North Koreans
September 1953

enough to be my father. One was a Catholic, one a Jew and I the Protestant. The Sergeants had on remnants of their uniforms in which they were captured over three years before. On each side of me was a grizzled veteran, displaying no emotion whatsoever. Then tears of joy began streaming down each of their faces and years of my pent-up emotions, likewise were unleashed. Our transition from ruthless tyranny by atheistic captors to the freedom of a loving God began."

Richard was asked what food he wanted. His answer: "Ice cream."

PAUL LaBARRER SUTER

"We thought all the prisoners were dead. All that moved were their eyes. I will never forget the smell and all the dead bodies."
Paul Suter

S/SGT. PAUL L. SUTER
1940-1945
FIELD ARTILLERY OBSERVATION BATTALION

This is a story of a soldier who was stationed in Hawaii when the Japanese carried out this savage surprise attack. He later landed on Utah Beach at Normandy, and then fought in the Battle of the Bulge. His name is **Paul LaBarrer Suter**. He is age 94 now, a very special man and a hero of World War II. Paul graduated from college in 1937 and became a history teacher. He said, "History kept telling me that Hitler and a few others were really going to mess the world up." He joined the National Guard in 1939 and a short time later requested that he be transferred into the regular army. The recruiters gave Paul a choice of assignments. He was offered either Hawaii or the Philippines. He said that this was probably the smartest decision that he ever made when he chose Hawaii. Those who chose the Philippines later were forced to surrender on April 9, 1942 and many died in the Bataan Death march or became prisoners of war for 42 months. Paul's grandfather Suter was a staunch Baptist, an admired teacher who taught him many lessons. His parents were married in 1913. His father, an artist, took his young bride to New York where he worked. Paul was born the following year in Brooklyn. He said that this is hard to live down among his southern cousins. His father was a multi-talented commercial artist who taught Sunday school with colored chalk and large chalk board. He was able to hold the class spellbound as he spoke and illustrated the Bible lesson. At age 15, Paul was baptized into the Baptist church. The family later moved to Summit, New Jersey into a beautiful Tudor- style home.

Following graduation from Summit High School, Paul enrolled at Brothers College of Drew University at Madison, New Jersey. After two years at Brothers College, he decided that his future would be in teaching, not preaching. He then entered Upsala College in East Orange, New Jersey, receiving his teacher's certificate in 1937. He was a Baptist, entering into a Methodist Institution, then transferring to a Lutheran College. Paul engaged in several sports but excelled in fencing, becoming the captain of the team. He studied under the famous Olympic Star, Anthony Scafati.

On July 11, 1940, Suter requested a discharge from the National Guard to enlist into the regular Army. He immediately was sent to Fort Slocum, New York. They were marching past a long row of barracks with other recruits yelling "Suckers! Suckers!" The next week his section was on maneuvers. Paul's job was driving a truck. To his surprise, on Wednesday, July 25, 1941, he boarded the USAT *Hunter Liggett*, picking up about 200 soldiers at Charleston, making a total of 1,200 soldiers. They traveled through the Panama Canal, finding the city of Balboa very pleasant. The trip carried the troops along the coast of San Francisco and under the Golden Gate Bridge. His new station was Fort McDowell, Angel Island, California. Angel Island was a hilly place, covered with poison ivy. Fort McDowell was a casual post with troops arriving and departing in almost a continuous flow. Next, they left for Hawaii. As the ship went under the Golden Gate Bridge, Suter said the beautiful sunset was breathtaking.

When Suter arrived in Hawaii, he was assigned to Battery E of the 13th Field Artillery. Their motto was "Without fear, favor or the hope of reward." The Artillery Regiment was formed at Camp

Stewart Texas. It had been equipped with 4.7mm Howitzers, (horse-drawn) in preparation for combat in World War I.

Suter thought he was in paradise. From Honolulu, he would take a bus to Waikiki Beach, tour the beautiful Royal Hawaiian and Moans Hotels. He had a very interesting experience one Sunday. Paul and his friend Albert Lewis were wearing fresh uniforms and really looked sharp. A prominent Japanese motion-picture actress, Suzuki Sumiko, got out of a car for cameramen to take pictures of her on the beach. After they took several pictures of her, she had the officials' motion to Paul and Albert to pose with her. Later they wondered if the actress was actually a spy.

On Sunday, December 7, 1941, Suter, along with many other soldiers was eating breakfast at a mess hall near Wheeler Airfield. Wheeler was the fighter base adjacent to Schofield Barracks. They heard a horrible commotion about 7:55 a.m. He said to one of his buddies, "Can't they stop maneuvers on Sunday?" Shortly after he had asked this question, an airplane came over with a big red ball on the side and wings and a big grin on the face of the pilot. For Suter and the United States, the war had just begun. He fought alongside his buddies to prevent the Japanese from destroying the fighter base at Wheeler Airfield.

Combat readiness required that each man fulfill designated tasks. They raced across the quadrangle to the supply room, hoping to dodge the bullets. The flying bullets seemed to add wings to their feet. The supply sergeant was issuing weapons such as the BAR's (Browning Automatic Rifles).

The Post, Schofield barracks was named in honor of a celebrated soldier of the Civil War, General Schofield. By the mid-30's, Schofield Barracks had become America's foremost Military training camp. It was located on a tropical island almost indescribable in its beauty, truly worthy of its name, "Paradise of the Pacific." Oahu was born out of two giant extinct volcanoes. The mountains and great volcano rims form a virtual wall rearing thousands of feet into knife-like heights to hide in the low white clouds.

After Suter's duty ended in Hawaii, he left on August 18, 1942. The military sent him back to the States for schooling. He was promoted to corporal. His new assignment was the Quartermaster School near Cheyenne, Wyoming. Later, he went by rail to Fort Bragg, North Carolina, and reported to Major Gardonyi of the 15th Field Artillery brigade.

In December 1943, Suter was sent to Europe to start training for the invasion of Western Europe. The United States and Allies were preparing for the Invasion of Normandy. The invasion of Normandy was originally scheduled in 1943 but delayed until June 6, 1944.

Suter had a date with a "good looking lady," a British Officer in early June. They were watching a movie but his friend was very solemn. Paul told her that he should be the one with a long face because he had a pass for London and would not be able to see her for a few days. He said, "I will never forget her response." She said, "This is goodbye and I am quite sure you will not get to London. She told him that this would be their last date. We will never see each other again." He said that she was right, "I never saw her again." This British lady either had some inside information or had a woman's intuition what was about to occur. The fact is that her unit, in order to mislead the German reconnaissance planes, would often pack up and move out for several days. However, they did not move the kitchen. On this occasion, the kitchen was being moved along with all the other equipment. She had to believe the invasion was on.

There were five beaches that the Allies were to land on. Suter's unit, the 13th Field Artillery Observation Battalion, landed on *Utah Beach* on D-Day. Their mission was to locate the German artillery and direct US artillery fire against the German positions. His unit was assigned to the VII Corps of the US First Army. His commanding officer told him that they would have to cut the Cotentin Peninsula. The history of the Normandy invasion will be covered in a different chapter.

The next two paragraphs are in Paul Suter's own words.

It was 5 June 1944 and we were briefed on time and destination. We were to hit Normandy Beach (area called Utah) at "H" hour + 12. The 4th Division also received briefing to bring their artillery ashore. The 4th Infantry Division landed on Utah Beach at "H" hour + 12 with the 13th Field Artillery Observation Battalion. D day (6 June 1944) was cool and windy, the aftermath of the storm which had passed over leaving a rough sea.

We boarded the landing craft and were given little brown bags to be used only if seasick. Thank goodness I had no need for the bag; but, stepping off into rough sea, waist deep in cold water did provide a jolt. We moved some yards inland from the beach to a designated area for the night. I was ordered to return to the beach for the purpose of guiding the remaining units to the assembly area. As darkness fell I began to realize that being wet and cold, with occasional flares and burst of gun fire, digging a foxhole in the sand gave me no comforting thoughts. The troops continued landing throughout the night. By dawn of 7 June 1944 the 13th Field Artillery Observation Battalion entered combat.

Sometime later, Suter was staying with a family in a Belgium village. Christmas packages had arrived and they wondered what to do with them. So they decided to have a party and share their gifts with the people. A small girl came up to Suter and gave him a necklace that she had been wearing. She told him that it might save his life. He never saw the little girl again but in his memoirs he stated that he still has the necklace.

Paul Suter had now survived the attack on Pearl Harbor and the invasion that was the turning point of World War II, Normandy. But his military commitment did not end on Utah Beach. There were other battles that he was involved in as his unit moved across Europe, with the goal to defeat the Germans and bring the war to an end. One of the worst battles in terms of casualties was Suter's next. This was *The Battle of the Bulge*. On December 17th, it was reported that the Germans had broken through the Allied lines. The weather was unbearable. The US soldiers found themselves improperly equipped and short of ammunition. It was reported that there were approximately 81,000 American casualties, including 38,446 wounded, 23,554 captured and 19,000 killed.

Their job was to stop the advancing Germans, but with what? The German tanks were superior to the American tanks; the Germans had white camouflage uniforms which kept them from being detected in the snow; the American troops did not have camouflage. They had to as Paul stated it, "advance to the rear." The Germans used American-speaking troops dressed in MP uniforms to lead the Americans into a trap. The German tanks were running out of fuel. Their goal was to advance to where the American fuel storage was located, capture and then refuel their tanks. This failed. The fact that the Germans ran out of fuel is the only thing that stopped their advancement. They were eventually pushed back to their original lines.

(Photo courtesy of Paul Suter)

One of the most memorable moments for Suter was one that he has never erased from his mind. His unit liberated a POW (prisoner of war) camp. The smell was unbearable.

The people who were barely living were skin and bones. At first Paul thought everyone was dead. As he and the other

American soldiers walked throughout the barracks, the so called dead bodies' eyes began to follow them. The eyes were all that moved. Paul said of all the combat that he had experienced, this was the worst sight he had ever seen. The Nazis had been extraordinarily cruel and are said to have killed millions during World War II.

This paragraph is in Paul Suter's own words.

The weather was changing and I had a strong feeling that something was about to happen and it did happen. Germans in white camouflage appeared to be everywhere. I was told that the Germans had mobilized three armies. The German offense had exploded around us. We were moving in the wrong direction. We were hammered day and night. We were driven back. The Germans had created a salient 50 miles deep. The action was referred to as the "Battle of the Bulge". All towns fell to the Germans except one—Bastogne. It was 16 December 1944 when the Americans at Bastogne were ordered to surrender by the Germans. The American reply was "NUTS!" The effort to close the salient was aided by the arrival of Patton, General Commander of the third Army. The German offense was a strong effort, a desperate effort to reach the great allied supply depot. The Germans were running low on everything. They threw all they could muster into one great and desperate effort. The allies attempt to stop them was just as desperate. Allied tank units were no match for the heavier and stronger German tanks; but the delay was long enough for them to run out of fuel—to bring the entire German offense to a stop. Their armor looked like a vast parking area. The Great German offense was over. The Battle of the Bulge was over.

Suter's unit was to advance to the Elbe River to link up with the Red Army. The Soviets took out their canteens and began celebrating. He wondered, why celebrate with water? But Suter soon learned that their canteens were filled with Vodka. Suter decided to celebrate with the Soviets and took his first drink of Vodka. He said that it nearly took his head off. He quickly decided that Vodka was not for him.

Here at the Elbe River, the Germans began to surrender, so many in fact they didn't know what to do with them. The Germans wanted to surrender only to the Americans, not the Soviets. Because of the battles between the Soviets and the Germans, the Germans were afraid what the Russians would do to them.

(Paul Suter's medals)

One funny story that Suter related was during a time he was in his favorite bed-a foxhole without pillow or blanket. When he complained about having a toothache, a buddy suggested that he take a chew of tobacco. Some say that chewing tobacco will ease the pain. Suter said, "Man, did it make me sick. I don't know what was worse, being sick, or having a toothache."

After five years of active service in the US Army, Paul Suter received his honorable discharge in May 1945. Paul was heavily decorated as indicated by the medals in the picture. He became a certified internal auditor and pursued a career in banking in New York and Florida. He married a lady who was a co-worker, Susan Robinson Wilsey on March 6, 1948. Paul and Sue live at Smith Mountain Lake in Virginia. They have two sons, Bruce of New York and George of Florida; daughter, Paula Meighen of Moneta, VA; and four grand-children.

1939 BUICK SURVIVES PEARL

There are many interesting stories about the day of the attack on Pearl Harbor. Everyone who survived has a different experience to tell about. However, there is one story whose subject is unable to talk about its experiences. This is about what happened to a 1939 Buick Convertible. The story was printed in the *Martinsville Bulletin* in Martinsville, Virginia on December 7, 2006. The headline read, ***"Car survivor pays tribute to Pearl Harbor,"*** by Jim Stegall. Permission was given by the owner, Mr. A.C. Wilson of Martinsville, and Jim Stegall to print this story.

"If A.C. Wilson's 1939 Buick could talk, what a tale she would tell. In 67 years, she has traveled from sea to shining sea in this country. She has crossed the Blue Ridge Mountains, shuttled passengers to the Metropolitan Opera in New York and sailed the Pacific aboard a boat, where she often cooled her engine as the sun set on the gracious shores of Hawaii. But the journey wasn't always beautiful sunsets and scenery. It actually started with a trip to the very depths of hell. On a crisp Sunday December morning 65 years ago today, she waited patiently in the parking lot of Dock C at Pearl Harbor, her owner serving aboard the USS *Pensacola* on duty at sea. Often US sailors on the island stood gawking at the beautiful 1939 Buick Special convertible, but not on this day. Most of the sailors on the island were still asleep. The parking lot was virtually empty. Nobody seemed to notice the small plane that suddenly flew overhead, reflected in the shiny, gun-medal grey finish of the 1939 Buick.

"But hours later, the tranquility was gone. Planes roared overhead, bombs exploded nearby and the very color of the car seemed to turn from grey to jet black, reflecting the dense smoke from burning US warships in the harbor. *The Japanese were attacking Pearl Harbor.* And the classic Buick, owned then by

RESPECT

Navy Officer Julian Venter, of Connecticut, was in the midst of the attack. Six days later he returned to Pearl Harbor. The attack, he thought, probably demolished his car, a gift from his parents after graduating from Yale. He feared the worse. His car was sitting in the parking lot right where he left it, amidst unbelievable destruction. But there was not a single scratch on it. Today, the car is owned by A.C. Wilson, of Martinsville, Virginia, a retired quarry owner. He didn't acquire it until 1973. But he credits his 91 year-old cousin of nearby Radford with preserving the car and its "historical value."

"Mary Ingles Bullard was the young bride of Naval Aviator George C. Bullard, who was assigned to duty in Honolulu in late 1941. He and his best friend, Julian Venter, the Buick owner, were on the Pensacola during the attack. Mary lived alone in a rented cottage while her husband was away. The day of the attack, Mary Bullard recalls, she "could see the planes and the smoke rising" on the opposite end of the island. 'But I thought they were our planes,' she said. Later she heard on the radio that 'Hawaii is being attacked by enemy planes, presumably Japanese and this is the real McCoy,' they said.

"We gathered in the streets and there was a girl with a dog. I had a black cat, so we stayed at my house. You waited with a blanket and listened for some news. Coconuts were falling from trees on the house and it scared us to death. It was totally dark. At a time like that, you don't know what to think," she said.

"The next day the Navy brought her some food. And her husband at sea didn't know of her fate. "I wasn't about to leave," she said. "I wanted to be near my husband." The *Pensacola* returned to port a few days later and Mary drove, "across the mountain" to meet him in their Model-A Ford. "He didn't even know I was still there," she said. There were no phones. He couldn't call."

"George Bullard was overjoyed when he saw his wife. Officer Venter reacted similarly, finding his 1939 Buick unscathed. But faced with enormous duty of fighting a looming war, he made the Bullard's an offer they couldn't refuse. He gave them his car in exchange for their Model-A which he sold for $500 that he donated to the Red Cross.

"Like many soldiers, Officer Venter felt he might not survive the war. Disposing of the car seemed the right thing to do. The Bullard's accepted his offer and Mary started driving the car around Hawaii, recalling now the age of 91 that the convertible "was just transportation." She drove it working for the Army as a "Plotter," spy work to keep an eye out for potential Japanese infiltrators on the island. Meanwhile, her Navy pilot husband was attacking Japanese ships in the Pacific. In time Mary returned to the US, the Buick in tow aboard ship. Mary's mother, Pamelia, traveled to San Diego by train from Virginia to meet her.

"She and I drove that Buick across the country back to Pulaski County, Virginia," she said. 'We'd drive half a day each. We had dozens of flats. People stopped to help and thought we were from Hawaii because of the car tag. We finally made it home in about 10 days.' As the war went on, Mary developed a close kinship with the '39 Buick. She missed her husband. The car held a special place in her heart because it had survived the historic attack on Pearl Harbor. Then the sad news came that her husband, George, had been shot down by anti-aircraft fire in the Pacific. He had ventured away from his squadron to attack a Japanese ship when it occurred.

"His fate remained a mystery. But after a 19-month ordeal, George Bullard was reunited with his wife in New York on Armistice Day. He had survived two weeks on a Pacific Island without water, only to be captured by the Japanese, who beat him severely. After the war, George Bullard rose to the position of Rear Admiral at the Pentagon. Mary and George had four children and continued to drive the famous 1939 Buick. Whenever relatives came to visit, they wanted to see the historic car that survived the Pearl Harbor attacks. And friends called often and asked, "How's the Buick doing?"

"In 1966, George Bullard suffered a fatal heart attack repairing a fence on the family farm in Pulaski County. And it was around the time that Mary drove the Buick for the last time. "It got so it wouldn't shift gears," Mary said. "So we just parked it in the barn." Over the next 10 years, the World War II relic became a home for chickens, birds and groundhogs. Its body rusted and the convertible khaki top rotted into rags.

"Cousin A.C. Wilson often expressed an interest in the car when he visited Mary on the farm. And knowing that A.C. had a lifelong love of Buicks and preserving old cars. Mary called him one day in 1973. "It's time for you to get the Buick," Mary told A.C. After writing a check for $300, which was more than she wanted, A.C. had the Buick towed to his home in Martinsville. And while he credits Mary with preserving "a real piece of history," A.C. Wilson deserves credit for returning the car to its original form.

"He spent nearly 20 years finding Lewis Jenkins of North Wilkesboro, who owns a restoration company. It took more than a year and nearly $100,000 of A.C. Wilson's money to completely refurbish the 1939 Buick. A.C. had a public showing of the car after its restoration in 1993, inviting Mary, family, friends, and even Julian Venter, the car's original owner. He is delighted with the nearly $100,000 restoration, except for one minor detail–a red stripe on the side chrome (a dealer option) that was missing. A.C. had it added.

"Julian Venter died a few years back. Mary Bullard, 91, lives alone in a big, rambling home in Radford, another family keepsake. Her grandmother had it built nearly 100 years ago.

When she discusses the 1939 Buick that survived the Pearl Harbor attack with A.C, she'll often say, 'This car is talking.'

(Photo courtesy of A.C. Wilson and Jim Stegall)

"Nowadays the Buick rests protected in a friend's garage. Occasionally A.C. and his wife Lucy, take it for a spin. "It gives us a great sense of pride," he says, "not just for it beauty, but for what it represents." Five years ago his wife added the crowning touch to the restoration project. Unbeknownst to A.C., she searched far and wide for an original Hawaii license tag for the car. Shopping one day at a flea market in Abingdon, she nonchalantly challenged a vender, asking, 'I'll bet you don't have what I'm looking for?' After telling the vender what she wanted, he sifted through his wares and amazingly produced a 1941 Hawaii license tag. Lucy couldn't believe her luck. 'You've made my day,' the vender told Lucy, who paid him $100 for the rare find. Lucy placed the tag under the Christmas tree that year for her husband. Finally, the restoration of A.C. Wilson's 1939 Buick that survived the Japanese attack on Pearl Harbor was complete." [Mr. Wilson brought his Buick to Bedford, VA for a parade. The parade was canceled due to rain. He took the car out of the trailer and allowed Paul Suter, a Pearl Harbor survivor to have his picture taken in it.]

This 1939 BUICK was on the dock at Pearl Harbor Dec. 7, 1941 and Survived the Bombing!

CHAPTER THREE

THE FIRST SPECIAL SERVICE FORCE

USA.–CANADA

The FORCE was on line for 99 days before being relieved. They painted their faces black and roamed through the German positions. One German soldier wrote in his diary "The black devils are all around us and we never hear them come." Bill Story

WILLIAM STEER STORY

If you study every war, special highly trained units in each conflict are organized different from other military units, and are tasked to engage the enemy without knowing the fate of the men in their outfit. During World War II, one of these unique units was formed. This is a brief history of *"The First Special Service Force"* as provided by William Steer Story, a

Canadian, who was one of the original members of the Force. Some of the facts in this chapter are from a book written by Lieutenant Colonel Robert D. Burhans. (The copyright privileges were waived).

My initial visit to meet this Canadian hero was over lunch at the Red-Wine & Blue restaurant at Smith Mountain Lake. Although I had seen the movie *Devil's Brigade* featuring William Holden about one of The Force's important victories, I was not familiar with Story's unit nor did I realize how important they were during World War II. I was truly fascinated. My interviews occurred in Story's home.

William "Bill" Story was born at Grace Hospital (Salvation Army) Broadway Ave, Winnipeg, Manitoba, Canada on June 6, 1921. Bill was a graduate of Gordon Bell High School, and a member of the Winnipeg Canoe Club. He took part in the Gordon Bell opera in his school days and was a member of the Westminster church choir. His parents were Mr. & Mrs. W. Morley Story of 834 Wolseley Avenue, Winnipeg, Manitoba, Canada. Bill entered service in January 1940 at Winnipeg, Manitoba, Canada although he had served at McGregor Barracks in the Militia in 1938-1939. During his training at Fort Harrison, he was a young, enthusiastic 21year old soldier who always honored and showed respect for his parents. He was a bright young man, intelligent, but "gung ho" when it came to performing his duty. Yet he was a compassionate person. Story wrote long letters to his parents regularly that they kept for him. You will find inserted in this chapter a sentence or more from various military posts where he served. He always addressed his letters to "Mum and Dad." Even with the meager income Story received as a member of the Canadian Army, he would send presents to his parents from time to time. When they did some remodeling on their home, Bill would express a sincere interest, yet concerned about the cost and where the money came from.

The Force, a highly trained unit, was given special assignments and was feared by the enemy. These men were a living example of the close friendship and co-operation that exists between the two countries. This is in reference to the *First Special Service Force,* composed of volunteers from the Canadian and American Armies–said to be one of the finest units ever assembled in the history of either army. Trained in secrecy, and later, given little publicity, this group has been variously described as the "Hands across the Border Fighters," the "Joint Canadian-American Task Force," and by the enemy, *"The Black Devils."*

Their Shoulder Flash was a Red Spearhead bearing the insignia USA-Canada. The Unit sprang from an idea of Lord Louis Mountbatten's, and was born in a conversation between Churchill and General Marshall at Chequers on April 9, 1942. Their training never ended. They learned all the commando tricks. They learned to march 57 miles in 24 hours with full packs. They became ski troops, qualified as parachutists and were whisked from Vermont to Florida to Montana to find the right ground for learning new skills. The Force was armed and clothed with US equipment, drilled English-style, saluted either flat-handed like the British or finger-tips- to- forehead, G.I. fashion. Every enlisted man was a noncom except for a few privates. Most top sergeants were Canadians; most junior officers were from the US.

The Force was activated on July 20, 1942 at Fort William Harrison, Helena, Montana, and trained there until April 13, 1943. They moved to Camp Bradford, Norfolk, VA from April 15-May 22 for amphibious training. While training at Camp Bradford, the Force beat the time set by the Marines by 20-seconds. The day after completing their training at Camp Bradford, they were sent to Fort Ethan Allen, Burlington, Vermont, where they completed their training on June 27, 1943. The Force arrived at the San Francisco Port of Embarkation on July 4.

The Force flag, the first North American flag, was made of red silk with a black dagger on a white shield. The dagger would be used for hand- to- hand combat.

The Force had a glamorous career laid out for it: Suicide raids into Norway to destroy hydroelectric plants producing Heavy Water for the use in the development of atomic bombs; raids on key power plants scattered throughout Europe, and even a parachute raid on Berchtesgaden to kill Hitler.

In June 1942, select volunteers from the American forces in the United States and from the Canadian Army both in Canada and overseas, were brought together for the first time in Helena. In the early months of their training, Canadian came to know American, as American did Canadian—not only to know, but to understand and to appreciate the qualities of the other. In this they were aided in no small measure by an influx of Montana friendship and goodwill.

From the outset, two Americans and two Canadians were quartered in a tent together and soon Canucks were seen walking downtown arm-in-arm with their American buddies. In the strenuous months of training, and the long weary months of combat that lay ahead, the friendships that were made in those first days grew, flourished and endured.

From the Aleutians to Africa, through the rugged mountain peaks of Italy before Cassino, to the Anzio Beachhead; first to enter the Holy City, Rome, and spearheading the invasion of Southern France–these Canadian and American boys ate, slept, fought, loved and died together in the defense of the personal liberty and freedom of speech of their two countries. Few of the original members returned.

Colonel Robert Tyron Frederick, who became a Major General at age 37, commanded the Force from July 20, 1942 to June 23, 1944. Frederick became the youngest ground forces general and the youngest division commander in World War II. Frederick decided on the Force name, an innocent-sounding name taken out of the air. He wanted to cover the identity of the Force by not using common attack group names such as "Commando" or "Ranger" or "Parachute Infantry." These highly trained men were known as strike units which the Force was to be but the colonel wanted their identity and missions to be kept secret.

Robert T. Frederick had spent most of his life preparing for

Major General Robert T. Frederick
Commanding General, First Special Service Force
20 July 1942 to 23 June 1944

such a chance. He had joined the National Guard at 13, at 16 had a reserve commission as a second lieutenant of cavalry, was graduated from West Point at 21 and in 1939 attended the Command and General Staff School. To discuss the complicated problems of organizing a combined Canadian-American combat outfit, he went to London and then to Ottawa. Impressed by his inspiring personality and his military knowledge, Ottawa said they'd go through with the business if Frederick himself would command the Force. The US War Department agreed.

Frederick picked a training site near Helena, Montana. Officers were touring army camps looking for men of extra-good physique such as lumberjacks, trappers, cowpunchers and tough outdoor men. Frederick wanted the toughest of toughest men. He naturally had a lot of problems in training the men in many skilled areas. Frederick imported experts to teach officers and men in these many areas.

Frederick was a tough, smart and respected commander. The men would have followed him anywhere. An example of his leadership occurred on June 4, 1944. He led a scouting group of seven men in an armored car across Rome to the Margherita Bridge, one of the main German lines of retreat across the Tiber. His mission was to seize the bridge and let no retreating Germans cross. The fight began when the first German vehicle lumbered out of the darkness. Tommy guns chattered and tracer bullets flew like supercharged fireflies. Frederick saw a German rush to throw a grenade; his automatic roared and the German fell dead. A gust of German bullets swept the defenders. General Frederick's driver dropped, shot through the brain. Another Force soldier fell. Bullets hit Frederick's right leg. Five Germans were dead, six more wounded; 11 surrendered. The remainder of the Germans fled. Most generals demand aggressive personal leadership by their subordinates in combat; Frederick not only insisted but made it his business to get it. Frederick was wounded eight times-probably the most wounded General in the war–and he never left the battlefield.

Frederick was awarded eight Purple Heart's, the Silver Star for courage at "La Defensa", and the Distinguished Service Cross for conspicuous gallantry. He was one of the most decorated men in World War II. Yet his greatest pride was in the swell job that his Canadians and Americans did, fighting together as a unit.

When new men would join the Force, Frederick would welcome them by saying *"We welcome you to our ranks knowing that you are the kind of soldiers who will fight with only the thought of victory in mind. We know that you will take the same pride in successful accomplishment of the mission as do the men you have joined."*

Next, this group needed a patch. One suggestion was "Braves" to denote the various sub-units as Indian tribes. This idea was not accepted. In searching for a suitable patch, they looked at shapes of pine trees, buffalo heads, coonskin caps, and tomahawks. In desperation the "Indian Spearhead" was selected. The patch was to be a Red Spearhead surcharged with a white "USA-CANADA" shown. Outsiders called the Force the "Bow and Arrow Boys."

On July 2, 1942, the Army Ground Forces were instructed by Brigadier General Edwards to activate the First Special Service Force. His instructions included "to give highest priority to Force housing, equipment, and training facilities." Colonel Frederick realized that the different training and skills this group had to master, that the dropout rate would be high. For this reason he requested 30% more troops than would be allowed him. Major D.D. Williamson of the Canadian Army arrived to work out the details of Canadian participation in a US Army unit. The conference lasted for three days before an agreement was made. Army Ground Forces directed Ninth Corps Area at Fort Douglas, Utah, to activate the *First Special Service Force.* The Force headquarters were moved to Fort Harrison, Montana. On July 20, 200 men were sent to the post to keep the utilities running, post guards, and in general take care of the needs of the trainees and the post.

Colonel Frederick was the first officer to make a parachute jump followed by the other officers after 15 minutes of instruction. During the summer Lieutenant Colonel John McQueen broke his leg in a jump and had to be replaced. Volunteers joining the Force began arriving. The Canadians from Calgary from Western Canada and Ottawa from Eastern Canada began arriving at Fort Harrison to join the Americans in what was to be the most difficult training requirements anyone could imagine. By the end of August, most men had gone up in a C-47 airplane and practiced all the necessary commands before exiting the plane.

In a letter dated September 16, 1942 to his parents from Ft. Harrison, Story wrote, "We were paid yesterday–not as much compared to what Americans get but it was something." (American soldiers were paid more than the Canadian soldiers who were in the same training program. This caused a little resentment initially but the Canadian government would not make an adjustment in their pay). Bill went on to say in his letter, "Our work down here is beginning to get more strenuous. They are weeding out a lot of the fellows now that cannot keep up with the rest." In a letter dated September 28th, he wrote, "Some 20 men from our company will have to leave."

The operation was named *"Plough Operation,"* which was a secret operation code. The qualifications of these men were designed for them to achieve combat goals that no other unit was capable of. They were required to master all of the infantry small arms, be able to drive the Weasel (a snow- driven vehicle), became a qualified paratrooper and qualify as a skilled skier. In addition, they had to master some other skills and demolitions.

[Fort Benning, Georgia has been one of the main training schools for paratroopers. It still is today. The program in years past was a five- week course. Physical fitness is a must for the duties of the airborne. At Benning, you learn to jump off a platform to achieve a good PLF (parachute landing fall) to help you land properly; jump off a 34 foot tower to practice proper door position in the airplane, count 1,000, 2,000, 3,000, at which time your parachute should open; look above, below, and all around you to check to see if there are other parachutes around you then prepare to land. From this tower, your riser is hooked up to a cable that carries you to a dirt mound where you stop. All these commands must be accomplished during this brief period or up you go and do it all over. Men who quit the airborne training washout usually during the 34- foot tower jumps. Next, you get the feel of being free and floating to the ground from the 250-foot tower. Your chute is hooked to a ring. They take you up near the top, have you check the wind and release you. Benning also has a wind machine to train the new trooper what to do after landing and when the wind drags you along the ground. You lie on your back and they turn the machine on to inflate the 'chute. As you are dragged along the ground, you pull your knees up to your chest, spin around to a standup position and then run around the chute to deflate it. Then there was the "harness" training. This is where you are suspended with a tight harness holding you up in a very uncomfortable position. In the early days, each person would learn to pack his first five parachutes; five jumps were required for you to receive your silver airborne wings. Future troopers were also trained in gliders. The training today at Fort Benning is only three weeks. Packing your own chute is out and glider training is obsolete.]

The Force did not have the time or luxury for this extensive training. Story said it wasn't necessary. There were no towers for practice jumps and they were not required to pack their own parachutes. But the physical training was more vigorous. The Force men were given 48 hours of training before their first jump. Their second jump was 24 hours later. This ended their paratrooper training. They were qualified. If anyone froze in the door and failed to jump, they were disqualified and immediately transferred to another post. The men described this system as "separating the sheep from the goats." After these men qualified as paratroopers, they were proud to have their airborne wings pinned on them by Colonel Frederick. Bill Story said the only training preparing them to jump was harness training and brief mock-up in a C-47. He said Colonel Frederick jumped in his bedroom slippers. Their paratrooper boots had not been issued at this time.

Bill Story did not express his feelings concerning his first jump until he wrote to Tommy from the Anzio Beachhead, Italy, on February 23, 1944. In this letter Bill was giving Tommy a review of places he had been, training he went through and in general an overview from June 1942 until the present. He wrote, "We were there to learn how to jump, how to fight in enemy terrain, how to make use of Commando tactics. We had only a short time in which to learn. So we trained and we marched, and we used the mock-ups, and we dreamed of the day when we would be able to take our first jump. It wasn't too long after arriving that we donned our 'chutes and were taken by truck to the airport, where the big C-47's waited to carry us back over the jumping field at camp. Boy was I scared. There was one consolation to that—everybody else was just as scared as I was. So we filed into the plane, found our seats, fastened our safety belts and waited. The plane took off, and in no time at all, it was over the field. We circled once. Then it came–"Stand Up; Hook Up"; "Stand in the Door"; "Go"; and in less time than it takes to tell, I was at the door, had a glimpse of the ground below me, and then was out into the void, falling. It wasn't the sensation of falling that you get when you have a nightmare, rather, it was a floating, hazy feeling as the earth seemed to revolve around and around you. I was brought out of that reverie by the jerk of my 'chute opening. Looking up, I saw that magnificent canopy above me, and knew that my worries about a 'chute failure were over. I enjoyed the sensation of slowly drifting downward for a few minutes, so I thought. (Actually it was only a matter of a few seconds). Then, on looking down, I saw the ground coming up to meet me. I suddenly realized that there were a few things that I was supposed to do before landing. I had time to start doing those things, and then, with not too great a bump, I was on the ground. Thus my first parachute jump; without a doubt, the greatest thrill that I have ever experienced. There was nothing in those later jumps to equal that first one."

Only one of the six C-47 aircraft remained to provide parachute training for the group of replacements that came in from both armies. The men had made their qualifying jumps. When combat conditions required it, they could jump again, singly or in groups. Every man received instructions on the vehicles, learned the characteristics and worked out the "bugs" that cropped up in the Weasels. The radio men were working long hours on communications. S-3 had designed a combat course complete with simulated land mines of dynamite, overhead fire, and other realistic touches. Instructions continued on the M-1 rifle, the light mortar, the flame thrower, and the Johnson gun. There were also long weekly marches that continued throughout their training at Fort Harrison. Each man had to have mental and physical toughness, and an initiative that surmounted all obstacles.

Story wrote in a letter dated October 6, 1942 the following, "I'm going to buy a camera and a typewriter. Then I want a good knife and blackjack. Don't be alarmed I'm not going into burglary, but I am getting a few weapons to protect myself with when we get into action. I am also going to get a revolver. I have been chosen along with some other chaps in the company to take a radio course....learning the Morse and international codes....I have also been chosen for another job the facts of which I cannot give you."

October 27, 1942, Ft. Harrison: "I went to church yesterday morning and then to dinner at the Manse. Mrs. Morel is an English woman but she learned to cook in New England...I made rather a glutton of myself. In the evening I went to the youth fellowship meeting in the church. We had quite a time there.....Things are beginning to hum around here at last. We start our ski training tomorrow under the instruction of a group of Norwegian Army and Air Force Officers....The civilian laborers are leaving the camp this week. Our secret work should start in two weeks or so....I have a feeling that our pay will come through this month. Latest rumor is that we are to receive $30 per month plus 1st class trades (.75 cents per day) which gives a total of $52.50 per month."

November 6, 1942–"I went down to choir practice last night. They want me to sing the solo in "Rudyard Kipling's Recessional." Story sang that solo and received many compliments from the members of the church. If fact, the pastor, George Morell, of the Saint Paul's Methodist Church of Helena, wrote to his parents and said, "Your son did himself proud yesterday when he sang the solo parts in the anthem. The people enjoyed him very much." Author's note: Bill Story continues to sing today, 65 years later in his church choir and with the Smith Mountain Lake Singers in Virginia.

Long hard days continued for the men of the Force. In early December, storms came roaring through Mullan Pass and over Sawtooth Range, bringing snow for the cold-weather training The unit had been taking training exercises from Captain Kiil's Norwegians on skiing techniques without snow. Many of the men, particularly the French-Canadians from Quebec and the Maritimes, were highly skilled on skis. By Christmas, everyone had gained at least the rudiments of skiing, and every combat man could drive the Weasel. With the mountains near Blossburg, Montana, Captain Kiil and his staff took each regiment up to Blossburg. For two weeks, each man strapped on skis before daylight and skied until dark. Captain Kiil reported at the end of February that 99% of the Force was competent skiers by Norwegian Army standards.

While the skiers were training at Blossburg, other winter exercises continued. The men were instructed in raids, snow operations, and the use of cold-weather equipment. The Second Regiment parachuted into a patch of barren hills called Prickly Pear, behind the enemy lines and moved to attack the bridges and tunnels at Mullan Pass. The First Regiment parachuted behind the "enemy lines" near Fort Harrison Their mission was to blow up the Hauser Lake Dam and Lake Helena Bridge.

December 15, 1942, Bill wrote, "My Christmas here in Helena will be my first one that I have spent away from home. It will be pretty lonely for all of us."

December 29, 1942. Ski Camp, Blossburg, Montana. "Dear Mum and Dad; Well here I am out here about thirty miles from Helena, living in a box car along with the rest of the fellows....I have some good news. The Colonel called me into his office yesterday and told me that I was leaving sometime this week for an intelligence school at Ft. Belvoir, Virginia."

In January Colonel Frederick visited General Buckner in the Alaskan Department. The Alaskan Scouts, the only troops in Alaska at the time, were preparing to land on Adak and Amchitka, and later, Attu and Kiska. General Buckner wanted the Force in his department. General Eisenhower wanted "Frederick's Plough Force" for operation "Husky." It was in March and there were objections because before the Force could be committed, they had to complete amphibious training.

The Force completed its last three weeks at Harrison with 20 mile marches, rope-climbing classes, sorting, packing and cleaning up. The independent spirit of the people in Helena and the state of Montana remains as it did when they took gold from the pockets along the Last-Chance Gulch. The Force wanted to say goodbye to the good folks at Helena. On April 6 the 2,300 hundred strong marched with pride through their city. They left Fort Harrison on April 11th on five passenger trains for Virginia.

HEADQUARTERS FIRST SPECIAL SERVICE FORCE FORT WILLIAM HENRY HARRISON, HELENA,   MONTANA, 6 April 1943. TO: OFFICERS AND ENLISTED MEN

I wish to compliment all members of the Force for the fine appearance made at the parade in Helena this afternoon. People, including both military and civilian spectators who saw you were high in their praise of your appearance, eagerness and soldierly bearing. To the praise of these others I add mine.

These excellent showing made by the Force reflects credit on not only those officers and men who actually marched, but on every member of the Force. The men whose duties required them to be elsewhere during the parade, contributed just as much as those who were in formation. It is only through the wholehearted effort and performance of each individual that outstanding results are achieved. I felt very proud of the Force, and I know that you took pride in doing the job well. Signed by: Robert T. Frederick Colonel, First Special Service Force, Commanding

RESPECT

The commander had received a letter from one father whose leg had been pulled. It read:

"Dear Sir: Corporal_____ of your command has indicated his desire to marry my daughter. Both my wife and I are very fond of the lad, but we want to make certain of some things before giving permission. We want to know if it is true that Corporal_____ owns 3,000 acres of land in Alberta, stocked with 5,000 head of gophers. Yours truly_____"

Story wrote on May 25, 1943 from Camp Bradford. "This is a wonderful life in this camp. All of the training has been in the water in some way or another. We go down to the beach to take a swim. The other day, the whole regiment went down to Virginia Beach and spent a whole afternoon swimming in the breakers." He continued, "I was just thinking of how much ground I have covered with the Army during my year in the service; from Winnipeg to Vancouver, Nanaimo, and to the Pacific Ocean; from Nanaimo to Vernon to the Okanagan Valley, Vernon to Calgary; Calgary to the United States, Helena and Fort Harrison. Helena to Camp Ritchie and back again, Helena to Camp Bradford and the Naval Operating Base, and now, in a few days, we are off again." "Altogether since our organization, we have learned parachuting, mountain climbing, engineering, skiing and a lot more about soldering. To top it all we have also trained as an amphibious unit. Our training roster calls for training in dessert warfare, and jungle warfare before being sent overseas."

From Ft. Ethan Allen, Burl, Vt.–Sept. 28, 1943. "Last week I met a girl who works here on the post, and along with a couple of other First Sergeants, who had met similar girls, we had a very nice time. Over the weekend, we went dancing, and Sunday afternoon we all went on a picnic. This was the first picnic that I had been on in almost four years. The girls down here are very nice, but you still can't beat the Canadian girls. They have it all over these Americans. For one thing, most of the Canadian girls that I have run into during my Army career, are much better educated, and speak a much better brand of the King's English than these Americans do. Their grammar down here is terribly poor. I have heard more bad grammar down here than I ever thought was spoken by a nation supposed to have as high an educational standard as the United States has."

In one letter it was obvious that Story wasn't too happy and even considered leaving the Force. He wrote, "I have finally come to the stage, where I want to leave this unit. I am not alone in this desire. Most of the Canadians are fed up with always having to do things the American way, and with always having to stay down here in the states. The uniforms are very nice, the pay is good, our work is interesting, but it still is not all that it was cracked up to be when we first joined it. There is something lacking. As the unit is half Canadian and half American, we would like to see 50-50 proposition in everything we do. The Americans do not see it that way. I'm getting fed up.....I am going to blow my top to the Colonel. I myself have an ace-in-the-hole. Now that George is in the air force and because he is my older brother, he can claim me into his branch of the service." Bill went on to say, "I am quite sore about the whole matter and I want to do something about it. We will be here for about another month, I believe. That should give me some time in which to act." Evidently Bill had second thoughts about leaving the Force as indicated in his next letter.

Ft. Ethan Allen, Vt. 5 October 1943. "I have recovered from my dismal feelings about this Force. Couldn't get away from it if I wanted to, anyway, the Colonel is not letting anybody return to Canada unless they really have to go because of sickness or similar matters. We have one man down here in the hospital with a very serious illness. The only thing that would cure him was this new drug called *penicillin*. I presume that you have read the articles that have appeared in Readers Digest. If you have, you will know that it is very rare and very expensive and is denied civilian use at the present time. They used the drug on this man and it cured him inside of a week."

The Army faced a problem never before encountered or even visualized. In addition of the combination of the Canadian and American military training to fight together, the variety of skills would be needed for the Force to become a combination infantry, armored-engineer-parachute-mountain force. There was no precedent for this type of unit. The code title given to this military project was *"Plough."* The Force commander had a Canadian executive. Two of the regiments were commanded by American officers; the third by a Canadian officer. The initial target date given to Plough was December. The training schedule to meet all their goals was vigorous. Only the toughest would survive this training. Outlined are three phases of their training:

(1) From August 3rd to October 3rd, their training included, parachute training, weapons, demolition, small-unit tactics and achieving top notch physical condition.

(2) From October 5th until November 21st, they studied tactics and problems.

(3) The remaining time was used for skiing, rock climbing, living in cold climates and operation of the snow vehicle. They were up at 4:30 a.m., breakfast at 6:30 a.m. then calisthenics. This was followed by running through the one and a quarter mile obstacle course before 8 a.m.

Each trainee and all officers were required to qualify on the carbine, light machine gun, sub-machine gun, pistol and grenade. Discipline was not only very important but a matter of self- pride. The men had Sundays off and usually went hunting or fishing.

The plan called for paratroopers to be dropped with a special vehicle over the snow covered areas of Europe. The British Engineers estimated it would take four years to develop such a snow driven vehicle. Gen. Marshall and others met at Churchill's summer home on April 9, 1942 to discuss this idea and hear the story of Pyke. It was estimated that 600 of these vehicles would be needed for the first six months. Many types of snow machines were tried but failed to meet the required standards.

This was a very important Englishman, a genius, who provided important information for this special operation. His name was Geoffrey Pyke. Between World War I and World War II, Pyke practiced his profession of psychology. During World War I, he was captured twice by the Germans and escaped both times. He prepared a paper called, "Mastery of the Snows." In his report he outlined the fact that mastery of the snow was as important as of the sea. Vehicles such as a cross-country snow machine were essential. Norway's hydroelectric stations would have to be destroyed because of their value to Germany.

Rumania was supplying three million tons of oil to the Axis every year. Intelligence estimated that there were 5,000 oil wells within a 50 mile radius of Ploesti. The first attack on this city was in August 1943. During that bombing, the Allies lost 44 heavy bombers out of the 178 who participated. Because of the importance of these oil wells, Germany had surrounded the city with heavy artillery in key locations. They built circular defense belts of barbed wire, machine guns, and artillery placed in pillboxes. If the Force attempted to blow up these oil rigs and refineries, the problem was how to evacuate the men from Rumania. The Weasel could be used for a time when they were moving toward Turkey. But the problem was that the snow would then disappear leaving them to fight against German tanks.

Initially Frederick was given the task to evaluate the "Plough" plan by General Eisenhower. Frederick was a thorough man, an officer who was highly respected, the ideal person to analyze the plan. His report indicated that the plan was not practical. General Eisenhower refused to sign the report because plans had been made to go forward with Plough.

Fighting was not isolated. Fighting was going on in many places. Because of the demands by the military in other areas, the needs of the Force could not be met. Intelligence continued on Norway. Targets from all over Norway would demand a number of parachute jumps in separate places. Even though Winston Churchill and Lord Mountbatten had continued to show interest in the plan, it was decided to let "Operation Plough" die. A cable came from the Force offices stating, "Suspend Current Planning." Colonel Frederick left Fort Harrison and returned to the United Kingdom. He wanted to clear up any existing problems. His report was also sent to the American General, Dwight D. Eisenhower. The decision was made to allow the Force to continue, concentrating on Norway. Eisenhower called Colonel Frederick and ordered him, "Frederick, you take charge of this Plough project. You've been over the whole thing. You're in charge now. Let me know what you need." It is interesting that the officer who had given many reasons why Plough was not a workable military plan, fell heir to raising, training, and commanding a task force bent on demolishing enemy installations in various parts of Europe. The Plough project was discontinued for two reasons. First, the Norway government decided blowing up their installations would bring hardship to the people of Norway; secondly, the British refused to allow the Force to use their planes to drop the snow machines. The new operation was named, "*Operation Torch.*" The new Allied plan was headed for North Africa.

In a newspaper article dated June 29, 1943 from Ottawa, the decision of the Force to invade Norway was revealed. It read, "Disclosure that the famous 1st Special Service Force of Canadians and Americans, which fought through Italy and in southern France, was originally assembled in 1942 for an invasion of Norway that didn't take place, was made in a defense headquarters release last night. Without elaboration the release said the Force was "originally assembled back in 1942 for a specific purpose of invading German held Norway–a venture which was later abandoned."

Breaking one of the strictest publicity blackouts of the war, the release said it was not until the Canadian contingent of 47 officers and 700 men had joined their American comrades at Helena, Montana, that the two groups learned they were to be organized, trained and sent into action as a mixed Canadian-United States force.

Kiska was the next scheduled action for the Force. Kiska was very similar to the other islands of that chain. There was an inactive volcano on the northern tip. The sole economic value of Kiska was a fox-trapping rights licensed out to trappers in peace-time for $9 a year. Colonel Frederick wanted the Force to land scouts on the island but the Navy denied his request.

Everyone was on edge. Countless question were asked of the old-timers who covered the Attu show as to what gear to take, how to dig foxholes in the least possible time...etc. Secrecy was the word for days in advance. It seems that a possible Hollywood production was planned for this battle. Camera crews were on hand for the preparation for the great battle on Kiska as heroic American doughboys dashed ashore into the devastating machine-gun and mortar fire. The best estimates of the enemy strength placed the Japanese on Kiska at 11,925. The night of the landing, the tide was high. It was a foggy night. The men of the Force began climbing down the nets, each carrying from 90 to 100 pounds of ammunition, rations etc. They climbed into rubber boats and began paddling toward the beach. The first boats landed at 1:20 a.m. Where were the Japs? Why weren't they firing? Patrols were sent out to explore the island. The patrols found empty caves and huts, but they didn't locate any enemy. Could the Japs be planning a surprise attack? They had evacuated Kiska. It was a dry run for the

Force, however, the maneuver proved to be very valuable for future action.

"Most unique fighting unit in history, the Force which first saw active operation at the Aleutian island of Kiska which the Japs abandoned is reported to have disbanded. But some of its members will likely see action again with Americans when they operate with the 6th Pacific division. What the force had expected to be its first battle action-Kiska in August 1943–turned out to be it last rehearsal. It wasn't three months later, thousands of miles from Kiska, in the rugged Camino mountain range south of Cassino, Italy, that the force got its introduction in spectacular fashion, to the real thing."

Major General, USA Charles H. Corlett in a letter said, "*In the occupation of the Island of Kiska, the First Special Service Force was under my command. They performed all missions according to plan and even though no actual enemy was encountered, their missions were difficult and dangerous. They landed in rubber boats at unknown beaches during the hours of darkness against what was presumed to be hostile shore. They moved across difficult terrain and positions where cleverly-concealed traps had been left by the enemy. They reached their objectives on schedule according to plan.*"

Naples-Foggia (September 9, 1943 to January 1944)

The Special Service Force's next mission was in Italy. The Force was trained for mountain and cold weather fighting. Throughout November, the entire US Fifth army had been stopped in its tracks by a series of heavily fortified mountains, most formidable of which were the peaks of Camino and La Difensa. From these towering vantage points strong German forces had been able to beat back every Allied effort to advance past them, and every attempt by British and American regular infantry to dislodge them. Such was the situation when the TFSSF (The First Special Service Force), newly arrived in Italy, moved up to the front. Still green, and still without actual battle experience, their orders were to scale the 3,000 foot peak of La Difensa, and wrest it from the veteran 11th Panzer Grenadier division solidly entrenched on the top. They sent one Canadian and one American to scout a way for the regiment to rope their way up and at dawn the Germans discovered themselves cut off, with the Special Service Force at their rear. Once Story had a close call when a phone line went dead. He went out to investigate and found the point where the line had gone dead. Just then, he heard in the distance the sound of German Nebelwerfers being launched. Story said that the Germans had seen Russian Katyusha rockets on their Eastern front, thought that they were a good idea, and built their own version. Story could see the red glow from the rockets. The glow disappeared, right over his head. The rocket engine's had cut out and what had gone up was about to come down on top of him. Story lay flat on his stomach. The rockets exploded around him and pieces of shrapnel ricocheted off rocks, and with their force spent, bounced off his helmet. When it was over, Story looked up and saw a large chunk of metal imbedded in the ground, inches from his head.

Fourteen machine-gun nests fell to the FSSF within four hours and by dawn the heights were in Allied hands. For the next six days and nights, during which its Canadian commander was killed, the force held on under terrific shelling and mortar fire, throwing back all German counterattacks and mopping up the surrounding heights. Not until Dec. 9, with La Difensa and nearby positions cleared of the enemy, was the FSSF finally relieved. The Force pulled back after taking heavy casualties. Not long after, the Force found itself on the front line at *Anzio.* They were on the front lines for 99 days before being relieved. They painted their faces black and roamed through the German positions. The diary of a dead German paid them their most cherished tribute: "The black devils are all around us every time we come into the line and we never hear them come." The Force worked hard and bloodily to maintain the legend, pasted their divisional stickers on the bodies of Germans they knifed and on enemy equipment they disabled. When Allied forces broke out from the beachhead, the Force spearheaded the attack led by Robert Frederick wearing a bandage around a neck wound.

Sergeant William Steer Story was promoted to the rank of First Lieutenant on December 5, 1943. Story said that a runner came to his tent to have him report to headquarters. His commander advised Bill that he had received a battlefield commission, to tear off his sergeant strips and put on a bar. Bill said, "a gold bar?' His commander said that a second lieutenant was not qualified to lead, for him to put on silver bars. There was a newspaper clipping dated January 20 with the headlines reading, "Winnipeggers promoted as Big Battle Rages." It read as follows: "With the 5th Army in Italy. In the thick of battle, amid hills bearing a striking resemblance to the Laurentians, but not quite so peaceful, eight young Canadian non-commissioned officers of the combined Canada-United States special force fighting the German's, suddenly became officers. As Tommy guns stuttered and rifles barked midway up a snow-capped mountain, orders reached the front that eight men had been made first lieutenants in this commando-like unit. Those commissioned included Sgt. W. S. Story of Winnipeg."

ANZIO (Operation Shingle) January 29, 1944

The US VI Corps began attacking out of Anzio on January 29th. The US Third Division continued to advance. On February 3rd, the Germans counterattacked at Anzio but gave up on March 3rd. On June 3rd, Hitler granted his commander permission to give up Rome. On June 5th, the US Fifth Army entered Rome after a long and costly battle to both sides. The Germans reported 25,000 casualties while the allied forces had 40,000 casualties.

The Force was reinforced with additional American and Canadian volunteers. The Force was a powerful attraction for

Canadian sergeants because they were now drawing pay at the US Army rate. They also got better food and better clothes. After training the new volunteers, the reinforced Special Service Force returned to Anzio. Polish troops captured Monte Casino, to the south, breaking the German Gustav Line. This opened the door for a breakout from Anzio, spearheaded by the Special Service Force. Story said that the first day was "tough." This was the first time that the allies had seen German Tiger tanks in Italy and bazooka rockets would not penetrate their frontal or side armor. But the Tigers were slow and clumsy. Story added, "We were the first Allied troops into Rome." The Force had captured seven bridges over the Tiber River, clearing the way for other troops.

For 98 days, the Force held ten miles of front, an area which ordinarily would demand five times their number. Germans on patrol were bushwhacked, Indian style; dozens went out only to vanish; finally the Germans pulled back their patrols for five miles, whereupon Frederick staged a raid with tanks and armored cars, killed 50 Germans and captured 60, with the Force having only one casualty-a Canadian who sprained his ankle leaping off a tank.

On January 30 orders came for the Force to move immediately to the port staging area outside Pozzuoli. They begin moving by 3:00 o'clock that afternoon. So they suddenly moved from Santa Maria to ancient Pozzuoli near Naples. The Force unloaded in an open field two miles west of Anzio. They went into the line on February 2 under VI Corps. The strength of the Force at this time was 68 officers and 1,165 enlisted men. Their mission was to defend the right flank of VI Corps. The sector that the Force had captured had seven enemy divisions with elements of three others.

General Alexander had laid plans to capture Rome. Anzio Beachhead forces were meanwhile being cocked and primed to join the drive at the proper moment. At Anzio, the Force, with the divisions, was preparing to "crack the egg" in one of the three plans: *Operation Grasshopper; Operation Buffalo* and *Operation Turtle.*

The Force Beachhead casualties totaled, 54 killed or died of wounds; 51 missing and 279 wounded in action. These statistics will never tell the Force's Anzio story.

The Force pushed on, but so suddenly and rapidly that they were through the German defense's and well on the road to Rome before any second line of defense could be organized. The FSSF had the mission of breaking into Rome and seizing the railway station and eight of the Tiber bridges. At first, it looked like the Force would be unopposed. The men were enjoying the flowers and wine, when the Germans started shooting shells down the road. This was the start of the German delaying action in what they claimed was the open city of Rome. By night, the Force was into the heart of the city, their objectives taken, after a wild day of mingled acclamations and fights. The Force seized all bridges intact, arriving so suddenly that the Germans didn't have time to set off the explosives. This was the last of the dramatic successes which this superb fighting force achieved in Italy. They went from there for a rest period in the Alban Hills before starting their training for Southern France.

The Force distinguished itself in Italy by capturing the strongly held peaks of La Difensa, Mount Sammuere and Mount Major to help break the deadlock at Cassino. When they flung into the Anzio beachhead, it helped in the break-out there that led to the capture of Rome. For three weeks a first class American division had been trying to take "Mt. La Defensa," 3,000 foot key to the German position at Cassino. But ice, snow and a deadly German defense stopped them. Making a reconnaissance patrol, General Frederick discovered that one part of the peak was so steep it could be scaled only with ropes. The Germans thought this impossible. A few nights later, Frederick and his men started up the mountainside. At dawn they hid out about halfway up, so close to the enemy that they could smell German food and hear the Germans talking. It was almost zero weather; the men had no blankets; they dared not even move for fear they might be seen and annihilated. For nearly twelve hours they lay motionless. Their clothing froze to the ground; they could not eat. When night came they scaled the sheer cliff with ropes, and at daylight swarmed on the Germans, panicking the Nazis so that they fell back six miles to Cassino. The cost was 75 SSF casualties.

After Rome, Frederick became a major general at the age of 37, and took command of the airborne for the invasion of Southern France. Colonel Edwin A. Walker, one of the regimental commanders, took over and led the outfit in its toughest fight yet, a landing in rubber boats on Levant Island, which guarded the approaches through Cavalaire Bay.

Before the Special Forces reached Rome, it had lost more than half the men who sailed from Kiska, including two regimental commanders, and nearly all battalion C.O's. At Levant, where the Germans fought bitterly from their camouflaged hideouts, the casualties struck deep again. By then, because Canadian replacements were fewer; the outfit was more than two-thirds US and many of its officers were ex-noncoms commissioned on the battlefield. Fighting men had a word to explain the outfit's success. The word was "guts."

Bill Story wrote a letter to his parents, dated June 10, 1944, somewhere in Italy. Here is a part of that letter. "Well, I suppose you have already heard of the part that we played in the capture of Rome. The going was tough for the first little while, then we got "him" on the run, it became a bit easier. The Force moved at a phenomenal rate of speed, and every time caught the Jerry where he least expected it. At one town the boys moved in and captured over 300 prisoners without firing any more than half a dozen shots. We traveled at top speed towards Rome to catch up to the Kraut, catching his fleeing trucks and supply columns before they could escape. I stopped one night with my platoon near a supply train that had been knocked out by our fighter bombers. What a time we had that night–food galore, sardines, bread (black of course), bully beef, candy, cake and cigars. The next town we moved into, we actually captured some German sentries who were all unaware that we were anywhere in the vicinity. They certainly let out some squawks when they understood that the Tommy gun shoved in their ribs meant business. Believe me I have quite a tale to tell just as soon as I can tell it. We are sleeping in pup tents. The food is good and the weather is wonderful."

The Special Force was detached from the US 5th Army and transferred to the 7th Army for operation *"Anvil,"* the invasion of France's Mediterranean coast on August 15, 1944. The island of Levant with its batteries of German guns, mortar and machine gun posts, must be knocked out before the main invasion of Southern France gets underway. Slowly the rubber boat is pulled away from the ship's side to be soon swallowed in the darkness. On the shoulders of these 40 men, Levant bound, rested the immediate success of the invasion plan of the Combat Group. They must get ashore and, like the mountain goats, they have virtually become by hand and foot scale the cliffs and secure the heights. The Force went in five hours before the main force to take two islands, Port Cros and Levant that defended the main landing beaches. This was difficult because they encountered some thick-walled Napoleonic-era forts and they had no artillery. The big guns of a British battleship finally took care of the problem. The German troops that they encountered in Southern France were of poor quality and retreated rapidly. Of the original FSSF which Fredericks took into Kiska one year to the minute before the Force hit Southern France, there was probably 45% left with the Force when it left Italy. Employing and expending these highly specialized men as "standard" infantry may seem over costly, but like paratroopers and rangers, they are so highly trained they are among the best infantrymen in the world. They have baggy pants and dirty faces and a few of them go a long way.

The Special Service Force disbanded in France on December 5, 1944. Story said that the time for small, elite units like theirs has passed. Story and the airborne qualified Canadians went to England where they joined the 1st Canadian Parachute Battalion, attached to the 6th British Airborne Division. They made a combat jump at Wesel, Germany. Story said, "We landed right on top of SS troopers." The battalion commander, Colonel Jeff Nicklin, got hung up in a tree, right over the SS unit's headquarters. He was machine-gunned to death before he could cut himself free. This was a tough loss for Story. Nicklin had been his high school football coach for one season.

At precisely 2:00 p.m. on August 11th, commandos were told for the first time, their invasion objectives would be the Islands of Port Cros and Lefant, five miles off the southern shore of France. Their mission would be an island invasion under the cover of darkness and without the usual terrific air bombardment and naval fire support.

A newspaper article written by Sgt. George Powell, Staff Writer, *The Maple Leaf*, gave this account. "Allied troops, which smashed ashore on the southern coast of France, are firmly established along an extensive beachhead between Caunes and Toulon and all initial objectives have been taken. While few details were given of the fighting along the French Riviera beachheads, it was stated operations were going according to plan and the bulk of leading Allied infantry divisions had been landed. Initial assault on the beaches was carried out in the main by the US 6th Corps. It was revealed for the first time last night that Allied troops encountered serious opposition at one point. A second group of airborne infantry was dropped from troop carriers Tuesday. It was declared that British and American glider and paratroops had been successful in blocking German reinforcements. The second series of airborne landings which met no air or ground opposition was one of the largest operations of its kind." [The skies over the new beachhead in Southern France, somewhere between Nice and Marseilles, break into bloom as parachutists saunter earthward on their way to work for the Allied nations. The silk-born soldiers were carried to their destination by C-47 aircrafts.]

Canada had been represented in southern France by some of the best Canadians in the armed forces. The Force swarmed ashore on the islands of Levant and Port Cros, dominating left flank of the original beachhead in southern France.

Before Anzio, this combined Canadian-USA combat group was so hush-hush, it was almost completely unknown, even in army circles and those who knew it, nicknamed the Force, "First Special Tourist Force," or "First Special Nervous Force," because it started from so many places, reached so many others, and then did its job in complete obscurity. Its men swear the name was deliberately chosen for security and obtained through confusion with the special service division which provides movies, magazines, photographs and recreation rooms for troops. They took a lot of ribbing.

The Allied armies in Italy knew the men of the Force because of their baggy-panted mountain uniforms and shoulder patches. They finally released their organizational name and history after landing in France. The Germans at Anzio probably knew them best of all. Documents abandoned by the Germans in their flight north from Rome showed that the German command gave prisoners taken from FSSF top priority–the Germans caught only 23 of them alive, although most of their combat occurred well behind the German lines. The Germans continued to try to obtain information on the Force. The Canadians reached the Baltic Sea at the end of the war, where they met the Russians. The German Army surrendered at 2:41 a.m. on May 7, 1945.

On June 18, 1945, Story was back in Winnipeg, Canada. In a letter from the Department of National Defense -Army, dated 17 September 45, Winnipeg, Manitoba, it reads:

TO WHOM IT MAY CONCERN

Lieut William Steer STORY

The marginally named Officer was taken on Strength the Canadian Army, Active effective 2 Apr 42 and was Struck off Strength the Canadian Army, Active effective 17 Sep 45 under authority A G Radio Pers 4877 4B3-7 dated 15 Aug 45 on being returned to Reserve Status at his own request.

Signed A. Thomson Lt. Col., Officer Commanding (No. 10 District Depot CA)

The Canadians serving in The First Special Service Force along with the Americans whom they trained with, fought with and died with were not awarded the same medals as the US Soldiers. This too became a concern and a kind of sore spot. After all Story and his Canadian buddies believed they should be entitled to the same honors. One of the awards was the CIB (Combat Infantry Badge), a prestigious infantryman's badge that was established by the US War Department in 1943. The American members of the Devil's Brigade were awarded the CIB in 1944.

World War II ended. US Army Chief of Staff of the Armies George C. Marshall was satisfied that his introduction of the Bronze Star Medal (BSM) and the subsequent tying of it to the Combat Infantryman Badge (CIB), was working. US Soldiers–front line veterans of WWII were applying for and receiving the CIB followed by the Bronze Star. But there was one group of soldiers who had served in a US Army unit-THE FIRST SPECIAL SERVICE FORCE, under a US Army commander, Major General Robert T. Frederick, a West Point graduate, who were rejected when they applied to the Awards Branch of the US Army; when they applied to the Secretary of the Army; and when applications on their behalf were made by their fellow Force veterans. Sixty plus years passed. While efforts slackened, they never ceased.

Appeals gained support from US Army Special Forces to whom the battle honors won by the Force had been transferred along with its distinctive Crossed Arrows and its V-42 Combat Knife. Its red Spearhead shoulder patch with the V-42 Combat Knife superimposed in place of the USA/CANADA lettering was adopted by the US Army Special Operations Command at Ft. Bragg, N.C. At Ft. Benning, GA, home of the Infantry, the US Army Chief of Infantry supported the position of the Canadians. There was still no response. And for a

RESPECT

very good reason–the US Army had no military records of the Canadians of the Special Service Force. General Frederick wanted the Canadians to join the US Army but the Canadian Government refused. They did approve their Force Canadians receiving US Army medals of valor: Bronze and Silver Stars; Distinguished Service Crosses. Many were awarded.

The Canadian members were denied at the time despite 40 years of effort by the First Service Force Association lobbying the US Congress. The good news finally came some 60 years later when the CIB (Combat Infantry Badge) was approved for the Canadian Force soldiers, in May 2005. It was also decided that the CIB would be presented to next-of-kin of deceased Force veterans.

Bill Story and the Canadian Devil's Brigade survivors were honored during one of their Reunions on August 14, 2005. Another comrade honored with Story was Alan Lennox who was twice blown up by land mines while serving with the elite Canadian-American army unit in World War II. Now 60 years later, his bravery has been recognized by the US government. The 84 year old was among about 100 Canadian veterans and representatives of the Devil's Brigade—the crack First Special Service Force remembered in history and by Hollywood—who received the US Army Combat Infantryman's Badge. Lennox's eyes welled up and his voice cracked when asked to describe how it felt to finally receive the honor. Lennox, who is from Winnipeg, said, "I feel it right now in my heart." Lennox signed up for the unit at the age of 21 and fought the entire length of the war from 1939-1945. He added, "I was quite aware of what we were getting into in this unit. It was strictly attack, attack, and attack. That was our duty."

After years risking their lives in hand to hand combat for the Allies, the Canadian members received fair dues during this special presentation when they were awarded the CIB badge previously only given to American soldiers.

The other medal awarded to Americans that eluded the Canadians for 63 years was the "Bronze Star." For their combat activities in July and August, 1944, the American Army soldiers in Story's unit were awarded the Bronze Star. During the 2006 Force Reunion in Helena, Montana, the Commander of Special

Forces announced that in keeping with General Marshall's order that the CIB award would be accompanied by issuance of the Bronze Star Medal. In February, 2007, all surviving Canadian members of the Force were awarded the coveted medal by the US Department of Defense.

Other medals awarded by the Chancery Office, Office of the Governor General of Canada to William Story are listed here:

>>WWII Victory Star   >>'39-45 Star

>>North Africa Star >>Defense of Canada Medal w/Volunteer Clasp

>>King George VI Medal-Victory WWII

>>125th Anniversary of Canadian Confederation

>>50th Anniversary of Queen Elizabeth II Coronation

>>USA Bronze Star   >>USA Combat Infantryman's Badge (CIB)

>>"Kings" (battlefield commission) awarded for attack on Monte La Defensa

>>Liberation of France Medal (Government of France)

>>Liberation of Italy Medal (Government of France)

The *"Devil's Brigade"* has been mentioned when referring to Story's unique unit. This was a name given to them when Hollywood made a movie about their World War II combat experiences. This movie was made on the Force's mission on the Monte la Difensa campaign in Italy in December 1943. This is where the Force broke a German stronghold on a 1,000 meter peak by scaling the back of the mountain over two nights. Prior to the Devil's Brigade arriving and scouting the problems there, 26,000 men had died trying to take the hill the conventional way. Hilton added, "We were the only one with guts enough to do it in the dark, and that put us in position to surprise the Germans in the morning." They went up the 600 feet of the vertical face of the mountain in the dark. During their annual Reunions, much of the conversations expressed are about their combat experiences. Norm Beech of Calgary said that "We didn't know what training was up here in Canada compared to what we went through down in Montana. We learned stuff we would've never learned in units here." The Devils Brigade is known for having never lost a battle, taking orders from the top ranks of Britain and the US between August 1943 and November 1944. This unit's twenty-two successful exploits, especially its first overseas campaign, prompted the Hollywood movie made in 1968. Hilton, age 89, with a laugh at the Sheraton Eau Claire said, "But have you ever seen an esprit de corps like this before?" The head of the commandos in England said he had never seen an outfit with more or better esprit de corps. He said, "It's because we never asked each other if we were Americans or Canadians–that didn't matter because we were Force men."

RESPECT

During the Forces 50th Reunion in 1996 at Dearborn, Michigan, the address for the Memorial service was given by Rev. Herb Morris, a former Force member, at the Hyatt Hotel. It is appropriate to include his address and prayer.

"Fellow Comrades of the battlefield, members of the Force Family, and friends, since before those days in which Moses told Pharaoh "Let my people go," from time immemorial mankind has sought to free itself from the shackles of despots and the forces of evil that threaten our happiness and take away our freedom.

Two centuries ago, our Nations received this heritage of the quest for liberty. Often we have been called upon to defend those beliefs around the world and never have we failed to respond when duty and devotion called us to service. Today we pay tribute to all who have participated in the great battle with the forces of evil, but most especially the members of our beloved First Special Service Force. The world may take little note of the exploits of the Force in World War II, but we remember and recognize the important contribution made by our buddies for the benefit of mankind.

Over 50 years ago, Sir Winston Churchill and President Franklin Roosevelt caused this unique brigade to be organized from volunteer fighting men of the United States and Canada. Bonded together under the command of Gen. Robert T. Frederick they formed the most audacious combat unit ever devised. Fueled with the desire to fight for liberty and democracy against the forces of totalitarian tyranny, they went through rigorous paratroop, ski, mountain and amphibious training.

We remember our major encounters with the enemy as if they were yesterday. The fighting in the Italian mountains; enduring over three months of patrol activity on Anzio beachhead; suffering under ferocious artillery while liberating towns such as Artena; being the first allied combatants to enter Rome; landing in rubber boats on the Hyeres Islands prior the Southern France invasion; and liberating the mountainous area north of Toulon as we moved across to the Franco-Italian border. Through it all, God was with us and we were victorious. Later, members of the Force continued to fight in northern France and Germany, and removed the Nazi from Norway. During these engagements most were wounded at least once, and many died. As we mourn the loss of those who fought with us we also remember and give thanksgiving for the wonderful days of victory and the presence of our Creator.

Today we represent not only that heritage but the loyalty we feel for our brave comrades who are now only with us in spirit. We stand as an assurance that their sacrifice will never be forgotten. We will courageously carry on with a strengthened resolve in the warfare against the evil of tyranny, and for the virtues of liberty, equality, and democracy. We represent our two countries, as partners in the struggle for permanent peace and justice for our nations and all mankind. By our actions today, we complete the fight for which our fellow combatants gave their very lives. We are here as well to memorialize those comrades who have gone to their eternal home in this past year. We know they rest from their labors, but their works do follow them. We say to those braves of old, "Well done, good and faithful servants -enter the joy of your Lord."

The years pass and new generations come forward in the drama of life, but let there be no fear. We will not, like old soldiers just fade away. As Force Troopers of over half a century ago, we continue to live courageously in this new day, for we remember the sacrifices of our buddies and the debt we owe those who gave their lives for those values we hold so dear. Partners in war are aware of the costs, and do not take lightly the price of peace. Freedom may cost, but it is worth the cost. Permanent Peace may require sacrifice, but it is worth the price. We know liberty demands vigilance against oppression and the tyranny of tyrants. We will truly stand on guard for our nations. If you will allow me a personal note, I will never forget volunteering for the Force and returning home with the inspiration of that experience to become part of the Clergy.

As the poet has said so well:

Lord teach us to believe,
That we are stationed as a post,
Although the humblest 'neath the sky,
The place where we are needed most,
And that at last if we do well,
Our humble services will tell.
Lord grant us faith to stand on guard
Uncheered, unspoken, alone.
And see beyond such duty hard,
Our service to the throne.
What'ere our task, be this our creed.
We are on earth to fill the need.

Let us lift high the lamp of liberty and never, ever, forget the sacrificial love of others for us. PRAYER Almighty Father of us all, as you are present with those who become partners for peace, reignite us with that spirit of enthusiasm and purpose, which forged our nations into a common and victorious task, that in these days, we might contribute to a positive and lasting peace. AMEN.

It was reported by the *Independent-Record* newspaper that Major General Robert T. Frederick, former commander of The Force, then commanding officer of the 45th Infantry Division, returned to Helena to discuss plans for the construction of a special memorial in the new park for the First Special Service Force. The General planned to meet with the Mayor and the Memorial park committee while in Helena. The General expressed his happiness at being able to visit Helena again and renew his old acquaintances. When speaking at the banquet held in his honor, he said, "The first special service force was and I say with pride and respect for many a gallant outfit–the finest military unit ever assembled in our history. My greatest regret is that all of my men are not with me tonight, especially those who will never return. We left in Italy and France some of the finest men I've known-men who stood out not only as soldiers but as citizens." He added that there the figures showed a 250 to 300 percent casualty rate for original force members. Frederick laughed about how some of the men "borrowed" various pieces of furniture such as overstuffed chairs and lugged those 14,000 feet to their dugouts on Italy's towering mountainsides.

Columnist George Gamester wrote this story about "How a school dropout became a hero to his family and his country."

You know what they say, folks: It takes all kinds, winners and losers, rich and poor, saints and sinners. Then there's William Magee. Was he a devil or an angel? Well, he has been both, from heroic episodes on the battlefield, to sunny times at the park, where he helps kids learn how to better help themselves. The story about Magee is a doozy with enough blood and guts for a war movie.

We begin with a 14-year-old Grade 9 kid at Parkdale Collegiate, holding up his hand in French class, asking to be excused. "Very well, William" intones Miss Gavin. "But hurry back. You can't afford to miss any more French." This was in 1937. Times were tough. Willie's father, a stationary engineer, dies of pneumonia. Suddenly, he's the bread winner for his ailing mother and his five siblings. He dropped out of school to work six days a week as a newsboy. Then he gets it into his head to join the military for adventure. The recruiters laugh. Tell him to come back when he is grown.

It's different in '41. Canada is at war, and a determined 17-year-old can sneak in and assign his $1.50 a day pay to his mother. Willie signs with the Toronto Scottish Regiment. An officer said to Willie, "We like your spunk, Magee. So we've prepared to send you to the University of Toronto, where you can get an education and earn your commission. What do you say?" "Not me! I want action." Within weeks our hero is training for the paratroops. This is the 1st Special Force, an elite strike unit made up of Canadians and Americans whose exploits were chronicled in a popular 1968 film, *"The Devil's Brigade, staring William Holden.* .He seriously injures himself on his first training jump along with another young Toronto hell raiser.

He was sent home but vows he'll be back. After a series of adventures involving unauthorized leaves of absence, fistfights, a court martial and the loss of 129 days pay, he's shipped back to the Devil's Brigade.

After adventures in North Africa, some near-death experiences in the nasty fighting around Cassino and Anzio, and a triumphant march into Rome, Magee finds himself in a pickle in Northern Italy. He finds himself pinned down by crossfire from three machine guns; his platoon is warned not to try to rescue two wounded comrades lying in no man's land. Magee ignored the warning. He zigzagged to his buddies, with bullets humming all around. He bandages their wounds and carries them to safety through withering fire. For this brave act, he is awarded the Silver Star.

While in France, he writes to Miss Gavin, his French teacher. He said, "If only Magee had listened! "My military ventures have taken me to Tdrois-Rivieres, Casablanca, Oran, Corsica, Iles D'Hyeres, and now Provence. How I wish I'd learned my French! Please read this to your students. Tell them they never know when they may need it."

Later, Magee received the Bronze Star for helping to knock out enemy strongholds and capturing 31 prisoners. When asked why he got into so much trouble, he said, "It was the times. Any day could be your last so you didn't think ahead. You lived by the day." Magee became a family man, a successful businessman.

William Story, a resident of Smith Mountain Lake, Virginia continues using his talents, his experiences to share with others. An unusual thing occurred recently. The account of this remarkable story was written by Rob Lyon of the *Smith Mountain Eagle*. The headlines read: "Lake barbershop chorus members' paths cross again after chance meeting during World War II. Then: **"Love of singing reunites soldiers 50 years later."**

Roy Rardin and Bill Story both fought in the same war and came from cold-weather climates and loved the music of Irving Berlin. They met briefly in a military hospital in Italy in 1943 during World War II. After the war they went their separate ways never imagining their love of music and barbershop singing would reunite them at Smith Mountain Lake some 50 years later, their memories are still fresh and they were naturally surprised when their paths again crossed, at first not sure what it was they remembered or seemed familiar about the other.

"I thought he looked familiar," said Story, describing how when he saw Rardin in 1992 at a rehearsal of the Harmoneers. Story said during a break in the rehearsal he went up to Rardin and started talking with him. He "kept probing" Story said and the two finally realized they had met briefly while both were hospitalized in Italy.

Rardin, a native of Green Bay, Wis., had been severely wounded by a grenade while serving with the US Army. He recalls the blast blew off his helmet and caused a severe injury to his leg. Using his skills learned as a Boy Scout, Rardin said he "half crawled and rolled" down a hill and made it back to safety.

Canadian native, Story had been in the same areas of Italy, attached to the same unit as Rardin. With remarkable detail, Story remembered several of the battles he was in as the Allied forces fought the German soldiers.

During his combat service, Story said he was commissioned a first lieutenant. He later served as an intelligence officer going on dangerous missions behind enemy lines. On one mission Story was wounded by a piece of shrapnel, developed jaundice and was sent to a hospital.

It was then Rardin and Story happened to meet for the first time. Story recalls officers were given maroon robes to wear while the enlisted men wore blue robes. Story knew of a friend who had also been wounded and went looking for him on the floor with the enlisted men. He found the friend while only two beds away was Rardin who spoke briefly with Story.

While at the hospital musician Irving Berlin visited and performed several of his now-famous songs for the patients. Rardin said he also got the autographs of other famous stars of the day, including one from Humphrey Bogart.

Both men eventually recovered from their wounds and left the hospital. Rardin was sent back to the United States and admitted to another military hospital to continue his recuperation. Story went back to the battlefield.

After his military service, Rardin got married and lived and worked in the Green Bay and Gary, Ind. areas. When he moved he has enjoyed the music ever since.

Rardin moved to Lynchburg in 1978 and found a barbershop chorus there. It later folded and he began singing with groups in Danville and then in Roanoke. Finally, in 1992, a small group of men in the Lake area decided to form a chapter here and Rardin has been a member since the beginning.

Story also recalled his love of music which began when he was a boy. He sang in choirs and also did solo work. His career with US Steel and in public relations took him to New York and Washington, D.C. Story became interested in barbershop singing while working in Washington but then lost interest when his first wife died.

His retirement brought Story to the Lake and he heard about the Harmoneers. That's when he was reunited with Rardin almost 50 years later. The men had had no contact with each other since their chance meeting in the hospital. Since their second meeting they have shared their life stories with each other and have recounted some of their experiences from the war years. Rardin and Story even learned they went over to Europe on the same ship, only at different times during the same year.

The active retirees still enjoy barbershop singing. The two men served as co-chairs of the recent Harmoneers concerts which played to full houses for both performances. The concerts had a patriotic theme, using music from the World War II era. Their amazing story shows how friendships can last a lifetime.

Bill Story married Gayle Robertson on August 24, 1943. They had five children and eight grandchildren. After Gayle's death, Bill married Patricia Vete on February 5, 1978. Retired now, they live at Smith Mountain Lake in the Blue Ridge Mountains at Moneta, VA. After completing his military obligation, Story graduated from the University of Manitoba in 1948; and went on to earn a Masters in Business from the University of Chicago. He remained in the United States and became a US Citizen in 1960.

THE LAST PARADE   The Force rode back to Villeneuve-Loubet to disband. General Dwight Eisenhower became the SHAEF Commander (Supreme Headquarters Allied Expeditionary Force) in 1943. Plans were being made for the invasion of Normandy which D-Day was June 6, 1944. The days for a small unit like the Force were numbered, in fact, outdated. The plans now required divisions not quick strike groups like the Force. They had suffered with over four hundred killed and missing, with total casualties over 2,300. With the battles they fought in; the victories achieved; who can question the fact that the First Special Service Force was the best fighters in the world. The combination of Canadians and United States soldiers serving together for two and one half years proved to be truly the "Devil's Brigade" who lived together as one. It was never "Canucks" and "Yanks". (From book by LTC Robert D. Burhans–The First Special Service Force)

"Only a few days remained, the first days of a cold December in 1944, when the men wandered idly from battalion to battalion seeking out old friends for a last word and a last drink together. Nice was the place, in those early December days, to say good-bye. They were a short few days. The end came quickly on December 5th. At 2:00 P.M., the Force gathered on the Loup River flats under a warm sun with the old chateau atop Villeneuve-Loubet looking down, a silent spectator on a small disbanding Force. First the chaplains read a prayer for the final dead who had fallen from Hyeres to Menton to join the honored dead of other campaigns. Then the colors moved forward–United States, Canadian, and Force–to remain a minute whipping in the breeze while the Adjutant read the inactivation order.

Slowly the red Force flag with its black dagger on white shield was wound to its staff and the casing slipped over it. Then the Canadians withdrew from ranks and formed their own battalion to march past, behind their own colors, the US contingent standing with empty ranks to review the passing of their comrades.

The next evening 37 officers and 583 other ranks boarded trucks for Marseille and boarded ship for Naples. Seven other officers had already left to join Canadian parachute units in the United Kingdom. The Force as history would know it had finally dissolved. An epitaph is not appropriate, for it did not die that afternoon at Villeneuve-Loubet. Its memory is still young in the hearts and minds of families who gave their sons to its ranks, and in the heart of every man who wore the red Spearhead."

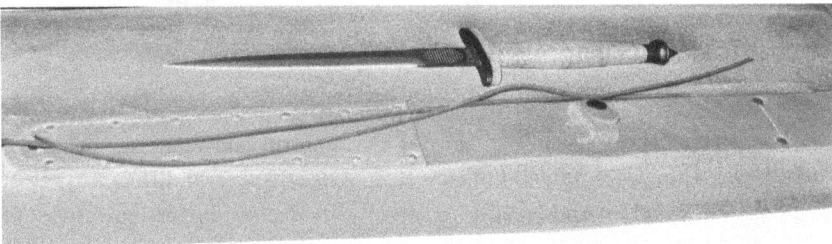

V-42 commando knife used by the Force. (Photo courtesy of Bill Story)

It can be summed up in the words of Sholto Watt of the *Montreal Standard,* who knew the Force best of any man outside it: *"I can testify to their spectacular power and efficiency, their marvelous morale and their never-failing spirit of attack. They were exactly what one would expect from North America's best–an inspiration to see and a terror to their enemy.*

But the importance of the First Special Service Force in world history, and their influence on the future, are much greater than even their outstanding military merit would deserve. The significance of this Force is that it was the first joint force of its kind, drawn from two neighbor democracies, and that it was a brilliant success throughout. It is by no means fanciful to see in it the prototype of the world police of that world community which has for so long been the dream of men of goodwill. Their legend [is] a feat of arms which will remain celebrated in military history which should be remembered even longer–

The picture above is an example of the uniform and equipment that the Force used. They were trained in many categories and several different types of weapons for combat and ready to meet the enemy under any type of circumstances.

The next picture is Private Spalding, an MP, with a German prisoner. The Force, called "The Black Devils" by the Germans, captured many Germans

during their surprise attacks behind the enemy lines. Lieutenant Bill Story was
an original member of the Force, a Canadian, now an American citizen, a hero.

Private Spalding of the MPs surveys a captured Superman

The Force was first again
(Photos courtesy of Bill Story)

WEASEL

CARRIER, CARGO M29; CARRIER, CARGO, M29C

SO PUBLICATIONS

CHAPTER FOUR

NORMANDY INVASION
D-DAY JUNE 6, 1944

It has been reported that England's Prime Minister Tony Blair was asked this question by a member of his Parliament: "Why do you believe so much in America?" Blair's answer was, "A simple way to take measure of a country is to look at how many want in and how many want out. Only two defining forces have ever offered to die for you: 1. Jesus Christ, 2. The American GI One died for your soul, the other for your freedom." In this chapter the evidence of the Prime Minister's statement rings true.

President Franklin D. Roosevelt

The invasion of Normandy on June 6, 1944 was called "The Greatest Invasion." It has been the subject of many books and movies. The intention here is not to recount all the details of this important battle, but to share some other events that took place prior to, during and following the invasion and the true experiences of some of the heroes who participated.

The invasion of Normandy was the turning point of World War II and disrupted Hitler's plans to dominate the world. President Franklin D. Roosevelt led the nation in prayer over the radio for six minutes on D-Day. [D-Day was first used in World War I to indicate the day the battle started.]

Some troops had trained for two years planning to land on the beaches of *Utah, Omaha, Gold, Juno, and Sword.* The Code name for this operation was *"OVERLORD,"* which lasted D-Day plus 80 days and ended on August 25th. Lt. General Fredrick Morgan, was the architect of Overlord, which evolved over a three-year period.

General Dwight D. Eisenhower)

Following a six-year study by a staff member of the National D-Day Memorial, a researcher found 4,391 recorded deaths; 2,477 American and 1,914 Allied deaths. The names of each of these brave men are listed on bronze necrology tablets in the Gray Plaza at the National D-Day Memorial located in Bedford, Virginia. During operation Overlord, the Allies landed over 2,000,000 men. The total casualties of the Allies were 209,672 with 36,979 killed. The Germans had over 1,000,000 soldiers with 240,000 killed or wounded; and 200,000 captured or missing.

The first man to go ashore at Normandy was a British agent, Red Wright. On May 27th, Wright went ashore with a group of scouts in a rubber dinghy to link up with the French Resistance. They were given old clothes and false papers and were armed only with pistols. The French carried out nearly 1,000 acts of sabotage on June 5th and June 6th. Nothing prior to and during the invasion went as planned, in spite of the fact that some soldiers had trained for more than a year without having any combat experience. One of the training programs that went sour was called *"Operation Tiger."*

Hitler and some of his generals in 1943 believed the main invasion would take place at Normandy. However, after several deceptions by the Allies, the Germans concluded that another location had been chosen. Field Marshall Rommel was one of the top German officers. In preparation for a possible attack at Normandy, the Germans laid 4,000,000 mines along the five beaches and also installed 500,000 obstacles which included "hedgehogs" (steel structures). The hedgehogs were to damage the landing crafts while injuring or killing the troops they were carrying. On the ridge overlooking the beaches were Germans manning machine guns, mortars and heavy guns to stop any Allied advancement from the beaches.

Field Marshall Erwin Rommel said, *"In the short time left before the great offensive starts, we must succeed in bringing all defenses to such a standard that they will hold up against the strongest attacks. The enemy must be annihilated before he reaches our main battlefield. We must stop him in the water, not only delaying him but destroying all his equipment while it is still afloat."*

The invasion by soldiers landing by the Higgins landing crafts began at 6:30 a.m. The rain was to stop and the wind quit blowing for a 36 hour period, according to a British Captain James Stagg, Eisenhower's meteorologist. Stagg was under a lot of pressure. One Admiral told him that if he didn't give them a good weather report that they would hang him from a lamp post. Stagg later said, "If all conditions were met by all the commanders, that the invasion would not have taken place for a hundred years, and maybe not even then." With this favorable report on June 5th, the order was given by General Eisenhower, "O.K. Lets Go."

(Hedgehogs on Normandy Beaches)

The land invasion started at 6:30 a.m. on June 6th. It must be remembered that around 10:30 p.m. on June 5th, British paratroopers and glider-men took off at one minute intervals in 733 aircraft and 355 gliders. The British were the first troops to land in Normandy. The first British soldier to land in Normandy was Lt. Bobby de la Tour. The British gliders were called *"Horsas."* Each glider could carry 30 combat soldiers. The British also had gliders called *"Hamilcars"* which had 100 foot wing spans that had the capability of carrying light tanks into battle. The 7th Parachute Battalion landed sticks of 21 men. The British missions were to blow up two bridges over the River Dives; hamper the German counter attack; capture two bridges intack and capture the guns located at Merville. These big guns were in a position to shell the British soldiers when they landed on Sword Beach the next morning. The 1st Canadian Parachute Battalion was credited with blowing up one of the bridges over the River Dives.

Ninety minutes after the British aircraft were airborne; there were 13,500 American paratroopers and glider-men from the 82nd and 101st Airborne Divisions on their way to Normandy to land in the middle of the night. The 82nd was commanded by General Matthew B. Ridgeway. Ridgeway was 49 years old at the time. His troops had experienced combat at Salerno and Anzio. [Ridgeway was the General who replaced General Douglas MacArthur on March 24, 1951 after President Harry Truman relieved MacArthur of his command in Korea.] General Maxwell Taylor commanded the 101st Airborne in their first combat experience. Twenty-one C-47s were lost and four gliders unaccounted for. One of the deceptions used prior to the 101st combat jump was called *"Operation Titanic."* "Oscars" which were dummies made to look like airborne troops, were dropped. The Oscars had firecracker - like explosives that went off on impact. At first, the Germans thought the invasion was on.

The Higgins landing boats were loaded with the troops from the ships anchored in the Channel. When the soldiers landed on Omaha Beach, many were killed and wounded; the others were pinned down by the German machine guns and mortars.

About three miles from Omaha Beach was a 100 foot cliff called "Ponte du Hoc Cliffs." From this position, the Germans had the Americans pinned down on the beach causing heavy casualties. Two hundred-twenty-five men from the 2nd Ranger Battalion had the mission to climb up these cliffs under heavy fire and extreme danger to silence the German guns and blow up their ammunition dump. Ninety men made it to the top of Pointe du Hoc by 7:30 a.m. and achieved their missions by 9:30. To let their headquarters below know that their mission was accomplished, they radioed this message, "Praise the Lord." General Omar Bradley said, "Every soldier who landed on the beach were heroes." The stories in this chapter are about some of those "heroes."

In 1943, Hitler who prided himself to have intuition was convinced that Normandy would be the target of the invasion as did some of his officers. Due to deceptions by the Allies, the Germans came to the conclusion that the main invasion would take place at some other location. Field Marshall Rommel who had planted thousands mines along the five beaches was prepared for an attack. On June 4th Rommel, because of bad weather, was convinced that the invasion would not take place at this time. In fact, Gerd von Runstedt, Commander of the German Armies sent this message, "There is no immediate prospect of the invasion" Rommel who was called "The Desert Fox" because of his successes in Africa, went home on June 4th to be with his wife whose birthday was on June 6th, the day of the invasion.

Two Panzer Divisions were in reserve and if used, the Normandy Invasion may well have turned out differently. Hitler's officers were afraid to wake him and by the time he woke up at noon, it was too late to use the tanks effectively. Hitler had taken a sleeping pill and was asleep in his Bavarian retreat

On June 1st Eisenhower moved his command post to Portsmouth, about one mile from his main headquarters at the Southwick House. On June 2nd, Winston Churchill, the British Prime Minister came to the Southwick House. Churchill was sulking because he couldn't go ashore on D-Day. He had received a letter from King George V1. The letter was in the King's handwriting, dated May 31, 1944. A copy of the letter was given to the author for the National D-Day Memorial by Allen Packwood, Director of the Churchill Archives Centre, Cambridge. The letter was written from Buckingham Palace. The contents of the letter are: *"My dear Winston, I have been thinking a great deal of our conversation yesterday and I have come to the conclusion that it would not be right for either you or I to be where we planned to be on D day. I don't think I need emphasize what it would mean to me personally, and to the whole Allied cause, if at this juncture a chance bomb, torpedo or even a mine would remove you from the scene; equally a change of Sovereign at this moment would be a serious matter for the country and Empire.*

"We should both I know love to be there, but in all seriousness I would ask you to reconsider your plan. Our presence I feel would be an embarrassment to those responsible for fighting the ship or ships in which we were, despite anything we might say to them.

" So as I said, I have very reluctantly come to the conclusion that the right thing to do is what normally falls to those at the top on such occasions, namely

to remain at home and wait. I hope very much that you will see it in this light too. The anxiety of these coming days would be very greatly increased for me if I thought that, in addition to everything else, there was a risk however remote of my losing your help and guidance. Believe me. Yours very sincerely, George R.I."

Eisenhower had become a heavy smoker while attending West Point. His orderly, Sgt. McKeogh, checked on him in his trailer at 7:15 a.m. on June 6th. The sergeant found the commander in bed reading a western novel with his ashtray completely full. Evidently western novels were a means of relaxing this great general, the future 34th president of the United States. "Ike" had just given the most difficult order of his military career. Nothing more could be done now but wait for the reports from his commanders.

EISENHOWER'S ORDER OF THE DAY

"SOLDIERS, SAILORS AND AIRMEN OF THE ALLIED EXPEDITIONARY FORCE: You are about to embark upon the great Crusade, toward which we have striven these many months. The eyes of the world are upon you. The hope and prayers of liberty-loving people everywhere are with you...Your task will not be an easy one. You enemy is well trained, well equipped and battle hardened. He will fight savagely. But this is the year 1944. The tide has turned! The free men of the world are marching together to Victory! I have full confidence in your courage, devotion to duty and skill in battle. We will accept nothing less than full victory! Good luck! And let us all beseech the blessing of the Almighty God upon this great and noble undertaking." General Dwight D. Eisenhower, June 6, 1944

Prior to the Normandy Invasion, the servicemen were subject to propaganda. Of the 12 Americans indicted for treason after the end of World War II, seven were radio broadcasters. On May 11, 1944, "Axis Sally," with her sultry voice, made her most infamous broadcast. She introduced herself as "Midge at the mike." She pretended to be an American mother who dreamed that her son was killed in the English Channel. Describing the meaning of D-Day, she said, "It stands for doom, disaster, death, and defeat,

Dunkerque or Deppe." Axis Sally was born Mildred Elizabeth Sink in Portland, Maine but took the name Mildred Gillars after her mother remarried.

Her dream was to become an actress but she was not successful. She became an announcer in Europe and later an announcer and actress in 1935 in Berlin, Germany. Mildred was in Germany in 1945 when the Germans surrendered. She was captured and returned to the United States in 1948, having been charged with ten counts of treason. The sensational trial lasted for six weeks, ended on March 8, 1949. She was sentenced to 10 to 30 years in prison. She was paroled in 1961 and later taught music to kindergarteners at a Catholic school in Columbus, Ohio.

Gillars, or "Axis Sally," fell for Max Otto Koischewitz and became his star propaganda broadcaster. During the programs on which she served as a DJ, she played music, and then used remarks such as, "Damn Roosevelt! Damn Churchill! Damn all the Jews who made this war possible." She would visit POW camps, telling the American POWs that she represented the American Red Cross.

Using this fake identity, she would obtain information from the prisoners, and then change it to use on the air when broadcasting as propaganda.

"TEN MEN AND A BOMBER" by SSGT ED MULL
("IT WAS JUNE 6, 1944...D-DAY")

This is a story entitled "Ten Men and a Bomber" written by SSgt Edward G. Mull who was a tail gunner on a B-24 Bomber. Mull had just completed his 51st mission. His squadron put up 13 Bombers for this mission, only three returned. Their raid was on Bresnov, Rumania. This is Ed's memory of that historic day. It had

been a long day. Ed's story will walk you through what just one day was like for these men serving on bombers.

Ed Mull was born in a small town, Maryville, Tennessee on May 1, 1923. He entered the US Army Air Corps on January 9, 1943. While home on leave, he married Ruth Louise Haun on

August 13, 1943. Ed was flying missions out of Italy when he was notified about the birth of his son, Edward G. Mull, Jr. Ed and Ruth had a daughter, Holly Ann Mull, who was born on March 13, 1946, after the war ended. Ed also had another son, Kevan Knight Mull, by another marriage.

Ed took his basic training at Keesler Field, Mississippi; then he was assigned to Laredo, Texas for gunnery training. During this intense training, Ed learned about the 50- caliber machine guns as associated with the consolidated A-engine, B-24 aircraft. The 50-caliber soon would become the life savers for Ed and all the other crewmembers on his B-24. After numerous weeks of concentrated training and mastering crewmember status as a tail gunner, he was transferred to overseas duty. It was there that Ed and the other nine crewmembers trained together so that they knew each other well and became a family of "Ten Brothers." His entire crew was assigned to the 15th Air Force, 459th Bomb Group and 756th Bomb Squadron in Italy.

Ed and the crew flew a total of 51 missions, each of which could have been an individual story. However, he chose to take notes on his last mission. This is how he reported this day.

The C.Q. slipped into our tent very quietly, almost apologetically, and one by one, he began awakening the six of us, "O.K. fellows, it is time to rise; this is your day to fly." He touched each of us gently to make sure we were awake, and like a ghost, he slipped out between the tent flaps and disappeared into the darkness of early morning. Each of us was wide awake now; we stretched, lit a cigarette and began to face another day; another mission to where we knew not.

We took our mess kits and stepped out into the cold dark air of southern Italy and slowly trudged our way to the mess tent, each of us still not speaking a single word; each of us too busy with thoughts of the coming mission and the sobering effect it had on us. As usual, we could hear the rattle of pans and voices of the other men and the noise of cooks as we came near and fell into chow line. As usual, the food was lousy, but we choked it down with the help of bitter coffee—our hunger subdued the knot we felt in our bellies.

Back at our tent, we awaited the 6X6 Army trucks that would take us to or briefing rooms some distance away. It was still dark and cold as we huddled together in the back of the trucks. There were ten of us in the crew; four officers and six enlisted men, all sergeants. Our briefings took place in an old winery building; the air filled with strong, sweet and moldy wine kegs, long ago emptied by the Germans. We sat on metal bomb crates on the dirt floor while up front an officer stood and described the country we would be flying to, but we were not to learn the exact town or type of target we would be bombing. We would learn all of this when we met the officers on the flight line, prior to takeoff. We were told by the briefing officer about how many enemy planes we could expect and the type of German aircraft we would encounter. He was wrong almost all of the time and we wondered why we should be awakened so early to hear such drivel when we would get all this information from the officers at the flight line. However, it was a routine we had to endure because it was the Army way of doing things.

From briefing, after a prayer from the Chaplain, we loaded back on the trucks and were taken to the "Parachute" building, as we called it, where all of our flight gear was stored, which included flight suits, "Mae West's," boots, helmet, goggles, gloves etc. We walked back to our tent as the sun was coming up and began dressing for the flight.

We were carrying most of our gear to the plane which we would put on as we ascended because the suits were full of heating wires to keep us warm in the 60 degrees below zero that we would encounter at high altitude. One by one we slowly gathered at our plane, which was a huge 4-engine B-24 Aircraft, fully loaded with bombs, gasoline and ammunition.

"Hi gang" said the pilot as we approached. "Everyone feel O.K. today after a good night sleep?" He questioned. Our pilot was always concerned about each man and how each one of us was "up" for the mission. He was a tall straight man from Virginia and took every detail upon his shoulders as commander of plane and crew. His name was Apperson, but we called him "App." We each called each other by last names with no mention of rank unless the C.O. (Commanding Officer) was close by.

Today, we learned, we would be bombing the oil fields in Romania, the most dreaded and feared of any target we would ever fly over. It was heavily defended by hundreds of anti-aircraft batteries, and the Germans put more fighter planes up than any other target we had in our range of bombing. The very word "PLOESTI" sent cold chills through our bodies, and if any one of us was still sleepy, he was wide awake now. We knew that today we would see death.

It was broad daylight now as we crawled into our planes. We could now hear the roar of many planes as propellers spun and the engines roared into life of the many other bombers that would make up our formation. Slowly the big awkward looking planes left their hardstands and taxied one by one behind each other toward the rock and gravel runway for takeoff, an event that was almost fearful as the bombing run itself. As our turn came to take off, we braced our bodies firmly against the planes' bulkheads in case of a mishap on takeoff.

When the nose of the overloaded B-24 pointed down the runway, the pilot kept the brakes of the "big bird" locked before moving the ship into takeoff. The engines roared wide open with propellers properly set, super chargers running at full R.P.M. and the fuel setting at full RICH. The plane roared and vibrated like a beast gone mad. When the pilot was satisfied that all was O.K., he released the brakes and we started moving down the runway. The airplane was straining with everything she had; the loud roar was even louder now and the gravel from the rough runway began bouncing off the belly as the propellers stirred up a powerful torrent of wind from the back wash.

As we rumbled on, I peeked over to our ball gunner, who was wedged tightly against me. His eyes were closed; his lips moving in obvious prayer. I joined him, praying also, as we awaited the great relief of liftoff when we left the ground. At the moment of being airborne, the landing gear was raised giving us added speed. The wing flaps were raised a bit and we could feel the tension leave us as we banked to the left to start forming up to join the other planes, and the rest who were climbing behind us. When all 47 planes were in the air, each one moved to his assigned slot and into proper formation.

We headed east which would take us across the Adriatic Sea on our way to the target. We flew low while over water to conserve oxygen, as it took us about an hour to fly across the sea and we were in no danger from the enemy. Before reaching the coast of Yugoslavia, we began to climb to a higher altitude. The temperature started getting colder as we put on the rest of our heated suits and additional gear we had to wear.

I started my dressing that morning with long heavy underwear and wool pants over that. Next was the electric flight suit that worked like an electric blanket. The boots and gloves were also wired, and over that would be leather gauntlets for hands and fleece lined leather boots for the feet. A "Mae West" was next which fit over the head on the shoulders and strapped around the waist; an inflatable life vest, which would keep us afloat in case we had to bail out or scuttle the plane over water. The parachute came next, which was a backpack or front snap-on type depending of which position you flew at your particular station. Over all this came the "flak jacket," a heavy body protector that, hopefully, would deflect shrapnel or gunfire from the enemy planes. It snapped on in sections so it could be released quickly before a "bailout," since it covered the parachute. Our oxygen masks, made of rubber, were carefully fitted to keep outside air from leaking in. This was important because   outside air and oxygen were automatically mixed, and varied according to the altitude we were flying. We could also breathe pure oxygen by means of turning a "bypass" lever. We often did this in situations of high excitement when breathing was faster. Our fleece-lined helmets and earphones covered our entire head when the oxygen mask was firmly in place. Goggles covered our eyes and no piece of skin could be exposed in the extreme cold, which would cause dangerous frostbite.

The pilot ordered each man to his gun position and to test-fire our guns while still over the sea. I took myself to the rear of the plane. I was the tail gunner. We aimed our guns into an open spot, so as not to endanger any others. It was a great relief when both of my guns fired, because a failure of a gun meant that it had to be fixed, which was not always easy while in flight. Settling into my turret, I began checking everything out. In a few minutes the pilot came over the intercom. "Pilot to crew, pilot to crew- call in your crew check." This would take place every 20 minutes or so. It began with me in the tail, "Tail gunner O.K." Next would be the words of **Siler** the left waist and **Powell** the right waist. Then from the ball turret- **Lilley**. In the nose was **Kap** to check in. Then checking in were **Russell** the bombardier, **Sutro** the Navigator and **Evans,** the co-pilot. This was an important procedure in the event someone would become unconscious due to some malfunction. If unconscious long enough, a man could suffer brain damage or even death.

Now they were nearing the coast of Yugoslavia. They were slowly climbing and were above 20 thousand feet. Later the group would turn to the right then take a different course to keep the Germans guessing which target they planned to bomb. This procedure would keep the German planes guarding several targets. The formation closed tighter as they traveled deeper into enemy territory and moved closer to the target. There were ten 50 Caliber machine guns on each bomber so their fire power was enormous. They could fire 300 to 400 guns in any direction depending on the number of bombers involved. When approaching the "I.P."(Initial point), the pilot would say "Ten minutes to the "I.P. fellows." For the bomb run, they would run straight and level.

Sitting in the tail turret for many hours, with no space to move around, left much time to just sit and deal with your own thoughts as the "thrum" "thrum" "thrum" of the powerful engines and propellers kept grinding us through the sky. In my mind, I could turn the noise of the planes into beautiful music. Yes, it was crazy I knew, and I never mentioned it to anyone. I could plainly hear Bing Crosby sing "Too-Ra-Loo-Ra-Loo-Ra" or hear a waltz by Wayne King. My mind could stay in this mode until the voice of the pilot came over the intercom. Now, the adrenaline began to flow and we prepared for anything. We would be dropping our bombs in about 25 minutes. Our own fighter escort had been with us for the past half hour covering our formation. The escorts were mostly P-38s and P-51s.

Suddenly, the fight was on. Five enemy planes popped out of the blue from five o'clock high diving toward us in single file. At the same time our fighter escort dropped their auxiliary wing tanks and dove downward to meet them. I yelled "Fighters at five o'clock" into my mike, and swung my turret to the left. I gave the enemy planes proper deflection in my gun sight, waited until the first one was in range, and I started short and steady bursts of fire. It was the main purpose of the enemy fighters to get a lucky hit on the bombers and knock one or more out of the formation. If this happened, the bomber became a lone and vulnerable target for the enemy planes. Most stragglers would try for a few minutes to defend themselves, but after a brief exchange of fire, the smart crewman "bailed out." When this happened, we made a point to count the parachutes, hoping there would be ten.

There existed an unwritten "code" between enemy airmen: if a stricken plane's crew wanted to parachute, they would drop or lower their landing gear and the attacking plane or planes would hold their gunfire until the men bailed out. This courtesy was also true when an enemy wished to escape their beaten craft. I saw this happen many times. The purpose of both sides in the air was to destroy the machines, but let the flyer save his life if he could.

Each gunner had more targets than they wanted. To my left, I saw a B-24 from another group, out of formation and on fire. Their number three engine was blazing and the men were bailing out through the left waist window away from the fire. I counted the chutes but one was draped over the left vertical stabilizer, the crewman hanging by his "chute shrouds", helpless and doomed. I felt sick to my stomach. Our left wingman suffered a direct hit, exploded and went down in pieces; it was gone in the twinkling of an eye. No one had a chance to jump.

"Pilot to crew, pilot to crew," the voice came over the intercom. "We are now on our final approach." To the flight engineer he said, "Check bomb bay doors for open position." Now we could see large puffs of smoke drifting by our plane. We were flying into heavy anti-aircraft fire. "Flack, 12 o'clock level" was the message from the nose gunner. His words were always calm, without emotion. The enemy fighters were gone now; they rarely flew into their own canon fire. We are now sitting ducks for the anti-aircraft gun batteries 28,000 feet below. They were bursting close to us now. The concussion rocked the bomber in every direction. From the tail turret I could see the shrapnel pop holes through the tail section. There is no place to hide, and I wished to be back in Tennessee by a quite lake.

We finally heard those wonderful words, "bombs away." Then the entire formation turned sharply to the left and went into a very steep dive. By changing direction, speed and altitude, the anti-aircraft guns on the ground were thrown off a correct aiming point since they had to shoot where they thought they would be in 18 to 20 seconds. Now the air battle was on again with the enemy fighters waiting for them. Before they could tighten up their formation, an M.E.110 German fighter plane came boring in straight from the rear at six o'clock. He was 800 yards from me, firing all his guns. With my heart in my throat I leveled my guns. I poured my gunfire into him. It was him or me. At about 300 yards his nose flipped up and for a few seconds he just hung there in a stall. I must have pumped three or four hundred rounds straight into his belly; he burst into flame, slid under us and went into a dive. This was my first kill. Looking down at the target, I could see a black cloud of burning oil. Red flames covered the entire target area. I counted more than thirty five parachutes floating slowly into the smoke and fire. Enemy fighters still dogged us but our own escort planes were giving them hell.

I thought the action was lessening somewhat, when I was suddenly jolted violently from an impact beneath. A piece of flack ripped upward through the turret. I saw a hole four inches from my left foot. The shrapnel swiped my left ammunition belt and blew a hole through the top of the Plexiglas roof. Another sick feeling in my gut swept over me. I fired at two or three enemy fighter planes but they soon left. Apparently none of the crew was wounded. I was dying for a cigarette. If all went well, we would be home in about three and a half hours. I witnessed one more tragedy. A B-24 from the rear of our formation had his number two engine on fire. He left the formation. We were flying over rolling farmland now which was a good place to bail out. Suddenly, one man jumped and his parachute opened normally. I started yelling into my oxygen mask and started screaming, "Jump, you poor bastards, jump!" I became fearful for their lives. One more man jumped, then a fourth. About three minutes later, the ship exploded in a huge ball of fire. They didn't know what hit them. The desire to have a cigarette was over whelming and I began to break a forbidden rule of safety. I unsnapped the right side of my oxygen mask, pulled it away from my face and started smoking. I would take one draw off the cigarette then place the mask back over my face for oxygen. It was good to have this horrible mission behind us. We counted as many holes in the plane as we could see from inside and knew it would be days before it would fly again. The pilot's voice came over the intercom again. "Pilot to crew, pilot to crew." "We just heard over the radio that the invasion has just begun at a place called *Normandy*." We heard the news without excitement because we knew there were many more missions to fly.   **IT WAS JUNE 6, 1944 - D-DAY-NORMANDY.** SSgt Edward G. Mull was a member of the 459th Bomb Group and 756th Bomb Squadron; 15th Army Air Corps.   Ed was awarded the Air Medal, The European-African-Middle Eastern Campaign Medal, The World War II Victory Medal, The Efficiency-Honor Fidelity Medal (The Good Conduct Medal), and the American Campaign Medal.   Ed was discharged on September 10, 1945. Ed married Mary Helen Colter on August 18, 1979. They had a happy marriage until his death on April 26, 1997. Helen Mull lives in Florida.]

ROBERT ELWOOD TORRENCE

"Bullets were whizzing by my head, shells going off around us; landing crafts being sunk by the Germans. I looked up and said, 'Lord, do I have to go into this?' " Robert Torrence

This story is about the experiences of Robert Elwood Torrence who landed on *Utah Beach* on D-Day, June 6, 1944. He served in

combat in Normandy, Northern France and the Rhineland with "B" Company, 116th Infantry Regiment 29th Infantry Division. This story starts with a personal interview by the author with Robert in his home in Concord, Virginia on April 17, 2007. He was 90 years old at the time of this interview. His mind is sharp as a tack. His southern accent was so thick that you could cut it with a knife; he was a true southern gentleman. Robert was born on this

farm on December 27, 1916 to Calvin D. Torrence and Lois C. Cheatham. He and his wife, Julie Fielder Torrence have lived in the same house all of their 61 years of marriage except for four months. They have 90 acres which was originally a part of 200 acres under a land grant by Thomas Jefferson to Joseph Terence (family name changed later). This was in consideration for the sum of 20 shillings sterling paid into the treasury of the Commonwealth, on January 15, 1774, when Jefferson was the Governor of Virginia. Governor Jefferson, on September 1st, "set his hand and caused the seal of the said Commonwealth to be affixed at Richmond" to the document.

Since childhood, Robert has been called "Nice" by his family and friends. He attended Sherwill Elementary School through the fifth grade at which time he started riding a school bus to the Concord Elementary school and high school.

Robert became a member of the Virginia National Guard, 1st Battalion of the 116th Regiment in Lynchburg, Virginia. On February 3, 1941, the once-a-week evening drills came to an end. On that day the Blue-and-Gray guardsmen entered upon a life of full time military duty under the provisions of the Act of Congress. Major General Milton A. Reckford signed the order instructing all units of the Division to convene at Fort Meade, Maryland on February 13th. The recruits began their 13 weeks of basic training in March. The division left for maneuvers in North Carolina on September 13 arriving at Fort Bragg, North Carolina on September 27th after a stopover at A.P. Hill Reservation near Fredericksburg, Virginia. While training, the men were not afforded the luxury of sleeping inside barracks. They had to endure the daily elements that North Carolina provides. That included the hot sun, rain, pine trees and ticks. This training could be miserable at times.

Robert grew up on a farm. He was reared by parents who had a lot of common sense and learned to work with his hands. He seemed to have a built- in skill with mechanics. Prior to becoming a soldier he drove a five-ton truck delivering groceries for a firm in Lynchburg. This experience provided him an opportunity to become a jeep driver in the Army for Company B. Most of the other soldiers in his unit were unable to drive a vehicle.

During maneuvers, living out in the field, the men were unable to get their hair cut. Unless they had a neat haircut, the captain would not allow the men to go on pass. A light went off in Torrence's head. He got the idea of becoming a part-time barber to earn some extra money. After all, $21.00 army pay each month wasn't very much. The men who came early were charged one dollar; late comers would be charged two dollars. Most of the haircuts were simple without any imagination. However, plain haircuts didn't satisfy Robert's whim or his humor. He and his

buddies decided on a special cut for seven of the men. He used his clippers to remove all the hair from seven who became skinheads. He left enough hair on each one, making a design to spell the word" victory," one letter on each man's head.   They would line up on each other's backs spelling victory. The men went into a public restaurant to enjoy a leisurely meal. They sat nonchalantly ate unhurriedly, watching the civilians glancing at them with funny expressions on their faces. The civilians were probably wondering where these goons came from. Needless to say, the captain was displeased with their sense of humor, but did not administer disciplinary action.

In early December, Nice and his unit were traveling back to Fort Meade when they stopped at South Hill, Virginia to eat. It was there that they heard that the Japanese had bombed Pearl Harbor. Their plans were shattered. The men, on arriving at Fort Meade, expected to be given a pass to go home and be relieved of active duty. That was not to be. Security of vital areas and coastal defenses became the team's Division's first wartime assignment. The 116th Combat team's assignment was the defense of the Chesapeake Bay section of the Atlantic Coast.

Additional training for the 116th became urgent. In January 1942 they participated in amphibious training at Cape Henry near Virginia Beach, Virginia. In mid-April, units of the 29th Division set out on foot and motor marched to A.P. Hill Military Reservation. After two months of training, the men of the Blue-and-Gray were again in North Carolina on another maneuver. From North Carolina the unit moved again, this time to Camp Blanding, Florida.

Major General Leonard T. Gerow met with his regimental and battalion commanders on September 6th to announce orders had been received for overseas duty. From Camp Blanding the troops were moved by train to Camp Kilmer, New Jersey; from Kilmer they went to the New York Port of Embarkation. The passage overseas was made in two groups. The first group which included the 116th Combat Team sailed on the morning of September 27th aboard the *Queen Mary*. They arrived in Scotland on October 3, 1942. The *Queen Elizabeth,* which carried the remainder of the

Division, sailed on October 5th. The two liners safely navigated the U-Boat patrolled waters of the Atlantic but not without incident.

The *Queen Mary*, the ship that Torrence was on, was one day from land. On October 2nd, the *Queen Mary* was met by two English corvettes and several other cruisers of the Royal Navy to escort her through the dangerous waters near the British Isles. They were not only in range of submarines but also of the Luftwaffe. As the *Queen Mary* and her guardian ships, bristling with antiaircraft guns, were heading north toward Great Britain, one of the cruisers, the *Curacao*, commenced a zigzag course in front of the *Queen Mary*. As the cruiser attempted to pass from starboard to port side it was caught in front of the speeding liner. The 83,000 ton *Queen Mary* knifed into her 4,390 ton protector, cutting her squarely amidships. Men aboard the *Queen Mary* could barely feel the jar. As the stricken cruiser passed under the huge transport it sounded to the men on the *Queen Mary* like the bottom of a rowboat scraping a log. In a split second, the *Curacao* reappeared in two parts. The aft section sank in less than a minute, while the fore section stayed afloat only a few minutes and then went down. Torrence said that he was shocked as he watched sailors thrashing around in the waters. He then realized that he had witnessed casualties of the war for the first time. The *Queen Mary* never stopped, because stopping would have made the ship and several thousand soldiers aboard a sitting target. This tragedy took the lives of 332 British sailors. The damage to the *Queen Mary* was a hole large enough to drive a truck through. The ship was patched up and returned to New York for repair. Robert's comment was, "It was quite an experience."

The 29th stayed in Scotland just long enough to march from the docks to the railway station, carrying their heavy duffle bags on their shoulders. The train ride took them to Southern England to Tideworth Barracks, an old British Army cavalry post on Salisbury Plain, near Andover and the cathedral city of Salisbury. Torrence and his buddies trained in England until the Normandy invasion when they landed on Utah Beach.

Prior to the Normandy invasion there were seven planned rehearsals for beach landings to be held on *Slapton Sands*. This was called *"Operation Tiger."* This was a military training exercise simulating the planned assault on Utah in France. The plan of exercise Tiger incorporated a short movement by sea under the US Navy, disembarkation with Naval and Air support, a beach assault using service ammunition, the securing of the beachhead and a rapid advance inland. Paratroops were to be dropped, as well as engineer's deployed to clear obstacles protecting the beaches. The exercise was to be on the southwest coast in the Devon area. On April 27, 1944 just prior to the sixth practice landing, there were some 300 ships and 30,000 troops gathered about 2 a.m. Nine German fast torpedo boats attacked. In this attack, 198 American sailors were killed, 552 soldiers were killed and 89 were wounded or missing, for a total of 839 troops. All were buried in secret; this tragedy was not made public until sometime after the war ended.

On April 28, 1944, Corporal Robert Torrence was the driver of his jeep which was towing a trailer loaded with supplies. His jeep, as with other vehicles that became inundated with sea water, had been waterproofed. A vertical pipe of several feet had been attached to the exhaust pipe. The alternator, the battery, and any other vulnerable parts were coated with grease. When the operator of the landing craft Robert was on lowered the ramp, he entered the water that reached his shoulders. The four-wheel-drive jeep just hunkered down and carried its load.

Meanwhile, across the English Channel at Cherbourg, German U-boats of the 5th and 9th Schnellboote flotillas were preparing for a patrol run along the southwest coast of England. The U-boats were over 90 feet long, had a crew of some 20 men, and could cruise at 35 knots (40 statute miles). The armament varied from 20 mm to 40 mm guns; however, each boat had a pair of fixed torpedo tubes firing forward, and four torpedoes aboard. The Germans had intelligence from their airmen that there was naval activity in Lyme Bay.

General Dwight D. Eisenhower gave the command for the land invasion of Normandy to start at 6:30 a.m. on June 6th. Torrence was a member of "B" Company, 116th Infantry Regiment of the 29th Division. "A" Company, from Bedford, Virginia, landed on Omaha Beach. They suffered heavy casualties. Company A started with 170 men in their company; 91 were killed, 64 wounded, leaving 15 men to continue fighting.

Company B landed on Utah Beach at 7 a.m. Torrence said as the landing craft that he was on approached the beach the action was unbelievable. There was the sound of bullets whizzing by his head, shells going off all around them; landing craft being sunk by the Germans who had started preparing for this invasion in 1943. He looked up and said, "Lord, do I have to go into this?" It seems like his prayer was answered immediately. Within a short time, the craft that he was in turned around and went back into the channel. The craft Torrence was on was loaded with a jeep and a bulldozer, but it also had a large amount of explosives loaded on the top. If a shell had landed at the right place, not only the men aboard would have been killed, but the important cargo would have been lost. Each jeep had a 50- caliber machine gun mounted on it,

When Torrence was asked what he remembered most when he landed on the beach, he said, "There was so much I couldn't take it all in. When I went in they had cleaned up the dead and wounded; some soldiers went in over their heads and drowned and were floating in the water, and some of the tanks mounted on special floatation devices sank." There were 29 Sherman tanks which were badly needed on the beaches, with only two making it to the beaches. The Germans sank two; 25 sank for failure of the devices that were made for them. Torrence added, "It was the biggest mess that you ever saw."

There was one area that neither the Germans nor the Allies could take. It was called "No man's land." Torrence said that dead bodies lay out there for weeks. He used a jeep and trailer later to haul off the bodies. One man was left in a wheat field for several days. When they picked him up, he fell to pieces.

When the operator of the LCVP (Landing Craft Vehicle Personnel) dropped the exit ramp, on the second try to deploy its personnel onto the beach, they were about 300 yards from the beach. Corporal Torrence was the first to move forward, again having the water sloshing around his shoulders. Four jeeps with trailers and one bulldozer followed. There were no small-arms enemy firing on the beach as was the case when he had attempted to land earlier. The Germans on the high ground had been killed, had been captured or had withdrawn to establish a new battle line by now.

The troops needed supplies, particularly ammunition, water and K-rations. German snipers were everywhere and a moving jeep was an easy target. The Normandy breakthrough in the battle to take Brest was an experience that Torrence remembers vividly. One of the forts protecting the city and submarine pens was Fort Montbarey. Torrence's buddy, Sergeant Odell "Toad" Padgett was with the unit assigned to capture the fort. Padgett had survived the initial landing on Utah Beach but his fortune changed. While searching a building, Padgett was mistaken for a German soldier and was shot by one of his own men. The sergeant staggered outside and said, "I think I got shot," and passed out. He said that the next thing that he knew he was on the hood of a jeep. The driver of that jeep was his good friend Corporal Torrence. Risking his own life, he drove through enemy fire as he took his friend to safety. The field doctors were unable to help Padgett before sending him to a hospital. Torrence said that he would never forget that day. He said that the night Toad got hit, he prayed all night.

Padgett was hospitalized for almost a year and never returned to combat.

A feature article was written in the *News & Advance*, Lynchburg, Virginia by Terry Scranlon on June 4, 1998, which gives an account this story. The article's heading read, "D-Day Evokes Vivid Memory. Madison Heights Man Shot after Siege on Normandy." (This story was provided by Robert Torrence).

"If it weren't for Robert Torrence, Odell Padgett says he wouldn't be alive today. On June 11, 1944, Padgett took a bullet to the chest, and Torrence, his best friend and jeep driver, carried Padgett off the battlefield to safety. 'I thank the good Lord every day of my life,' Padgett said, 'if it wasn't for him I wouldn't even be here.' At the hospital, Padgett said, the doctors didn't expect him to live. But he refused to go quietly. 'If you're waiting on me to die you forget it. I'm not going to die,' Padgett told doctors that night."

"Both men grew up in Lynchburg and were good friends before the war. They trained together and fought together in France. Padgett tries not to dwell on the memories. 'I don't like to talk about it. I just want to forget it,' he said. 'It was just too terrible.' Because of that he no longer attends the ceremonies for veterans. However, he still remembers the choppy waters of the English Channel and the bodies on the Beach. He said, 'We stepped over bodies in the water like wood floating back and forth on the beach.'

"Corporal Torrence delivered supplies to the front for B Company men during four campaigns, Normandy, Northern

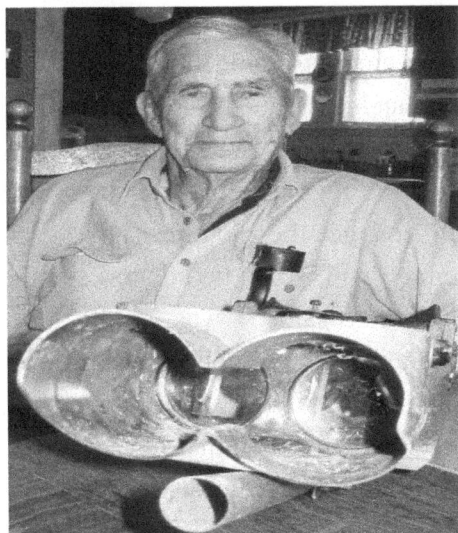

France, Rhineland and Central Europe. The frontline infantrymen depended upon jeep drivers to deliver their daily needs, water, food and especially ammunition. They admired their buddies who often faced hazardous and dangerous situations. A jeep driver was subject to artillery and snipers; consequently, supplies were often delivered to the front under the cover of darkness. Night runs were not completely danger-free either. The most intense fighting occurred beginning with D-Day, and lasting until early December.

"One day, Major Dallas told Torrence that they were out of ammunition and asked if he knew where the supply dump was located. Torrence said, 'I don't have any idea.' The major said to follow him and headed for the ammunition dump. After loading the jeep and trailer, they ran directly into the Germans. The Major turned his jeep around and somehow Torrence turned the jeep and trailer around on a very narrow road with shells and mortar rounds falling all around them. They got out of their jeeps and sought protection behind a slag pile. When told, 'If one of those shells had hit your jeep that was full of ammunition, you would have been in Heaven a long time ago.' Torrence smiled and with a laugh answered, "Yea."

On another day, Torrence and some others were trying to take ammunition to a farm house across a treeless field. The ground was covered with snow. The men had sleighs loaded with ammunition and were pulling the sleighs with a rope. When the Germans opened up on them, some used some regular army language, like shucks to it, dog gone it—well you get the picture. They rolled over in a ditch and covered the hole with some boards to keep the shrapnel from hitting them. Torrence said, 'I was laying there, ain't nobody here but me and if I am bombed, nobody would ever know what happened to me.' He called on the Lord again saying, "Lord I know you are here with me and that's all that I need.

Another time they were in Northern Germany with only a few men. The artillery and tanks had been pulled out. The colonel sent

Torrence to look for some weapons and ammunition. He didn't find anything. He looked in a ditch and found five dead Germans. After he had reported this to his officer, a tank was ordered to cover the ditch. The families of these German soldiers never knew what happened to their loved ones.

When the unit reached the Elbe River, they learned that the Germans had left their boats on the other side. Torrence said that they took their rifles and shot holes in the boats so they couldn't be used any more. At this point the Germans were surrendering in overwhelming numbers and the American troops didn't know what to do with them. That night Torrence went into a home to get some rest. The mattress was made out of feather-tick. He took off his clothes to go to bed, put his pistol and flashlight on a stand by his bed. There were still a lot of Germans around who had not made it across the river. Suddenly, he heard a lot of noise in the next room that happened to be the kitchen. As Torrence explained it, "It was the biggest racket you ever heard." He got up, picked up his pistol and flashlight to investigate. He found a big hog in the kitchen in the corner, eating. The Germans had been cooking but had left in a hurry. The hog was rolling a big pot around, making the "racket." Torrence said, "I tried to turn the hog around. I would open the door and try to run the hog out and he would close the door. Finally, I got on top of the eating table with a broom and finally got him out through the door. I would open the door and the hog would close it every time."

He said, "Things that happen like that, you remember." In this farm house, Torrence found some ham and eggs left by the Germans and had a feast. He also found a German set of binoculars. It was a large set, which would break down to use for artillery, the other for airplanes. (Picture on page 180)

Torrence told another story that was unusually humorous. During combat, it was necessary to find something to laugh about to ease the tension and stress of their battle experiences. The jeep of Major General Elwood Quesada, an Army Air Force officer, was blown up by a German tank. A sign was put on the jeep read, "Ground transportation of that well known Airman Pete Quesada after his contact with the ground war in the vicinity of Tessie Normandy." Later Major General C. H. Gerhardt, US Army wrote this letter, Gen. Quesada took his jeep up to and beyond the front lines. Saw a German tank—shortly an 88mm armor-piercing shell whammed through the jeep, twisted it into a mass of wreckage and hurled General Quesada and his companion in a ditch. When the jeep was recovered, recognizing it as a Mashing vindication of the Infantry in the eyes of the Air force. The jeep was recovered, wrapped in cellophane and tied up in a large bow of ribbon and delivered to the General with a note: "It is with regret I am compelled to return this package to you in its present form. It is our practice to take care of our visitors including the servicing of their equipment, but unfortunately in this case the enemy has us on the run trying to keep up with him and our maintenance sections are too busy moving tanks provided for the sight seer's convenience. It is thought with a bit of first echelon maintenance your vehicle can be put back into perfect running order.-Signed C.H. Gerhardt, Major General, US Army

After the drive inland following the beachhead landing, came the battle for *St.Lo;* followed by the Normandy breakthrough. This led to the *Brest Campaign*, the fall of Fort Montbarey and the surrender of Brest. Beginning October 1, 1944, the 29'ers were fighting Germans on their soil and conducted the November Offensive, which brought them to the west bank of the Roer River. For Meritorious service Corporal Torrence was awarded the Bronze Star Medal. The order read as follows:

TEC-5 Robert E. Torrence, 20363905, 116th Infantry, US Army; for Meritorious service in Military Operations against the enemy during the period 6 June 1944 to 6 December 1944 in Western Europe. During this period TEC 5 Torrence excelled in the performance of his duties and contributed materially to the fine record established by the organization of which he is a member. The high standards of courage, initiative, and discipline required by long periods of combat were met by TEC 5 Torrence in a manner that reflects great credit upon himself and the Military Service. Entered Military Service from Virginia.

One night Torrence was staying in the basement of a three-room stone house. There was only one road going into the next town. He was going up the road in his jeep with only his parking lights on, when he heard the sound of a tank approaching. As he got beside the tank, another jeep pulled around and hit Torrence's jeep head on. He was taken to a MASH unit for treatment. Two German nurses got the doctor. The doctor told him that he was just bruised, nothing serious but wanted to keep him overnight for observation. The German nurses checked on him every two hours during the night. He said that he didn't know where they came from but they were very nice and generous. Later, he was wounded when hit with shrapnel from a tank in Germany. He received a Purple Heart.

Robert Torrence departed from Germany for the States on June 16, 1945. He was discharged at Fort Meade, Maryland on June 22, 1945. His story had a romantic ending. About six weeks after returning home, Robert had a date with a young lady who was a friend and co-worker of Julie Fielder, a native of Franklin County, Virginia. The double date was on August 6, 1945 which happened to be Julie's 21st birthday. During the evening the "vibes" between Julie and Robert sparkled, and they began to date. They were married on December 8, 1945. They are the parents of four children, eight grandchildren and seven great-great grandchildren.

Robert Torrence received the following medals and ribbons: Purple Heart, Bronze Star, Combat Infantry Badge (CIB), Good Conduct Medal, Rifle Badge, Presidential Unit Citation, American Defense Service Medal, European-African Medal with 4 battle stars and 1 Arrowhead.

Some of the veterans from B Company, 116th Infantry Regiment still keep in touch with each other although, many have moved away from Virginia. A few years ago they held a reunion in Madison Heights, Virginia. Thirty-three attended. Imagine the joy, laughter and stories that took place that day. For five years these men had lived together as "brothers" in England, France and

Germany. Their Company Commander, William Williams of Cherry Hill, N.J., said, "We all felt B Company was the best company in the whole army. I couldn't have asked to be in a better company. They had a tremendous team spirit. They had become extremely well trained and fine disciplined, and they had a lot of guts." Tyberious "Peanut" Ferguson of Lynchburg said, "When I got homesick, they nursed me back to manhood. They would do anything in their power for me." Laughter dominated the day, but the veterans expressed sympathy for their friends who had died in the battle. Ray Coffey said, "I really never felt like I wasn't coming back, but it came to times when you just wondered. There were minutes when you didn't know if it would be your last."

ARY LEE JARVIS

"His helmet crumpled up on the back of his head when he fell face down. There was a hole bigger than my fist. He made two or three gasps...that was the end of him." **Cary Jarvis**

CARY JARVIS still has the images of that day, June 6, 1944 when his unit landed on Omaha Beach in the first wave with the 116th Infantry Regiment. He was a forward observer with the 111th Field Artillery Battalion, now a veteran of the Normandy Invasion. Cary remembers his comrades being mowed down, the deafening bombs, whizzing bullets, and a lot of shells exploding. He said during an interview, "Anybody says that war isn't hell, they're crazy." He knows why mines were called "bouncing betties" and how booby traps worked. He said, "We, of

course, wanted to get cover as fast as we could, get off the beach, because we could see the sand jumpin' up all around us, so we knew there was bullets hittin' in the sand. I saw a couple people get blown half in two, steppin' on those mines right in front of me. We were scared to keep goin' across the beach so we got on our hands and knees and was crawlin', feelin' with our fingers, to see if we could detect anything such as a bouncing Betties and avoid it."

Jarvis was born in Norfolk, Virginia on April 13, 1922. His parents were Cecil B. and Emily L. Jarvis. He joined the Virginia National Guard in 1939. The age requirement was age 18. Although he was only 17 at the time, he convinced the commander that he was older, raised his right hand and was sworn in. He liked having a uniform, enjoyed marching and to top everything, they paid him one dollar for each drill.

On February 3, 1941, Jarvis went into Federal service for one year. He became a member of the 29th Division at Fort Meade, Maryland. The outfit later went on maneuvers in North and South Carolina. He remembers the chiggers, ticks and mosquitoes. They trained with brown sticks because rifles were not available. When the United States entered World War II on December 7, 1941, the one year of service that Jarvis and his buddies had planned on was extended to over four years. He was discharged in September 1945.

In September 1942 Jarvis' unit sailed for England. By D-Day, he had been promoted to the rank of staff sergeant with about 30 men under him. His job was one of the most dangerous in the Army. He was a forward observer (F.O.). His job was to observe the enemy's position and direct artillery fire. Jarvis called in fire, aiming at a German coastal gun that could fire shells close to 20 miles. He said, "It must have hit the ammo dump or something right there by the gun. It looked like the whole world was blowing up. It blew up the gun. All the ammo there, everything blew up.

Planes that were trying to bomb it, then the P-38 Lightning's, when all that big explosion and smoke rose, had to go up in the air trying to get away from it." Many men who have served as an F.O. (forward observer) have been wounded or killed.

Late in the evening, they were about 300 yards off the beach. Germans on the hill were spraying them with machine guns all night. Jarvis had jumped into a ditch that had water in it. Their feet got wet and the men were unable to lie down that night. Jarvis said that the 81 Chemical Battalion set up mortars which caused the Germans to start running. He said that one guy commented "This is more fun than rabbit hunting."

Jarvis' lieutenant was killed on the beach. He said, "We were going across this real flat, open field. We was gettin' up one or two at a time and running in a zigzag fashion toward a hedgerow, which was 100-150 yards in front of us. There were two or three other guys that had already gotten up there and they hollered to us and said, 'Sergeant, when you come around this curve you'd better come fast, there's a sniper shooting at everybody.' When I started around that little curve where the hedgerow was, man, he shot at me. My heart, I guess, went right up into my throat. The bullet must have just missed my head. Then two or three infantry guys, they got ready to come up there. The first two made it up, and the third one got hit right between the eyes and fell right at my feet. His helmet crumpled up on the back of his head when he fell face down. There was a hole in his head bigger that my fist and he just made two or three gasps. And that was it. That was the end of him."

Jarvis said after his section moved across the beach next to the sea wall, they decided to jump into the first shell hole and take cover. However that didn't last too long. General Cota showed up and asked why they were there. The General asked "What's holding you men up?" Jarvis answered, "Snipers sir." His answer was, G.. D...., get up and get them." They crawled out and started above the seawall which had the emblem of a skeleton with cross bones stating "Achtung-Minen." It wasn't a lie because the whole field was mined. The men crawled on their bellies with equipment and those unbearable gas masks strapped to their legs. Incoming artillery from the Germans falling close by would detonate the mines and blow fire and dirt sky high. Jarvis continued to call for artillery support but none came. The guns had either sunk or were hit by enemy fire. Since the guns were lost, the men decided to help cleanup troops through the villages which the infantry had taken. There were still many German troops hiding and were sniping at the troops. Some were in houses, barns, culverts, anywhere to be concealed and do their sniping. Later they received new artillery guns and were able to do the job they were trained to do.

Jarvis shared this story, "Two or three of the guys in my section asked me about raiding the kitchen truck." He said, "No-no." 'Well, man, we're hungry, we're starving.' "Well, I was hungry, too." So after a lot of persuasion from them Jarvis said "alright." "We snuck on down to where the kitchen truck was, one of the guys pulled up the back curtain and jumped inside, grabbed a can, a gallon can, come jumpin' out and we ran to our truck. Right away, we was gonna open that can and devour whatever was in it. When we opened it up, we had a gallon of orange marmalade. I don't know why, I still like orange marmalade."

One night their officer asked for volunteers to check out a French Village for Germans. Jarvis volunteered. When they entered the village, the French people began yelling and pointed to a house where German snipers were hiding. Jarvis said, "We went in firing like John Wayne." Next they were directed to a cemetery across an open field. Jarvis and Sergeant Lawrence Moore separated with plans to meet in the back of the house. There was a deep ditch and they saw purple trousers that Germans wore. He checked it out and said "The Germans in the ditch were deader than doornails."

These were brave men just doing their jobs. They would stick their necks out with German shells coming in regularly. Someone would be killed or wounded every day. The men lived in fear. The question Jarvis and others would ask, "When do I lose an arm or a leg—a million-dollar wound and get to go home?"

The Germans had big 240 MM Coastal guns pointed at the sea. The shells were "hughmungas." You could see the huge barrels sticking up in the air. Jarvis said that he had his men run a telephone line up the hill and mount a scope on a tripod so they could focus on the gun. He later called for the two guns to fire on the German target the same time. He then made a correction and the next round hit an ammunition dump which also blew up the gun. The major stepped out of his tent and complimented Jarvis for this accomplishment. He received a lot of recognition from others as well.

When asked if he had been wounded, he said, "I was hit one time. The shell hit close by and drove clay into my back. I thought half of my back was gone." He felt his back knowing that there would be a lot of blood and maybe even his guts hanging out. He didn't feel or see any blood. Shrapnel from the same shell had clipped his lieutenant in the chin and thumb. The first sergeant relieved Jarvis and sent him to the doctor to be checked out. The doctor ordered him to take off his shirt but he told the doctor that he was all right. The doctor discovered that he was black and blue from the impact of the clay. Though Jarvis requested to return to his men at the front lines, the medical doctor ordered him to go back to Belgium to rest for three days. Although Jarvis was offered a Purple Heart, he refused. He regrets that decision today. If he had been awarded a Purple Heart, he would receive better treatment at the Veterans Hospital. He thought that he needed to lose a gallon of blood to qualify.

The Germans had broken through the American lines at the Battle of the Bulge. Jarvis was ordered to report to the colonel at Battalion Headquarters. His question, "What have I done?" He was ordered to attend a two-week class with some other soldiers. They slept in a cattle barn. Different subjects were taught by different men. Two days after he reported back to C Battery, three men were ordered to report to the colonel at Headquarters. The colonel was smiling from ear to ear when Jarvis and the other two men arrived. The colonel said, "I want to offer you men a battle-field commission to 2nd Lieutenant." Jarvis was shocked. The colonel said, "What about it, Sergeant Jarvis?" Jarvis replied, "I'm honored, sir, but have to refuse." "Why?" asked the colonel. Jarvis said, "I'm not a college graduate and I haven't attended officers candidate school. "What you need to know, look up in the manual," said the colonel.

Becoming an officer had some nice benefits. They were to receive $250 in a clothing allowance, a car with a driver, the privilege of going to the officers PX store in Belgium to buy a new uniform with gold bars. He added, "To look for wine, women and song, but we didn't find much."

CITATION FOR BRONZE STAR MEDAL

S.SGT GARY L JARVIS, 20366220, 111th FA Bn, US Army, for meritorious achievement in military operations against the enemy in Western Europe. From 6 June 1944 to 15 January 1945, S Sgt Jarvis excelled in the performance of his duties as Chief of Detail and Acting Forward Observer and contributed materially to the fine record established by the organization of which he is a member. The high standards of courage, devotion to duty and discipline required during long periods of combat were met by S Sgt Jarvis in a manner that reflects great credit upon himself and the Military Service. Entered Military Service from Virginia.

Jarvis and his wife Mary Ella returned to France in September 1997. While attending a reception in Brest, he met a Frenchman who was desperately trying to tell him a story. Not understanding French and the Frenchman couldn't speak English, they could not communicate until an interpreter helped. The interpreter told Jarvis that the man was a member of the F.F.I. and was captured by and interned by the Germans. He said there were 20 Americans or so who had been captured on D-Day, who were locked up where he was. The Germans had sentenced this man to death by hanging and hung him. He bent over to show Jarvis the scars on his neck to substantiate the story. The man had been hung on a tree and the limb broke.

Jarvis married Nellie Ashby on April 13, 1946. After her death, he married Mary Ella Jarvis on June 29, 1984. He has four children and two grandchildren. In addition to the Bronze Star, Cary Jarvis earned the Good Conduct Medal, NOBC Medal-French Government, Normandy Campaign Medal (June 6-August 20, 1944), ETO Ribbon w/4 Battle Stars and one Arrow Head, American Defense Medal, American Campaign Medal, Freedom Medal, Army Occupation Medal.

Jarvis was asked by his family what he would like to do for his 85th birthday. His daughter, Thelma Peterson, suggested a helicopter ride or cruise, or maybe a trip to the Outer Banks, where the Virginia Beach native loved to deep-sea fish. However, he was quick to reject the fishing idea after last year's birthday trip to the Outer Banks yielded no fish. Though they all sounded appealing to Jarvis, he told them that he would like to take a road trip in their three Model A Fords from their home in Virginia Beach to the D-Day Memorial at Bedford, Virginia. He and his wife Mary Ella along with seven family members loaded their A Model's and started the long, slow journey. The names of his family were Ken Simmons, Catherine Simmons, Charles Peterson, Erika Peterson, Thelma Peterson, Walter Jarvis and Cary Douglas Jarvis. Jeff Reid, a writer for the *Smith Mountain Eagle* filed a story with his newspaper on April 18, 2007 about this venture of Jarvis and his family. Jeff titled the article:

"Road trip a piece of cake for 85-year-old D-Day vet."

"Since Henry Ford introduced the Model T automobile in 1908, there has always been a special bond between man and machine. The smell of motor oil and the roar of a combustion engine as you made your way down a country lane, freedom yours for just a few gallons of gas. Though the early automobile was not built for speed or comfort, it still allowed motorists to travel great distances and explore the beauty that abounded them. It wasn't until 1927 when Ford introduced the Model A that could travel at speeds of 65 MPH on a four cylinder engine and get between 20 and 30 mpg. That is when the automobile as we now know it today was invented.

"Today, the sight of an early automobile still evokes imagery of a time when life was slow and simple, of country fairs and picnics by the lake, quality time spent with the ones we love. So Jarvis, an antique car enthusiast, wanted to make this journey in Model A cars. It was not an ordinary trip. Jarvis, who is a member of a Model A Club in Tidewater, would supply two of the automobiles, his son, Walter, adding a third. The trip would not only be special to Jarvis because it would be a good way to catch up with his children and grandchildren, but because of the Memorial holds a special place in his heart.

"Several years ago, Jarvis' daughter, Thelma, gave him a tape recorder for his birthday, asking that he record his memories of World War II. The painful memories of D-Day were something that he rarely discussed until he attended the dedication ceremony at the National D-day Memorial in 2001. One day Thelma's mom called her to say that "Your Dad is sitting in the front seat of his Model A, a car just like the one he'd had before he joined the National Guard and the Army, and he has the recorder." On the tape, he shared memories of fighting inland from the coast of France and supporting the Battle of the Bulge. Author's note: (Thelma provided the CD of Jarvis' experiences to the Author).

"As in battle, Jarvis' return to the D-Day Memorial didn't go exactly as planned. Jarvis and eight family members left Virginia Beach early Friday morning and were due to arrive at Smith Mountain Lake in plenty of time for a 5:30 dinner engagement with a family friend. After replacing a carburetor on one of the cars, and nearly 9 hours on the road, one of the Model A's developed engine problems near Shop Rite. However, Jarvis' son Walter was able to get the car road worthy again after tinkering with the points.

"Though the journey had to be cut short because of time restraints and vehicle problems, the family was still able to visit the National D-Day Memorial. Volunteers Bob VandeLinde and Bob Lindell waited patiently with two golf carts, and escorted the family on a personal tour of the grounds. Jarvis' grandchildren, Erika and Charles Peterson, were snapping pictures and asking questions of guide Lindell, especially when he mentioned the 29th Infantry, the unit their grandfather fought in.

"After the tour, Jarvis seemed to be at peace, as though he had completed a different kind of mission, a conflict that wasn't waged on the battlefield, but from deep inside. He added a moment of humor, when asked about the Model A he left behind. 'I guess we'll award it the Purple Heart when we get back home,' he said.

Tired and hungry, he described the biggest hardship of the journey as driving 30-40 mph on the main highways, and the antiquated steering system causing the car to jump all over the road. Yet one believes he would do it all over again.

"We can learn a lot from Cary Lee Jarvis, not only about the personal sacrifices he and so many soldiers made on June 6, 1944, or of the horrors of war and the price we must pay for freedom, but about the importance of family, and slowing down every once in a while, to take in the beauty that God has blessed us with." (This concludes the article by Jeff Reid).

FELICE PHIL NAPPI

"I was with the 2nd Bn. of the 175th Inf. Reg. when I landed on Omaha Beach, Normandy, June 6, 1944. The really true heroes are all those young men under ivory crosses who made that supreme sacrifice." Phil Nappi

PHIL NAPPI was born on January 23, 1920 in Mount Vernon, New York. His father was Nicolo Nappi; his mother, Margaret Graziano. Phil entered the US Army on May 8, 1942 and after serving for 35 months, was discharged in September 1945. He took his basic training at Camp Wheeler, Georgia, and then served with the 29th Infantry.

After additional training at Camp Blanding, Florida on October 5th, Phil and his buddies were on the *Queen Elizabeth* headed for England. He was in the communications platoon, serving as a radio operator. The unit made several dry runs which included practice landings at *Slapton Sands*. They trained in England and were selected to land in Normandy on D-Day. He drove a jeep with trailer.

When the LCM dropped its ramp, Phil said that he was surprised that they were about 50 feet from the beach. He drove the jeep into the water but didn't get very far when his jeep let him know it wasn't a boat. It just bobbed up and down; then gave up in disgust. Phil's buddy was quite excited, yelling that he could not swim. Phil said, "I assured him that we would not abandon our craft. So I got up on the hood and started thumbing a ride. A LCVP saw our dilemma and brought his vessel alongside for us to ride in with them." Phil and his buddy were not able to locate their unit until dusk.

The second night they began to settle down for the day and suddenly they were receiving incoming German 88s. He said, "I guess it was our 'baptism of artillery' fire. It was 'pretty scary' an experience that we would go through many more times." There were several men killed and wounded during the shelling. The next day they were on the highway heading for "Isigny" which had a bridge that his outfit was asked to secure. After meeting this objective, Phil's unit began a slow but costly advance for their next objective, St. Lo.

Early in the morning on June 29, 1944, Nappi was wounded by shrapnel from an 88 shell for which he received a Purple Heart. He was taken to a field hospital. After being treated, he was flown to a general hospital in England. Phil said, "By the middle of August I was back in France and caught up with his outfit in Holland." The Holland operation was *Operation Market-Garden*. His unit was on the Elbe River when the Nazis threw in the towel.

In addition to the Purple Heart, Nappi was awarded the Bronze Star, Good Conduct Medal, and Combat Infantry Badge. About five months after returning home Felice Phil Nappi married Irene

Amoruso on February 3, 1946. They have three children, Linda Louise, Marilyn Ruth and Peter Andrew.

EDUARDO ALBERTO PENICHE

"I went airborne and landed on DZ "American Dream"
Ed Peniche

ED PENICHE, a member of the 101st Airborne Division, the "Screamng Eagles," landed on *Utah Beach*, and was wounded twice in the Battle of the Bulge. Ed was awarded two Bronze Star medals for heroism. He was born at Progreso, Yucatan, Mexico on June 28, 1925 to Ariosto B. and Amanda Carvajal Peniche. His story reveals many of his experiences including the fact that he became a successful professor, a man who could speak five different languages. A facinating story of another hero and his lifes journey.

In a letter to the author, Ed wrote, *"I do not consider myself a hero, but I sure proved to be a good and well disciplined soldier and, thanks to my fervent spiritual strength, I was able to serve in the ranks of one of the most outstanding divisions ever fielded in combat. I always did my duty to the best of my abilities. And by the grace of God, our Lord and Creator, I survived the war, a bit battered, yet in one piece and well enough to become an Expert Linguists in five languages, and capable of earning three college degrees, and eventually, becoming a full fledge*

American educator. Yes, indeed, I did land on DZ 'American Dream'!!!" (DZ means drop zone) This picture shows Ed when recuperating from wounds sustained at Bastogne. Notice his airborne wings, patch on his hat and his jump boots with trousers bloused.

Peniche's story begins when a teacher saw great promise in his ability. By the time he was 15 years old, it became apparent that he possessed certain academic skills that could not be honed by the school he had been attending. He entered the USA, legally, on a student visa in December 1942. His aunt and uncle, Mr. & Mrs. Edward G. Menendez, both US citizens and residents of Paducah, Kentucky, sponsored him. Ed had to prove that he deserved the student visa and that he was free of communicable diseases and had no criminal record. This process took two years before he obtained a visa.

In January 1943 Ed entered the Paducah, Kentucky school system to meet the requirements for a US high school diploma. His school work included three daily hours of English, Monday through Friday with Mrs. Cooper, whom he called "My guardian angel;" plus other academic subjects such as math, civics, and US History. World War II was in its second year. That year Ed was required by law and as a legal male resident, to register with the Local Board 109, McCraken County. On September 16, 1943 he was inducted into the US Army.

Ed was sworn in into active duty at Fort Benjamin Harrison, Indiana, then was assigned to Fort Bragg, North Carolina for Basic Training. Florence Gibbs wrote a letter to the Mexican Government advising them of Peniche's military status. Following Basic Training and advanced training in Field Artillery, Ed was given a ten-day leave, during which he visited his parents in Mexico.

By the end of April 1944 he left for his overseas assignment, arriving in Bristol, England in May. Ed volunteered for airborne duty and was assigned to the 101st Airborne Division. Before D-Day, Ed and hundreds of other replacements were asked by a tough-looking paratroop officer to volunteer for the airborne. He mentioned that paratroopers would receive an extra $50 a month. At first, Ed was rejected by the airborne. He was 5' 3 ¼" and weighed 127 pounds, one inch too short and a number of pounds to light for the airborne. Four of his classmates threatened to leave if Ed was not accepted, but the sergeant at the front of the line held his ground. The sergeant consulted with his lieutenant, was ordered to measure again, and in a matter of seconds Ed grew an entire inch.

Under accelerated airborne training, Ed qualified both as a parachutist and gliderman; jump training still required the five basic jumps plus all the rigorous physical training. The glider training consisted of three glider flights under tactical conditions, loading and unloading the glider. He served in combat with the 101st from D-Day 1944 until VE-Day 1945. During that time he participated in four major campaigns., Normandy, Central Europe, Ardennes, and Rhineland. He said, "It was my destiny to be assigned to the Screaming Eagles." He became a member of the 81st AT/AA Airborne Artillery Batalion, which provided support to the Parchute Infantry Regiments.

Ed's staging area was at Pont Llan Fraith, near the port of Cardiff, Wales, UK. By May 28th they knew their destination would be France, but the actual landing area was not revealed at that time. On May 31st they took their equipment, vehicles and material to the Port of Cardiff where they loaded everything aboard a converted Liberty ship named either the SS *Robert Perry* or the R*obert E. Anderson*. K rations was the only meal during their trip.

Initally, they were told that they would depart on Sunday, June 4th. Their departure was delayed a day due to the weather. On June 5th in the early evening, they joined a larger convoy en route to the coast of France. Many of the troops by this time were seasick.

There were a lot of ships on the open sea. In fact, over 5,000 ships participated in the Normandy Invasion. The message came over the ships radio that the invasion of Europe had begun. The men were briefed, given maps of France and advised that they were to land on Uncle Red Beach, *Utah Beach*, France, early that evening of June 6, 1944.

However, due to circumstances which Ed said were never explained, by mid-afternoon their task force sailed to the vicinity of Omaha Beach. They were to land at Utah Beach where the airborne assault forces, parachutists and glidermen had landed the night before. The ship Ed was on disembarked onto LSTs and landed on Utah Beach at 7 p.m. on June 9, 1944. (D-Day + 3) The beach, although battered, was secured. Despite this unfortunate "detour," and the sinking of the *SS Susan B. Anthony* off Omaha Beach with much equipment lost, the historical record shows that the division artillery units and other combat support elements were able to be in place to provide timely and effective support to the infantry regiment during the battle of Carentan, June 10-13, 1944.

After the fall of Carentan and the successful defeat of the repeated German counterattacks, the 101st took a general defensive position of the area and they held their lines. Ed's unit moved to the vicinity of St. Saveuer Le Viscompt on or about June 26th. It was there that Ed celebrated his 19th birthday, in a foxhole, eating C rations. By the end of June the 101st was no longer in contact with the enemy. About July 7th, Major General Maxwell D. Taylor, their Division Commander, congratulated the men for a job "well done" and announced the unit would return to England. Their mission to Normandy, France had been completed. Ed said that although Utah Beach was not as bloody as Omaha Beach, their losses were 3,836 KIA, WIA and missing. Brig. General Don F. Pratt, Ed's Assistant Division Commander, was killed on a glider landing on D-Day.

After Overlord Ed participated in Operation *"Market Garden"* as a member of "C" AT Btry. 81st AT/AA Airborne Battalion. He landed in a glider at *Son,* near *Hell's Highway,* attached to the 502nd PIR on September 19, 1944. During their 72 days in combat in Holland, Ed's outfit fought in the bloody battle of *Ophesuden,* not too far from Arnhem where the British 1st Airborne Division was decimated by two German Panzer divisions. British Field Marshal Montgomery's ill-fated combined airborne-land assault on Holland resulted in heavy casualties. Along with 35,000 other paratroopers, Ed was deposited in the middle of the German army. His mission was to support the 502nd Parachute Infantry Regiment and to stop German tanks from overrunning the lightly armed paratroopers along the infamous Hell's Highway. Around 9 p.m., three or four German planes dropped a few bombs. The German bombers had a peculiar sound and they were referred to as "Bed Check Charley."

The next day Ed's unit was deployed to St. Oedenrode, which was being defended by the 1st Bn. 502nd. Col. John Michaelis, the commander of the 502nd, was all over the battlefield. He ordered Ed's unit to fire a few rounds against the top of two or three wind mills, which might have been used by the enemy as Observation posts.. They fired a few white phosphorous shells into some haystacks and set them on fire. There was a German half-track under one of them, another one had a tractor. The next day, Col. Michaelis was wounded.

The shelling and the automatic weapons fire was intensive. Ed and Francis Papaleo were prepared with their bazookas; Ed was the gunner, Francis the loader. On D-Day+6, September 23rd, the rest of the Divisions Artillery arrived by glider. The traffic heading north kept on moving, but the weather turned a bit nasty with rain and heavy fog. D+7, the enemy cut the road once again. The second platoon was ordered to move back to St. Oedenrode. Holland is a very flat country and being on any road made one an easy target. Ed said that it took two days to open the road. For this they received a bonus, their first mail since leaving England.

By D+10, the 101st and the 82nd Airborne Divisions had accomplished their missions. Following the fight for Hell's Highway, Ed's unit was moved up to Northern Holland to a place called the Island, a place between the Lower Rhine and the Waal rivers. They served there with the British where Ed learned to like tea mixed with powdered cream. The division opened a place near Nijmegan from the front lines for hot meals, haircuts, showers and a time to relax. Ed added, "Historically, our division is better known for our gallant stand at Bastogne during the Bulge—but let me assure you that in this so called Island we experienced some of the heaviest artillery barrages of the war from early October to the end of November 1944. And it was while we were here that, after Hell's Highway, we ended up in a 'Hell Hole' called Opheusden." Not all of the units of the 101st fought here. Everything entered into play; artillery, air support, mortars, automatic weapons etc. The heavy 50- cal machine guns were used for direct support of the infantry units. Ed said that a friend told him that he had seen a German cut in half by 50-cal. Bullets.

Maybe Opheusden was an insignificant little village, but for Ed and the others who fought there, it was Big Time, a real "BITCH" of a fight. It was in an orchard near there that Ed saw human flesh hanging on the trees…and on a secondary road, he saw three pigs feasting on a dead German soldier.

Operation Market Garden was conceived and planned to be carried out by the newly organized First Allied Airborne Army: British 1st and 6th Airborne Divisions; US 82nd and 101st Airborne Divisions; 878th Airborne Aviation Engineer Battalion; Polish Parachte Brigade. The US units would operate under the XVIII Airborne Corps commanded by LTG Mathew B. Ridgeway. D-Day was set for Sunday, 17 September 1944.

This is former PFC Ed Peniche's account about his unforgettable glider ride into Holland. (You can also read Jim Bryant's story about landing in Holland in the "Glider" chapter.)

"We were in Southampton firing our AT guns when we were ordered back to garrison; this was on Wednesday, 13 September 1944, I well remember, it was my mother's birthday. The very next day we moved to the marshaling area at Greenham Common, that evening we were given the "Big Picture" for the operation. My battery was attached to the 502nd Parachute Infantry Regiment for AT support. We understood from the briefing that we were to land on DZ/LZ near Son located north of Eindhoven. The overall mission was to keep the highway open so that the British Second Army could rapidly deploy to link up with the 82nd in Njimegan and the British 1st in Arnhem.

"We loaded our glider on Saturday, September 16th. One glider would carry the AT gun (a British Six-pounder), the other glider would carry the prime mover (1/4 Ton, Jeep). Joe O'Toole, our squad leader, was the loadmaster. We confirmed that all the tie downs were correcly secured. One cardinal rule about a glider flight was that everything had to be properly arranged in relation to the 'center of gravity' of the glider. After we finished loading, the glider Pilots came to check everything and, when we got the OK from our pilot, I asked him permission to write on the side of the glider. He said, 'Fine', and with a heavy piece of chalk I wrote 'The Yucatan Kid!'

"The Pathfinders and the Parachute Infantry regiments departed on Sunday, 17 September 1944. Market-Garden was on. Bad weather and the limited number of tow aircraft prevented us from departing on September 18th; we departed on Tuesday, September 19th. It was still foggy when we lifted off, but I remember flying over a corner of London which was our RP because it was there that I noticed that we constituted an Air armada; there were literally hundreds of planes and gliders in the sky. We were heading toward the channel and then toward Belgium. I was riding on the "jump" seat of the glider; the AT gun was riding quite well. We also had six boxes of AT shells. I remember thinking about ack-ack fire!

"We reached our second RP (or IP) somewhere near Brussels and from there we headed toward the target area. Through some clearings we could see long columns of British trucks and tanks heading towards Holland. As we headed for the DZ, (drop zone) the ride started to get bumpy and interesting. Before too long we saw the "puffs" of ack-ack fire; German 88s no doubt. Some of the explosions were quite visible. At the distance, to the left of our formation, a glider seemed to disintegrate in a big explosion; there were many small pieces. One of the tow planes was on fire; its glider cut loose. I was enthralled and excited by all this; suddenly, our pilot gave the signal that we were going to be released. Upon being released there was a deep silence and we glided into the LZ.; (landing zone) we were lucky, our landing was rough but without serious damage. I saw a glider go into the trees and another glider tilted to the left and crashed; on the far side of the LZ automatic and rifle fire could be heard. While we were getting the gun out, we came under enemy mortar and MG fire. By this time it was about 1630; British and American fighter planes were strafing the enemy. This was combat in all its splendor; as soon as the Jeep arrived, we hooked up the piece and moved toward the assembly point. The road had been cut-off and we were being fired upon from both sides of the highway.

"The glider ride was over; the task at hand was about to begin along Hell's Highway. Little did we know that we were going to be there for 72 days and suffer heavy casualites. The US Airborne Divisions were withdrawn a week after Thanksgiving of 1944 and went to Northern France."

After surviving Market Garden, the true mettle of this Mexican-born American paratrooper came to the fore during the *Battle of the Bulge.* It was at the height of this battle and the heroic stand of the 101st Airborne Division, that the 2/502nd distinguished itself defending a portion of the Bastogne perimeter against the repeated assaults by elements of the 9th SS Panzer Division. In constant danger of being overrun, the 57 mm antitank guns of C Battery were all that stood between the German panzers and the frontline infantrymen.

BASTOGNE (December 1944. White Christmas -Red Snow!)

The chronology of the events narrated here came from notes jotted down in Spanish by Ed Peniche for his father. Soldiers were prohibited from keeping diaries or unit photographs while on the front lines in the event they were captured. Ed jotted brief notes to keep track of time and surroundings and weather. Here is a brief account, not in its entirety. Ed expanded on his notes during the two months that he was recovering from his wounds in a hospital in England. Of the four major combat campaigns, Bastogne is the one that affected Ed the most. The freezing weather terrified and tortured the soldiers day and night.

Saturday, December 16—Word about the German offensive in the Ardennes came to us that Saturday night. We heard about it after midnight from the US Army MPs who were out in force clearing out bars, bistros and bordellos in the city of Reims in northern France; there were plenty of 2 ½ ton trucks available to take the men of the 101st and 82nd Airborne Divisions back to their barracks. There was, of course, a lot of bitching and complaining, and some of the troopers, drunk or not, were using profanity to express their dissatisfaction. And why not? We had just come to France for R&R barely two weeks before after 72 days of continous fighting in Holland to liberate the Dutch people from Nazi occupation.

Sunday, December 17th—Upon getting back to camp there was a lot of activity. We were cleaning weapons, drawing ammunition and rations, packing personal belongings, pack bed rolls and musette bags, underwear, socks, toilette articles, towel, mess kit and gear, etc. Don't forget gas mask and first aid kit. We had a break for religious services. I went to Mass with Joe O'Tolle, Joe Fair and two or three others. After lunch, we went to the motor pool area to check out our ¼ ton primemover (Jeep) and to the gun shed to clean and "bore sight" our anti-tank gun. Our piece was a 57mm actually a British Six pounder with double protective shields for the AT gunner and gun crew. The move to the front lines would be different than Normandy and Holland where we landed behind enemy lines by glider or parachute. We were going to Belgium by trucks.

Monday, December 18th—We left Camp Mourmelon about 1700 by a "cattle" truck. I was assigned to Co. "D" 2nd BN, 502d Parachute Infantry Regiment. We traveled all night with black-out lights. The long convoy was moving rapidly, under the circumstances, yet we managed to get two or three "pee" calls; As we approached the Bastogne area we were able to hear at the distance the sound of the artillery, ours and theirs! I guessed.

Tuesday, December 19th—By early Tuesday morning, still dark, we were at the edge of the village of Longcamps, 5 kms north of Bastogne. The 2nd BN, 502d PIR was straddling the main road that led from Bertogne to Bastogne. We established a roadblock on the portion of the highway connecting Bertogne to Longchamps with the assistance fom "D" Company. Our AT gun emplacement was on the right hand side of the road. We could hear sounds of a gun fight. The message to the German attacking forces was clear, the Screaming Eagles are here to fight. By daylight, Francis Papaleo and I, who constituted the AT squad bazooka team, places the edge of the road and judged various possible positions to cover the road block. Our gun was well dug in. Darrell Garner and I shared a foxhole.

Wednesday, December 20th—About 1430 hours, we engaged a German Recon unit that came to the road block and we destroyed one of their vehicles and damaged another of their half-tracks as they tried to turn around. Our position was on a knoll with a clear view of the valley sloping down between Longchamps and Monaville. The weather was turning colder and some snow began to fall.

Thursday, December 21st—We woke up with a heavy blanket of snow and the cold weather was making us feel miserably uncomfortable. The snow stopped falling about mid afternoon, but the temperature got much colder.

Friday, December 22nd—The heavy blanket of snow covered our entire sector and we were surrounded by the enemy. We were with "F" Co and Co. "D" had moved to our right. They were being shelled by the enemy self-propelled guns. It was incredibly cold; the water in our canteens was freezing. We also had to rub each others feet to prevent frostbite. From our foxholes, despite the horrible weather, it was fascinating to gaze at the wintry scenery, the snow was pretty deep and very white. The wind had picked up, it was much colder. I was terrified by the thought of freezing to death; being a 19 year-old soldier from the Yucatan in southern Mexico, I had never experienced snow on the ground, much less standing and sleeping on frozen ground.

Saturday, December 23rd—Our lines came under heavy mortar barrages; the activity to our right flank also intensified. Our P-47s bombed and strafed the German positions directly to our front. We also knew for sure that we were completely surrounded by the Germans when we saw our C-47s (cargo planes)dropping supplies inside our perimeter. Seeing all those planes and parachutes seemed to us that we were witnessing a miracle, it was a warming and beautiful sight.

Sunday, December 24th—Our P-47s and P-38s came over at daybreak. We were told that the enemy had given the division an ultimatum to surrender but it had been refused. We got a big kick when we heard that General McCauliffe had said 'NUTS" to the enemy. We also knew that things could get worse. That night, Christmas eve, the Lufftwaffe bombed Bastogne twice. Yet, on that unholy night, history has recorded an unforgettable mass that took place in town; wounded Airborne soldiers shed tears at the tune of "Silent Night." The Germans POWx were visited by Gen. McCauliffe himself as they were singing "Stille Nacht" and "O Tannenbaum." He wished them a Merry Christmas.

Monday, December 25th—In the forward area of the perimeter, in the MLR (Main Line of Resistance), what is called today FEBA, (forward edge of the battle area), in that place where the outcome of the battle is finally decided. Clinging to our foxholes in the frozen ground, we sank into deep thoughts and emotions. I thought mostly about home in the Yucatan in southern Mexico, where we never have snow; I thought about my family here and my relatives in Paducah, Kentucky. I was wearing a sweater , OD color, which had been sent to me for Christmas in early December by my cousin, Marie. (I still have it). That night, the enemy activity increased. The Germans were planning to launch a major attack against the northwestern sector of the Bastogne perimeter; the area defended by the 502d Parachute Infantry Regiment. Bastogne, indeed, would make a worthy Christmas present for the fuhrer. It was going to be, indeed, an unholy night for the 502d.

Suddenly, around 0300 a.m. the first barrages crashed against our positions, a few German planes droned over regimental headquarters and dropped bombs. Minutes later, wearing snow suits, the first grenadiers crep forward against our lines, supported by a few tanks. The fire fight on our left flank intensified. "A" Co. 1st Bn, was catching the brunt of the assault. The enemy was determined to break through, but the "Deuce" was not about to yeild easily. Champs and Hermoulle were the objectives, no doubt about it, it was a major assault.

As the ground shook under the impact of the heavy shelling, the snow covered battlefield soon became an spectrum of bright flares and deafening explosions and machine-gun tracers. The attack was on, it was Christmas Day already, lying face down in the bottom of my icy foxhole. I remember praying both in English and Spanish. A few mortar rounds exploded in front and behind our position, yet the activity to our left was gaining intensity. Our outposts between Longchamps and Champs had been reinforced and our machinegunners were delivering flanking fire against the attacking German infantrymen. Our own parachute infantry was also being deployed to meet the enemy threat; these men were the brave rifles from Co "E" 2nd Bn. 502d P.I.R. To me personaly, this was a defining moment in my life as a soldier and as an American, to see well disciplined , courageous fellow soldiers well motivated to follow orders under the most hellish of circumstances yet, without hesitation, at that very trying moment everyone seemed to know what had to be done and they DID IT!

Tuesday, December 26th—Bastogne was relieved on Tuesday, December 26th by the 4th Armored Division of General Patton's Third US Army. The Ardennes was, of course, not the first time that American soldiers had fought under adverse conditions. At the birth of our nation there were cold, tired, and hungry soldiers at Valley Forge, but at Bastogne and throughout the *Battle of the Bulge,* the resourcefulness and dependability of the American fighting men were highlighted by the GIs themselves. Were we prepared for Bastogne? I believe we were; we certainly were well trained and well led, and above all, we had the Airborne esprit-de-corps which always prepared us to fight facing the enemy from all sides as we did in Normandy and in the Liberation of Holland during *Operation Market-Garden.*

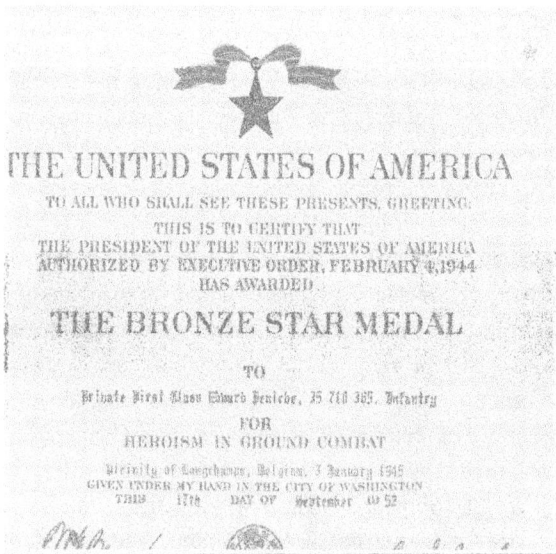

THE UNITED STATES OF AMERICA

TO ALL WHO SHALL SEE THESE PRESENTS, GREETING:

THIS IS TO CERTIFY THAT

THE PRESIDENT OF THE UNITED STATES OF AMERICA AUTHORIZED BY EXECUTIVE ORDER, FEBRUARY 4,1944 HAS AWARDED

THE BRONZE STAR MEDAL

TO

Private First Class Edward Penichet, 35 710 385, Infantry

FOR

HEROISM IN GROUND COMBAT

Vicinity of Longchamps, Belgium, 3 January 1945 GIVEN UNDER MY HAND IN THE CITY OF WASHINGTON THIS   17th   DAY OF   September 19 52

Success in the perimeter was achieved not by chance, or because of air superiority, it was won by officers and NCOs (from Generals to Sergeants) who provided exemplary leadership and by soldiers who knew how to follow orders, and yet had the initiative to act on their own when necessary.

The siege of Bastogne, Belgium was a frightful experience never to be forgotten, and hopefully, never to be repeated again. Misery on the battlefield was compounded by the severe winter of that year. YET, despite the adversity of war, all those involved were able to find warmth, strength, and comfort in man's eternal hope for universal fraternity and man's eternal search for divine guidance. As for me personally, like that of my fellow soldiers, it was my destiny to take part in and survive that gallant feat of arms; and, as miserable and terrifying as the experience was, it enriched my life forever because I learned to have faith and trust in my superior officers and in my fellow soldiers; it enriched my life because I learned first hand about the true spirit of America, by never hearing anyone ever express the word 101st Airborne Division, and I am proud for having been there. I had had my first white Christmas in that small Belgian town, and there were enough lights to last me a life-time.

Final thoughts of Ed Peniche. "I did survive the siege, but little did I know that on 3 January 1945, during a ferocious all out attack against our front by the 9th SS Panzer Division, Sgt. O'Toole, Darrell Garner and myself were to fall among the many wounded during that bloody engagement. Sgt. Silva, however, as well as quite a few other dedicated and brave parachutists from the 2nd Bn 502d Parachute Infantry Regiment were destined to be killed in action that very afternoon. The German attack was repulsed; there were heavy casualties on both sides. For the men of the 2nd Bn., it was their finest hour. As I left the battle area in an ambulance heading for a field hospital in Arlon, I knew that I had stood there rubbing shoulders among American's finest citizen-soldiers. I still thank our Lord for sparing my life and granting me the privilege to remember them and to honor them till the end of my days!

Repeatedly, during the battle, while under intense artillery, tank and machine gun fire, Peniche ensured the resupply of ammunition to his squad's 57mm AT Gun. Even though wounded, he continued to make the perilous journey from ammo dump to gun position until the gun was destroyed by enemy artillery fire. Aware that two members of the gun crew were seriously wounded and unable to withdraw, Peniche returned to the position guiding medical aid men to his wounded comrades. For this action, Peniche was awarded the Bronze Star w/V. The order read as follows:

BY DIRECTION OF THE PRESIDENT-THE BRONZE STAR MEDAL WITH "V" DEVICE; IS PRESENTED TO SERGEANT FIRST CLASS (THEN PRIVATE FIRST CLASS) EDWARD A. PENICHE; UNITED STATES ARMY.

For distinguishing himself by heroic achievement in action. On 3 January 1945 in the vicinity of Longchamps, Belgium, strong forces of enemy infantry and tanks launched a determined attach on his unit. As a member of a 57mm antitank gun squad, aware of the great danger involved, he volunteered to carry *ammunition forward to his gun. Exposed to the most intense enemy artillery, tank and machine gun fire, Private First Class Peniche performed his difficult task. Although wounded, he continued his work. When two members of his squad became seriously wounded and the gun was destroyed, he again exposed himself volutarily to enemy fire in order to report the situation and guide medical aid men to the casualties. His actions were in accordance with the highest standards of the military service*

Peniche was wounded in action at Longchamps in the outskirts of Bastogne, on 3 January 1945. In the annals of the 101st Airborne Division, 3 and 4 January 1945, are registered as the bloody days. It was here that he became a hero. Ed Peniche fought heroically at a roadblock, during the Battle of the Bulge. His six-pounder anti-tank gun destroyed three German panzers and helped knock out seven more. The ten destroyed German tanks broke the back of the Nazi attack. The enemy attack began with a heavy artillery barrage. As the first enemy tanks began to come out of the woods to their direct front, Sgt. O'Toole, Ed's squad leader gave him a warning order, "You will fire at my command." He kept his binoculars trained on the roadblock. The leading German tank, a mark V, Tiger tank, approached the roadblock and as the other tanks moved forward, O'Toole ordered Fire! They then engaged the enemy. The first round bounced off the tank, but the second round took its turret off, followed by an explosion. As two members of the German crew tried to leave the tank, our machine gunners, to the right of our emplacement, mowed them down. They destroyed the second tank, and damaged a third one, and all hell broke loose around them. The Germans zeroed in against Ed's position, and soon they were outgunned. They were being hit with everything the enemy could fire. It was at that moment when all the guns on the line seemed to explode all at once. Sgt. O'Toole got hit and dropped in his foxhole. The shelling was so heavy, that the ground was trembling. Peniche felt a sting on his left leg, but continued to man the gun while Darrell was tracking and firing the piece. Suddenly, Ed's gun took two direct hits, the gun recoiled and Ed was thrown back. He suffered a severe concussion which momentarily blinded him, and he was also bleeding from his nose and ears.

Ed crawled to check on Sgt. O'Toole. O'Toole had been severely wounded and was bleeding profusely. Darrell had also been hit by shrapnel, his jaw and shoulder were badly cut. Voices and moans of other men could be heard. Ed looked down and saw mud and blood on his trousers. Everyone needed medical attention. Ed remembers praying in English and Spanish as he crawled toward the CP (command post) beyond the ridge. He reported the situation to the CP. Ed received medical treatment.

Joe O'Toole and Darrel Garner, as well as others were evacuated from the battle area and soon were being taken by ambulance to a field hospital. The wounded were being evacuated according to the severity of their injuries-head wounds, chest wounds, stomach wounds, loss of limbs, etc. Once Ed's jaw and shoulder were moved back in place, and his leg wound was cleaned, he was held overnight and evacuated at dawn on January 4, 1945. His tag read, "Severe concussion; and foreign body left leg." The medic fixed his leg so he couldn't bend his knee. He thought at the time that he might loose the use of his leg. Ed was transferred to a field hospital in Arlon, Belgium. He said, "I was so frightened that it was showing, and as I was placed on a table, a nurse with a very soft and melodious voice asked me 'How are you feeling soldier?' I answered, 'Not so good.' After the medic removed his combat boots and socks, the blue-eyed nurse said, "You are going to be all right." She pulled a folded map out of Ed's pocket and said, "You might want to keep this and show it to your grandchildren someday." This made Ed feel much better. The Battle of the Bulge resulted in over 81,000 casualties. Ed has shown the map to his grandchildren. He donated the map to the 502nd Infantry Regiment combat memorabilia at Fort Campbell,

Kentucky, where the 101st Airborne-Air Assault Division is always ready to defend and protect America.

After Ed was wounded, he risked his life to crawl back to headquarters to request reinforcements. He was awarded the Purple Heart and two Bronze Stars for valor. He returned to his unit two months later, just in time for the final assault against Germany. (An airborne Monument/Marker was dedicated at Longchamps, Belgium. The marker honors the 2nd Bn 502nd PIR/101st ABN.DIV. The site is officialy known and listed as the "Stele PENICHE").

Col. Bill Weber, Ret., editor of *The Airborne Quarterly* and a hero of the Korean War, wrote this about Ed Peniche: *"This country of ours has good reason to be thankful for the 'Peniches' from amongst our people who 'stand to be counted' when they are needed. Then, today, and, God willing, in the future, our nation will be blessed with such men. In this century that is about to close, we have marched to the 'sound of the drums' many times. And, it is a given that the generations that will follow us will hear those drums again! That we have preserved our way of life in due, not to the politician—not to our industry—not to our wealth—but rather due to America's 'Peniches', be they ground, air or sea!* Weber added in regard to the monument dedicated at Longchamps: "I doubt that many in our nation will learn of what happened on January 3-4,1945 and July 25,1999 in Bastogne and even fewer will ever pass the **"Stele Peniche"** and know for what it stands! Hopefully, some future historian will read these pages and learn and report the way it really was!"

When World War II ended, Ed Peniche returned to his native Mexico, where at the tender age of 21, he was a cofounder of the Mexican Army Parachute Jump School in 1946. He also served as an officer in the Mexican Presidential Honor Guard and was an instructor of Military English at the Mexican Command and Staff College. He resigned his commission in the Mexican Army in 1951.

Following a five-year stint in the Mexican military, Ed applied for an immigrant visa with the US Embassy. He contacted his friend, Wilbur "Tex" McDonald from Dallas, informing him that the wait might take two years or more. McDonald, who had been a captain with the 82nd Airborne during the war, wrote to his Texas senator, Lyndon Baines Johnson, Chairman of the Armed Forces Committee. Tex wrote, "This young fellow entered as a replacement in Normandy, landed on Hell's Highway, and was wounded at Bastogne and no one asked him to wait. He didn't wait. He went forward. And now our embassy is going to make him wait for two years." He was issued a visa, according to Ed "right now." With a permanent immigrant visa in his possession, he returned to the United States in February 1952, and to the US Army Airborne, being assigned to the 503rd PIR, 11th Airborne Division, Fort Campbell, Kentucky. On February 25, 1953, in full Airborne regalia, Ed became a US citizen.

Ed and Deanie Peniche. (Photo courtesty of Ed Peniche)

In 1952 he had met a girl named Deanie, who was a high-school girl; Ed was age 27. He believed that the action and best chance of meeting girls was in Nashville at the Grand Ole Opry. He said, "Then I met Deanie at lunch. It was in a very nice restaurant, downtown. I told her I was going to be in uniform with my jump boots. Well when Deanie walked in, so help me God, I thought she was floating. I thought I was seeing the image of an angelic...angelic.

She was slender with that high school freshness, that purity, you know. Man, she knocked me off my feet. No kidding." "So all of a sudden, I didn't want to go to Nashville. I was taking a bus 80 miles to Paducah. Before I knew it I just fell in love with this girl."

Ed received his next assignment. They were sending him to Formosa to train the new military under Chiang Kai-Shek. In light of this, he pressed his relationship with Deanie and eventually asked for her hand in marriage. Getting her consent was easy. Her parents on the other hand... 'I was very nervous approaching her father and her mother, especially. The mother told the father, "You say no." After three hours of talking, I turned to Deanie and

asked her, "Deanie, do you love me?" She looked at her father and said,"Yes." "Then would you marry me and be my wife, already?" "Yes." So I tell her parents, "Mr. and Mrs. Baggett, we love each other. I want your blessing so I can marry your precious daughter."

"I understood why. Look, I am ten years older than Deanie, I am a soldier. What the heck am I bringing to the table? You know, I would hesitate having my daughter marrying a soldier, someone who drank. They'd seen me drink beer and someone had seen me smoke a cigarette." Mr. Baggett had been giving Ed a hard time because he was a Catholic, but never said anything about him being Mexican. Permission was given. Ed and Deanie were married on October 6, 1953. Their son Carlos was born while they were serving in Taiwan; John Michael was born while Ed was stationed at Fort Benning, Georgia. Their third son, Franklin Eduard was born in 1959 while Ed was serving in Vietnam. By this time Ed could read and understand both French and Vietnamese. The Pentagon was searching for linguists among those serving on active duty. President John F. Kennedy, in an effort to democratize Latin American counties, opened the Inter-American Defense College. They needed people fluent in English, Spanish and Portuguese. Ed was one of two names considered. In 1962, he was relocated to Washington, DC. He worked for three different generals at the Inter-American Defense College.

In 1967, the Peniches moved to the Canal Zone in Panama where Ed was editor of the translation pool at the US Army School of the Americas. He would edit and or translate US Army manuals into Spanish and Portuguese. Three years later, Ed left

the service and returned to Kentucky. He earned undergraduate degrees from The George Washington University (1966) and the University of Nebraska-Omaha under the US Army fellowship (1969). He received a Masters Degree at Murray State in Spanish American Literature in 1971: More post-graduate work was done at the University of Virginia (1973-1974) and UT-Austin (1978). Ed taught as a college professor in Kentucky, Virginia and Texas. In 1996 he was awarded the title of Professor Emeritus at Central Virginia Community College in Lynchburg, Virginia, where he taught for 22 years. In October 1998, he received a Teacher of the Year award from Mrs. Laura Bush, then First Lady of Texas. On Wednesday, December 14, 2005, the Honorable John Abney Culberson of Texas recognized Ed Peniche, American Soldier and Educator, before the US House of Representatives.

His military decorations include the Bronze Star with "V" and Oak Leaf Cluster, Purple Heart, the Joint Service Commendation Medal, and the Army Commendation Medal. His ETO medal has four battle stars and arrowhead; his Vietnam medal has one battle star. Ed was also awarded commendations from France, Belgium, Holland, Nationalist China, Vietnam and Mexico.

"What are a few more weeks after (waiting) 62 years?" **Deanie Peniche** Ed's wife was refering to the fact that Hurricane Humberto was the reason that plans delayed the presentation of the second Purple Heart to her husband. He was wounded twice during the Battle of the Bulge. Ed's military records are now complete. Sources attributed this oversight to misspellings and transposed numbers in Ed's medical records. Unlike his first Purple Heart presentation, this one was attended by his children and grandchildren and his wife of 54 years, Deanie, as reported by the *River Oaks Examiner* on September 13, 2007. Ed added ,"My problem was compounded because upon being honorably discharged from the service on 11 December 1945, my three year student visa had expired and I had to return to my native Mexico to obtain a new Visa."

VMI offered him a guaranteed two-year contract. Instead, Ed found himself face-to-face with CVCC Dean, M. Douglas Reed. Reed offered Ed a one-year contract and told him if he was any good we may keep you." Ed retired from Kingwood College in May 1998. Ed lives in Houston, Texas today. A soldier, educator, father, grandfather, and an American hero. Yes, Ed Peniche you landed on the right DZ (dropzone) **"American Dream."**

JESSE R. HOFFMAN

"When I arrived on Omaha Beach, D-Day +3, we came upon a stack of dead GIs piled in huge stacks about 40 feet long and 5 feet high." **J.R. Hoffman**

This is a story of a combat medic from Nitro, West Virginia who landed on *Omaha Beach,* June 9, 1944. J.R., as he prefers to be called, entered the US Army on June 25, 1943 in Huntington, West Virginia at age 18. After medical basic training at Camp Grant, Illinois, he sailed on the *Queen Elizabeth* on December 14, 1943 landing in Glasgow, Scotland. After serving as a dental technician with the 9th Field Hospital, he went to a staging area in England preparing for the Invasion of Normandy.

After landing on Omaha Beach, about ¾ miles inland is where he came upon the gruesome sight of stacks of dead GIs. The bodies had been tagged and prepared to be taken away for burial. J.R. began to wonder at that time what his life would be like as an Infantry Medic in the 30th Infantry Division, 119th Regiment, Company I. He served in Normandy, Northern France, Ardennes and the Rhineland.

J.R. was born at Elkridge, West Virginia on December 26, 1924. At age 15 he began working in the CCC Camp. After returning to his home state after the war, J.R. met Lavania Workman. They were married on September 6, 1947. It seems that J.R.'s sister had told Lavana all about her brother trying to be a matchmaker. The first time she actually saw J.R., he was riding by her house on an old plug horse with a big chew of tobacco. He worked for the Monsanto Chemical Company in Nitro for 31 years.

The Allies began a drive to St. Lo, France in July 1944. J.R's unit was pinned down by German 88mm artillery. Someone from one of the hedgerows began to call for a medic. The soldier thought he had been shot in the head but on examination, J.R. found out that a rock had hit the man in the head from the explosion and he was not injured. B-17 bombers missed their target and their bombs landed on the 119th Regiment, almost wiping out their division. Among the 111 Americans killed by our Air Force was General McNair. This took place on July 25, 1944.

J.R. was separated from his unit for about six hours because he was taging the dead and helping the wounded. After completing his duty, he began to move out to find his outfit. There were two houses alongside the road in that bombed-out area. Suddenly, two German soliders came out of the house. J.R. didn't carry a weapon because he was a medic. The Germans walked toward him with their rifles over their heads wanting to surrender. The Germans were taken prisoner by his platoon.

J.R. said, "We had a new lieutenant and as we jumped off he got about 55 yards and went down. I crawled out to him and found that the top of his head was gone. I told Sgt. Holden who was a good friend to the lieutenant what happened. Sgt. Holden got so upset that he took off his helmet, threw it down, kicked, stomped, screamed, hollered and cursed. It took about 15 minutes to get him quiet. Why he was like that, I don't know because bullets were flying everywhere. After we moved out, one of our buddies got a 88mm shell, probably between his legs. J.R. added "All I could find was part of his stomach."

One of the things that you don't do as a soldier, is to disagree with one of your officers. I think being a West Virginian gave this soldier extra courage. J.R. had a disgreement with his captain. The captain ordered him to bury the few remains of a GI, which he refused to do. The captain threatened him with a court martial if he didn't follow his orders. Two infantry GIs told the captain that if he court martialed J.R., it would be the last man because it was this medic's job to take care of the wounded. The captain walked away.

In was hot in July 1944 on this push for St. Lo. Again they were pinned down by heavy 88mm fire. J.R. heard someone calling for a medic. He crawled about 100 feet to find a 17 year-old soldier who thought he had been wounded. It seems that one of the 88mm shells had hit the top of the hedgerow and knocked a small tree into a pool of water. The water, hot from the blacktop road, had splashed on the soldier's hip and buttock. No combat wound here.

J.R. was wounded the first time on July 31st during a heavy 88mm shelling. He received three pieces of shrapnel in his left leg. His buddy was also peppered with small pieces of shrapnel. J.R. gave himself a shot of morphine and bandaged his leg before being taken to a field hospital. On the way his captain gave him a bundle of 57 letters from home which lifted his spirits. He was flown to Hereford, England to a hospital to be operated on. The operating began at 6 a.m. About 6 o'clock that evening, J.R. came to enough to know someone was slapping him in his face. He said, *"I remember rising up on my elbows and the major that operated on me was standing at the foot of my bed. He looked like he was swirling around in milk. He was bald headed, so I called him a 'bald headed S.O.B.' The doctor came in the next morning and sat down on the side of my bed. He took my hand and said 'We almost lost you son.' He went on to say he went in on the wrong side of the shrapnel and had to back up and make another incision. I was waking up so they gave me ether on top of the sodium penethol and almost gave me too much. After that, all the staff were very nice to me."*

J.R. was released from the hospital on December 14, 1944 and sent to Achen, Germany. He joined M Company as a medic. He arrived at Achen on his 20th birthday, December 26th. Next his unit joined in the *Battle of the Bulge* on December 28, 1944. Night fighters were bombing his unit when suddenly a soldier ran out to the middle of a field and started praying. All he said was "Oh God, not now" over and over.

It has been documented many times about the weather conditions during this important battle. J.R's platoon moved to the top of a mountain where everything was so frozen they were unable to dig foxholes for protection. J.R. said ,"My sergeant and I dug down in the snow and cut pine branches to cover us for the night. I stayed awake all night, kicking my feet together, probably because I was so nervous. My sergeant went to sleep. When he woke up, he said, 'Jess, my feet are burning up.' I took his shoes and socks off and his feet were blue up to his ankles. He had blisters on his toes half an inch long. His feet had frozen during the night. We called the litter bearers and they came and took the sergeant away. He never returned to the outfit. My feet were frost bitten that night too."

"Next we went to the town of Malmady, Belgium where the Germans had recently captured 78 American GIs, lined them up in a field and killed them with a 50-caliber machine gun."

J.R.'s unit went to another town in Belgium called *Spa*. Here they were able to take a hot bath. One soldier in J.R.'s platoon picked up a grenade. The grenade exploded, blowing off both of his hands. [A family in Spa appreciated the protection from the Americans. One man gave J.R. a calling card which he still has after 63 years. The card was from Mr. & Mrs. Joseph Leroy-Job, 37 Desnie-Spa. On the back of the card was a note to Jesse Hoffman thanking him for the protection.]

In another small town they were awaiting a German attack. At daylight someone started to yell that the Germans were coming. One GI was in a truck, handing down machine guns to GIs on the ground. He accidentally hit the trigger blowing off the hand and almost a leg of one of the GIs. J.R. patched him up the best that he could. They were located in a building that had been dug into a hill. From there, they could see the Germans coming. Along with the American soldiers, there were some Belgian civilians in the house. J.R. had a German soldier's watch in his pocket but hid it in the ashes of a stove. If he were captured, the watch would probably mean his death.

A small window was located in the back of the building. The Belgians climbed on top of each other below the window, making a human staircase. Eight GIs and J.R. climbed on top of them and slid through the small window. They went over the hill to where the road the Germans would come down. J.R. helped to set up an aid station in a train depot. They also set up a 155mm artillery and aimed it down the road. They could hear the Germans coming. The first German weapon was a tank. The 155mm opened fire and knocked out the tank. The disabled tank blocked the road, which allowed our P-51's and P-38's to start their bombing run. They were able to knock out 178 German pieces along the road.

On January 25, 1945, J.R. was wounded for the second time. This time he received shrapnel in the shoulder and knee. He received one Oak Leaf cluster for his Purple Heart ribbon. After being treated in a field hospital, he was moved to Leige, Belgium. This hospital was not much safer than the battlefield. The first night in the hospital J.R. said that a German buzz bomb hit the hospital, killing a doctor and a nurse. The bombs were coming in about every hour. The German target was a coal mine located near the hospital. The wounded were moved to another location after the continuous bombing. Later, J.R. was moved to a hospital located in Hereford, England. After he was released from the hospital, he was sent to a rehabilitation center in Abergavenny,Wales. The news came that the war was over when he was on his way back to Germany.

J.R. was sent to Chrispendorf, Germany where he and two other medics set up an aid station in a large two-story house. He stayed there until he rotated to the states. J.R. said *"We had been there about three weeks when they sent a man 40 miles on a bicycle to get two of their nieces. One girl was 15 and the other was 16. One girl played the guitar and the other played the harmonica. The man made Schnapps (a kind of German beer) and his wife made wonderful sweet bread. They had us upstairs every night eating sweet bread, drinking Schnapps and listening to the music the girls played. To our honor, we never touched the young girls. We had fresh eggs every morning when no one else in our company did. I stayed there until I was shipped home for discharge on October 16, 1945. When we left for home, the man, his wife and their neices cried like we were part of the family. I know without the grace of God I would not be here today. There were so many people back home that prayed for me."*

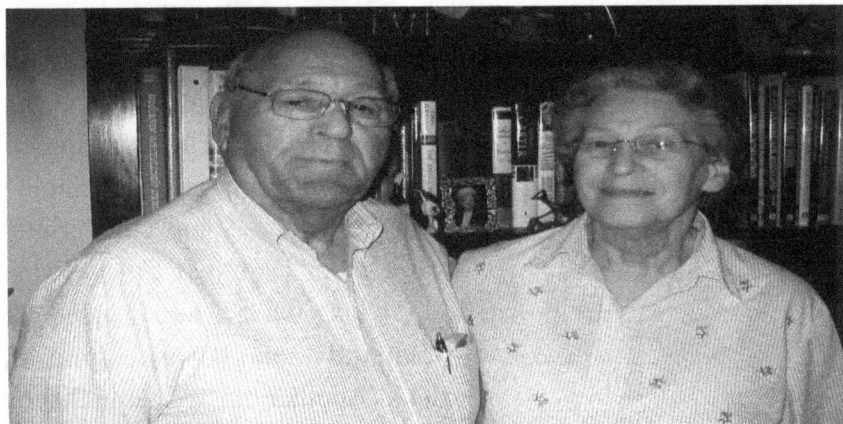

J. R. and Lavania Hollman

He said "After I came home in 1949 they found a big tumor in my shoulder. When I was wounded in January 1945, they didn't remove the shrapnel. When the tumor was removed, the piece of shrapnel was in the middle of the tumor. That shoulder still bothers me." He added, "Thanks Bob for including me in this book. Lastly, I thank the Lord for sparing my life."

J.R. and Lavania's only son, Charles David Hoffman, age 22, was killed in Vietnam on November 4, 1970. He was a member of the 101st Airborne. Charles was awarded the Silver Star, Bronze Star, Purple Heart and Good Conduct Medal.

Listed are Veterans who served in Normandy but whose stories and experiences are printed in other chapters.

PAUL SUTER, a 94-year-old veteran was a school teacher before World War II. He decided to enlist in the US Army instead of waiting to be drafted. After basic training, Suter had a decision to make. Its unbelievable but the army gave him a choice of assignments; either the Philippines or Hawaii. Which would you have chosen? He selected duty in the beautiful islands of Hawaii. In 1940 he was stationed at Schofield Barracks on Oahu and was there at the time of the **Japanese attack on December 7, 1941.**

S/SGT. PAUL L. SUTER
1940-1945
FIELD ARTILLERY OBSERVATION BATTALION

Suter returned to the States for additional schooling before being sent to England. The invasion of Europe had been in the planning stage for quite some time. Suter was a member of VII Corps of the 1st Army when they landed at **Normandy on D-Day, June 6, 1944.** Another bloody battle that he survived was the **Battle of the Bulge. [Suter's story is printed in the chapter "PEARL HARBOR."]**

JAMES E. BRYANT was a member of the 325th Glider Infantry Regiment who participated in the invasion of Normandy, Market Garden-Holland, and the Battle of the Bulge. The CG 4-A Glider carried Bryant and his buddies into battle. Jim made a career out of the service; he also served in the Korean War. He was born in South Hampton County, Virginia. He is the author of a book entitled, Flying Coffins Over Europe. For bravery, Bryant was awarded two Bronze Stars, a Silver Star and a Purple Heart. [**Bryant's story can be read in the chapter, "GLIDERS."]**

EVELYN KOWALCHUK, now age 87, has a remarkable story to tell about her experiences. She became a Flight Nurse who flew into **Normandy, D-Day + 3** to become a true "Angel" of mercy to the wounded soldiers. She was born in Jersey city, N.J. She and her group were transferred to the European Theater, sailing on a ship called *Saturnia*. The ship had 25 nurses and thousands of GI's and Officers. To use her expression, "We had a ball." She flew into Normandy on a C-47 aircraft. The planes had been converted into hospital planes; each caried 24 litters. **[Evelyn's complete story appears in the chapter, "NURSES."]**

ROBERT "CAL" MOORE, Jr., now 89 years-old, lives in Appomattox, Virginia. He was a pilot on a CG-4A Combat Glider into **Normandy, Market Garden-Holland,** and into the **Rhine Crossing-Germany.** Cal soloed in a Taylor Cub Aicraft at the age of 16 and became the youngest "barn stormer" in the state of Virginia at the age 18. He was a member of the 9th Air Force in Europe during World War II. In addition to flying gliders, Cal also flew the C-47 aircraft. The United States trained over 6,000 glider pilots who started flying sailplanes. He said, *"We got in formation South of England and headed across the English Channel between Utah and Omaha Beaches. The sight of the men*

going ashore was horrible." **Cal's complete story can be found in the chapter on "GLIDERS."]**

TOMMY L. HARBOUR, from Milton, West Virginia. Tommy was a member of the US Coast Guard who landed men on Omaha Beach at Normandy on D-Day in a LCVP (Landing Craft Vehical Personnel) Age 19 at the time of the invasion, he was in charge of the motor on boat PA33-4. On D-Day, Harbour's boat left his ship, the USS. *Bayfield,* about four hours before H-hour and went to a Navy transport, where it was loaded with 14 men and a "mud hen" (M29 Cargo carrier.) The heavily ladened landing craft arrived on the beach about 45 minutes after the initial assault.

Grounding on a sandbar about 50 yards from the water's edge, Harbour and another coast guardsman lowered the ramp preventing Harbour and his mates from closing it and allowing more water to enter the boat, finally swamping it. His boat sank. The soldiers waded safely ashore with the rising tide lifting the other LCVP from the ramp so the "mud hen" could be driven off. Harbour jumped from his landing boat and swam until he was hauled aboard a nearby LCM. Transferred to another LCM, Harbour rode it for about a mile while other German mortars scored near misses.

Arriving back to the *Bayfield,* Harbour was assigned to another LCVP and returned to the beach about 5 p.m., staying there until about 5 a.m. Harbour remembered picking up the bodies of men who had been killed in battle. He said, "We put the bodies in the ship's freezer until we could turn them over to the army," "It was really sad." Harbour continued, "I guess I am lucky to be alive. I took part in four major invasions without a scratch. The roughest part of the war was losing your buddies. You really get close to each other in that kind of situation."

The LCVP on which Harbour was a crew member, landed some of the troops of the 116th Infantry Regiment from Virginia. This fact was proven by a video showing a soldier leaving his boat on Omaha Beach. One of the soldiers left his 30 cal carbine on the boat when landing. Harbour was able to take the carbine home with him after the war. He kept the carbine for 63 years and decided to donate this valuable item to the D-Day Memorial Museum in Bedford, VA on June 6, 2007. The Carbine was valued at $6,000.

On June 6, 2008, Tommy Harbour while visiting the National D-Day Memorial in Bedford, Virginia, donated his original white Coast Guard Uniform which was issued to him in May 1943.

USS *BAYFIELD*-PLAN OF D- DAY

On D-Day, the USS *Bayfield* was anchored 13 miles off the Cotentin Peninsular, the Flagship of Rear-Admiral Don P. Moon who oversaw the landing of the US 4th and 90th Infantry Division.

6 June 1944 TUESDAY

2400- Commissary Officer will send coffee and sandwiches to men at General Quarters Stations.

0030- Breakfast for Boat Crews and Troops on mess deck. Men must not go on deck-use passage through compartments)

0030-Breakfast for troop officers in Wardroom

0200- (Approximately)

    Anchor in Transport Area

    Set Condition One Able

    Lower All Boats-Boats carry out orders

1. Damage Congrol and repair 1 and 2 will see that no unauthorized person goes on deck and that complete darkened-ship condition prevails throughout. When troops are ordered on deck-watch openings closely.

2. All Hands will wear impregnated clothing and carry all equipment.

3. As soon as boats are lowered prepare to debark troops and equipment promptly as LCM's and LCVP's come alongside.

4. Prepare to receive casualties.

5. As soon as Boat Teams are debarked, lower starboard and port accommodation ladders.

6. Food will be delivered at the General Quarters Stations.

7. BE PREPARED TO EXECUTE ALL EMMERGENCY ORDERS PROMPTLY, CALMLY AND QUIETLY.

    Signed by G. A. Littlefield, Commander, USCG. Executive Officer

[This copy of the Order of the Day had turned brown over the years and difficult to read if scanned.]

(The rest of Tommy Harbours' interesting story can be found in the chapters, **"Higgins Landing Craft" and "Iwo Jima."**)

Tommy Harbour proudly displays his medals

WORLD WAR II MEMORIAL
WASHINGTON, D.C.

It took longer to approve the Memorial for World War II Veterans than it did for them to win the war. On D-Day's 57th anniversary, the government urged a federal judge to let work move ahead on a World War II Memorial.

Yet Washington still didn't have a memorial to honor their service. Legislation finally received approval and was signed by the President. This battle began in 1993 when Congress authorized construction of the memorial on the National Mall.

Former senator Bob Dole, a disabled World War II veteran led the campaign to raise $170 million in private donations for the project. Dole said *"Our generation saved the world, and the Mall was a part of it." This is the artist drawing of the memorial.*

CHAPTER FIVE

NURSES

The stock market crash of 1929 caused soup lines to become the order of the day for the skilled and the unskilled alike across the nation. Franklin Delano Roosevelt was elected as President of the United States in 1932. He promised a "New Deal" for Americans that would provide them security "from the cradle to the grave." The New Deal program did not end the Depression. The war in Europe and the American aid to the Allies, and ultimately, US entry into World War II after the bombing of Pearl Harbor revitalized the nation's economy. World War II became the defining moment in the lives of an entire generation of Americans. The rise of Adolf Hitler and the Third Reich, the attack on Pearl Harbor, Rommel's Panzers rolling relentlessly across North Africa, June 6, 1944-the D-Day invasion at Normandy, the Marines struggling to raise the American flag on Iwo Jima and the horrors of the liberated death camps, are images of World War II that are horrifying.

Nurses were among the veterans of this war. Serving on battle-fronts from North Africa to Italy to Normandy to Corregidor and Bataan, the nurses of World War II contributed much to the care of the wounded, the morale of the fighting men, and the development of nursing as a profession. In all, approximately 57,000 nurses served in the Army Nurse Corps and 16,000 in the Navy Nurse Corps by V-J Day. A total number of 4,644 nurses were stationed along the European front in 1944; 4,000 were serving on the Pacific front in 1945. By the end of the war, 201 American military nurses had died, 16 from enemy fire.

The Japanese attack on Pearl Harbor on December 7, 1941 caught America by surprise. Nurses were stationed at Pearl Harbor when the attack occurred. A plan was implemented to expand the Army Nurse Corps and recruit more student nurses as cadets. However, prior to this attack, while Hitler was sulking around Europe pretending to save Germany, the military minds in Washington were stonewalling women's organizations about women being in the military. Fortunately Congresswoman Edith Rogers and Eleanor Roosevelt thought otherwise. On May 28, 1941 Congresswoman Rogers introduced a bill to establish the Women's Army Corps for service with the Army of the United States. This bill was dissected, bisected, stalled, lost, amended, sandbagged and all but trashed until General George C. Marshall took an interest. Some government department cooperated but the Bureau of the Budget continued to stall in spite of pressure from Mrs. Roosevelt and General Marshall and other groups. Still in late November 1941 there was no definitive action. General Marshall ordered the War Department to create a women's corps. Pearl Harbor reinforced this order.

Many nurses were involved at Pearl Harbor even though the Army Nurse Corps listed fewer than 1,000 nurses on their roll when the attack occurred. Military service took men and women from small towns and large cities across America and transported them around the world. Their wartime experiences broadened their lives as well as their expectations. After the war, many veterans, including nurses, took advantage of the increased educational opportunities provided for them by the government. World War II changed American society irrevocably and redefined the status and opportunities for the professional nurse.

The nurses worked under tremendous pressure following the morning raids. The Japanese attack left 2,235 servicemen and 68 civilians dead. There were 82 army nurses serving in three Army Medical Facilities in Hawaii at the time. Hundreds of casualties suffering from burns and shock who were treated by Army and Navy nurses. The nurses at Schofield Hospital and Hickam Field faced overwhelming numbers of wounded personnel. The chief nurse at Hickam Field, 1st Lt. Annie G. Fox, was the first of many Army nurses to receive a Purple Heart and the Bronze Star. [The Purple Heart was established by George Washington in 1782 during the Revolutionary War. The Purple Heart was called "The Badge of Merit" and instituted to reward troops for "Unusual Gallantry." The Purple Heart was a purple cloth heart edged in silver braid and was to be worn over the left breast of the uniform. Only three awards were known to be issued by General George Washington two are known to exist today. The Purple Heart as we know it today was reestablished in 1932 to coincide with the 200th anniversary of the birth of George Washington.

The original criteria for the Purple Heart were published by the War Department, circular no. 6, on February 22, 1932. This circular states that the medal would be awarded to anyone serving in the army who had received combat related injuries. The Purple Heart was not authorized by the US Navy until 1942. Any soldiers, sailors and marines who had been wounded prior to 1932 were eligible to apply. During World War II, there were an estimated 954,000 battle casualties (non-fatal and fatal). During the Korean War there were approximately 103,200 non-fatal casualties; and during the Vietnam Era, including Vietnam, Cambodia and Laos, the attack on the Pueblo, Dominican Republic and Cuba, 200,700 Purple Hearts awarded.]

Four days after the bombing of Pearl Harbor, and 23 years after the idea of women in the military was born, the Bureau of the Budget stopped objecting to women in the uniformed services. Finally on May 14, 1942, the bill to "Establish a Woman's Army Auxiliary Corps" became law and Oveta Culp Hobby, wife of the former governor of Texas, was named director. With a nudge from Eleanor Roosevelt, the Navy got its act together and began authorizing a Women's Naval Reserve and the Marine Corps Women's Reserve. The Coast Guard followed soon after. The first director of the WAVES (Women Accepted for Volunteer Emergency Service) was Lt. Commander Mildred McAfee, President of Wellesley College. The SPARS, which came from the Coast guard motto, *Semper Paratus-always ready,* were led by Lt. Commander Dorothy C. Stratton. The Marine Corps Women's Reserve was headed by Major Ruth Cheyney Streeter. The WAAC was changed to the WAC to establish it as part of the Army, not an auxiliary, by a second bill dated July 1943 and signed into law by President Roosevelt.

Six months after the Japanese bombed Pearl Harbor, 12,000 nurses were on duty in the Army Nurse Corps. Few of them had previous military experience, and the majority reported for duty ignorant of Army methods and protocol. A four-week training course was authorized for all newly commissioned Army nurses. This program stressed Army organization, military customs and courtesies, field sanitation, defense against air, chemical, and mechanized attack, personnel administration, military requisition and correspondence, and property responsibility. Over 2,000 nurses trained in a six-month course designed to teach them how to administer inhalation anesthesia, blood and blood derivatives, and oxygen therapy as well as how to recognize, prevent, and treat shock. To qualify for an Army nurse, one had to be a graduate of an approved nursing school, less than 40 years of age, unmarried, and female.

There were a number of male nurses but they were overlooked by our government. In fact, only 40% of qualified male nurses served in medical units. Most of the men were drafted into service.

Caring for German and Japanese prisoners of war proved a special challenge to American nurses. The German POWs were often quite young, many under 18 years of age. The language barrier was difficult to cross; one German soldier misunderstood the concept of taking blood samples and thought the nurses were attempting to execute him by slowly bleeding him to death. Nurses in the Pacific faced similar challenges in caring for the Japanese POWs. One nurse recalled being on suicide watch over a downed Kamikaze pilot, who felt his honor, had been lost when he survived his mission. However, even in the worst of conditions, the nurses managed to put on a brave front and cheerful faces for the fighting troops.

Christmas was an especially difficult time for all the service personnel, but the nurses on all fronts went to great length to make the holiday homelike. A good example of how the nurses tried to bring some happiness to the troops after the Battle of the Bulge, when the nurses decorated a Christmas tree, complete with tinsel and American and Belgian flags. The Battle of the Bulge started in December 1944 when Field Marshal General Gerd von Rundstedt of the German Army launched an all-out western front. This is one of the battles in which the 101st Airborne was deeply involved. Most of the medical units were forced to pack up and leave. However, five nurses with the 67th volunteered to stay overnight with 200 patients too weak to withstand the move. The next day they were able to evacuate within hours of the arrival of the Germans.

As the war escalated in the Pacific, women were sent to New Guinea, Leyte, and Manila in the Philippines as well as the China-Burma-India Theater. A Japanese suicide plane bombed the hospital ship USS *Comfort* off Leyte Island. In the attack six nurses, five medical officers, eight enlisted men, and seven patients were killed, and four nurses were wounded. Often ignored by history is the story of the women prisoners of war taken captive during World War II. Sixty-eight Army nurses and 16 Navy nurses spent three years as prisoners of the Japanese. Many were captured when Corregidor fell in 1942 and were subsequently transported to the Santo Tomas Internment camp in Manila, in the Philippines.

Santo Tomas was liberated in February 1945. Five Navy nurses were captured on Guam two days after the bombing of Pearl Harbor and interned in a military prison in Japan. The names of these five nurses are: Lieutenants (jg) Leona Jackson, Lorraine Christiansen, Virginia Fogerty and Doris Yetter, under the command of Chief Nurse Marion Olds. Later in 1942 they were transported to Japan. They were held for three months in Zentsuji Prison on Shikoku Island and then moved to Eastern Lodge in Kobe. They were repatriated in August of 1942.

Through 1941 the United States had responded to the increasing tensions in the East by deploying more troops in the Philippines. The number of army nurses stationed on the islands grew proportionately to more than one hundred. Most nurses worked at Sternberg General Hospital in Manila and at Fort McKinley, seven miles outside the city. However, a few nurses were at Fort Stotsenberg, seventy five miles north of Manila, and two worked at Camp John Hay, located 200 miles to the north in the mountains. Several nurses worked on the island of Corregidor. The Japanese attacked the Philippines on December 8th, Philippine time. Clark Field adjacent to the army hospital at Fort Stotsenberg, suffered a three hour air raid during which planes, barracks, and field shops were-bombed. The hospital escaped damage, but the large number of casualties from the air attack overwhelmed the small staff.

The chief nurse at Sternberg sent several of her nurses to Stotsenberg to help cope with the emergency. On December 27th, they were ordered to evacuate to Manila. All the nurses reached Manila except the two nurses at Camp John Hay, who were taken prisoners by the Japanese. General MacArthur ordered the nurses to the island of Corregidor. MacArthur planned to hold Corregidor and the Bataan Peninsula. He sent 45 nurses from Corregidor to the Bataan Peninsula to prepare two emergency hospitals for the US and Filipino forces fighting on Bataan. The hospital consisted of

16 wooden buildings. There were more than 1,200 battle casualties who required major surgery within a month.

The Japanese bombed one of the Hospitals on March 29th, scoring a direct hit on the wards and killing or seriously wounding over one hundred patients. One nurse remembered the force of the bomb. *"The sergeant pulled me under the desk, but the desk was blown into the air, and him and me with it. I heard myself gasping. My eyes were being gouged out of their sockets, my whole body felt swollen and torn apart by the violent pressure. Then I fell back to the floor, and the desk landed on top of me and bounced around. The sergeant knocked it away from me and gasping for breath, bruised and aching, sick from swallowing the smoke from the explosive, I dragged myself to my feet."* The sight that met her eyes was appalling. Patients had been blown out of their beds. Bodies and severed limbs hung from the tree branches. Although the nurses knew that nothing could be done to prevent further air attacks, they carried on. Supplies and food were not available. The troops were suffering from malnutrition, dysentery, beriberi, and dengue fever. The hospital was originally built to accommodate 1,000-patients, now had over 5,000. The day before the US and Filipino forces on Bataan surrendered to the Japanese, the army evacuated its nurses to Malinta Tunnel Hospital on the island of Corregidor.

Maj. General Jonathan M. Wainwright, who commanded the US forces on Corregidor, decided that surrender was inevitable. General MacArthur had been ordered to Australia. He grieved over the fact that he had to leave his friend Wainwright at Corregidor. He ordered many of the nurses to Australia. On April 29th, 20 nurses left the island on two Navy planes. Only one of the planes reached Australia. The second made a forced landing on Mindanao Lake, and all were taken prisoners by the Japanese. On May 3rd, a submarine picked up ten Army nurses, one Navy nurse, and the wife of a naval officer and took them to Australia. Three days later, the US Army on Corregidor surrendered to the Japanese. There were still 55 Army nurses working at Malinta Hospital.

In July the Japanese took the nurses to Santo Tomas Interment Camp in Manila where they joined the ten nurses whose plane had made the forced landing on Mindanao Lake. The 67 nurses remained prisoners of war until they were liberated in February 1945 by US troops. When General Wainwright became a free man, he was so thin and weak that he barely existed. He was awarded the Congressional Medal of Honor on his return.

In January 1942, ten Navy nurses and 68 Army nurses were captured by the Japanese in the Philippines. The Navy nurses were taken to Los Banos; the Army nurses to Santo Thomas. The Los Banos prison was located on the campus of the College of Agriculture of the University of the Philippines. The college was located 25 miles south of Manila, deep behind enemy lines, and along the southern shoreline of a huge island lake, Laguna de Bay. There were approximately 2,200 prisoners in Los Banos made up of nurses, Protestant missionaries and their families, Catholic nuns and priests, doctors, engineers and other professional people and their families. The plan to rescue these prisoners just before the Japanese had planned to kill them (ditches had already been dug,) was by paratroopers from the 11th Airborne Division. Their commander, Maj. General Joseph Swing, was given orders on February 4, 1945 to liberate the people in this prison camp. Due to his units fighting in other areas, the date was postponed. On February 23, 1945, the 11th Airborne parachuted into enemy territory in one of the most brilliant rescues and the finest of its type in the war. All the prisoners were saved. [One of the prisoners was Diana Russell Cantrel. She said once she failed to please the Japanese and they pulled her fingernails out. The next time she displeased them they hung her over barbed wire for a night and two days without water. She was three years old. Diana lives outside Washington, DC today.

In a letter to the 11th Airborne Division she wrote: *"Thanks guys. Thank you for my children, birthdays, weekends, snow, hot buttered popcorn, day's at the beach, the voting booth, a full refrigerator, falling in love, hot baths with soap, each reminded me of you."*] When, after three and one half years American forces liberated the POW camps, General Douglas MacArthur was on hand to greet the returning nurses. The psychological warfare inflicted upon the captured Americans by the Japanese was almost too much to endure. On several occasions, the nurses were lined up against a wall with their hands above their heads, execution-style, only to be let go at the very last second by a Japanese officer, who regarded this as a great joke. One nurse tells the story of an American doctor who was caring for a fellow POW and begged the

MacArthur returns to the Philippines

Japanese to allow him access to medical supplies necessary to save the patient's life. Two officers appeared to agree with the doctor and led him outside the barracks on the premise of getting the supplies. The nurses inside the compound heard two pistol shots; the doctor was never seen again. In the end, it was the nurses' own will to live, plus the encouragement received from their POW patients, that saw them through the years of confinement. One

Army nurse remembers, "The men called us angels and would say if you angels can take it, we can take it."

Nurses received 1,619 medals, citations, and commendations during the war, reflecting the courage and dedication of all who served. Sixteen medals were awarded posthumously to nurses who died as a result of enemy fire. Thirteen flight nurses died in aircraft crashes while on duty. Sixteen women received the Purple Heart for being wounded by enemy fire, and 565 women received the Bronze Star for meritorious service overseas.

BLACK ARMY NURSES

The Army Nurse Corps accepted only a small number of black nurses during World War II. When the war ended in 1945, just 479 black nurses were serving in a corps of 50,000 because a quota system imposed by the segregated Army during the first two years of the war held down the number of black enrollments. In 1943, for example, the Army limited the number of black nurses in the Nurse Corps to 160. Army authorities argued that assignments available to black nurses were limited because they were allowed to care only for black troops in black wards or hospitals. But unfavorable public reaction and political pressure forced the Army to drop its quota system in 1944. Subsequently, about 2,000 black students enrolled in the Cadet Nurse Corps program, and nursing schools for blacks benefited from increased federal funding.

The first black medical unit to deploy overseas was the 25th Station Hospital Unit, which contained 30 nurses. They went to Liberia in 1943 to care for US troops protecting strategic airfields and rubber plantations. Malaria was the most serious health problem the troops encountered. The nurses felt superfluous, and the unit morale declined. The nurses were recalled late in 1943 because of poor health and poor morale. Some were sent to general and station hospitals in the United States; others went to the 383d and 335th Station Hospitals near Tagap, Burma, where they treated black troops working on the Ledo Road. Another group of 15 nurses deployed to the Southwest Pacific Area in the summer of 1943 with the all-black 268th Station Hospital. In June 1944 a unit of 63 nurses went to the 168th Station Hospital in England to care for German prisoners of war. By the end of the war, black nurses had served in Africa, England, Burma, and the Southwest Pacific.

Nurses served all over the world taking care of wounded soldiers, trying to bring each one some happiness while caring for them. One nurse said that regardless of the situation, they tried to laugh occasionally, then go to their tents and cry. Only men who served and were wounded in combat can fully appreciate these "angels."

Nurses served in North Africa. On November 8, 1942, there were 60 nurses were attached to the 48th Surgical Hospital. They climbed over the side of the ship, down a ladder into small assault boats. Each boat carried five nurses, three medical officers, and 20 enlisted men. The nurses were required to wear helmets and a full pack just like the soldiers. The only way to distinguish nurses from combat personnel was that the nurses did not carry weapons and wore Red Cross arm bands. The D-day operation was named TORCH. The nurses had no choice but to wade ashore along with the soldiers. Enemy snipers were in position to shoot anyone trying to make it ashore. The nurses set up hospital in buildings without electricity or running water. The doctors had to operate by the light of a flashlight held by a nurse. There were many casualties and insufficient beds. Some wounded soldiers were lying on the concrete floor. Medical supplies were short in supply. This all occurred at a coastal town of Arzew in North Africa.

Nurses who served in North Africa learned a lot about bombs, snipers, hostile fire and the ability to evacuate their patients on a moment's notice. Each field hospital usually had 18 nurses assigned to it. Some patients' wounds were more severe than others. After providing emergency treatment or surgery and the patient was strong enough to be moved, the doctor would order this soldier to be transferred to another hospital where further treatment could save his life. The soldiers might be transported by hospital trains, hospital ships, or aircraft. Nurses would accompany the wounded men of each of these modes of transportation. The hospital ships were white with large red crosses painted on them so the enemy would be able to distinguish them from other ships. The Germans didn't always honor the Hague Convention, which protected the ships from bombing. On at least three occasions that a hospital ship was bombed by the Germans during the invasion of Italy and Anzio. Each time a hospital ship was bombed, American nurses would suffer wounds. Not only were the Germans guilty of attacking unarmed hospital ships, but the Japanese were as well. A good example was when Japanese pilots attack the USS *Comfort* in April 1945 off Leyte Island. Twenty-nine people were killed in this attack which including six army nurses.

Nurses performed well in the Sicily operation. The Sicily operation was named *"Operation Husky."* On January 10, 1943, the American and British paratroopers made a night jump into Sicily prior to the allied forces making an amphibious landing. The allied forces were commanded by General George Patton and by British General Sir Bernard Law Montgomery. Three days after the invasion of Sicily, nurses from the 10th Field Hospital and the 11th Evacuation Hospital arrived. The nurses worked 12 hour shifts. As always in an operation like this there were many casualties for the doctors and nurses to attend to.

Following the action at Sicily, the allied troops consisting of two US and British Divisions made a landing at Salerno on September 9, 1943. After heavy fighting and defeating the Germans, the allied forces continued to move toward Rome through Naples, Cassino, and Anzio. By June 4, 1944, the

Germans finally gave up Rome. Meanwhile, a British hospital ship named H.M.S. *Newfoundland* was moving toward Salerno carrying nurses, and was bombed by German planes. Before the ship sank, all 103 nurses were rescued. Four nurses were awarded the Purple Heart from wounds they received.

The Army nurses were also involved at Anzio. The US VI Corps began attacking out of Anzio on January 22, 1944. The US Third Division continued to advance. On February 3rd, the Germans counterattacked at Anzio but gave up on March 3rd. On June 3rd, Hitler granted his commander permission to give up Rome. On June 5th, the US Fifth Army entered Rome after a long and costly battle to both sides. The Germans reported 25,000 casualties, while the Allied forces reported 40,000 casualties. The 33rd Field Hospital and the 95th and 96th Evacuation Hospitals landed at Anzio with the assault force, ready to take care of the wounded. Again the German pilots failed to observe and honor safe passage to hospital ships. On January 24th German planes attacked three British hospital ships. The *St. David* ship had 226 medical personnel and patients on board. Only 130 survived which included two army nurses. On February 7th, a German plane trying to avoid a British Spitfire dropped a bomb that made a direct hit on the 95th Evacuation Hospital, killing 26 personnel and patients, including three nurses, and wounding 64 others.

Whenever the air raid sirens at Anzio sounded, the patients who could do so would put on their steel helmets and would get under their cots. Again on March 29th the hospital was bombed, killing four patients and wounding several doctors, nurses and patients. Because ammunition dumps, airstrips and other important facilities were located near the medical units, quite often the German bombs hit the hospitals and medical installations, thus earning for the area the nickname "Hell's Half Acre." Many soldiers believed that they were safer in foxholes on the front lines than in the hospitals. The nurses were in constant danger in Anzio.

The casualty rate was high during the time from January to June. During this period the hospitals admitted 25,809 battle casualties, 4,245 accidental injuries, and 18,074 medical casualties (disease).

CAPTAIN ANN BERNATITUS, NC, USN (Ret) STORY

[Information from the Department of the Navy]   Why become a nurse with the understanding that they would be exposed to combat and may be killed by the enemy? Captain Ann Bernatitus, NC, United States Navy, (Ret.) shared some personal reflections recounting her service in the Philippines including Bataan, evacuation from Corregidor on USS *Spearfish* (SS-190); and service on USS *Relief* (AH-1) during the Okinawa campaign and the return of America prisoners of war from Japanese-occupied China. These reflections are recorded in the Naval Historical Center. She wrote the document on November 26, 1975.

Captain Bernatitus when asked said that she always wanted to be a nurse. She trained at the Wyoming Valley Homeopathic Military Hospital in Wilkes-Bare. During her training, someone came from the army to talk about nursing. That's when she got the idea about joining the navy. This was during the Depression and there were no jobs for nurses. After she graduated, jobs were not available. She applied for a six-month postgraduate course in operating room technique. The captain's training was from 1931 until she graduated in 1934. She received a telegram stating there was an opening at the New Rochelle hospital in New York for $80 a month and board. She took the job because she was trained for the operating room. Her next position was from an x-Army nurse who served during World War I. The pay was $70 a month at the Nanticoke State Hospital. In the meantime, she had written for an application to join the Navy Nurse Corps. This was in 1936. There were 325 nurses in the Nurse Corps at that time. She took her physical exam the first of September, and on September 25th she was on her way to the naval hospital in Chelsea, MA. For the first six months there was a rule that nurses were put in a ward with an experienced nurse. The new nurses were neither officers nor enlisted people. During the first six months at the naval hospital her duties included supervising, keeping the books, and counting all the blankets, the thermometers and perhaps even the glasses. They also had to scrub the floors. An inspection was held every Friday by the captain and chief nurse.

After two years at this assignment, she received orders to report to Annapolis. Life there was good. The nurses had separate quarters and the food was good. They lived in a building that was probably 100 years old. The nurses were allowed to date the midshipmen. She was stationed at Annapolis for about two years. Several opportunities became available to attend schools to improve her knowledge or to learn new skills. Captain Bernatitus wanted to go to the Philippines. Instead of signing up to attend another school, she wrote down that she wanted to be assigned to the Philippines. Permission granted.

The captain wasn't much of a sailor. She was seasick all the way. The trip began at Norfolk with stops at Guantanamo Bay, through the Panama Canal, Pearl Harbor, Midway, Guam and the next stop, the Philippines where she arrived in July1940. The United States wasn't at war, so she didn't have any idea what her future in the Philippines would be. She didn't know what to expect when she arrived there. But life was good in the Philippines for the nurses.

When Pearl Harbor was attacked, they started putting sandbags around the hospital where she was stationed. One morning on December 9th the Japanese planes came in to bomb Nichols Field. After that bombing, they were ordered to transport the patients to a hospital in Manila. General MacArthur declared Manila an open city a short time later. Because of her training in the operating room, she was sent along with some surgeons to Bataan on Christmas Eve. The unit that she was attached to included Dr. Carey Smith and Dr. Farley. They were taken to Jai Lai to join a convoy to Bataan.

Another navy nurse, Dorothy Still, saw her sitting on the curb all alone and asked her what she was doing there. She told Dorothy that she was waiting to go to Bataan. When asked where Bataan was, she said she had never heard of Bataan. In the group were 24 Army nurses, 25 Filipino nurses and Bernatitus. During their trip to Bataan, the bus would go through small villages. The people would cheer them and flash the sign "V" for victory. Many times because of Japanese planes overhead, they would have to get out of the bus and dive into some ditch for protection.

Captain Bernatitus, in Bataan, became a member of Dr. Smith's team and worked in the operating room only. At first casualties were heavy and the operating room stayed busy. The wounded would come in dirty, many with lice. The doctors did a lot of leg amputations because of gas gangrene. The wards were open but the OR (operating room) was in a building. They were getting a lot of patients with malaria and dysentery, patients who did not require surgery. The second time that the Japanese had bombed this area they hit one of the wards. The nurses had to cut the ropes of the men who were in traction so they could get under their beds for protection. She didn't get along with the Army nurses very well so she mostly kept to herself. Even her relationship with other Navy nurses later became strained. She believed this to be because she was promoted to junior grade and became a chief nurse. After she came home, she was promoted over some other nurses who had 15 years service. There was unwanted friction between them.

On April 7th, they were bombed again. On the 8th, they were transferred to Corregidor. This is when the front lines collapsed. She took everything that she owned in a pillowcase. She was less afraid on Bataan than on Corregidor. When the Japanese bombed, the whole place shook. She was located in the Malinta Tunnel.

The main tunnel was where Generals MacArthur and Wainwright had their headquarters. She said that she never saw MacArthur, that he was egotistical. When she arrived on Corregidor, she had dysentery and didn't work very much.

She was experiencing constant daily bombing. One day, she learned that she was selected to be evacuated from Corregidor. Two PBYs picked some of the nurses up. She met with others after dark in Wainwright's headquarters. They were told because of the Japanese bombing, their departure would be delayed. Wainwright shook their hand and wished them Godspeed and said, "Tell them how it is out here." At that time, she got in a car and was driven to a dock. They were loaded on a small boat to take them to a submarine. The boat had to maneuver through mine fields. At first, the submarine wasn't available because they weren't sure if Corregidor had fallen. There were six Army officers, six navy officers, 11 army nurses, and one navy nurse. There were also one civilian woman and others. The trip on the Navy submarine, the *Spearfish* (SS-190), took 17 days. Just before getting off the submarine, each nurse was given a bucket of water to take a shower. You can imagine what a treat it was arriving in Australia and having the privilege of getting a bath.

After nearly four months of fighting, Bataan fell on April 4, 1942. Approximately 20,000 Americans along with 120,000 Filipino troops were forced to surrender. A total of 3,500 Marines escaped to Corregidor. These soldiers who survived were prisoners of the Japanese for three- and- one -half years. However, during the Bataan "death march," it is estimated that between 10,000 and 14,000 Americans died or were killed by the Japanese.

[In my book entitled, *A Tribute To Lincoln County Veterans,* a newspaper article was quoted as saying this: "*Private James Edwards, son of Mr. & Mrs. H.H. Edwards of West Hamlin, West Virginia, who was captured by the Japanese on Corregidor more than 40 months ago, has been liberated from Tokyo prisoner of war camp. Captured on May 6, 1942, Private Edwards was interned in a prisoner of war camp in the Philippine Islands until early 1944, when he was transferred to a Tokyo camp."]* In the article by Capt. Ann Bernatitus, she stated that she was liberated from Corregidor on May 3rd. This was just three days before Private Edwards was captured and the fall of Corregidor.

After a short time in Australia she expressed a desire to go home. The paymasters paid her for the clothes that she had to leave on Corregidor. With the money she bought some civilian clothes. She flew to Melbourne to get the *West Point* (AP-23) troopship back. There were extra benefits for being a Navy nurse on a Navy ship. They gave her one of the best staterooms. They went through the Panama Canal again on their return to New York where they arrived in July.

When this Navy nurse returned home, she received a hero's welcome accompanied by a parade by the townspeople, a dinner at the high school and a nice gift. After that wonderful experience, it was back to duty. She went to Bethesda and was there when President Roosevelt broke the champagne bottle to initiate the new facility. This famous hospital was opened on August 31, 1942. At Bethesda, since there were a lot of senior nurses, she got pushed around. She alternated on SOQ (Sick Officers Quarters) with another nurse. Then they used her to sell war bonds and visit factories.

The captain was awarded the *"Legion of Merit"* by Admiral Bennett when she arrived in New Orleans. They were pleased with her presentation although someone else wrote her speeches. Albert Murray did a portrait of her and it is hanging in the Pentagon. Her next assignment was to report to a hospital ship *Relief* (AH-1) in San Francisco on November 3, 1944. She landed at Buckner Bay, Okinawa in April 1945. She was the chief nurse and in charge of all the nurses on the ship. In the battle of Okinawa, 50,000 Americans landed on this island on April 1, 1944. This was one of the bloodiest of the war, in fact. United States losses were the heaviest of the war, with total casualties 25,000, and nearly 7,000 dead.

Next, the *Relief* was guided past ten floating mines. They were en route via Okinawa for Dairen, Manchuria to pick up prisoners of war. On September 11, 753 prisoners came aboard. Before coming aboard they had to be deloused, fumigated and then showered. The supply officer who was in charge of the food, told her that he would give the former prisoners of war sandwiches. She told him "If you can't give them a steak dinner and ice cream or something, we ought to be ashamed of ourselves." The one thing they couldn't get enough of was bread and butter. For some reason, they dropped the former POWs off at Okinawa.

[It is possible that one of the prisoners from Manchuria, who was picked up in the 753 prisoners by the *Relief*, was a cousin of the author. Sherrill Brookover survived the Bataan death march along with two other soldiers from Hamlin, West Virginia. The other two, Okey Pack and James Edwards were prisoners in the Philippines and later taken to Japan. Brookover was sent to Manchuria.]

They then arrived at Taku, China on September 30th to provide medical facilities for the First Marine Division. They arrived in San Francisco with 361 passengers and 386 patients on November 30, 1945. This was her last trip. The *Relief* made one more trip to Japan and was decommissioned at the Norfolk Naval Shipyard on May 11, 1946 and sold for scrap on March 23, 1948.

Back in the United States, Captain Ann Bernatitus was assigned to Brooklyn, New York for a short time. She attended an 18 month course at the Philadelphia School of Occupational therapy and served in various hospitals and Veterans Administration duties.

Of course, this outstanding lady, Navy nurse, a true hero, retired. This is a story of just one nurse and the duty stations she was assigned to all over the world. The available records do not reflect her marvelous accomplishments during her time as a navy nurse. She assisted in saving of lives, bringing smiles to wounded soldiers and marines, and in so doing, she made many unknown personal sacrifices. Take time to find a combat nurse and say thank you for serving.

EVELYN CHAYCHUK KOWALCHUK-FLIGHT NURSE NICKNAME "CHAPPIE"

"We landed in Normandy on D-Day + 3. I had never seen someone who had both arms, or both legs amputated." **Evelyn Kowalchuk**

This is a story about a very special lady whose story has captured the interest of everyone who has had the pleasure of meeting her. It is a story that needs to be told so that people for generations to come can appreciate what she and her friends who were Flight Nurses experienced during World War II. Evelyn's is a story of dedication, commitment, service, courage and sacrifice. This is in part an account as told to Hazel Burnett by First Lieutenant Evelyn Kowalchuk. Among her many honors, she was awarded the French Legion of Honor, an award bestowed upon only ten other women in the United States. She is one of 11 surviving flight nurses who served in World War II during the Normandy Invasion.

Evelyn was born March 29, 1920 on Van Winkle Street, in Jersey City, N.J. as Evelyn Chaychuk of Ukrainian descent. Her parents arrived from the Ukraine in 1915. She had two sisters. As most men, Evelyn's father wanted a son, but had to settle for three daughters. In fact, when Evelyn was born he expected a son, and disappointed, he left home. During his absence, the neighbors and church helped the family. When her father learned that there were other families with daughters only, he returned home. Jobs were difficult to find. They were very poor. Her father became a house painter, and her mother cleaned offices at night to help. They managed to rent a four- room apartment for $27.00 a month for the family. It was called a train apartment, with a front door and back window only. The family moved to Newark when she was four years old. She graduated in 1938 from Newark High School.

Evelyn always wanted to be a nurse. She walked about six miles to attend a college prep high school. After school she worked at Woolworth 5 and 10 cent store for $1.75 a day. After graduation from high school, she started nurses' training at Newark Memorial Hospital. It was a small hospital. She trained with 13 other nurses. After the attack on Pearl Harbor on December 7, 1941, Evelyn applied for the army, navy, Marine Corps, and coast guard. She later joined the US Army in 1942 with the rank of second lieutenant, a rank given to all volunteer nurses. Many of her nurse friends had already joined the service but she had never received an answer from any military branch. This was very disappointing to her as well as something that she didn't understand. Evelyn's older sister told her that her mother had been receiving the applications and tearing them up because she didn't want her daughter to enlist in the military. Not wanting to give up, Evelyn then gave her sister's address and finally received an application to join the Army Nurse Corps.

Her first base was Ft. Monmouth, NJ. Her uniform was a navy blue jacket, robin's- egg- blue skirt and black tie, white shirt, black shoes and bag and the insignia was air corps. She was transferred to Atlantic City where the hospital was a converted hotel. This plush environment didn't last long before she was sent to Seymour Johnson Field.

The chief nurse would list on her bulletin board from time to time locations in the US states where nurses were needed. One day there was an opening for an Air-Evac nurse. What was an Air-Evac nurse? No one seemed to know because it was something new. Being curious or just adventurous, Evelyn signed up for the Air-Evac and went to Bowman Field, Kentucky for training as a flight nurse.

The idea wasn't exactly new. As early as 1932, Lauretta M. Schimmoler, envisioned and Aerial Nurse Corps of America. She suggested an organization composed of physically, qualified, and technically trained nurses, who would be available for duty in air ambulances. She had tried to convince the upper echelon of medical doctors of her idea but was unable to at that time. In 1940, Mary Beard, Director of the Red Cross, acknowledged that Schimmoler was promoting something that was needed. Mary Beard approached the Air Force Surgeon General David Grant, to develop the concept of a flight nurse as part of the medical team. Without Grant's personal interest, it is doubtful that the military's indifference's could have been overcome.

On February 18, 1943, the first formal graduation of flight nurses was held at Bowman Field Base Chapel in Kentucky. In his address to the first class, General Grant said, "*Your graduation marks the beginning of a new chapter in the history of nursing. All evacuation of the sick and wounded is already an accomplished feat requiring only trained personnel for rapid and extensive expansion.*"At the end of his address, realizing that no one had thought of an insignia for the flight nurse, he took off his own Miniature Flight Surgeon Wings and pinned them on Lt. Disihron.

He said that the insignia of the Flight Nurse would be similar but with a superimposed letter N.

This was an eight-week training course which included bivouac-and setting up tents. Their training also included classroom instructions, marching, drilling, flying time, practical experience, plane loading, gas mask drills, aircraft identification, oxygen indoctrination, air evacuation nursing, air medical physiology, mental hygiene and military indoctrination. The training was to equip the flight nurses in connection with the evacuation of the sick and wounded. To become a flight nurse, graduate nurses were also required to apply for a commission in the Army Nurse Corps. They were required to spend a minimum of six months in the Army Unit Base Hospital before applying for admission to the Medical Air Evacuation Training.

Evelyn said, "We were early birds, the pioneers of air evacuation. We did not fight but we were taught to protect ourselves and our patients." The wounded soldiers received excellent care by the front- line doctors, nurses, and medics, before they were evacuated.

The Air Evac nurse had to be 52 inches to 72 inches in height, weigh 105 to 135 pounds, and aged 21 to 36. Physical fitness was important because most of their work was done in the air at altitudes of 5,000 to 10,000 feet. The flight nurse school at Bowman Field, Kentucky, was officially recognized by the United States Army on June 25, 1943. At that time a curriculum was systemized to acquaint medical officers, enlisted men, and flight nurses with their special responsibility for administering medical treatment. The ground commander would not concede its significance until the end of the Korean War in 1953. Evelyn said that they flew for ten years, and saved lives because some of the wounds were only a few hours old.

During December 1942, while battles were raging in North Africa, Guadalcanal, and Stalingrad, graduate nurses all over the

United States began their training at Bowman Field. Evelyn completed her eight-week Air Evac training, the second class of flight nurses to graduate. There were 125 nurses in each class. The nurses were divided into groups of 24 with the 25th being the chief nurse. At this time there was no Air Force but having joined the Army, she was now in the Army Air Force.

Evelyn's group was transferred to the European Theater of Operations (ETO). She expressed her luck in not being transferred to the Philippines. They traveled overseas on an Italian Ship called the *Saturnia*. The trip took 12 days. On the ship were 25 nurses among thousands of GIs and officers. To use her expression, "We had a ball." They landed in Moganberry, Scotland, and then went to Spanhoe, England. In Salisbury, England, a 1,000 bed Quonset hut hospital was set up. Four hundred patients were in traction from injuries from gunshot wounds in their spines. Twenty-two nurses were placed head to toe in Quonset huts. Later they moved into small houses in Catesmoor, England. Every room had a fireplace but they didn't have any wood or coal to burn. The officers' club provided a place to meet others, relax and for a short time forget about their duties.

Rumor had it that June 6th was coming up but they were never told anything specific. However, on June 6, 1944, she heard the roaring of plane propellers on the field. She said, "It was an awesome site to see all these planes lined up to go over to Normandy with the paratroopers." The nurses waved at the men and prayed that the troops would all come back safely. Her group was advised on D-Day +3 that they would be going to Normandy with supplies and to take care of the wounded.

Now, D-Day + 3, was Evelyn's and her fellow flight nurses time to go to Normandy. They flew over on C-47 and C-46 aircraft.

The aircraft had been converted into hospital planes; each carried 24 litters. Brackets were brought down, and the litter was strapped in. They took with them supplies such as shells, boots, blankets, medical supplies, barrels of gasoline, powered milk, powered eggs etc. Evelyn had never been in an airplane before. The C-47s landed at Omaha Beach on a temporary bulldozed metal strip for taxing and takeoff. These metal mesh strips were called "waffle." The propellers continued to run, never shut off. Young pilots made quick decisions whether to stay or take off.

(Photo courtesy of Evelyn Kowalchuk-with nurse friends)

After unloading the supplies, the crew strapped 24 Americans into Evelyn's plane. The litters were four deep and three wide, 24 in all. She said that they acted as a sister, mother, or aunt to the wounded soldiers, and very important, the nurses spoke English. Evelyn said, "They were all wounded. I will say that actually when I was in training, we had an amputation of a patient's leg because of diabetes. I had never seen someone who had both arms, or both legs amputated. At one time we had a patient come on the plane with his mouth wired. I had never had a patient like that in training. He had a bandage around his neck and if he felt nauseous we were to cut the wire so he could throw up. He never did." The wounded men had such courage; no complaints, no one cried out for attention but all were patient and cooperative.

The nurses redressed their wounds and gave them morphine or mineral oil. The mineral oil was for burns. It was the duty of the flight nurse to inform the pilot of the type of patients that were on board. If they had chest wounds, head injuries, or abdominal wounds, since the C-47's were not pressurized, the pilot could not fly more than 5,000 feet, sometimes having to fly at treetop level. The nurse's reinforced amputee dressings when bleeding was noted, dealt with pain, fear, anxiety, and shock, and only had morphine and Phenobarbital to administer. For the patients who were in body casts or who had their jaws wired, scissors were tied on a string around their necks and it could be cut if the patient felt nauseated. Many patients suffered burns from bomb fragments, bullets, and shrapnel. Others had large areas of torn tissue, damaged nerves, and trauma to blood vessels. Mines caused amputations.

Evelyn said that when they landed on one of the beaches, they saw hundreds of white crosses, dead husbands, fathers, sons, sweethearts, brothers, all young men with aspirations and plans for the future. All were gone now. They saw wrecked gliders with their wings torn off and other debris on the landing strip all the time not knowing what tomorrow would bring. Yet they knew it would bring the same ugliness as the day before, if not worse. They did their job under incredible circumstances.

In order for their plane to take off with the 24 wounded soldiers, they were required to have a fighter escort. If there was a dogfight with the Germans, or if it was too dark, they weren't allowed to take off. They could see shells exploding and could feel the ground shaking. The nurses would sleep in unusual places such as under the plane, under the ambulance, in jeeps or in fox holes. Because of the bombing, they didn't get much sleep regardless.

The flight nurses saw beautiful buildings and homes destroyed and normal life interrupted. They saw wrecked ships that never reached the beach. They pretended not to be afraid but they were terrified. Evelyn made many trips to France, Belgium, Holland and Germany. She flew with the 315th Troop Carrier, 310th, 34th, and 309th, to evacuate wounded to England then to the USA. On one occasion she let a young soldier who was bleeding badly rest his head on her lap and she sang an old Ukrainian lullaby to him. In all her flights, her crew did not have a single soldier die.

Between D-Day and V-E Day, over 350,000 patients were flown from the fast- moving front to a general hospital in England or France. The European Theater of Operations had a record of 4,707 patients evacuated from the front lines in one day. Between 1942 and the end of 1944, 1,514 nurses and 970 enlisted men were educated and trained using a minimum of five different aircraft to transport 172,000 sick and wounded soldiers.

Every nurse who served in World War II, whether in a field hospital, near the front lines, general hospital, Navy ships, overseas or stateside, proved time and time again that women could work effectively under the most trying conditions such as mud, heat, and many hours without baths, sleep, or meals. It didn't matter, they all did their jobs. Evelyn was a member of 818th Medical Air Evacuation Transport Squadron.

Evelyn's commander sent a v-mail to her mother telling her how brave she was sleeping in a fox hole. Her mother didn't know what a fox hole was. As a Catholic, she went to church to say a Novena, she said her Rosary and prayed that her daughter would be safe and out of the fox hole where the foxes were! Evelyn's brother-in-law explained to her mother what a fox hole was.

Evelyn was given the nickname of "Chappie" for chaplain because of her dislike for swearing.

At times, Evelyn and the other flight nurses would make two or three trips a day. The airplanes would be loaded with the necessary supplies at a different location then would pick up the nurses. The wounded servicemen would take out their wallets and show the nurses a picture of their mother, father, wife, and talk about their family. They didn't talk about their wounds. Some of the men with minor wounds would be treated at the hospital and sent back to their units in a few days. She said, "Memories are precious, sometimes painful. Our training never taught us what we were to come upon. It was a physical and emotional draining of body and soul. It was an intense mental challenge for a young nurse almost fresh out of training."

When one of the nurses was killed, they held the funeral in silence. There were three services, Protestant, Catholic, and Jewish. They were required to stand at attention, not allowed to move a finger or wipe a tear until all three services were finished.

At times it was necessary to treat wounded German soldiers. They were loaded on the planes last. The American GI's weren't too happy about this. Many of the German soldiers were about 13 or 14 years old. These young Germans were afraid that the shots given by the nurses would kill them. They were told that if captured, the Americans would give them a shot to kill them.

Some of the pilots went to London, England to celebrate the success of D-Day. While in England, they saw two English Spaniel puppies and decided to buy them. They were given two worming pills and instructed to worm the two-month puppies later in the week. While on one of her trips to Normandy, one of the pilots asked Evelyn if the nurses would like to have a puppy. Thinking it might bring some happiness to the 25 nurses in her group; they accepted his gift, not knowing the puppy had taken both pills and was very sick and could hardly stand up. Since the nurse's puppy wasn't expected to live, they named him "Sad Sack–Lord Sad Sack" to make him more royal. After getting well, Sad Sack would visit the hospital giving the patients some happiness. Evelyn was scheduled to return to the States in December 1944, but her plans were changed. A canvas bag and a small parachute were made for Sacky. After they arrived in Newfoundland, Sacky couldn't stay with her. Luck would have it that Captain W.J. McIntyre, a pilot, was going to the States. He agreed to take her puppy with him and call her mother when he arrived in the States to pick Sacky up. Sacky stayed with Evelyn's nephews until she came home from service. A newspaper thought this story would be of interest to the public. The article was called "A Doggy Immigrant." Although Lord Sad Sack was only seven months old, he had logged 26 ½ flying hours. The Kowalchuks' had this special dog for many years until he was killed by a car.

After France was liberated, Evelyn's group went to live in France. They were housed in chateaus without furniture so it was necessary to sleep on cots. This was in a little French village called Villa Coublay which was about half way between Paris and Versailles. One day Evelyn and her roommate went to the cellar to look around. They found a tunnel that led to another chateau which had beautiful furnishings and paintings. A caretaker discovered them and in no certain terms let them know they were trespassing and not to come there anymore.

Evacuation began from France and Belgium to England and to the United States. For this trans-Atlantic flight, larger planes, C-54s were used. They picked the wounded men up in France or Belgium, then took the northern route to England. From England they flew to Scotland, Iceland, Newfoundland, and ended up at Presque Isle, Maine. Evelyn's flight always ended up in New York because this is where they would pick up blood to take back for transfusions. In New York they would pick up doctors, flight nurses, or technicians. When in New York or Presque, Maine, the nurses were ordered not to call home. You know, "Loose lips sink ships."

Nurses frequently demonstrated their ability to remain calm in unpredictable and dangerous situations. For example, *flight nurse Reba Z. Whittle's* C-47 was caught by flak and crashed behind enemy lines in September 1944. Every member of the crew, including Whittle was wounded. The Germans provided their prisoners with medical care and upon their recovery incarcerated them in Stalag IXC. Whittle's captors allowed her to nurse other POWs throughout her captivity. Whittle was held as a prisoner of war for five months until her release in January 1945.

They landed at Cherbourg on Christmas 1944. They had taken a planeload of boots for the troops who didn't have any more leather on their boots. Evelyn said "When we got back to our quarters we just lay on our beds, and didn't think we had any more tears left. We cried for hours." Fun was a word almost eliminated from their vocabulary. The only place they could go for a little pleasure was the officers' club. The pilots and co-pilots with whom they flew would be there. Out of the 25 nurses in her group, ten of the nurses later married one of the pilots or co-pilots. However, none of the nurses quit. All 25 of the nurses were together until the end of their tour. Of course if any of the nurses married or became pregnant, they were replaced. These nurses were young, yet knew the importance of a free country. They were patriotic and called it *esprit de corps.*

Perhaps the importance of the flight nurses or the sacrifices they made can be summed up by a New York overseas reporter, Ted Malone. He wrote: "This is Ted Malone. Maybe this is a good time to remind you that American girls have about as rugged a time in this war as anybody; dodging bombs and bullets, getting lost in the front line, going down on emergency plane landings with litter patients and German prisoners, ditching in the cold waters of the choppy English Channel, missing their meals, losing their sleep, and even sometimes losing their lives, working side by side, regardless of danger, with the rest of the American Army. This is all more or less standard operation or procedure the line of duty for the Medical Air Evacuation Squadron. Becoming pretty much of a commuter these days, I've had the privilege of flying with many of these Air-Evac crews made up of nurses and technicians on their daily missions back and forth between front lines and base hospitals. They go in planes packed with ammunition and supplies for the troops and take back plane loads of litters rushing injured boys to hospitals where they can be given the best medical aid known to science with in only a few hours of their injuries. This is something new in war fare-Air-Evac of the wounded. It is saving thousands of lives and also costing a few. Some of these lives are nurses. December 11, 1944, top of the evening broadcast. Nurses in the Army are soldiers in every sense of the word. Most of them will live to tell you more stories when it is all over, but some of them gave their lives fighting for your boys and fighting for you. This is Ted Malone, overseas returning you to New York."

When asked about Evelyn's most memorable experience, she said,' "*I guess it was the first time that I saw a young man being put on my plane who had lost a leg. They put his boot on the stretcher with him which I thought was unnecessary. It hit me as being cruel, but I guess they wanted him to have his boot when he went home, but he didn't have a foot to put in it. I always remembered that young man didn't complain and took it like a soldier would. We were not too much older. He was a brave soul and to have his boot on the stretcher with him to go home was unforgettable.*"

Evelyn shares this story that was written by Martha Vroeman, a registered nurse in France in 1945. The army nurse: "*A small boy asked his mother as they walked in to the hospital ward, what is a nurse? She said that a nurse is the one who takes care of the sick. She was anxious to get to her husband's bed as she passed other visitors by. The boy's father had come from a battlefield where the enemy had left him to die. He looked at his son who kept watching the nurse and a vision passed before his eyes. A nurse so bright was there that night they were bringing the litters in. She was dressing men's wounds and easing their pain, not once, but again and again. The man looked at his son who kept watching the nurse and with a tear in his eye he said, "A nurse, my son, is so many things. She really is hard to define. She's relief from pain. She's legs for the lame, and often she is eyes for the blind. She's the one who can smile when the going gets tough. She takes Army life with a nod. It's easy for her to be kind to these men for her commanding officer is God."*

In 1946, after the war was over, Evelyn came home. Instead of remaining in the nursing profession in a hospital, she took a civil service examination, passed with flying colors and chose to take a job as a public school nurse. During this time, she met a man at church, started dating the man who became her husband, Andrew W. Kowalchuk. They were married on January 10, 1948. She discontinued working for a period of four years. During this time she had two sons, Peter Andrew and Ivan James. Her younger son, Ivan, had a mission in life. He wanted to be a marine. He died a marine in 1981 while scuba diving in California for the Marine Corps. She returned to nursing in 1967 until she retired in 1988.

Evelyn's husband decided that they should move to Florida after they retired. In the meantime, a nephew who lived in Huddleston, VA invited them for a visit. They liked the lake, bought a house in 1989 and have lived here since that time.

An article was written about Evelyn Kowalchuk in the *Smith Mountain Eagle* by Melody Tinder. The article's headline read, **"Evelyn Kowalchuk receives French Legion of Honor"** It read, *"Last Wednesday in a special ceremony at the National D-Day Memorial in Bedford, Evelyn Kowalchuk of Huddleston who served as a flight nurse during World War II and D-Day, received the French Legion Of Honor medal, an award bestowed upon only 10 other women in the United States. Julia Child was the last recipient."* Evelyn's unit was awarded the AIR MEDAL on April 27, 1945. The citation stated, *"The Air Medal is awarded to each of the following named officers and enlisted men, organizations and residences, as indicated, for meritorious achievement while participating in aerial flights. During the periods indicated these individuals served with distinction on difficult and dangerous air evacuation missions flown in unarmed and unarmored aircraft. Charged with the responsibility of ministering to wounded personnel being evacuated by air from combat and communications zones to rear areas, they exhibited a high degree of courage, technical proficiency and devotion to duty, often under the hazards of unfavorable weather and when attack by hostile aircraft or ground forces was probable and expected. Their achievements are exemplary of the finest traditions of the armed forces of the United States."*

She also received the Normandy Invasion medal, the ETO ribbon, the American Theater Ribbon and has credit in the campaigns of Normandy, Northern France, Rhineland, Ardennes, and Central Europe.

The National D-Day Memorial located at Bedford, Virginia was dedicated on June 6, 2001. This special lady, Evelyn

Kowalchuk had the privilege of escorting President George W. Bush to the speaker's podium. An estimated 24,000 people attended this memorable event. Many men who were present had landed in Normandy on D-Day. You could feel their emotions and see the tears trickle down the faces of these brave men. Many attendees had survived operation *Overlord*, still very proud to have had a part in saving the world from a madman like Adolph Hitler and his henchmen. Pilots who flew missions were there. As they approached the podium the President offered to shake Evelyn's hand. The story goes that she said to the President, "Mr. President, I'm not a hand shaker. I'm a hugger." At which time she gave President Bush a big hug. He in turn said to Evelyn, with a grin, "You are just like my mother."

Evelyn graduated from Jersey State College in 1971 with a BA degree; from Kean College in 1979 with a Masters Degree; and 32 credits over her Masters in the area of Guidance and Nursing. This remarkable lady remains active in the community today. She is a member of the American Legion Post 54-Bedford, VA, and the VFW. She gives speeches to college students and civic organizations.

MARY LANGSTON BOYLES

"The doctors and nurses worked through the night, getting their first break after 36 hours of non-stop duty. We cleaned up a bit, changed clothes, grabbed a bite to eat, and back to our duty stations again." Mary Boyles

According to an article in the *Smith Mountain Eagle* by Rebecca Jackson, "Mary Langston Boyles may be a tiny wisp of a woman, but she filled some mighty big boots during World War II an era that the 90-year-old Winston-Salem North Carolina resident recalls with sterling clarity." Now age 92, this special lady who was nicknamed "Skip," entered the US Army in January 15, 1941 at Fort Bragg, North Carolina as a second lieutenant. She only had a few weeks left on her scheduled one-year tour of duty, but her enlistment was extended for the duration of the war because of the attack on Pearl Harbor. Mary was born in Rio de Janeiro, Brazil, on April 2, 1916, the daughter of Dr. and Mrs. A.B. Langston, who were missionaries

Mary Boyles (L) and Evelyn Kowlachuk in Bedford, Virginia (Photo by Rebecca Jackson, reporter for the *Smith Mountain Eagle.*)

This is the story of another brave, dedicated nurse who cared for the wounded. Until age 15 ½, Mary attended a combination of Brazilian schools, American schools and some home schooling. She then came to the United States to complete her education. After attending Furman University, she enrolled in the Stuart Circle School of Nursing in Richmond, Virginia, which was affiliated with College of William and Mary. After graduation, she accepted a job in a hospital in South Carolina.

The United States was becoming more and more involved in World War II and the military was expanding daily in 1940, drafting large numbers; consequently, more nurses were needed. Young boys became men, wearing their uniforms with more pride and a deeper respect for the American flag. Troops were shipping out, intense training picked up, including self-defense training for nurses.

On April 29, 1943, Mary along with her nurse friends, sailed from New York and ten days later landed in Oran, North Africa. They were loaded into trucks and bumped and rattled to their first staging area. This was a desolate-rocky place. One general referred to it as "even unfit for goats to live," therefore, "Goat hill" became their home. The nurses lived eight to a tent and were rationed water, one canteen per day for all purposes and so the use of their helmets became more obvious.

Mary's first taste of battle came soon and at night. The guards came by quietly calling alert. The nurses jumped up, grabbed their helmets, put them on their heads and took off. What they neglected to realize was that their helmets were full of water with their lingerie. Next, orders came. They rolled up their sleeping bags and tents and were off to board a 40+ 8 train, which was filled with fleas. They arrived in a South Tunisia village called Karouqan, where they set up a hospital in a bombed out building and soon started receiving patients.

Religious services were held on Sunday by a chaplain. Mary heard planes flying overhead and was aware they were carrying paratroopers who were going to make a combat jump. She said, "I sang and I prayed." Later that same day, the nurses were alerted that soon they would receive a large number of casualties. The nurses reported to duty immediately and began preparing the ward-tents to take care of the wounded soldiers. Mary could hear the roar of the ambulances and trucks coming to the receiving dock at top speeds. All personnel moved quickly, lifting stretchers with bleeding soldiers, assisting those who could walk into the hospital. There were 114 wounded men who were treated that night.

Double-decker cots filled and stretchers were placed end to end on the floor, awaiting their turn in surgery as quickly as the operating room team could take them. Nurses worked patients- to-patients, while on their knees, giving aid and medication. Also standing on the edge of the double-decker cots they helped those on the top bunks. The doctors and nurses worked through the night, getting their first break after 36 hours of nonstop duty. "We cleaned up a bit, changed clothes, grabbed a bite to eat, and back to our duty stations again" Mary said. The hospital capacity was overflowing. The designated capacity was 125, but with the 114 newly wounded, they were overcrowded.

Kairowan was Mary's home until November 10, 1943 when the monsoon hit suddenly with tremendous force. The camp and hospital began to flood. Off came their shoes as they began to pack their equipment and move their patients. Everyone was moved to Bizerte, a staging area, where they stayed for 14I days in rain, more rain, mud, drippy tents and boredom as they waited for their orders.

Their new orders came. They would be leaving North Africa and go to Italy. They boarded a beautiful white hospital ship, which had the Red Cross plainly displayed. This gave them a false sense of security because the Germans had plans of their own. Enemy planes were spotted coming in their direction. Orders were given to grab their helmets and back packs and go over the side of the ship and down a wiggly rope ladder to open barges that were waiting. The Italian fishermen became excited when the nurses were ordered off the barge and waded ashore. Army vehicles were waiting for them. They climbed in and the flaps were drawn. Orders were "no smoking and no talking." A short time after Mary and the others left the Red Cross ship; they heard a tremendous noise and a flash of light. The beautiful-white ship had been sunk by the Germans. They were very lucky. The hushed voices of the nurses were heard singing, "Near my God to Thee," not realize that they were singing the funeral hymn for some of the men in their unit.

From December 1943 until August 1944, Mary's new home would be in Segezia, Italy. As our combat troops moved into combat, so did the nurses. They moved to Leghorn, then to Florence. While in Leghorn and doing night duty as supervisor, Mary had a religious experience. Rounds had been made and double check of the prisoner patient-tent. Mary came out into the open field, and heard the roar of an enemy plane hovering above. It was "Bed check Charlie," a frequent visitor from the German Air Force. It became obvious very soon that this was not a routine visit because a flare was dropped, lighting up the entire tent village with a very white light. Mary stood in the open field, completely visible to the pilot of the plane and her entire being in the presence of her Maker. Strange, but, fear did not take over. Instead, she felt a sense of peace and an affirmation that God was near, caring and protecting her.

During the *Pisa* campaign, there was a lot of sniper fire causing an increase in head and spine injuries. As Mary's specialized field was neurosurgical nursing, she was sent on temporary duty to join the Surgical Unit. The assignment was a busy, busy one and interesting in that it was quite an international experience. There were American, British, Brazilian, Italian soldiers and, also German prisoners of war. The short tour in Pisa was the most distasteful one, according to Mary. The patients were the Army's bad boys (rapists, looters, etc.)

When Mary returned to her unit, they had moved to Florence. Everyone loved Florence. She was now ready for some R&R (rest and recuperation), which was spent in Sorrento, Italy. The 91st Division was assigning some of their officers to Sorrento during this time. Mary met a Chemical Officer, Lt. Col. Julian Boyles. Julian and Mary became friends.

Mary and Julian were married on December 15, 1945, and started their new lives together. They had six children, all grown. Now, Julian's days on earth are over. Mary is 92 years old and finding much in life to enjoy. She said, "I'm proud to be an American and honored to have been able to serve and stand beside many true and loyal men and women."

World War II ended in Europe when Germany surrendered on May 7, 1945. However, the war in the Pacific continued. A B-29 Bomber named the *Enola Gay* took off from Tinian with Colonel Paul Tibbets the plane commander. On August 6, 1945 a bomb named *Little Boy* was dropped on the Japanese city of Hiroshima. The entire city was destroyed, killing more than 75,000 people and injuring thousands of others. Following that bombing, on August 9th a bomb named *Fat Boy* was dropped on Nagasaki. It is estimated that over 35,000 Japanese were killed. The Japanese Emperor Hirohito got the message. On August 14, 1945 Washington reported, **"Japan surrendered unconditionally tonight. History's most destructive war is over.**

KOREA-"THE FORGOTTEN WAR"

Only a few years after World War II ended, another war, called a "conflict," started in Korea. On June 25, 1950 the North Korean Army used its force to invade South Korea. Ten Infantry Divisions from the North Korean Peoples Army (NPKA), came across en masse, the border, the 38th parallel, using tanks and weapons furnished by the Russians. More than 5,000,000 Americans fought in Korea. America had 36,913 killed in action; 103,284 wounded in action; 8,177 missing in action and 7,000 prisoners of war in just three years. The war ended with the signing of the armistice on July 27, 1953. The toll of the enemy was heavy. Over 400,000 Chinese and 215,000 North Korean's were killed in action.

RESPECT

THE "RAKKASANS" AT KOJE-DO ISLAND

Many fascinating stories relate to the Korean War. Books are filled with these stories, but none perhaps more interesting or less written about than the prison camp riots at the Koje-Do Island Camp. Koje-Do was one of the prettiest possessions of South Korea. It was a small fishing village located across from Pusan Port. The United Nations, with tens of thousands of North Korean and Chinese prisoners, needed a place where escape would be difficult. Koje-Do was chosen. Enclosures were built with as many as 7,000 prisoners in one enclosure, living in tents, Quonset huts and great flat- story huts with corrugated sheet metal roofs.

The North Koreans who were held in Compound 76 were alleged to be the toughest and most cruel agitators. Col. Lee was their leader. The POWs staged daily riots. They would goose step and perform bayonet drills with wooden sticks. They would throw rocks, sticks, etc., at the UN guards. On May 12, during a riot, they seized Brigadier General Francis T. Dodd and sentenced him to death. In order to save his life, General Dodd signed a document agreeing to cease the alleged mistreatment of prisoners.

On the morning of May 12, 1952, General Thomas Trapnell received orders to move the 187th Airborne Regimental Combat Team to the island of Koje-Do. [Bob Kiley who has a home at Smith Mountain Lake was a paratrooper with the 187 ARCT.] As the troopers unloaded, they were astounded at what they saw. Tens of thousands of NK (North Korea) and CCF (Chinese Communist Forces), POWs (prisoners of war) were lined up along the barbed wire fences looking out in anger. The prisoners were out of control. The Rakkasans got to work immediately. There were early morning runs with the paratroopers yelling "Airborne" as they passed the fences. Sanitary conditions were bad. 50 gallon drums cut in half were used as toilets which had to be emptied every day into the sea.

Intelligence revealed that Compound 76 was the key danger spot on the island. They established an Observation Post overlooking Compound 76, which was manned 24 hours a day. On June 14, 1952 at six o'clock in the morning, Capt. George Essex summoned POW Colonel Lee to the main gate. He was ordered to prepare his men to move to another compound. He refused. Support Company began lobbing tear gas and concussion grenades into the compound. Engineers cut a hole in the fence. First Battalion Rakkasans poured through the breach, forming skirmish lines. A tank was driven into the breach. With gas masks, MI rifles and bayonets, the paratroopers began to move slowly forward.

The POWs began throwing sheet- metal spears, barbed wire nails, Molotov cocktails, rocks and sticks at the paratroopers. Near the entrance, Captain Garrett spotted a cluster of POWs running into a tent. Just beside him was Corporal John F. Sadler, Company A, who carried a flame thrower. Captain Garrett yelled, "Son, burn that tent down." Corporal Sadler complied and seconds later he was shot in the groin by a homemade POW gun. He died of shock within minutes. Some prisoners were killed. The 7,000 prisoners were pushed to one side. Some POWs wanted to surrender to the paratroopers but their leaders would stab them in the back with knives and spears.

This riot was over in two hours. Forty POWs killed and 130 wounded. The Rakkasan intelligence found more than 1,000 Molotov cocktails, thousands of knives and spears, and scores of barbed wire baseball bats. They found tunnels leading to other compounds. They found thousands of dollars of currency and a telegraph set in working order. They found more than 50 bodies of POWs secretly executed and thrown down wells in the compound. They found bodies of hundreds buried in unmarked graves. Most important, the paratroopers found an enemy operation plan for the mass breakout of all 70,000 POWs.

The next morning the Rakkasans deployed across the road to Compound 78. The 6,800 POWs were given 30 minutes to organize and march out peaceably. They formed and moved out as ordered in order not to have a repeat of yesterday's action. The Rakkasans (had moved to quell the planned breakout just in time. A few weeks later, *Life Magazine's* cover showed a picture of Jaj Korn, Rakkasans Intelligence Officer, grabbing POW Col. Lee by the hair of his head, amidst the carnage of Compound 76.

When the flag-waving stopped and Johnny came marching home, GI Jane was out in left field without a ball game. The war was over and there was no place for women in the military in the minds and hearts of many. In typical government fashion, politics prevailed for three years the question of women as an integral part of the military. Two GI expressions that mean respectively: Situation Normal All Fouled Up (SNAFU) and Fouled Up Beyond All Recognition (FUBAR) certainly applied to the situation regarding women in the service. As the political football of women in, or not in the peacetime military, was a subject tossed from the sidelines to the goal posts and back, many women advocates emerged among others. Present-day servicewomen owe a lot to Eleanor Roosevelt. When Mrs. Roosevelt taught school she posted on the wall one of her mottos, *"Be all that you can be,"* later used in army recruitment ads.

There were 120,000 women on active duty during the Korea era. In addition to the nurses serving in Korea, many women served in support units nearby, in Japan and other far eastern countries. When General MacArthur landed at Inchon, Army Nurse Corps officers also came ashore on the very same day of the invasion. Thirteen Army nurses of the 1st MASH and those of the 4th Field Hospital made the landing, and by the end of 1950 over 200 Army Nurse Corps officers were in Korea.

General Eisenhower finally helped clear the folderol away by strongly recommending that women become a part of the US military. He was backed by several other senior officers who had worked with women during World War II and had nothing by praise for their efforts. On June 12th, then President Harry Truman signed on the dotted line, putting Public Law 625, The Women's Armed Services Act of 1948 into effect. It opened the door for dedicated women to serve their country in peacetime. One thing that this law did not do, that is often misinterpreted, is create separate women's branches, corps or forces. Then two years later, as the overall numbers for women in the military dropped to a post-war low, the North Korean war started. President Truman ordered troops into South Korea and within a few days the Army Nurse Corps was also there. To many people the word MASH means a long running hit television program in the '70s. To hundreds of women who served in Korea, at the real Mobile Army Surgical Hospitals, it was no party.

By this point of time in the 1950's, almost a million women had worn the uniform of the United States Armed Forces. They had been prisoners of war; they had been wounded; they flew planes, planned strategies, nursed the casualties, and died for this country. Hundreds of women flew air evacuation, caring for the wounded during every bumpy air mile. One of the women who served was Captain Lillian Kinkela Keil, a member of the Air Force Nurse Corps and one of the most decorated women in the US military. Captain Kinkela flew over 200 air evacuations missions during World War II as well as 25 trans-Atlantic crossings. When the Korean conflict erupted she donned her uniform once more and flew several hundred more missions in Korea. She was the inspiration for the 1953 movie, *Flight Nurse* and served as a technical advisor to the film. Lillian's decorations include the European Theater of Operations with Four Battle Stars; The Air Medal with Three Oak Leaf Clusters; The American Campaign Medal; The United Defense Medal; and Presidential Citation, Republic of Korea.

VIETNAM WAR

Vietnam is a war that divided America. This was America's longest war on record, lasting eight years and five months (August 1964 January 1973). Wars have always forced soldiers to commit and witness terrible acts; to remember shooting someone and to see him die; to stick a bayonet in someone and see the blood gushing out and the man taking his last breath; to reach your objective only to see dead bodies all over the area, some still on fire with their flesh burning from the dropping of napalm bombs that preceded the attack.

The first Congressional Medal of Honor (CMH) awarded from the Vietnam War era was awarded to Captain Roger Donlon (retired as a Colonel). Donlon made the following remarks about military service: *"There is no doubt that the youth in America today would benefit from one or two years of national service. One of the biggest drawbacks of the military today is the concept of the all-volunteer force. It's just drawing from too small a segment of America and leaving out too much of our society."*

When you are being shot at, you start shooting back. It is either you or the person shooting at you. It is a matter of self-survival. But the wet jungle, the underground caves, the uncertainly of where the enemy was and when they would attack, proved to be very difficult for the American soldier in the Vietnam War. These were brave men who served in Vietnam.

The Vietnam War Memorial "The Wall" was dedicated to these brave men and women, in Washington, DC on November 22, 1982. One count lists 58,226 names on this wall of men killed in action. According to the records in the American War Library, the Vietnam War cost $111 billion. There were 153, 336 wounded in action.

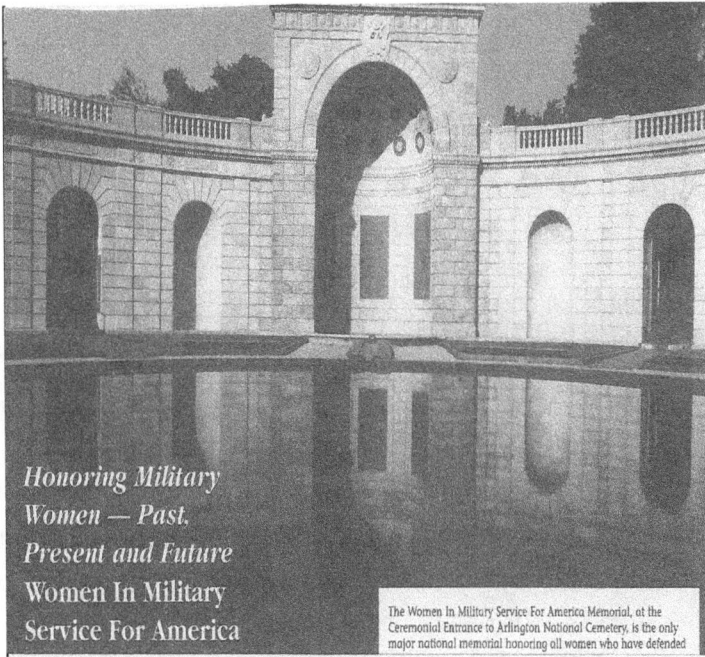

Honoring Military Women — Past, Present and Future Women In Military Service For America

The Women In Military Service For America Memorial, at the Ceremonial Entrance to Arlington National Cemetery, is the only major national memorial honoring all women who have defended

(Women's Memorial dedicated on October 18, 1997)

Women served in greater numbers during the Vietnam War than in any previous time in our history, yet there are inaccurate records provided of their importance. Women serving as WACs, Marines, Air Force served in impressive numbers. Records indicate that there were over 6,000 brave women from all branches of service who served in the medical field. They saved many lives with their skills, devotion to duty and personal sacrifices.

CHAPTER SIX

GLIDERS

This chapter is about one of the most interesting, yet most dangerous means of transporting troops to a combat zone ever used. Featured are James E. Bryant, Arthur J. Lee, pilots George Hess and Robert C. Moore, Jr. Bryant was a member of the 325th Glider Infantry Regiment during World War II. He participated in the Invasion of Normandy and Holland, landing in a Waco glider. Moore was a flight officer with the US Air Corps and a pilot on a Waco glider and a C-47 aircraft. He piloted a glider that made combat landings in Normandy, Holland and the Rhine. Lee, who

(Photo courtesy of R.C. Moore, Jr.-Waco CG-4A Glider) took his glider training in France, was a member of the 17th and 82nd airborne. He served in France and Germany. Hess, a glider pilot, made six landings in the Burma Theater. This is a brief history of gliders and the story about these men who survived. The American Waco CG-4A transport glider statistics are: wing span

83 feet-8 inches; length 48 feet- 33/4 inches; height 12 feet -7 ½ inches; and weight empty 3,790 pounds. The capacity is 16 men, or one jeep and 4 men; or one 75 mm howitzer and 3 men. The towing speed is 120 mph; gliding speed 75 mph.

Gliders, often referred to as "Flying Coffins," were developed and used in combat during World War II. "Flying Coffins" was an appropriate name for them because of the construction that allowed little or no protection for the troops. They were unarmed and unpowered aircraft, the only aircraft designed to make a crash landing. Gliders were made out of three-quarter inch plywood, usually pine, oak or mahogany, steel tubing and canvas.

Estimates of the number of glider pilots trained were between 6,000 and 6,500. Their silver wings resembled regular pilot's wings except a large "G" in the center. Instead of the "G" standing for glider, the proud pilots referred to it meaning GUTS. Just imagine that you were flying something, landing in enemy territory, looking for a field to land in, to make crash landing, yet knowing it was a one-way trip. Yes, it took guts and the glider pilots and men had plenty. After landing, the pilots picked up their M-1 rifle, or carbine, and then became fighting infantrymen.

The glider pilots and troops they carried into action have not received the attention or gratitude that they deserve. They sometimes were the first to land in a combat area. They made assaults from Sicily to Europe and the Far East. When paratroopers made a combat jump, they usually landed over a broad area, the gliders could deliver a lot of troops to a specific area, behind the enemy lines, ready to engage the enemy and secure important objectives. After midnight on June 5th, and before the Invasion of Normandy, which occurred at approximately 6:30 a.m., June 6, 1944, the United States launched 1,662 airplanes with over 800 C-47s, towing 512 gliders into Normandy. Most of the gliders used in this invasion were never used again.

In the beginning, the glider troops were not accepted by the paratroopers. There was plenty of friction between the two. Many men serving in glider units were transferred in and did not have a choice. At first, this was when the 82nd Division, an outstanding division served in World War I, was split into airborne and glider units. The reason for the jealously and friction between the two outfits was the fact that the airborne units had a special patch to wear on their hats and were paid $50.00 hazard pay extra each month. Those men serving in glider units believed going into combat in a "Flying Coffin" was just as hazardous as parachuting behind enemy lines and deserved equal benefits. This rule was changed in 1944 when the glider-men were authorized a special patch and $50.00 hazard pay.

America believed it necessary to develop and use gliders in combat situations because of a successful operation by the Germans. It was still dark on the morning of May 10, 1940 when Nazi Germany unleashed a secret weapon. The German secret weapon was the combat glider capable of landing in short, rough fields and delivering armed combat troops ready to fight. The treaty of Versailles (France) was signed on June 28, 1919. In that treaty, the German army was limited to 100,000 men but did not have a provision for an air force. Within a year, the Germans began to train sailplane and glider pilots.

German glider troops used 11 gliders holding only 78 combat troops in an assault and captured the Belgian fortress of Eben Emael. This fort, the key to the defense of Belgium's against German armored forces, controlled the approaches to the Mense River and Albert Canal. The Germans landed, placed demolition charges at strategic points, and disabled most of the Belgian guns and crews in the first few minutes of the assault. Within hours, the Germans had forced the surrender of the fort's 780-man garrison, at a cost to the glider troops of six dead and 20 wounded. The victory was made possible by the elements of surprise and audacity and the ability of the German glider pilots to silently land their loads within the fort.

Though Germany was the first World War II power to use gliders in combat, other countries, especially the US and Great Britain, hastened to catch up. Winston Churchill in England and General Hap Arnold in the US made the creation of airborne forces, parachute and glider, their personal spheres of influence and interest. In approximately two and one half years, the United States had designed a combat CG4A Glider, and had trained pilots. The pilots started training with sailplanes, small gliders, and small aircraft for a dead stick landing. The small aircraft had their engines removed.

Much has been written about the World War II paratrooper and rightly so. However, history has largely ignored the glider pilots and glider borne troops who constituted vital elements of our airborne divisions. Gliders delivered troops, weapons, equipment and supplies in the airborne assaults in *Sicily* (July 9 1943). This was the first allied airborne operation in World War II. Allied gliders took off that night from an airfield in *Tunisia*. The destination was Axis-held Sicily; their cargo, British airborne troops. In spite of the many difficulties encountered on a first mission of this nature, enough of the gliders got through to complete the mission successfully.

This is an account of one glider pilot on that mission. *"We cast off at 10:20 p.m. We faced flak on the island. The flak was getting thicker and their course took them over one of the anti-aircraft guns. Fortunately none of the flak hit my glider. As we crossed the shore line, I could see a glider bouncing on the shore to his right. The moon was covered by haze and their visibility was poor. They had cut at 2200 feet and now were at 1,000 feet just over the shore line. I could not make out the landing zone, so I had to glide straight ahead, hoping for the best. At 500 feet the pilot could distinguish certain fields; and I let down in a small field with trees in it. As we landed, we ran into a tree, but were fortunate to hit it with the wing stopping us abruptly. No one was injured on the landing."*

In February 1944 gliders carved another niche for themselves in *Burma.* The allies devised a plan to concentrate a force behind Japanese lines to cut enemy rail and river communications. There were no handy roads and the landing area was unprepared. Gliders were picked to fly certain troops, airborne engineers and equipment into the selected areas by night. Their job was to seize and prepare landing strips so that additional troops and equipment could be flown in by transport planes. Although only a limited number of gliders were used, the operations were successful and troops and cargo were poured into the rear of the enemy positions. Most of these missions were accomplished at night. The Japanese were completely surprised and the overall operation successful.

This is one pilot's memory of that landing. *"We were too high but no choice, so a violent slip got us into the edge of Broadway about 120 MPH, not much control here. I had been told to turn left and to be used as a hospital ship. We hit a log buried in the grass and tore off the left gear and swerved right into position to the left side of the field (sheer luck!)." "We buried some men the next day, one was a good friend."* (Lt. George Hess, a glider pilot who made six landings in Burma, story is in this chapter).

Moore shared this pilot's memory of his landing in Southern France. *"Then we came in over the landing zone. There was no mistaking it this time. Hollywood never made a scene like this. I was given a perfect tow over the center of the field at 500 feet. We had a bird's eye view of the burning planes, smashed gliders, collapsed parachutes, shell bursts, men running, dodging, dying. The whole panorama of war with our reinforcements being funneled into it, like circling down the cone of a tornado to the point of contact with the ground."*

On December 26, 27, 1944, *Bastogne,* Belgium was the next mission for the gliders. Military history has recorded the heroic efforts of American forces in this action at Bastogne. However, few historians give more than a casual mention of the part that gliders and glider pilots played in this important action. Flying their frail aircraft into a hail of enemy flak and ground fire, the glider pilots who participated in this battle carried to the besieged defenders badly needed ammunition and medical supplies that enabled them to hold out and secure the ultimate victory.

Gliders were used in *Germany* (March 24, 1945) crossing the Rhine. This aerial invasion of Germany at Wesel, on the Rhine River, was the final ETO glider mission. On that date some 1,348 American and British gliders crossed the river strongpoint and delivered the final, fatal blow to the Axis forces. Robert Moore, from Appomattox, Virginia, was one of the pilots making this important mission. Some of the pilots have shared their views of this landing. *"Several slugs go through the fabric of your glider sounding much like a dull drum beat, but no one is hit. Tensely, your eyes dart about as you look for a landing place, for high tension wires, and for other gliders. Now you are down to a 100 feet, and out of the corner of your eye you see a transmission tower, but no wires. Just ahead is a pasture with barbed wire fences and there are two gliders touching down. Ahead a glider rolls to a stop, disgorging troops on the run. Just past it is a burning glider with smoke and flames billowing into the air. Glancing to your right, you see a small woods and approaching it, two gliders on the ground, but rolling too fast. The first hits the trees, crumpling the nose and stopping abruptly. The big tail lifts up and then drops. The second glider pilot tries desperately to ground loop, but the right wing catches a tree and his glider is drawn into the woods also, with its parts flying all over. But you are concentrating on the approach and the landing. You flare, touch down, put it up on the skids, and quickly come to a stop. You have accomplished your primary mission. But while you are still moving, a rifle slug whined through the glider, and the airborne troops started scrambling out of the doors."*

Luzon in the Philippines (June 1945).The CG 4 as and a single CG 13 landed near Aparri in northern Luzon, carrying elements of the 11th Airborne Division. This was a first for gliders in the Pacific and the mission was successful.

One of the best kept secrets of World War II was the use of gliders to resupply the surrounded 101st Airborne Division at Bastogne, Belgium, December 26-27, 1944. One hundred CG-4A's, piloted by volunteers flew at low altitudes through murderous flak to bring vitally needed ammunition, fuel, food and an entire medical unit to the surrounded division. This airlift by gliders was credited by Major General Tony McAuliffe, the acting Division Commander, as allowing the 101st Airborne Division to hang on and beat back desperate German attempts to break through the heroic defenders. The glider pilots involved in this mission suffered a 35% casualty rate, one of the highest of World War II.

Each airborne division included one glider infantry regiment plus glider artillery, engineers, medics and other glider borne support troops. Original plans called for more glider infantry regiments but the large amount of ocean shipping needed to transport the crated gliders dictated more paratroopers and fewer glider units. The workhorse of the US gliders was the WACO CG-4A, called the Hadrian by the British Airborne. The CG-4A (Combat Glider-4A) was not lovely to look at, but the pilots said the Waco was delightful to fly.

The Waco glider cost varied with over 13,000 procured. They were crewed by two pilots, however many times they flew with only one pilot. The normal tow speed was 120 mph, with a maximum, 150 mph. The tow planes were the twin-engine C46 Commandos; or the C-47 Sky-train transports.

The crash program to create production gliders finally settled on a design submitted by the Waco Aircraft Company of Troy, Ohio. Production started in 1941 of the popular Waco CG-4As. By the end of World War II, more than 13,000 had been built by 16 different companies. Most of the Waco's were built in Kingsford, Mississippi in a Ford Motor Company plant. The fuselage was built of steel tubing. The wings were of wooden rib construction and were covered in plywood. The floor was a honeycombed plywood pattern. The aircraft was covered in cotton fabric. The front of the Waco would open up creating a 70" X 60" opening into the cargo area, allowing the men, jeep, or 75mm howitzer or whatever to be unloaded. About 12,400 models of the CG-4A went to the Army Air Force along with 940 more for British forces. Through a reverse Lend-Lease agreement, Army Air Force units in Britain received some 2,600 examples of the Airspeed MK-1 Horsa, a larger glider capable of carrying up to 30 combat troops or 7,120 pounds of cargo. The gliders were towed by a 300-foot nylon rope. A glider snatch was accomplished by a C-47 tow plane flying just above ground level with a hook trailing behind from a cable which played out from a revolving drum in its fuselage. The hook snagged a glider tow rope suspended between two vertical poles sweeping it airborne behind the tow plane from a dead standstill to 120 mph in a matter of seven seconds.

In training, when the glider was cut loose from the tow plane, very often the pilot would turn the nose of the glider in a vertical position, sometimes causing the soldiers to get sick and throw up. This was a new experience for the men who were in training. Many had come from farms and small towns and had never been in an aircraft of any kind. When airborne, there was no noise except the sound of wind. A person had to have a lot of faith or be just plain crazy to go into combat in a glider. These men were true heroes.

(The "Snatch." Photo courtesy of George Hess)

Collectively, these transports and gliders represented the heart of the Army Air Force and allied airlift and airborne assault forces. That they preformed effectively in every theater, under the harshest environments of arctic, cold and desert or tropical heat, attested to their sturdy design and perhaps even more to the efforts of the aircrews and ground personnel who kept them flying. One surviving glider pilot remembered a harrowing landing in Germany when a phosphorous shell set his fabric-covered wing afire. As he descended through haze into the battle zone, he suddenly saw power lines directly ahead, but was able to fly his glider underneath them and complete a safe landing.

The gliders actually contained over 70,000 parts. They were shipped in large crates to England where they were assembled by English workers. If you visit the Cornish Pump and Mining Museum located at Iron Mountain, MI, you can view a video on how the Waco was manufactured and you can view film of the huge crates that were used to load the disassembled glider onto trains, which then transported them to areas for shipment overseas. This was a slow procedure and slowed the urgent need for the gliders in Europe by our troops.

US MARINE CORPS GLIDER PROGRAM, WORLD WAR II

Generally speaking, outside of a very small number of World War II era Marines, few know of the fact that the US Marine Corps did embark on a program to integrate glider formations into their airborne capability. However, though the Marines did activate and train four Para-Marine battalions, three of which saw combat only in a ground role, the glider program never went beyond activation of a Glider Group, which was oriented exclusively to experimenting with gliders and training glider pilots.

The Marine Corps' interest in gliders was closely associated with its parachutist program. Both programs grew out of high-level interest in the successful German invasion of Crete in May 1941. Secretary of the Navy Knox was particularly impressed with this new facet of modern warfare and directed that the Marine Corps determine whether it held any promise as a tactic in amphibious operations. The Commandant of the Marine Corps, General Holcomb, had indicated in October 1940 that one battalion of each Marine regiment would be designated as "air troops" to be transported by aircraft. The glider idea offered economy over powered aircraft, and permitted the landing of forces on terrain unsuited for general flight operations. Once committed, the Marine Corps wasted no time in exploring all approaches to developing a viable glider force.

The navy had experimented with gliders at Pensacola Naval Air Station in 1933. The results indicated that gliders did not make any substantial contribution to flight training as long as sufficient numbers of powered aircraft were available. In July 1941 a decision was made to train officers and 100 noncommissioned officers as pilots and co-pilots during the fiscal year 1942 in the Marine Corps. However, it was recognized that the 150 required glider pilots could not be siphoned from existing resources.

Schools were available for training. One school, the Lewis School, located in the Chicago area, charged tuition of $775 per man plus $2.00 per day housing and mess charge for officers and $1.50 per day for noncommissioned officers. The Lewis school was capable of handling 20 students. Despite a variety of problems concerning equipment, training, and facilities, the Marine Corps were on record by October 1941 as favoring expanded development of a glider capability. The course included cross-country towing. By mid-March 1942, the one-and-two man gliders had been delivered and were in use.

During the summer of 1942, a number of studies were made, and inspection trips taken, to locate suitable sites for development of glider bases. Four sites were chosen. First was Eagle Mountain Lake, Texas, which became the main glider training base for the Marine Corps. A second was located at Edenton, North Carolina but was never used. A third location was at Shawnee, Oklahoma but was never used for gliders. A fourth site, at Addison Point, Florida, was selected but never developed.

By 1943, the glider program had became a lesser priority and it was ordered that no further steps be undertaken in the glider program until more pressing needs in the Pacific were met. It then became apparent to the senior Marine Corps planners that gliders were not suited to the Pacific war. In the aftermath of the Guadalcanal battle attention was focused on planning for other island campaigns, and it was recognized that gliders would be impractical except under the most favorable conditions. The Commandant therefore ordered the termination of the Marine Glider Program, effective June 24, 1943.

UNIT HISTORY-325TH GLIDER INFANTRY REGIMENT

The 82nd Airborne, stationed at Ft. Bragg, North Carolina, is called the All American Division. From this division the 325th

Glider Infantry Regiment was born. The 325th Regiment became an official division on August 25, 1917 at Camp Gordon, near Atlanta, Georgia. This was a division composed of draftees who were from the South. The patch, the Double A, is the same patch that they wear today. During World War I, the unit moved to Camp Upton, New York but a short time later found itself in Lettaure, France. Steel helmets and gas masks were issued, as well as Lewis light machine guns.

The Regiment had its first encounter with the deadly mustard gas used by the German barrage of explosive and chemical artillery. The American offensive in the Argonne Forest was their last major offensive. After ten days of battle, the Regiment was able to punch though the German lines.

During World War II, the 325th, a Glider Infantry Regiment was formed and given the task of arriving in a certain location but often would wind up scattered for miles on a drop zone. Gliders and their tow planes were slow, fat targets. They had no armor to protect the men inside. Landing in a glider was also an adventure that amounted to little more than a controlled crash. Ditches, wire, fences, tree stumps or a host of other possible ailments could flip, twist, or gut an unfortunate glider.

The Regiment arrived to its first battle, not by air, but by sea. They landed at Salerno from the island of Sicily to reinforce some 18 miles south of Salerno. The 2nd Battalion was to re-board the landing craft and was attached to Colonel William O. Darby's Ranger Task Force.

BURMA 1944

The story of GEORGE HESS, Glider Pilot

"Transporting the men out of the battle zone was critical to survival. A glider could arrive at an Army Hospital within two hours, but it took a jeep three months over land." **George Hess**

In 1942 the Allies withdrew their troops from Burma to India and China. The Japanese now occupied Burma. It was in the jungles of northern Burma where the Waco CG-4A earned its spurs. Plans were made to liberate Burma and reopen the ground route to China. British Major General Orde Wingate accepted this tremendous challenge. In 1943 Wingate formed a Brigade called the *Special Force or "Chindits"* to attack the Japanese. After the monsoon season, on February 4 1944, the Chindits ,which consisted of six brigades of British, Scottish Black Watch, Gurkha and West African troops, and totaled about 23,000 men under the command of Wingate, received its mission from Field Marshal William J. Slim. This was the second Allied invasion of northern Burma.

Wingate called the plan *"Operation Thursday."* His plan called for two infantry brigades (77th and 111th) to be airlifted, while the 16th would walk in from India. His plan required about 12,000 men and 1,800 mules. Operation Thursday was set to go on Sunday March 5, 1944. Strongholds to be established were "Broadway," "Piccadilly" and "Chowringhee." It was the 900th Airborne Engineer Aviation Company's job to land their equipment by gliders and prepare airstrips behind enemy lines. (The 900th made more landings than any other glider-borne unit).They were to take off at dusk, each transport towing two gliders and flying 200 miles into Burma. The gliders cut loose over Broadway and landed in the dark. Troops fanned out to hold off any Jap attackers. At dawn engineers started the airstrip for powered planes.

The 900th Airborne Engineer Aviation Company was activated on June 3, 1943 and trained at Westover Field, MA. They were formed to provide a force that could be delivered by glider or transport plane and was capable of building or repairing airstrips. They landed in India on August 10, 1943.

Wingate decided to send all 80 gliders to *Broadway*. Broadway was 250 miles and 3 ½ hours flying time from Lalaghat. Each C-47 towed two gliders all overloaded with at least 4,500 pounds. Each team had two bulldozers, one grader, one jeep, one carryall, and engineer hand tools. The bulldozers shot out of the gliders and turned over several times after the gliders crashed landed. The two pilots and their engineer "co-pilots" were not killed. In all, 35 gliders crash-landed on Broadway that night. All but three gliders were wrecked, about 30 men were injured and 23 men killed. Gliders reached the jungle clearing at one- to- two minute intervals, setting down into the Buffalo grass, plowing into teakwood log ruts, water Buffalo holes, tree stumps, rocks and small hills. This resulted in their ripping off their landing gear, tearing out sections of the fuselage, chopping off wings, and smashing the pilots' compartments.

One of these gliders carried Brigadier General Calvert. It was the high glide speed that saved the general's life. As the glider dropped out of the dark night's sky, the pilot leveled off prior to touch down, setting the wheels into what he expected to be a smooth and level surface. His co-pilot yelled, "Wreckage ahead!" and both violently pulled the control wheels full back, forcing the glider into the air, jumping over the wreckage, slamming back onto the ground. This was a great example of skill.

By the time the Japanese attacked Broadway, the airfield was protected by 2,500 Chindits troops, well dug in, heavily armed, and able to beat back the Japanese attack. With the help of the Chindits, the 3,600-foot airstrip was ready the next day. The 14th Brigade flew in and was given the mission of preventing Japanese reinforcements from moving against the 77th Brigade at "White City." The 77th Brigade moved southwest out of Broadway toward

Mawlu. They destroyed a Japanese railway engineer detachment at Henu on March 16th and established the "White City." The Chindits cleared a 400–yard-long glider strip, and five gliders landed on the evening of April 3rd.

Even airborne soldiers needed pack mules. In specially prepared bamboo stalls, six mules were carried one of the aircrafts, three in gliders. After practicing at the India base, the mules usually became accustomed to air travel. However, one mule did kick a hole in the side of a glider at 8,000 feet—highest mule kick ever recorded.

For many years **George Hess** flew sailplanes around and over the Blue Ridges and Mountains of Virginia. Flying sailplanes was a great sport that didn't require great strength, but it was a sport of skill, concentration and knowledge. Hess said, "There is nothing like flying along under the clouds gracefully and quietly. No motor just the air swishing over the wings and around the canopy. There is a spiritual quality as well. Alone and close to God with the earth spread out below.

The Bible speaks of soaring with eagles. In Virginia we had to settle for hawks. It wasn't unusual for a hawk to come join us if he thought our thermal was better than his. What a thrill when that happened.

Beautiful Motorless Flight

O, God who made the earth and skies
And all that in between them lies,
Help me to see much more
That as I turn and wheel and soar
I really need to understand
I'm held there by Your unseen hand.
Your awesome power lies all about
It's up to me to seek it out.
So, as it puts me to the test,
I concentrate and do my best
To use it in the cleanest way
That I may much the longer stay
Suspended there in graceful flight,
And gain a little more in height.
And so, it is with life indeed,
That when we find we have a need
To rise above our earthy ways
We take the wings of prayer and praise
And use the power that You supply
To rise above and soar on high.

Dedicated To:

All World War II
Glider Pilots
and
Sailplane Pilots
Everywhere

By:

George D. Hess, World War II Glider Pilot
1st Air Commando Group
C. B. I. Asansol, India
Charter Member - Blue Ridge Soaring Society
Salem, Virginia

Because of the pure enjoyment and the spiritual blessing, I have written a poem dedicated to all World War II glider pilots and sailplane pilots everywhere."

During World War II, a young George Hess was one of 6,000; only 200 pilots flew into the enemy skies of Burma to deliver supplies and men. Hess was a member of the first Air Commando Group of the Army Air Corps until 1945. Now 85–years-old, he lives in Aurora, Ill. with his wife of 60 years, Linda, and their daughter and son-in law. Both George and Linda are retired from General Electric. George frequently wears his pin that bears the letter "G," issued to glider pilots.

During World War II, in just five minutes, the Army could train men during their time in the infantry to get into massive steel-structured planes. Paratroopers required much more training. And if they jumped at nighttime they often were separated, whereas if the group went in on a glider, "You put 'em in right away and go," according to the way George explained it.

Hap Arnold, who was the five-star general in charge of the Army Air Force, had a goal of training 15,000 glider pilots. Due to the lack of pilots, communities were authorized by Congress to train civilians to become pilots. George received his 30 hours of training in his home town, Marshall, MN. He immediately was taken into active duty. During his training, which began in 1942, his wife was working, making $15 a week. All George got out of his training for three months was breakfast. He trained in a 65-horsepower plane.

It was one thing to land a glider within enemy territory; it was quite another to get it out. To this day, the glider pilots who flew in Burma are known for the effective use of the glider technique called the snatch. Transport the men out of the battle zone was critical to survival. Those who were injured in combat were fortunate to be part of a glider's "cargo." Morale had to be kept high as soldiers fell in combat. A glider could arrive at an Army hospital within two hours, but it could take an Army jeep three months to make the same journey over the uneven roads.

Hess's active duty began in April of 1942. He was 25 years old but knew he would have to go. So instead of waiting, he volunteered. The temper of the country at that time was, "Hey, let's go get this over with." The attitudes and drive of these soldiers were characterized by a hunger to succeed and defeat the enemy. Hess spent eighteen months flying glider planes. He flew in seven combat missions and co-piloted C-47 tow planes. Hess served as a Staff Sergeant, Flight Officer and First Lieutenant in the Army Air Force.

Hess said, "I can't say I really got homesick. Sure, you wanted to be home, but essentially it wasn't like Vietnam. In Vietnam, you go and stay for a year then come home. This was a big mistake. We went to stay until the job was done. We wanted to get it over with, so we'd go home and stay home."

Hess closes his eyes as he remembers, with great detail, the days when he was stranded "in the boonies" near Calcutta. He and his co-pilot, Jack Keiser, had lost the plane's tow rope and the plane could not complete its mission. It was three days before the US Army Air Force found the men in the field. However, it took only a few short hours before the local natives discovered the foreign giant in their backyard. The natives returned the lost tow rope to the pilots and were awestruck by the enormous structure that lay before them. Worried that the onlookers would damage their craft, the two pilots used the rope as a boundary line for the onlookers. Over the course of ten days, between five and ten thousand natives came to gaze at the plane. George and Jack made a game of it by allowing only four to five people to go up and touch the glider at a time. If the onlookers crossed the rope line before it was their turn, the two pilots would playfully strike their bare feet. The natives found this funny and laughed along with them.

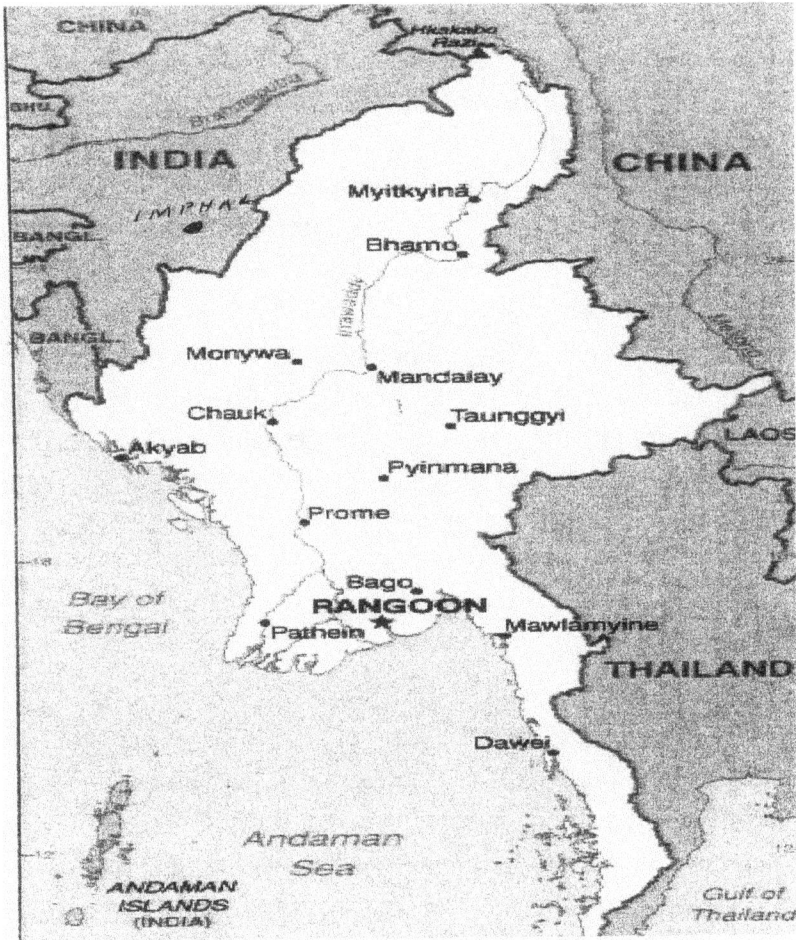

(Photo courtesy of George Hess)

Another experience that Hess shared was when he went to a port city in Eastern India to pick up a British anti-aircraft crew. Flying over any port city was a real adventure as the air was always full of vultures. Their destination was in Burma, north of Miktela. They were going to an airfield in the process of being built but not yet complete enough for powered cargo planes to land. This was another opportunity for a glider operation. They picked up the anti-aircraft crew of ten or 12 men, and after a 2 ½ hour flight landed them safely at their destination. When the troops were getting out of the glider, they heard a big hue and cry among the troops. A convoy was coming into the camp and that convoy was another British anti-aircraft crew. This crew had left the same port city to come by ground transport to join their British passengers. Hess said the kicker was that they had started three months earlier. It took the ground troops three months; the Glider transport, 2 ½ hours.

Even to this day, Hess remembers the cultural differences between what was familiar to him in America and what he witnessed through the natives. He remembers the lack of medicines, the need for sterilization of medical supplies and drinking water, the images of young teenage girls breastfeeding their babies, and frail bodies wasting away in the heat. Every day they were brought boiling water to drink by a native who knew a little English.

Living in a rustic area had their effects on the soldiers. George said, "There was one time when we were out for six weeks without any facilities; no place to write, no mess hall, no tents, no nothing. We lived mostly on canned sardines. As you sat under the Burmese sun in the hothouse canopy of the glider, the sweat really poured out of you. This was also compounded by the anticipation of the actual snatch. While you sat waiting you could hear the tow plane coming closer and closer, literally flying right up your back. We were loaded with walking wounded and two stretcher cases. They were mostly big black men from Africa. All the English they knew was 'gotta cigarette'?"

So the tow plane is flying up your back and finally he flashes by your right wing tip with his tail wheel running on the ground. "Please Lord, don't let his props hit," Hess said. Of course, he runs right through the loop and the stands knocking them to the ground. So you set them back up and go though the whole process again until he gets it right. You kept your cool as best you could because that's all you have to get you back safe and sound.

Hess said that you questioned some of the tow plane pilot's ability to complete the snatch properly. One of the C-47 pilots was Buddy Lewis who had been a fielder for the old US Senators baseball team in Washington, DC. Hess said that this guy was good and very considerate of the glider pilots who he was towing. Hess said, "As far as I know, he never missed a snatch." This was difficult to do. If the pilot came in too high, he missed altogether. If he came in to low, he would knock down the loop before the hook arrived.

In Burma, the air commando groups were furnishing air power transport and fighter and bomber power to the British ground troops. As the British were pushing South many Japanese troops were separated from their outfits and were living in the mountains, usually without food. They would wear Burmese clothes and try to assimilate into the Burmese population.

Yet another emotional World War II moment from Hess's experience came while working in conjunction with British troops. He related once while they were waiting to get their glider pushed back for their snatch, they saw two Japanese in Burmese clothes being interrogated. The British presumed them to be spies who were trying to assimilate into the Burmese culture. They could see the sweat pouring off the prisoners. As they watched, they could see why. The British were using many African troops in Burma. An especially large and muscular black man was walking around the Japanese as they were being questioned. He was carrying a big knife and kept testing the sharpness with his thumb as he shinned a big sneer at the Japanese. Hess said, "I have never forgotten the fear that radiated out from the Japanese. War is hell for sure." He never found out what happened to the Japanese prisoners but believed that the British killed them for being spies.

Hess said, "*We were pushing the Japanese out of Burma in the spring and summer of 1945. The Japs were vacating an airfield north of Rangoon which we wanted to use. In the process of vacating they blew many big holes in the runways. Our C-47s couldn't use the field so we had to take in bulldozers and scrapers with our gliders. As it so often happened there weren't enough glider pilots available. So they would assign anybody they could find to fly the right seat. Well, I got a corporal who had never been in a CG-4A. It was a fairly long flight so the corporal's main job was to keep me awake.*"

When Hess's glider was "cut off" he discovered that the stall speed was high and there would be no slow landing and it wouldn't be long until they were on the ground. Once they had landed, the glider didn't want to stop rolling. The delivery of their cargo was successful. This was George Hess's last flight of in a CG-4A. He said, "To some extent I was sorry it was over."

The day that Japan surrendered, Hess boarded a plane for the good old USA. He took a plane to India and then boarded a ship. It was a crisp October morning when he arrived in New York City. He said, "We were on that dumb ship 30 days, nothing but steel." When they entered the harbor they went past the Statue of Liberty and the New York skyline. Three women were singing "Sentimental Journey." He said he has never forgotten that. He has even written some different words and wants them sung at his funeral. A sentimental journey (pointing a finger up to heaven) is where he said he is going with a gentle smile and a small tear in his eye. As with most World War II veterans, very few of Hess's war buddies are alive today. He still keeps in touch with several of his wartime buddies including Jack Shipman, who lives in Oregon; and Tim Bailey from Iowa. He met a young man, Lawry, in Burma who he remembers, and believes that Lawry died while on a mission.

After the war, George Hess continued to fly gliders in the scenic mountainous areas of Roanoke, Virginia. Often these momentous flights inspired him to write poetry about the peacefulness he felt while flying recreationally compared with the stress of a combat mission. In 1965 George was caught in a rainstorm. He became disoriented, making it difficult for him to judge where the mountains were. He crashed into a mountain, destroying his plane. He spent three weeks in the hospital from the injuries that he received in the crash, but continued to fly after his recovery. It is difficult for George to fly alone today because of his age. It is difficult for him to get in and out of the plane now.

The glider pilots of World War II are a dying breed. There will be no future generations of American military glider pilots. The Defense Department ended the military glider pilot program in 1952. But the special purposes that World War II gliders accomplished in battle, and the extraordinary men who flew them, should not be forgotten. With men like George Hess, "the 'G' stands for GUTS. Hess is a true American hero.

NORMANDY

"Glider landings casualties were 497, with 61 killed, 422 wounded and 19 missing. Normandy proved to be the Divisions toughest campaign. The Airborne had heavy losses too." **Jim Bryant**

This story continues about **JAMES E. BRYANT**, a survivor of major battles in Europe during World War II and seven battles in the Korean War. James was born in Southampton County, VA in 1924 and was a member of the 325th Glider Infantry Regiment during World War II. He retired from the US Army in 1966 as a Command Sergeant Major. Bryant is the author of a book entitled, *Flying Coffins Over Europe*. [Published in 2003 by H.E. Howard, Inc., Appomattox, Virginia.] James Bryant gave the author permission to use material and quotes from his book in writing about his personal experiences. Bryant lives at Daleville, Virginia. He is a volunteer at the National D-Day Memorial.

To go into combat as glider-men took unusual courage. Walter Cronkite, a United Press correspondent at that time, landed with the 101st Airborne in a Glider during *"Operation Market-Garden."* Cronkite said this about the gliders, *"I thought the wheels of the glider were for landing. Imagine my surprise when we skidded along the ground and the wheels came up through the floor. I got another shock. Our helmets, which we all swore were hooked, came flying off on impact and seemed more dangerous than the incoming shells. After landing I grabbed the first helmet I saw and my trusty musette bag with the Olivetti typewriter inside and began crawling toward the canal which was the rendezvous point. When I looked back, I found a half dozen guys crawling after me. It seems I had grabbed the wrong helmet. The one I wore had two neat strips down the back indicating that I was a lieutenant."* Cronkite also said, **"If you have to go to war, don't go in a glider."**

Though the code name for the Normandy Invasion was "OVERLORD," the Code name for the Navy operation was "NEPTUNE," and the code name for the airborne assault was "TONGA" the code name for the Gliders was "MALLARD.

There will never be an exact count of those killed on D-Day. Countless died in water and never seen again. Many were killed in remote sunken lanes and hedgerows and discovered days later. Many were blown to bits. Who knows when or what day these men killed on? General Omar Bradley said that *"every man who landed on the beaches today were heroes."* Soldiers were cited for their heroic actions. Three Congressional Medals of Honor and 153 Distinguished Service Crosses were awarded to men who landed on Omaha Beach. One Congressional Medal of Honor and 61 Distinguished Service Crosses were awarded to soldiers who landed on Utah Beach.

The British, members of the 180th Airborne Infantry and Engineers were the first to land in Normandy. Their gliders were released at 6,000 feet, about three miles from the target. The lead glider was piloted by Sgt. James Wallwork, and it carried Major John Howard and 29 men. Only 150 men could muster for the attack on the guns at Merville. The British divided these men into four groups. Each German gun had 200 soldiers. Though the British action was successful, they suffered 50% casualties.

The British were instructed to notify their headquarters in England after the guns at Merville had been captured. The method that they used was by *"The Duke of Normandy."* The Duke happened to be a carrier pigeon. On June 1st, the pigeon was put into a medal box. On June 6th, he was transferred into another box and placed on the chest of a British paratrooper. You can imagine the confusion that was visited upon the poor pigeon by the flight, the sound of gunfire and the fact that the paratrooper landed on his chest and dented the pigeon's carrying box. Nonetheless, after the mission was completed, a message was attached to the Duke of Normandy to fly back across the channel to England. The flight took 26 hours and 50 minutes. Someone asked why it took so long. One British soldier remarked that the Duke probably took the scenic route to look over Berlin before returning to England. The

Duke of Normandy was awarded the "Dickin" Medal for its action. Two dogs were also parachuted into Normandy. One dog named Bing, landed in the top of a tree. Dogs were used because they could hear convoys, tanks, or gunfire before the soldiers. Bing also was awarded the Dickin Medal.

The Normandy Invasion was successful for the United States and her Allies despite the heavy losses and unplanned problems that occurred. A good example of this was the loss of tanks. There were 29 DD Tanks mounted on special floatation devices. These tanks were vital for the troop advancement on the beach. 22 of these tanks sunk, five were destroyed by the Germans, leaving only two made it to the beach.

James Bryant was still in high school when the attack on Pearl Harbor occurred. He and his classmates were too young to enlist although some indicated they wanted to. He became 18 years old on December 24, 1941 and was required to register for the draft. In February 1943 he received his induction notice and reported for duty on March 13, 1943. Jim's first station was Ft. Lee, Virginia. A short time later he was sent to Camp Butner, North Carolina. His first pay check was $17.00. The pay for a private was $30.00 a month. Maneuvers were held in South Carolina, and then he went to Tennessee for further training. He was assigned at this time to the 81mm Mortar Platoon. After relocating at Fort Pickett, Virginia, James shipped out to an unknown destination. Toward the end of April 1944, they sailed from Boston on the troop ship *John Erickson,* a former Swedish passenger ship. The trip lasted ten or 11 days. The weather was beautiful, which gave them wonderful views of both the English and Irish coasts.

When they arrived in England, a British military band welcomed the Americans. The next morning, interviews were conducted by the 82nd Airborne Division looking for glider-men. Jim had never heard of glider troops but found the assignment interesting. Later that day, he was assigned to the 325th Glider

Infantry Regiment. They were stationed outside of the city of Leicester (pronounced "Lester"), which was about two hours from London by train. The troops were housed in six-man pyramidal tents with outside latrines. The first priority was to take glider training. They trained with both the US CG4 (WACO) glider as well as the British Horsa Glider (AS51). Both gliders were towed by C47 aircraft.

Bryant described the gliders in his book. *"The CG4A glider was constructed of tubular steel with canvas covering and a plywood floor. It had been designed by Frances A. Archer of Weaver Aircraft Corporation (WACO) for the Army Air Forces. It could carry up to 15 fully equipped troops in addition to the pilot and co-pilot. It could carry a jeep, a jeep trailer, a small bulldozer and a short barrel 105mm howitzer. It could land on wheels or skis (if it had both), and the nose lifted for loading and unloading. Nearly 14,000 CG 4As would be built. Only four remain today with one at The Silent Wings Museum near Dallas, Texas; one at the 101st Airborne Division Museum at Fort Campbell, Kentucky; one at the USAF Museum at Wright Patterson Air Force Base, Ohio. The 4th Glider was assembled for the movie "The Longest Day."* This glider can be found at the Airborne Museum in St. Mere Eglise, France.

"The AS51 Horsa glider was constructed of plywood and had a tricycle landing gear. It could carry up to 36 fully equipped troops or two jeeps or a jeep and trailer. Loading was done through a side door or in some cases the nose lifted. The Horsa had a reputation for splintering during crash landings thereby carrying the name "Flying Coffins." One could literally get stabbed to death when a Horsa crashed. While the CG4A was preferred by American glider-men, the use of the Horsa in Normandy would far exceed the CG4A, probably because it had a larger carrying capacity. The CG4A while much smaller than the Horsa was more efficient and could take more punishment than the Horsa."

During the Normandy Invasion 520 Horsa and 347 Waco Gliders were used. The British, taking off approximately 10:30 p.m. on June 5th, used 733 planes and 355 gliders. The United States took off 90 minutes later, using 1662 planes towing 512 gliders.

The troops would catch one of the British double deck- buses into Leicester. There were pubs, dances, concerts for the British and American soldiers. It was in Leicester that Bryant first heard the paratroopers refer to glider-men as "Hermans." They would flap their arms when they saw the glider-men and taunt: "Look Herman—no motor."

By the end of May, Bryant's outfit was ordered to pack. They arrived at an air base and were "sealed," which meant they could not leave the base and all movements were supervised. Next came the briefing. The invasion of France would start on June 5th. The 82nd Airborne was to land east and south of the town of St Mere Eglise, some miles inland from Utah Beach. They were to seize the town which was a major communication center. The invasion was delayed one day because of the weather conditions.

With several briefings completed, the troops were issued ammunition, grenades of all kinds, several days of K rations plus a D ration, and a first aid kit which contained two morphine syringes. They were also issued a "cricket" used to identify the American soldiers from the Germans. On June 7, 1944, D-Day + 1 of the Normandy Invasion, Bryant's unit, the 325th Glider Infantry Regiment landed by glider and participated in the invasion of France. On June 9th, PFC Charles N. Deglopper from Bryant's unit was awarded the Medal of Honor for single-handedly defending his platoon's position. This would be the largest use of glider infantrymen up to that time. The code name for the 325th was "Hackensack." It consisted of 20 Waco and 30 Horsa gliders which carried 968 men of the 2nd and 3rd battalions into Normandy. Each glider's wings were painted with three white and two black strips as were all allied planes, trucks and jeeps. This was to keep from our troops shooting them down.

Bryant said "the night of June 6th, we slept by our assigned gliders. At 2 a.m., we ate a large breakfast of fresh eggs, ham, bacon and home fries." Certain fields were chosen for the gliders to land in. Rommel, of course had thought and planned for this. In some of the fields he had put poles painted green, held together by wire to cause the gliders to crash. These poles were called *"Rommel's Asparagus."* Some of the fields were flooded, so that when the paratroopers landed, many would drown. The 325th took off at 6:30 a.m., landing in Normandy about two hours later.

Bryant said that the C-47 airplane started down the runway. The tow rope slowly began to move and was fully extended in short order. In an instant, they were airborne with a P- 47 fighter plane as an escort. Their flight took them over Utah Beach. It was now time to prepare for their landing. Check your seatbelts. The pilot now was required to release the tow rope from the airplane. They could see the gliders in the field below that had landed the day before. A total of 16 Horsa and four Waco's, were destroyed during this mission, with 17 killed and 69 wounded or injured.

Bryant's battalion was temporarily attached to the 505th Parachute Infantry Regiment. They immediately took up defensive positions and dug foxholes along the hedgerows. It was here that Bryant saw his first dead trooper. Not much happened that night except occasional mortar and artillery fire. The next morning was different. Bryant's unit's mission was to capture a bridge over the Merderet River. The Germans were ready and waiting for their attack. Although small arms, mortars and artillery were used by the Germans, their machine guns caused the most problems. Bryant lost another foxhole buddy. He was hit in the chest with shrapnel causing blood to gush out. Jim went on to write, *"Some men simply could not accept the sight of death, mutilated bodies and bloodshed associated with war. Their minds would snap, becoming casualties as surely as the wounded. It was called 'battle fatigue."*

The La Poterie action was the 325th last major operation in Normandy. The unit was relieved by the 90th Infantry Division and returned to England. Here the glider-men received some good news. General Ridgeway had obtained through the War Department permission for the glider-men to receive $50.00 for enlisted men and $100.00 for officers, the same as the paratroopers received. They also were issued a special patch for their hats. Ridgeway was promoted to Commanding General, XVIII Corps (Airborne). James M. Gavin, at age 37, became the youngest Major General and Division Commander of World War II. For the division's action in the Normandy Campaign, General Eisenhower awarded the division the Presidential Unit Citation. The division would also be awarded the French Fourragere twice by the French Government.

Bryant said, "Normandy proved to be the division's toughest campaign." It sustained nearly 5,000 casualties. In this total, the 325th lost 280 killed and 714 wounded, injured or captured. There were approximately 272 parachute landing casualties with 36 drowned, 63 injured and abandoned to the enemy, and another 173 injured who were evacuated to friendly lines. Glider landing casualties were 497 with 61 killed, 422 injured and 14 missing.

One of the glider pilots recalled his experience in the Normandy landing. *"We had dropped down to about 100 feet as we crossed the beach and had climbed to between 400 and 500 feet over our "landing zone" (really no landing zone as it was up to us to pick any field we could get into). The damn trees were about 50 feet tall (as in all the hedgerows) and I was about five feet too low to clear them. A tall limb hit my left wing about the same time as my undercarriage snagged the tops of the trees. The left wing, catching as it did, pulled us in a turn of 90 degrees and we stopped at the base of the trees with the left wing still tangled and the tail section twisted upside down. Not one of us got a scratch."*

Another pilot wrote, *"When I was given the green light, I could see two gliders ablaze on the ground and others that had cracked up. No suitable LZ's were visible to my left or right. I picked a half plowed field half the size of a football field. Upon landing, my glider lost part of its right wing and I received damage to the nose section."*

OPERATION "MARKET-GARDEN"

The next glider assault for the 325th was during Operation *"Market-Garden."* Market was the code name for the airborne action. Garden was the code name for the ground troops. The First Allied Airborne Corps was set up in August 1944. This was their first mission. It consisted of the American 18th Corps (82nd and 101st Airborne Divisions) and the British 1st Airborne Division. Later the Polish 1st Parachute Brigade was added. The US IX Troop Carrier Command dispatched 1,899 gliders and the RAF some 697 Horsa in the largest single glider operation of World War II. The landings were successful. Some accidents happened. Two Hamilcar gliders nosed over on the landing zone, which meant the loss of two 17-pounder anti-tank guns. Some of the Horsa gliders collided with each other.

D-Day for Operation Market-Garden was September 17, 1944. The operation officially ended on September 26, 1944, D-Day plus 8 days. The withdrawal of the 1st British Airborne Division and a few Poles had reached the perimeter continued until Tuesday morning. For the British soldiers, Arnhem was a second Dunkirk. Arnhem was the main target of Operation Market-Garden because it was a good place from which the Ruhr could be assaulted. Also the Ruhr out of Arnhem would bypass the Siegfried Line.

Casualties were even higher than the British had suffered on D-Day, the invasion of Normandy.

Why did Market-Garden fail? This operation was a failure for several reasons: Allied radio communications failed, bad weather intervened, and intelligence data were flawed. The 2nd SS Panzer Corps had been discovered in photographs in Arnhem but the British ignored the report. Perhaps the most important reason for failure was the planning. It was on such a tight schedule that it was impossible to achieve. It is suggested that an operation should plan to achieve 25% of its objective. With Market-Garden, 75% had to be accomplished on schedule or it was doomed for failure. Market-Garden wasn't a complete failure however. The corridor helped the Allies to eventually liberate the southern part of the Netherlands.

With all the failures, Montgomery still called Market-Garden 90% successful and said, *"In my prejudiced view, if the operation had been properly backed from its inception, and given the aircraft, ground forces, and administrative resources necessary for the job, it would have been succeeded in spite of my mistakes, or the adverse weather, or the presence of the 2nd SS Panzer Corps in the Arnhem area. I remain Market-Garden's unrepentant advocate."*

Jim Bryant and the 325th Glider Infantry Regiment were an important part of the Market-Garden operation. The 325th landed among German positions. This glider attack turned the tide of the battle. After Normandy the unit continued to train in England to prepare for their next mission. Replacements came into the unit to replace those men lost. Lost or damaged equipment had to be replaced. The men of the 325th had to be combat- ready and on call. This call came sometime in late August. The mission was secret. During the briefing the following day, Bryant learned that the division was to land south of Brussels, Belgium to cut off the Germans who were retreating. British forces had overrun the landing areas and the mission was called off. The men didn't have any regrets.

About two weeks later, in early September, Bryant's division was put on alert again. Again they were "sealed." The division was part of a three-division airborne force and would land in the vicinity of Nijmegan (pronounced "Nee-magan"). Their objective was to seize two major bridges; the bridge at Nijmegan over the Maas River and the bridge at Grave, over the Waal River. The 101st Airborne would land in the vicinity of Eindhoven; the British 1st Airborne Division, with the Polish Airborne Brigade, would land near Arnhem to seize the bridge over the Rhine.

Picture of Glidermen killed when glider crashed landed.
(Photo courtesy of Jim Bryant)

The purpose of this operation, if successful, was to end the war in Europe. This was the brainchild of Field Marshal Montgomery. The 325th would use only the CG4A gliders. Their landing would be near the Dutch-German border. Some of the gliders landed in German territory. Their takeoff was delayed because of heavy fog. The fog lifted on September 23rd for them to become airborne in the afternoon.

They carried about 3,500 men, jeeps and guns. Because of heavy anti-aircraft fire, several gliders had to land prematurely. About 350 gliders arrived at Overasselt. The 325th Glider Infantry immediately headed for Groesbeck's woods to support the troops there. Bryant was a co-pilot on this mission, which gave him a bird's eye view. In the event of an emergency, the pilot gave Jim about a 30 minute crash course on how to land the glider. There was not any ground fire as they landed. His company relieved a company from the 505th PIR (parachute infantry regiment) and used the foxholes they had occupied. In the morning if anyone exposed any part of his body, a German sniper would take a shot at him. One trooper near Bryant's foxhole had half of his head shot off. The body wasn't recovered for several days. Food was scarce. The K rations they brought from England were gone. After a couple of days without food, they received some rations from the British. Bryant and buddy got a can of strawberry jam–nothing else. Another guy got crackers, so they shared.

Bryant's company began their attack following heavy artillery and mortar barrage. After a short time, they became pinned down and had to dig in for the night. Jim and his buddy were ordered to go ahead of their unit about 100 yards to set up a listing post. About 1:30 a.m., he heard noises coming from a German patrol. Five men went by them within 20-25 feet, too close to use their telephone. A few minutes later he heard shots from his lines. Eventually the patrol was eliminated.

In October, Bryant's company was relieved from their positions at Kieberg so they could prepare for their attack across the Mook Plain. The regiment suffered more casualties during the Mook operation than any other attack in Holland. After Mook, the regiment took up defensive positions and remained there until relieved by the Canadians in November. It was during this time that Bryant lost another buddy with whom he had shared a foxhole with. They had flipped a coin to see who would take a shower first.

His buddy won the toss but didn't return. He had been killed by a mortar barrage on his way back. During the Mook operation, Bryant discovered that a K ration in his right pants pocket had been split in to by a German bullet without injuring him. This was indeed a miracle. Because the Allies failed to occupy the area north of Nijmegan until spring, the Dutch suffered through the worst winter of the war and the worst in their history.

Bryant writes, *"In the final analysis, Operation Market-Garden was a complete failure. The British XXX Corps which was responsible to link up with the airborne forces simply moved too slowly, resulting in the complete annihilation of the British and Polish airborne forces at Arnhem. The taking of the major bridge at Arnhem was pivotal to the mission's success. The successes of the 82nd and 101st went for naught. The British also failed to heed intelligence reports that two German divisions were re-outfitting in the area. Additionally, the British commander was inexperienced in airborne operations and had only been recently assigned. Their main error was landing too far from the objective plus they lost vital communications equipment during the landings. On the other hand, it would have been a great Allied victory had it worked."* In the summer of 1945, Bryant's division was awarded the Dutch Orange Lanyard by the Netherlands government. It was the first time this award was given to a foreign unit.

THE BATTLE OF THE BULGE

(December 1944-February 1945)

During the Battle of the Bulge, the 325th dug in around the crossroads at Baraque de Fraiture and held. During the intense fight in December 1944, the 325th decimated two German divisions. On December 17, the commanders were told that the Germans had broken through Allied lines, and were rolling westward across Luxembourg and Belgium. This was the largest land battle of World War II. A total of 19,000 American soldiers were killed and about 61,000 were wounded. The fighting also claimed 120,000 German lives.

On December 24, 1944 during the Battle of the Bulge a funny incident occurred. An entire US armored division was retreating from the Germans in the Ardennes forest when a sergeant in a tank destroyer spotted an American digging a foxhole. The GI was Pfc. Vernon Haught, 325th Glider Infantry Regiment. He looked up and asked, "Are you looking for a safe place?" "Yeah," answered the tanker. "Well, buddy," he drawled, "just pull your vehicle behind me. I'm the 82nd Airborne, and this is as far as the bastards are going."(P 64-Flying Coffins over Europe)

Following the battle in Holland, the Canadians relieved the 325th on November 13, 1944. After an 18-mile march and boarding trucks to an unknown destination, the unit arrived at a French military base outside the village of Sissonne in northern France. Some of the men received three- day passes to Paris and Rheims. This proved to be a serious problem for the MPs because the 101st Airborne was stationed in Rheims. The 82nd Airborne and the 101st Airborne had barroom brawls every night. It is safe to say that there was not only competition between the two divisions, but there was no love lost between them either.

During the various wars, the USO provided entertainment for the troops. While waiting for their new assignment, Hollywood stars, Ingrid Bergman and Marlene Dietrich visited the troops.

Around midnight, on December 17th, Bryant's unit was alerted for another mission. As always rations and ammo were issued. At this time they did not know where they were going or what the mission was. It was Bastogne but they were ordered to the vicinity of Webermont. The 101st Airborne was given the Bastogne assignment. The 325th was assigned the duty to counter the offensive of the Germans which later was known as "The Bulge."

As in Korea, the weather at The Bulge proved to be a serious problem. The snow, fog, and freezing temperatures made it difficult for the men. Their clothing was inadequate as well. They were not issued sleeping bags.

Combat medics were well trained men who helped to save many lives of wounded soldiers. They were brave men who through the most difficult situations would leave the safety of their foxholes, run through heavy fire to care for someone who had been wounded. Here at the Crossroads, the first man to be wounded was Bryant's medic. He was hit with shrapnel in his back. After some treatment, the medic was taken by jeep back to an aid station. Bryant didn't know if he survived which is often the case when a buddy is wounded. The Crossroads was important point because two major highways converged there. After the attack started, General Gavin attempted to reach the Crossroads but was unable to make it because of the heavy German attack with mortar and machine guns that afternoon.

The German attacks continued into the night. Bryant and his company had used almost all of their ammunition. A new supply of small arms ammunition, grenades, 60 mm mortar shells, and bazooka rounds had been delivered by battalion supply. Bryant was ordered to find a jeep, pick up and deliver the ammunition to where the troops were located. He followed his company commander's orders but did so under a constant mortar and artillery barrage by the Germans. On perhaps their last trip of picking up the ammunition, Bryant and the jeep driver experienced enemy fire from close range. The jeep driver was killed. Bryant rolled out of the jeep on the opposite side where the machine-gun and rifle fire were coming from. His helper had remained in the jeep. Bryant told him to stay put. Evidently his helper was unable to hear Bryant's warning. As the helper attempted to get out of the jeep, a German bullet killed him instantly.

Bryant tried to crawl back to friendly lines but that didn't work. His own soldiers started shooting at him, thinking he was a German soldier trying to break through their lines. Now what to do? He was between the Germans and the American lines, both shooting at him. He realized that he was very cold and needed to move, so he decided to crawl past the Germans into the woods. Hearing noises believed to be German soldiers, Bryant covered his body with leaves and debris to camouflage his body beside a log. A German patrol was scouting the area when two of them stepped over the log where Bryant was hiding. After the patrol was out of sight he began moving through the woods again, but in the opposite direction from his unit at the crossroads. He ended up with the 3rd Armored Division at Manhay, a few miles from the crossroads. Bryant said of this experience; "I never dwelled on my narrow escape. But now, when I think back, it was possibly the most important few hours of my life. I am positive my survival was due to Divine Intervention. At age 19, all my decisions, which were many, proved to be correct." For this action during heavy enemy fire, Bryant was recommended by his company commander for the Silver Star. In his modesty, Bryant said, *"It was a great honor, of course, but I didn't feel then, and don't now, that my contributions were any greater than many others. Apparently, the Company Commander thought otherwise."*

SILVER STAR ORDER

"James E. Bryant 33628181, First Sergeant (then Private First Class), 325th Glider Infantry. For gallantry in action 24 December 1944 near BELGIUM when his company ran low on ammunition while defending a vital crossroads, First Sergeant Bryant went back for a resupply over the single open road. An enemy machine gun commanding this road opened fire on the jeep, killing the driver and one occupant. First Sergeant BRYANT secured as much ammunition as he could carry and returned to the surrounded

company then led a patrol which forced the enemy machine gun to withdraw. The courage, initiative and devotion to duty exemplified the conduct of First Sergeant BRYANT enabled his company to secure ammunition to hold its position eight hours longer and was a material contribution to the success of the action. Entered military service from VIRGINIA

The officer of the 3rd Armored Division questioned Bryant at length. They fed him a hot meal, let him sleep in the barn and returned him to the 82nd the next morning, the 82nd then took him to his regiment. He found that his unit had nearly been destroyed by the Germans that night. Out of 115 men from the 325th at the crossroads, only 20-25 had survived. Headquarters had denied the request of the company commander to withdraw. However, because of the seriousness of the situation, permission was eventually given. The sad part of this withdrawal was the necessity of leaving the seriously wounded and dead behind.

One of the most difficult times for a soldier is being away from home on Christmas. If the troops are off the front lines, the Army tried to provide them with good food, not K rations on Christmas day. This was no exception for Bryant's company. They received rations for 60 men, although less that 30 remained in his unit. The food was uncooked. They worked out a deal with a nearby artillery unit to cook the food for them and take half for their men. It worked.

General Eisenhower had placed Field Marshall Montgomery in charge of all the US troops on the northern shoulder of The Bulge. Montgomery ordered the 82nd Division to withdraw. Both Generals Ridgeway and Gavin objected. It was a wise decision for the troops. After they withdrew, Bryant was in a foxhole with his helmet laying about six inches from his head. The next morning he found a three- inch hole in his helmet from shrapnel.

The Regiment had earned a well-deserved rest. Just think how the morale would be improved by a hot meal, warm bed and a shower. Their rest area was in the town of Pepinster, Belgium. This was in January 1945. Bryant and a couple others were invited to stay at the home of Mr. and Mrs. Alphonse Dolne-Des Champs. Because of the war, the Belgians had very little food. The men staying with this family provided them with staple items such as coffee, sugar, butter and cooking oil. They also provided them with Spam. Bryant and the others stayed with this family for about two weeks.

Bryant said, *"Some miles from Pepinster, we launched an offensive to drive the Germans from what remained of 'The Bulge.' These attacks took us through dense Belgian forests and hills, through hip-deep snow and sub-zero temperatures. After Pepinster this was a cruel reminder of the hardships of war, so it took several days to get fully acclimated again. The winter clothing was still lacking, making it even more difficult to cope with extreme weather conditions. "*

The Germans continued fighting but began to withdraw to Germany. Bryant's regiment was suffering from trench foot caused by cold and wet conditions. During this period, two of Bryant's buddies were wounded. The battle continued. The Battle of the Bulge marked the end of hard combat for Bryant's division. In February, Bryant had a chance to go to Paris for R&R. He stayed in a beautiful hotel. He had bananas and oranges for the first time since leaving the States. While in Paris, he bought a print of "The Last Supper." Today, a prized possession, the print hangs in the dining room of his home.

For their action at The Bulge, Bryant's division was awarded the Belgian Fourragere by the Belgian Government. The 325th Glider Infantry Regiment is also honored by a monument at the Village of Manhay and another at Baraque de Fraiture.

The 325th got another non-airborne mission at the end of March. They moved to Cologne, Germany to relieve elements of the 86th Infantry Division. There were many dead, both civilian and military. The town was completely destroyed except for a cathedral, which was also damaged. Across the Rhine, thousands of German soldiers were trapped. This was called the *"Ruhr Pocket."* Bryant noticed a German flag flying on a building across the river. Bryant and three buddies decided to cross the bridge, which was booby-trapped, and capture the flag for a souvenir. They accomplished their mission and captured the flag but were "chewed out" for it by one of his officers.

Bryant and members of the 325th were assigned the duty of patrolling the outlying areas and farm houses looking for German deserters. During these raids, they found fresh eggs, which they hard-boiled and enjoyed. The Cologne mission ended with the elimination of the "Ruhr Pocket." The trapped German soldiers surrendered. Bryant was a private first class at this time. His first sergeant had been rotated to the States and Bryant was promoted to the first sergeant, the highest enlisted rank in the Company. He was 20 years old.

The 325th next assignment was to cross the Elbe River near Bleckede which was southwest of Hamburg. When they arrived, the 505th had already secured the site. The regiment's next objective was the city of Ludwigslust, midway between Hamburg and Berlin. Bryant said, "The formal surrender by the Germans was executed by the German 15th Army commander, General der Infantrie Von Tipplakirch, and our Division Commander, General Gavin, at the Ludwigslust Palace, the division command post (CP). An entire German army and their equipment, such as it was, surrendered to us. It was a pathetic army and the men looked drawn and half-starved. It was a defeated army. The German army surrendered officially on May 7, 1945 at 2:41 a.m.

One of the most difficult things to forget was when the American soldiers would locate a prison camp. Bryant's unit learned of a concentration camp near the village of Wobbelin. When they arrived, they were completely shocked. Many were dead, lying around all over the compound; and those who were alive were skin and bones and were starving. There were approximately 5,000 interned in the camp; with about 1,000 who were dead. They were not Jews. They were forced laborers from Russia and Poland. Bryant said, *"It was a horrendous sight, and the smell made many GIs physically ill. The smell of decaying human flesh unlike animal's, is one you never forget."*

Later, Bryant's division was selected as the US occupation force for the American sector of Berlin. In early August 1945, they boarded "40 and 8" boxcars (40 men-8 horses) for a train trip to Berlin. During this trip they encountered some unexpected problems. Earlier, the Americans had captured the bridge over the Elbe at Magdeburg and had rebuilt the bridge. Now the Russians were in charge of that area and delayed their train trip to Berlin. The Russians became more and more difficult to deal with. The Russians were fascinated with the American Mickey Mouse watch. A watch costing $5.00 would sell to the Russians for $100.00 occupation money. Bryant said that the Russians, not having seen toilets that flushed, would stand on the commode and flush it over and over.

Now that the war was over in Europe, the soldiers were anxious to come home. However, the point system was in place and the men who had accumulated the most points would naturally rotate home first. Bryant's division didn't rotate to the States until January 1945. General Gavin led his troops in a parade down 5th Avenue in New York City and later in Washington, DC Regretfully Bryant was not a part of these parades, which to this day he regrets.

On his return, Bryant landed in New York and was assigned to Fort Meade, Maryland. He was then discharged after 2 years, 9 months, and 12 days. The Army paid Bryant $556.98 due him, which included $100, a part of his mustering-out pay. Taking a look at the American soldier's age during World War II, it is almost unbelievable for a man to go through all that has been shared by Bryant. He was one week short of being 21 years old. Jim Bryant was discharged in 1945 but reenlisted in the Army in October 1946 and retired after 22 plus years of service.

The last paragraph that James Bryant wrote in his book, *Flying Coffins Over Europe* was: *"In 1994, I returned to Ludwigslust which had been in East Germany. It looked exactly the same as it did in 1945. No new buildings or streets, and I don't believe the houses had been painted since 1945. I returned because I had always been curious as to whether these victims were still buried on the palace grounds. To my surprise they were, and two monuments commemorating the event had been erected by the East Germans."*

Bryant served with I Corps Headquarters Company in Korea. He landed in Korea in August 1950 and remained there until January 1952. He shared one interesting story about an experience in Korea. In October 1950, the first Chinese soldier, who was fighting with the North Korean Army, was captured. The prisoner was brought to I Company to be interrogated. The problem was that there wasn't anyone who could speak Chinese. They contacted General Paik of the South Korean Army who spoke Chinese. General MacArthur flew over from Japan to observe. Colonel Thompson was giving the briefing to MacArthur, advising the general that there were Chinese now fighting in this war. General Willoughby, G2, also shared this information. Bryant was the first sergeant and the only enlisted man in the briefing. Bryant said that MacArthur immediately stopped the briefing, not accepting the fact that the Chinese had entered the war. MacArthur said that there were only a few helping the North Koreans. The General had assured President Truman that the Chinese would not enter the Korean War.

Author's note: [It was October 20, 1950 that my unit, the 187th Airborne Infantry Regiment, made our first combat jump in Korea.

We jumped at Sukchon and Sunchon, north of the North Korean Capital, Pyongyang. Our unit later occupied Pyongyang until December when the Chinese came across the border in mass.]

JAMES E. BRYANT'S DECORATIONS

Silver Star, Bronze Star w/Oak Leaf Cluster, Combat Infantry Badge, Army Commendation Medal w/4 Oak Leaf Clusters, Good Conduct Medal, North American Defense Medal, European-North African Campaign Medal w/bronze arrowheads and 4 battle stars, World war II Victory Medal, World War II European Occupation Medal, National Defense Service Medal, Korean Service Medal w/7 battle stars, United Nations Korean Service Medal, Presidential Unit Citation, Korean Presidential Unit Citation, French Fourragere, Belgian Fourragere, Netherlands Orange Lanyard, Glider Wings w/2 Bronze Stars (1 star for each combat landing).

GLIDER PILOTS

"The Germans, having planned for glider landings, had made square holes in the ground about two feet deep with grass growing in each one. From the air the glider pilot's view suggested a smooth landing. When a wheel hit one of the holes, it would cause the glider to flip over." Robert Moore

ROBERT C. MOORE, JR.

World War II glider pilots, none of whom had ever been such before and probably none will ever be such again; they are described as a hybrid breed like jackasses with no need to reproduce themselves; definitely one of a kind understood only by themselves and some completely beyond understanding. A few more years and military glider pilots will be an extinct species, remembered only by few. But they did exist and were involved in some mighty important and exciting military actions in World War II. These are some thoughts and experiences of another American hero, 90 year old, **Robert C. Moore, Jr.** of Appomattox, Virginia. He was a pilot on a CG-4A Waco glider who made landings in the invasions of *Normandy, Holland* and the *Rhine*. Moore was a pilot before entering the Army Air Corps. He soloed at the age 16 in a

Taylor Cub Aircraft in Lynchburg, Virginia. In the late 1930s, at age 18, he became the youngest "barnstormer" in the state of Virginia, flying a bi-plane Travel Air 2000. Moore and a friend, Birt Lee, took a wrecked airplane and over a three-year period restored it, buying a wing, a landing gear and other needed parts as money became available.

"Cal" was born on July 8, 1918 in Stapleton, Virginia. His parents were R. C. Moore, Sr. and Maude Gregory Moore. Cal joined the US Army Air Corps on December 3, 1941, just four days before Pearl Harbor. He was discharged on March 31, 1946 after a prestigious as well as an interesting military career. He took his four months basic training in Pittsburg, Kansas. During that time, he attended Kansas State University, studying Navigation and Meteorology. Moore served in Europe with the 9th Air Force.

He had two brothers, Lawrence W. Moore and William H. Moore, who also served their country in the military.

Uncle Sam awarded Moore his wings on February 1, 1944 at Lubbock, Texas. He then took commando training in Louisville, Kentucky for a month. On March 18th, he transferred to Laurinburg-Morton Air Field in North Carolina for flight training on landing a glider in a small field. This training lasted about one month. From North Carolina, he was sent to Ft. Wayne, Indiana for final processing before his overseas assignment. The men each received a seven-day pass before reporting to Camp Kilmer, N.J.

Moore sailed on the S.S. *Pasteur* from New York just before daybreak on May 7th. The sea was fairly smooth the entire trip. The ship dropped anchor in Liverpool on May 14, 1944 for two days. While in Liverpool, an English General spoke to the men, explaining how they should conduct themselves while in England. From Liverpool, they took a train to Stone, England, and then were assigned to their various squadrons. The next three weeks, they trained day and night. Three days before D-Day, the men were put behind a barbed wire fence for security purposes. They were required to pack all of their personal items into their footlockers and stencil their home address on the lockers, just in the event they did not return. The day had come for the *Normandy Invasion*, exactly one month after they had left the States. They watched the heavy bombers heading for Normandy. Moore said, "It gave us the impression that there would be nothing left when I got there." "But I was wrong," he continued.

When they started across the channel, Moore realized that all the training had prepared him just for this moment, his first combat experience. Moore took off at daybreak on June 6th to meet with other groups. As they arrived near the French coast, they could see the vast number of ships anchored and airplanes overhead. They saw a lot of fires along the mainland, and three minutes later, he was over his assigned target. The pilots said "goodbye" to the C-47 tow planes, and within one minute they were landing their gliders in German territory between Utah and Omaha Beaches. Moore was carrying a jeep, a doctor and four medics in his glider.

The pilots were told that the field they were to land on was a small field with "low" hedgerows. Surprise! Surprise! It seems that the pictures taken of the hedgerows were by P-38 pilots. The trees were like cottonwood trees about 80 feet high and difficult to fly over. The Germans, having planned for glider landings, had made square holes in the ground about two feet deep with grass growing in each one. From the air, the pilots' view suggested a smooth landing but the holes caused serious problems. When a wheel would hit one of the holes, it would flip the glider over.

After landing and unloading, Moore grabbed his M-1 rifle. (He later carried a Grease Gun, which had a 15 round clip.) After all, the enemy was not on the next hill, he is in front of you, in back of you and beside you. He tried to get back to the beach which was about eight miles. He hiked most of the way before catching a ride on a "duck" vehicle. He arrived at the beach about 10:30 a.m. While wading in the salt water, Moore discovered that he had blisters on his feet. He was picked up by a Navy LST. The Navy provided him with a new set of underwear and gave his feet medical treatment. The pilots were transferred back to their base in England. On the way, they saw several ships that had hit mines and sank.

As soon as the airstrip was built in France, Moore and crew started to fly in food supplies to the troops from England. The bulldozers had leveled many of the hedgerows between the fields, making their landing safer. Moore said almost everyone in England had a bicycle. He bought a bicycle for eight pounds and took it with him on a train or airplane for immediate transportation. The men continued to train preparing for the next mission.

On Sunday, September 17, 1944, about 9 a.m., Moore and his fellow pilots were airborne again in their Waco Gliders for a three-hour trip to Holland. This invasion was called, *MARKET-GARDEN*. They left the airfield from North London, flew across the channel. The day was clear, a good day to fly. His glider was carrying an anti-tank gun, its commander and four or five men from the 82nd Airborne. Moore said this was a very difficult trip because they had to fly about 80 miles over enemy territory. On this mission, he didn't have a co-pilot. He was leading the right echelon. As they came into Holland, for some reason they flew over the canal. In the canal were barges with guns shooting at them. The RAF pilots dived down and knocked the barges out.

Moore explained that there was a "double tow." When one glider was carrying a jeep and the other an anti-tank gun, the short tow was 350 feet long, and the long tow was 425 feet long. They were 75 feet apart and it was extremely important that both be cut loose exactly the same time. They had to land close so the jeep was available to tow the anti-tank gun into battle.

Moore made a good landing at Grospeck, Holland without any damage to the craft or injury to the men aboard. After unloading, he grabbed his Greece gun and stayed with the anti-tank crew as they moved toward their target, the bridge called "too far." Army paratroopers had already taken over the small town of Grospeck and had taken 150 prisoners. Moore stayed on the front lines for three days. The Anti-tank gun set up in a "Y" in the road so they could maneuver their gun to fire either direction. Then a German 88 gun located them and began firing on their location, requiring them to relocate. Moore relates an incident where he dug his foxhole next to a grocery store. The store was locked, but he having not eaten for two days, broke into the store. He found a can of peaches with the label stating the peaches were from Winchester, Virginia. Along with the peaches, he found some black (hard as a rock) bread. He soaked the bread in the peach juice and said, "It tasted pretty good."

Moore saw members of the 82nd Airborne alongside the road with concussions. He was very complimentary of the troopers in the 82nd. He said, "The men were well trained, never got excited, and just went about their business." He finally got word from the 82nd that he could go back through the line but would have to go alone. Moore said he stayed in ditches, not on the road. He used his five senses to survive. He traveled about 12 miles. On the way, Moore spent the night in a home with a family who fed him and were kind to him.

After they had taken the town of Beak, Germany, a lieutenant colonel ordered them back to headquarters. A shell hit in Moore's foxhole a short time after he had left it. He was then ordered by the light colonel to work in an ammunition dump. They unloaded ammo for three days. After nine days, he got a ride to Brussels on a GI truck; he then caught an airplane back to England. Before leaving, the sergeant of the anti-tank crew told Moore that he needed his 45 cal. pistol since Moore was going back to England. Moore gave the sergeant his pistol without any thought of repercussions. Moore said he later had to write about 15 letters to explain what had happened to his pistol.

Moore shared some of the glider pilot's experiences in landing in Holland. He said, *"Steve was the lead glider of the 3033rd Squadron on the third day of transporting troops from South England to Son 2, Holland. We had made it across the channel through low-lying dense clouds which often obscured to tow plane, 250 feet of tow rope ahead. They were ill-equipped, no intercom with the tow ship, no co-pilot, only one set of controls; no 'Mae West's,' no 'Griswold nose,' and no arresting chute were really not of much concern at this point. We were flying so low that the propellers were throwing spray from the churning waves over the windshields further obscuring visibility."* Another wrote, *"Some*

Jerry's in the left corner of the landing zone were firing one of our captured 50 caliber machine guns with tracers. The tracers were edging down the tow ropes from about ten yards behind the plane to about the same distance from my glider when I cut. I called for full spoilers and made a sharp turn to the left and didn't see any more of those. We landed safely." A third pilot wrote, *"Halfway across Holland, we ran into flak, and the tow plane behind me was hit and we had to crash land. The glider with Robert (Smokey) McCall at the controls landed in a pasture. The troopers helped unload the jeep they were carrying and they proceeded on an exciting drive through enemy- held territory to the landing zone. My landing was not too bad considering that I touched down in a turnip field. The wheels sank into the soft soil and we nosed up, tearing out part of the glider's bottom. Then the tail dropped into a normal position, the howitzer stayed in place, and no one was hurt."*

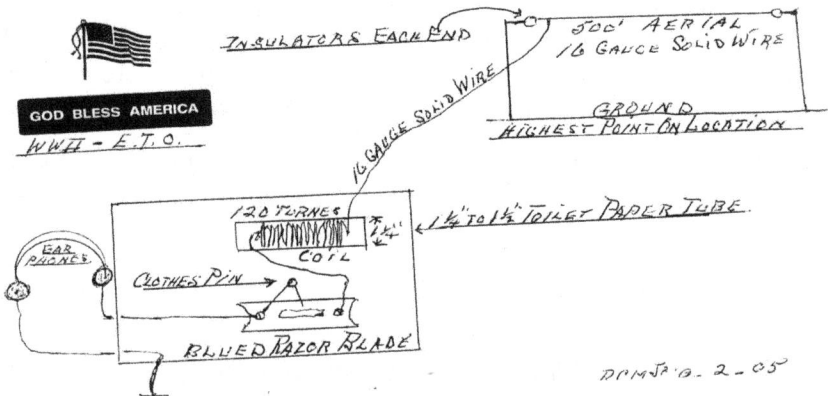

Moore said, *"After we got back we started packing to leave for Alencon, France. We were given a seven- day combat leave and went back to London, hiked a ride to Paris and stayed there for one day and a half. After we got back, we flew co-pilot on a C-47, hauling supplies to General George Patton. In about three weeks we moved to Chateudun, France in order to have a better field."*

Moore continued, *"We had to build a floor and sides for our tent as it was very cold. We had a hard time learning to speak French. The last of November, I went to Grove, Holland to get some gliders. Due to bad weather, we had to stay in Brussels for a week. After this, we got a lot of time flying C-47's."*

Having radio contact was simply not available. Using a touch of genius, Moore decided there must be some way to build a radio. He built what he named a "razor blade radio." The components to build this radio were: a clothes pin, blued razor blade, a toilet paper tube, 500 feet of aerial 16 gauge solid wire and ear phones. It worked.

Moore and fellow glider pilots were invited back to Holland on the 50th anniversary of the invasion. The Dutch called D-Day the "Day of Liberation." The ceremony lasted four days. Parades were scheduled in different towns and wreaths were placed in the cemetery. A big party was held for the men at Nijmegan. They had good food, a lot of cheese plus Holland beer and wine. After the feast, they moved to a large auditorium that provided a 26 piece orchestra, good music and singing. Moore said he was sitting on an aisle seat when the master of ceremonies put a microphone in his face and asked him what he thought of the celebration. Moore said he kind of stuttered then said, "My name is R.C. Moore, Jr. I am from the historic town of Appomattox, Virginia. I thanked them for their hospitality, the entertainment and good food." Then he added, "The thing that has impressed me the most was when we arrived, a girl gave each of us a flower and said 'thank you.' This was the highlight of my visit."

Moore's next combat mission was on March 24-25, *Rhine, Germany*. The tension was evident with the men. They knew another combat mission was imminent but didn't know when. Moore went to the motor pool and requested a jeep, a driver and a torch. He went to the airfield where damaged and unused airplanes were stored. He wanted a seat for his glider. With the torch, he cut out a seat from an airplane and installed the seat into his glider for his flight into Germany. Moore was going into Germany in a glider, with a seat from an army plane, a steel helmet, a flack vest and a grease gun and without a co-pilot.

The gliders usually flew at about 800 feet. Moore's glider landed ten miles east of Rhine and Weasel. There was a big smoke screen on the east bank protecting soldiers as they built a pontoon bridge. When the gliders got to the landing field, they couldn't see it because the smoke screen had shifted. They got the green light to go when they were about 1,100 feet. They broke loose from the tow plane to find the field through the smoke. Moore made another safe landing. His cargo this trip was a jeep along with five airborne personnel.

Moore said this was a fast invasion. This ended Moore's third and final mission. He hitch hiked a ride to the engineer's headquarters, to an air base, and back to England. They were given a seven- day rest at Bordeaux from April 3rd through the 10th. After the rest period, he was transferred to Verdun, France to haul supplies and prisoners for three weeks. During this time, they had a chance to see the inside of Germany. V.E. day soon came. The next trip was home. Moore stayed in England for eight weeks, which gave him the opportunity to tour England. He left Stone, England on July 17, 1945 and flew to the States by way of Scotland, Iceland, Greenland, Labrador and then to Connecticut, arriving on July 24th. He then went to Fort Meade, Maryland and was given a 30 day pass. Moore had 3,800 hours credited in flying gliders and C-47's.

Moore reported back to camp for final processing when he learned that the doctor decided to keep him because of combat fatigue. The short stay lasted six months in rehab. He was sent to Plattsburg, New York to the A.A.F. hospital. He called the love of his life to come to New York to marry him. On October 12, 1945, Robert C. Moore, Jr. married Roma Saul, whom he said was the most talented woman he had ever met. They had their honeymoon at Lake Placid, Montreal Canada and Vermont. Moore retired from General Motors, working in the Sales and Engineering department.

Moore's military decorations include: European African Middle Eastern Service Medal; American Service Medal; Distinguished Unit Badge; Air Medal w/2 Oak Leaf Clusters; Gp 123 HQ IX TCC, GO 33 HQ IX TCG July 44; World War II Victory Medal (109 points).

Another veteran American glider pilot painted a vivid picture of the stark terror they experienced. *"Imagine,"* he said, *"flying a motor-less, fabric-covered CG-4A glider, violently bouncing and jerking on a one-inch thick nylon rope 300 feet back of the C-47 tow plane. You see the nervous infantrymen behind you, some vomiting, many in prayer, as you hedge-hop along at tree-top level instinctively jumping up in your seat every time you hear bullets and flak tearing through the glider. You try not to think about the explosives aboard. It's like flying a stick of dynamite through the gates of Hell."*

American glider pilots were scheduled for *"Operation Eclipse,"* the Allied airborne offensive planned to capture Berlin. But, the glory went, through political default, to Russian ground forces. The pilots also were spared an invasion of Japan when the atomic bombs fell on Hiroshima. They proudly wore the silver wings with the letter "G" superimposed on them. The Defense Department ended the military glider pilot program in 1952. There will be no future generations of American military glider pilots. But men, heroes like Cal Moore and their memories, live on for their commitment, dedication to duty and bravery unequaled in serving their country.

One of the organizations that Cal Moore is proud to be a member of is the Glider Pilots Association. There were several attempts were made in the sixties to get this organization started. But the movement never got off the ground until the spring of 1965 when Earl Dust, of Champagne, Illinois, a glider pilot who was formerly a member of the 80th squadron of the 436th Troop Carrier Group, made a vacation trip between New York and Florida and visited all his old buddies from the 80th squadron. Earl decided to call for a reunion of ex-GPs in Champagne in May of 1966. Using a limited list of names that he had compiled, he put the word out and a total of nine GPs and their wives showed up.

A Steering Committee was formed, headed by Earl Dust. He located and appointed ex-Lt. Col. Frank Moore as "National Commander" and indicated that Moore's primary duty was to "search for, seek out, and organize." Finally, after months and months of hard work by Ginny Randolph and Bickett Ellington, the die was cast and a decision was made to call for the first national GP reunion. It was to be held in Dallas, Texas on August 13, 14, and 15, 1971. Sixty-five glider pilots were on hand when the meeting was called to order. Bickett Ellington was elected as the first National Flight Commander.

The following year in Las Vegas, 63 glider pilots were on hand. The Association has continued record growth with each annual reunion becoming "bigger and better." The membership grew to well over 1,500. Moore served as the Area Commander of the 47B VA (2) Area of the National World War II Glider Pilots Association in 2004. He is a member of the Blue Ridge All Airborne Chapter and was named the 1997 paratrooper of the Half Century. Robert C. "Cal" Moore, Jr. and his wife, Roma, had two children, five grandchildren, and one great grandchild.

ARTHUR LEE

Arthur served as a member of the famed 82nd Airborne Division. He was a member of the 325th Glider Regiment. Art was born in Ferry, New York on March 4, 1926. Art was drafted September 16, 1944 at the age of 18. He and his buddies assembled in front of the Court House on Grand Ave., Bellmore, NY at 10:30 a.m. His father happened to be on the Selective Service Board that sends out the nice letters for the "boys" to report. Art said, "I said goodbye to Pop and Johnny, he was crying. We went by the LIRR to New York City and then to Grand Central Terminal. They checked us out and we were transported to Fort Dix, NJ. I must admit I had some lonely moments thinking about home and my family.

After about two weeks, Art was sent to Ft. McClellan, Alabama, a long ride by train. When they passed through a town called Rome, Georgia, he said, "Pretty good that we were in Italy and the war isn't over yet." Friendships began to form at Ft. McClellan. Art met George Larsen from Hollis, Queens, Johnny Metzner from Rockville Center and a guy they called Rebel who had only been married for only three months.

Ft. McClellan was a training camp for GIs. Their training included marching, drill, bivouacking in the rain and of course the famous 30 mile hike. Metzner lasted about ten miles so to help his new friend, Art carried his M-I rifle to lighten his load. In December, Art heard about the Battle of the Bulge. This caused him and friends to become concerned because they had just completed their basic training and had enjoyed a ten day leave. From Camp Kilmer, NJ, Art was assigned to go overseas. He boarded the *Isle de France*, a luxury French ship. He said, "What a ship!" It wasn't the run -of –the- mill transport ship. The ship carried between 1,500 and 2,000 soldiers. The chow lines were a real challenge on a troop ship.

The ship would change its course about every eight minutes, trying to avoid the German U-Boats. About 5 o'clock one morning as they were approaching Scotland, the ship tilted about 45 degrees. Everything slid, mess kits, guys falling out of their five-tear hammocks. Little did the men know that the ship was dodging a torpedo? Some of the men became seasick because the Atlantic was treacherous in February with the waves coming over the hull of the ship. Art said that they pass the time away by holding crap games.

The *Isle de France* anchored near Glasgow, Scotland early in the morning in February. The countryside was green and beautiful that time of year. Glasgow is an old town with cobbled stoned streets, with brick and mortar buildings. The troops boarded a train and traveled south. Art said, "I remember passing an open crossing on a rural road. I can still see a small lad in his slicker and holding his school books; strange how some things just stick in your mind."

The crowds were waving and cheering Art and the troops as they passed through London. They enjoyed the attention. Next, they came to Southampton, a metropolis of cranes, boats and trains. The troops were amazed to see all of the activity in that area as they marched to the docks. They crossed the English Channel on a British ferry. The crossing took place at night with very few lights, an eerie feeling. The next morning Art landed at La Havre, France. His first impression was, "What a mess." Boats were half sunk in the harbor; the entryway was difficult to enter with all the "stuff" clogging the entrance.

The men were loaded on French train-boxcars. They began to wonder where they were going and what would be their assignment. The train arrived at St. Trom, Belgium. They were billeted in an old barnlike building. Art said, "I saw a big department store named Bazaar, and little did I know that years later my sister would be married to Walter Bazaar."

It was March and Art reached age 19. They had moved to a German town called Kempen und Kierfield. Art and his buddy decided to go to Liege, Belgium which was about 100 miles away. It was Sunday so Art and Johnny didn't have anything to do. They stopped by the Red Cross and enjoyed coffee and doughnuts with personnel from many other units. The bombed out areas were caused by the "buzz bombs" which were frightening as they flew overhead. Johnny had met a girl whom he wanted to see; Art decided to tour the area and see the sights.

When Johnny didn't meet Art at the appointed time, Art hitched hiked a ride passed Aachen, Germany. He ended up in Munchen Gladbach—two miles from the Rhine River. Art said that it was late and the MPs picked him up and put him in a German jail over night. Art said, "After my AWOL episode, I was put on KP every night for a week. This was a joke because after the second night the sarge in charge told me to take off, which I did."

Art and some other soldiers were called on about March 24th and asked if they wanted to join the airborne. The invitation was inviting because the pay for a paratrooper or glider trooper was an extra $50 a month. Art chose to serve in the gliders. The next day after the Rhine crossing they were transported by open trucks to an airfield somewhere and given their glider rides. Art recalls the glider being towed by a C-47 aircraft, the liftoff and ascent to 1500 feet before being released. He said, "Coming down was like an elevator ride and the trees seemed to becoming up at a fast rate. As we were coming to the clearing to land, another glider was ahead of us, and we were coming in at about 110 mph. All of a sudden, the other glider stopped and our co-pilot yelled at the pilot, "What should I do?" The pilot said, 'Go over him'." They had a close call, missing the other glider by about ten feet.

The next day Art's unit was convoyed across the Rhine near Wessel where the 17th airborne had landed less than 24 hours before. Art's unit joined with the 17th and also met with the 13th

Airborne. Art said, "That night we were near some shooting and the tracer bullets were flying all over." Foxholes then became their beds. They entered into Munster, a small town about forty or 50 miles inside Germany. Art said that they were warned to watch out for the kids who sometimes fought like gorillas. All they found in the town were kids and old people. There was a piano with a small boy trying to play. When they found out that Art could play, the boy was removed from the stool. Art played late into the night.

Art's first encounter with the enemy was the next day about 10:00 a.m. in the morning when his unit moved into a wooded area. A German machine gun opened fire. After ducking under some trees which had been cut down, they returned the fire and the Germans gave up. One of the men got hit in the buttocks. Try to explain a wound in the buttocks. About 11 o'clock, while moving along a railroad track, they could hear the 88s and the 42s steady, phom, phom, phom. Lt. Coffee was clipped in the chin from a machine gun. They continued to walk along the railroad track and came to a big clearing. The troops spread out and suddenly, another machine gun opened fire on them. Art said, "A bullet ricocheted off my helmet and I was there about ten minutes. It seemed like two hours. They began running toward a farm house for protection. On another similar occasion, a woman held out a white flag of surrender and when the men approached the farm house, all were killed by a German machine gun. No one could be trusted."

After entering the farm house, the 88s quit firing. Looking out, Art could see the P47s doing their job and taking out the gun emplacements. What a blessing! They stayed in another farm house that night. One of the guys wanted eggs for breakfast but didn't know the German word. Somehow he was able to communicate with the German farm girl who fixed them eggs for breakfast.

On the way to Munster, Art cut his thumb opening a can of K rations. He went to the medic to get a Band Aid. The medic asked him if he wanted a Purple Heart. Art said his thoughts went back to World War I when his father was shot and received a Purple Heart. He said, "No, just give me a Band Aid." Art's unit continued to march south. After he had walked about five miles, a tank came by and gave them a ride for a short distance. Some 6X6 trucks transported them back to Duseburg, Germany. They assembled at Duseburg then went to Dusseldorf. They arrived in Hamborne, Germany near the Krupp Works; this was the heart of the German war munitions area. It was now the end of April and World War II was nearly over. The fears that Art and others had in this town were the German kids called, "War-mach." These kids continued to fight. One of Art's duties was to guard about 100 Polish prisoners held in a schoolhouse. Art said they had been prisoners of the Germans. The Polish prisoners were now being guarded to protect the Germans. Art said, "If these Polish prisoners ever got loose they would start their own war with the Jerry's."

Art said, "On May 7, 1945, we found out the war was over in Europe and the next day the street outside was covered with broken bottles. Now was the time for peace." Germany surrendered at 2:41 a.m. on May 7th. Art stayed in Hamborne until June when he left for France. Art said, "I paid $10 for two packs of Camels when our rations didn't come in for a week. The next day I was smoking two "ciggs" in each hand, but who cared."

Art said, "I met a girl named Erna, little Erna Glass. I didn't know but she was age 15 at the time and had made her communion two weeks earlier. Somehow I went to her house right next to one of the Krupp factories. Her father and mother were there. They seemed very nice and we stumbled over German and English words. They were Russian and their sons were drafted and hadn't been heard from in a long time. Then I noticed a pan suspended from the ceiling and on it was rose petals. I asked him what are these for and he told me 'Tobac.' He was drying them to make cigarettes. I offered a pack that I had extra. He seemed to think I gave him a million dollars. I didn't see Erna much after that but I often wonder?"

Art's unit turned over the area at Hamborne, Germany on June 15th about 11 a.m. to the British. They boarded C-47s only to question their captain about their destination. Maybe to Japan or to the Pacific, were questions they asked. Their captain advised them that they were going to Luneville, a small French town. From the air they could see Paris. WOW! What a sight! The 17th Airborne settled in. It was R&R time. There was a stream nearby to cool off; a stadium for running and keeping in condition. After breakfast one morning, Art and some of the guys went to a nearby town called Nancy. It was a very old French town that was made famous in Napeolian's time. Art described the area in this manner. "Chariamaine, Napeolian's son-in-law was very influential in making the city beautiful. Especially interesting were the four main entries to the town park. There were iron grills and metal floral designs. It was very delightfully French. On one side of the entry was a small restaurant and don't you know someone was playing a saxophone American style. I must have stood there 20 minutes listening."

It was time for Art's unit to return to the United States. They were sent to Rheims, France to Camp Lucky Strike. On August 8th they learned about the atomic bomb being dropped on Japan. No one seemed to know what the atomic bomb was. The bomb called "Little Boy" was dropped on *Hiroshima* on August 6th killing more than 75,000 and injuring thousands others. The second bomb was dropped three days later on the city of *Nagasaki,* with over 35,000 Japanese killed. The Japanese surrendered on August 14, 1945. World War II was now over.

Art was then transferred to the 82nd Airborne, transported to LaHarve and to a Liberty ship for an eight day trip across the

Atlantic. On August 29th, Art and friends entered the New York harbor with horns blowing and people waving from a welcome home ship. He said that "It was fabulous!" Art went to Camp Kilmer, N.J., received $300 and a furlough. He later learned that he had been overpaid and was required to return the money to the good old US Army. When Art arrived home there was a welcome sign which said, "WELCOME HOME ARTY." There were a few tears shed. His mother served coffee and doughnuts.

Art married Jean Warner on July 17, 1948. He received the Good Conduct Medal, ETO ribbon with one battle star and the World War II ribbon. He was discharged from the Army on November 19, 1946. Art is a member of the "Blue Ridge All American" Chapter of the 82nd Airborne located in Lynchburg, Virginia.

This Horsa glider, (photo courtesy of Jim Bryant), had crashed on landing. The posts you see were called "Rommel's Asparagus." They were painted green and placed in the fields where the Germans had anticipated that landings would take place.

CHAPTER SEVEN

THE LADY FROM

VALKENBURG, HOLLAND

MARIE "TINI" PHILIPPI BOWER

The personal interview with the Bowers' began with the author at 1:30 p.m. on Friday August 3, 2007. I met in the home of Tini and her husband, George. George first offered me a strong cup of coffee.

Author Harry Mulisch said *"World War II will not be over permanently until everyone that has experienced it, has died."* **Marie Hubertine Philippi Bower** was born in Valkenburg, Holland, living under Nazi domination until the United States and their Allies liberated her town. This is her story shared with the author as she remembers the events during the invasion of her country. The operation was called *Market-Garden.*

When notified (few people had a radio) that two American, two British and one Canadian regiment were storming the five beaches in Normandy, France, the Dutch people began rejoicing because after nearly five years living in fear, living without much food, experiencing the deaths of their citizens by the Nazis, they now had hope-hope of freedom. The people of Valkenburg and the country of Holland had hopes of being reunited again with their loved ones, if they were still alive. The question was: When would the Americans come? It took three months and seven days for the first American soldier to land in Holland but it only took until

September 14 to remove the Germans from her town. The soldiers were from the 19th Army Corps. The code name was *Tomahawk*.

Even some of the German generals had given up on winning the war. To continue to fight seemed to be a lost cause. The officers had even tried to kill Hitler on July 20th but their plot failed. The Allies continued to move across France and on August 25th, freed Paris. The Germans continued to fight. One of the bloodiest battles since Normandy took place on the Cherbourg peninsula.

The people living in Valkenburg were beginning to sense that they would be liberated soon. On September 12, 1944, the first American entered Dutch territory. In some sections of town, the Dutch were able to start flying the flag of their country again. The hated Nazi flags had been removed.

During the war, the families had been issued ration cards for food. Tini's mother would trade her sugar ration for some other kind of food. During these years, cakes, cookies or pies, anything sweet for the Philippi family was not available. Their diet consisted mainly of sauerkraut, potatoes and black bread. No flour was available, only the Germans had white bread. On occasions the families could obtain horse meat. Tini said you could buy an egg on the black market for $2.00—if you had money. Her family worked on a friend's farm about three miles out of town, which provided their family with some food. Their sacrifices were not as great as some of the people.

Valkenburg is a Provence of Zimburg. This was an old, beautiful Roman city, with churches over 800 years old. The city had narrow streets with archways that made it difficult for the Allied tanks to drive through. Valkenburg was a tourist town with unique hotels, entertaining many visitors before the war. The town is located between two mountains where vacationers came to hike, climb or just relax in alpine beauty. The houses are built on sandstone. You could walk under the houses from one location to another. Sandstone caves were used by the citizens for protection during air raids. Valkenburg is located ten miles from the German border; and eight miles from the Belgium border. The people in the Southern part of Holland are Catholic; the Northern people are Protestant. Today if you visit this city, you will still be able to see evidence of the fighting there 64 years ago where memories have not been erased. One of the main events and tourist attractions was the Tour de France. When held in Valkenburg after the war, nearly 350,000 people attended.

(Photo courtesy of Tina Bower-Tina in white dress with family)

The Germans had taken over all of the schools in which to incarcerate labor camp workers. Tini said, "I didn't like school anyway." The Germans also occupied all of the hotels. The kids would throw rocks at the German soldiers. Tini's family home was hit by a bomb once but the bomb failed to explode. The family wore wooden shoes. Her father would put a strip of leather on the bottom to reduce the noise, especially when coming late to church. One Sunday the priest preached a sermon against the Germans. The next Sunday the German soldiers came into the church and arrested the priest. He spent 5 years in prison. The priest was never the same after he was released.

Tini's parents were Leonardus and Anna Maria Philippi. She had six brothers and one sister. The picture, taken in 1948, is all of the Philippi family except for Max who was in the East Indies. [A soldier sent the white dress to Tini from New Orleans.] Her father was a cabinet maker but during the German occupation, he made mostly caskets.

Tini came to America in 1961 as the governess for a Belgium diplomat. She said that she cared for his four children, did the cooking, washing and everything. Tini became a citizen of the United States in 1996 in Knoxville, Tennessee, after having taken her exam in Louisville, Kentucky.

Tini said that the air raids were frightening. When the siren went off, they ran for the caves. The town had a curfew every night. The curtains had to be drawn every night so that light could not be seen. One night Tini's neighbor was standing in his house when a German soldier came by. There was a little crack in the curtain that allowed some light to be seen from the outside. The soldier shot and killed the man through the window. The Nazis killed many of the Valkenburg citizens, sometimes for no cause at all. After the war was over, families who had been missing were found tied together in a common grave.

As the siege of Valkenburg began, the Americans learned quickly that the Germans were dug in and ready to defend their territory. The German trenches had been dug by forced laborers. Max, Tini's brother, had been arrested by German soldiers and forced to work in the labor camp for two years. He had been arrested because of a sleigh. One of the soldiers had taken Max's sleigh away from him to give it to his girlfriend. Max had slapped the German soldier. His job in the labor camp was mainly to dig foxholes or trenches and string wire. The Germans knew that the attack would come soon, so they were making preparations while waiting for the invasion.

The Germans began by blowing up all the bridges over the Geul River. They kept one bridge intact for an escape route. According to the book *The Liberation of Valkenburg*, its author reported that approximately 2,500 citizens found shelter in the Gemeentegrot in Cauberg hill (also used during air raids); 300 people in what was called the "velvet cave" and 1,700 people in the Catacomben and some in a coal mine. The Nicolaas Church tower was also used for shelter.

On September 14th soldiers from A Company, 119th Infantry Regiment came in marching on each side of the street. The Germans were known for wearing such heavy boots that you could hear them coming. On the other hand, the Americans wore soft-soled boots which could not be heard as they were walking. American soldiers were good to the people in Holland. Tini said, "The soldiers gave us white bread—a real treat since we only had been receiving hard black bread." They gave them chocolate, which made Tini sick from eating too much. Oranges were given to the children. Oranges were only for rich people and were a luxury for Tini.

Tini recounted that they were in a cave for six days and five nights during the battle. They did not have any lights except candles for three-days; they had no bath or rest room facilities; and they were given only one slice of black bread each evening. Everyone stayed in the caves during the heavy shelling.

Tini's brother Gier Philippi was a member of the Dutch Underground. These men worked under the cover of darkness, harassing the Germans, capturing prisoners to take their guns to use against them. The Germans were located on one mountain, the Underground men on the other. Members from the Underground were the first to leave the caves to see what damage had been done to the houses and bridges. They didn't stay outside the cave for an extended period in order not to expose themselves and be targets of the German snipers or machine guns. September 14th, the day of the Americans' arrival, was a very important day for Valkenburg. The people began dancing in the streets.

The next day was a beautiful September day; however the heavy fighting continued, not allowing the citizens of Valkenburg to experience their freedom yet. The Germans did not consider retreating. Most of the houses and business had been damaged or destroyed. Saturday, September 16th is believed to be the date that the Allies actually broke the German's backs. A German sniper would keep some to the troops pinned down, but not for long. The people saw a small plane flying low overhead. This plane was probably an L-3 observation plane used to determine the enemy position, strength etc. [The plane was called the *"grasshopper."* The observation plane had 65 horsepower and would fly about 87 mph; it was usually piloted by an enlisted man. The plane was made out of oil cloth and steel tubing, without any protection.]

By Sunday, September 17, most of the city was now free of the German army. Allied paratroopers landed near Eindhoven, Grave, Nijmegen and Arnhem, at the bridges across the rivers Maas, Waal and Rhine. This was the largest airborne operation during World War II with approximately 4,600 planes involved. The *Arnhem Bridge* "The Bridge Too Far" was not captured. This bridge is located about 1½ hours from Tini's home. Montgomery's plan had failed. Thousands of the Allied troops were surrounded. Of the original 10,000 men who arrived at Arnhem, only 2,000 reached the village of Driel. The rest were killed, wounded, or taken prisoner. However, four long, difficult and tragic years would soon end for the citizens of Valkenburg. The American tanks found a way to cross the Geul River. It is reported that one German, obviously drunk, continued to fire on the Americans. An American soldier shot and killed the German soldier. The last

German gun in the garden was put out of action about 4 o'clock that day.

In the Nijmegen sector, General Gavin's 82nd Division lost about 1,500 men. General Taylor's 101st "Screaming Eagles" lost about 2,100 men, killed, wounded or captured by the Germans. The gliders and paratroopers had landed in the middle of the German positions. This operation was a nightmare for the Americans. The worst part was that Arnhem was never reached despite all the men who gave their lives to hold the bridge or the perimeter. With all of the failures of *Market-Garden*, Montgomery still called Market Garden 90% successful.

Toward the end of the occupation, Tini said that the Germans became meaner to the people. One soldier came into their house for a drink, did not hurt anyone and told them that he just wanted to go home. Of the 28 Jewish families originally in town, only two families survived. Those local citizens who collaborated with the enemy had their heads shaved to expose them.

Tini said that the American soldiers were good to the Dutch people. She was now ten years old. The GIs gave them a mess kit and allowed the families to go through the chow line to experience decent food. What a treat!

The American engineers began to repair the blown-up- bridges. Valkenburg took years to reconstruct their city following the war. The restoration around the St. Nicholas Church took over 20 years to complete. After the war ended, Tini drove her uncle's truck and delivered bread. She wore pants, which was not the usual attire for a woman or young girl. A little boy saw her one day and said to his mother, "Look Mom, she's wearing pants." The Dutch families would invite American soldiers into their home to eat with them. The GIs brought the food.

While working in Washington, D.C., for the Federal Government, Tini met George Bower during a youth-adult club meeting. Tini's visa had expired which required her to leave the

United States. George signed her scrapbook at that time. They

were married on October 26, 1963 in Tini's home town, Valkenburg, Holland. They have three daughters and five grandchildren. George was born in Pennsylvania and served two years in the US Army.

Tina Bower Always Has Room For One More Child

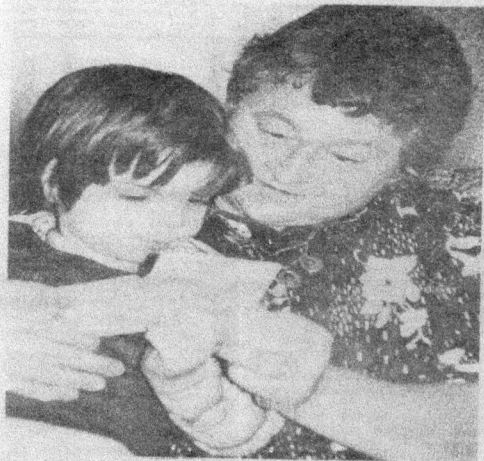

The American cemetery located in Valkenburg has 8,302 American soldiers buried there, with about 2,000 missing. Each Dutch family has adopted an American grave and puts flowers on the grave each year. Tini's family adopted Robert Erwin of Ohio. Fifty-years later an

American soldier returned to Valkenburg and found Tini' family home. Finding no one home, he went to the church where her sister recognized him.

Tini Bower is a very special lady for many reasons. For one thing, she had enough love in her heart that she wanted to share it with children. She started taking babies who had no place else to go in 1976. She and her husband, George, have stayed up many nights rocking a baby addicted to drugs back to sleep or cleaning up after children so abused and angry that they tore their rooms apart. Tini became a foster-parent in order to make a difference.

When Tini first started taking children into her home to care for, they were usually poor children from poor parents. Later she said the children had been abused and from families who neglected them, as she remembered a four-year-old girl who had been sexually abused. Tini said, "We didn't have much, but we had a family unit."

Tini and George are proud of their family. One daughter, Zita, lives in Richmond, Virginia; another, Rose, lives in Harpers Ferry, West Virginia, and Lisa lives in Wirtz, Virginia.

American soldiers entering Valkenburg

American soldiers in Valkenburg
(All pictures courtesy of Tina Bower)

Military cemetery at Valkenburg

CHAPTER EIGHT

HIGGINS LANDING CRAFT
UNITED STATES COAST GUARD

"SEMPER PARATUS" (ALWAYS READY) *"I made eleven landings in the Pacific as a pilot on a Higgins Landing Craft; and once blown out of the water by the Japanese."*
Frank Tucker

General Dwight Eisenhower, during a 1944 Thanksgiving Day speech said regarding the importance of the Higgins Landing Craft, *"Let us thank God for Higgins Industries, management, and labor which has given us the landing boats with which to conduct our campaign."* Think about it. Would the Normandy Invasion been successful without these landing crafts? Would the war in Europe ended in May 1945? How many more American and Allied forces would have died to end this war? The contribution and influence on amphibious warfare toward the Allied victory in World War II cannot be overstressed. Eisenhower also said, *"Andrew Higgins is the man who won the war for us. If Higgins had not designed and built those LCVPs, we never could have landed over an open beach. The whole strategy of the war would have been different."* The boats built by Higgins Industry were responsible for landing more Allied troops during the war than all other types of landing crafts together.

FRANK TUCKER
US COAST GUARD

FRANK TUCKER, a resident of Smith Mountain Lake, Virginia, another American hero, served in the United States Coast Guard during World War II. Tucker participated in 13 invasions in the Pacific as part of a crew on the Higgins landing craft. After one of his boats was blown out of the water, he helped save the lives of several soldiers. He was awarded the Bronze Star and the Purple Heart among other medals for his service during critical times in World War II. Tucker's story reveals the courage needed by crewmen from the Coast Guard to land the US Marines and American GIs on Japanese-controlled islands.

The United States Coast Guard is this nation's oldest and its premier maritime agency. The multiple missions and responsibilities of the modern Service are directly tied to the diverse heritage and the magnificent achievements of all the previous agencies.

The founder of Higgins Industries was Andrew Jackson Higgins. He was an outspoken, rough-cut, hot-tempered Irishman with an incredible imagination and the ability to turn wild ideas into reality. He hated bureaucratic red tape, loved bourbon, and was the sort who tended to knock down anything that got in his way. Higgins rose to international prominence during World War II for his design and mass production of naval combat motorboats–

boats that forever changed the strategy of modern warfare. Thanks to Higgins, the Allies no longer had to batter coastal forts into submission, sweep harbors of mines, and take over enemy-held ports before they could land an assault force. Higgins boats gave them the ability to transport thousands of men and hundreds of tons of equipment swiftly through the surf to less-fortified beaches, eliminating the need for established harbors. Tucker said, "Andrew Higgins designed racing motorboats used as rum-running boats during Prohibition. Then Higgins designed a fast patrol boat used by the Coast Guard to chase the rum runners."

A boarding party from the Revenue Cutter *Morris* prepares to board the passenger vessel *Benjamin Adams* on 16 July 1861 about 200 miles east of New York. The *Benjamin Adams* was bound for New York from Liverpool and carried 650 Scottish and Irish immigrants. The Revenue Cutter Service was originally established to enforce U.S. laws at sea and inspected incoming merchant vessels for compliance with those laws, as is illustrated here.

As late as 1930, Higgins was involved in the lumber importing and exporting business. By 1940 he was producing work boats and prototype landing crafts in a small warehouse located behind his St. Charles Avenue, New Orleans showroom. He expanded into eight separate plants in the city when the government started ordering his craft for military purposes. He employed more than 20,000 workers and produced over 700 boats a month. His total output for the Allies during World War II was 20,094 boats.

Higgins designed and produced two basic classes of military craft. The first class consisted of high-speed PT boats, which carried antiaircraft machine guns, smoke-screen devices, depth charges, and Higgins-designed compressed air fired torpedo tubes. Also in this class were the antisubmarine boats, dispatch boats, 170 foot freight supply vessels, and other specialized patrol craft produced for the Army, Navy and Maritime Commission.

LCVP

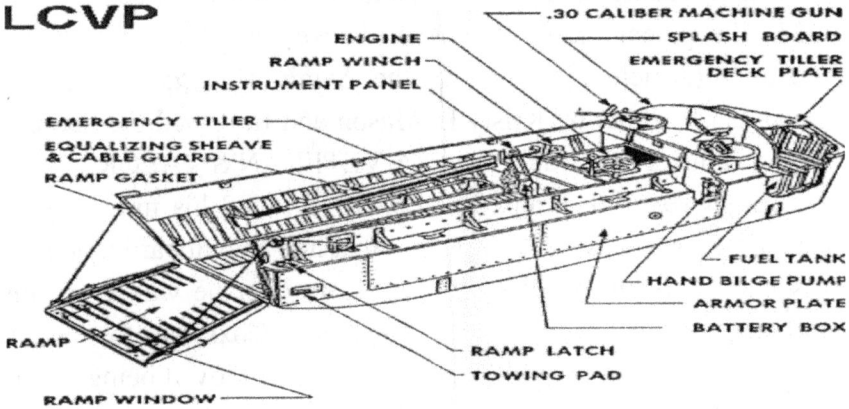

ENGINE
RAMP WINCH
INSTRUMENT PANEL
EMERGENCY TILLER
EQUALIZING SHEAVE & CABLE GUARD
RAMP GASKET
RAMP
RAMP WINDOW
.30 CALIBER MACHINE GUN
SPLASH BOARD
EMERGENCY TILLER
DECK PLATE
FUEL TANK
HAND BILGE PUMP
ARMOR PLATE
BATTERY BOX
RAMP LATCH
TOWING PAD

The second-class consisted of various types of Higgins landing craft (LCPs, LCPLs, LCVPs, LCMs), constructed of wood and steel that were used in transporting fully armed troops, light tanks, field artillery, and other mechanized equipment and supplies essential to amphibious operations. It was these boats that made the D-Day landings at Normandy and many others.

The Higgins landing craft is 36 feet long; 10 ½ feet wide and will attain the speed of 12 knots per hour. The LCVPs was made out of 3/4 inch plywood, mahogany, oak or pine. The craft had a crew of four men, either coast guard or navy. It would carry 36 combat troops or 12 combat troops and a jeep. The only protection the crew of this craft had was two .30 caliber machine guns which weren't much compared to what the enemy was attacking them with.

During Tucker's military career as a member of the US Coast Guard, he participated in the following invasions:
1/31/1944 Marshall Islands-Roi and Numur;   4/11/1944 Emirau; 4/20/1944 Cape Gloucester; 6/15/1944 Guam; 9/15/1944 Peleliu; 10/20/1944 Leyte;   1/9/1945   Luzon, Lingayen Gulf.1/29/1945 Subic Bay;   4/1/1945 Okinawa 4/7/45 Ei Shima

Frank Tucker was born in Taunton, Mass. on February 21, 1923. His parents were Ralph M. Tucker and Mary (Florance) Tucker. (Article appeared in the *Smith Mountain Eagle* on November 9, 2005, by Kristy L. Mason and furnished by Tucker). The headline of this article read, "A VETERAN'S VALOR."

"Eight-year-old, Frank Tucker would spend his mornings on Cape Cod's waters with his rowboat that had an outboard motor. It was merely a fun activity. Eleven years later he would use his skills to save lives while steering boats as a Coxswain for the US Coast Guard during World War II. 'I loved it. I loved being on the ocean and I still miss it. Can you believe that...60 years later,' he said while looking at numerous photos that replayed the events during 1942-1945. 'After December 7, 1941, when the Japanese bombed Pearl Harbor, that put us in the war and we had to win it,' said Tucker. 'I had been on boats all my life and I figured that's what I would be best at. When the war started I was in college. Everyone was being drafted, so I volunteered for the coast guard.

"At 19, Tucker boarded the USS *Aquarius* aka "16" US Coast Guard Cargo Ship. With over 100 to 150 ships in the coast guard, each ship carried over 30 boats to hit the beaches during the Invasions. He quickly became trained to steer a 36-foot long Higgins Boat Landing Barge that would carry 36 soldiers and four coast guard personnel. Days were filled with training and mock invasions for crew members and soldiers. When invaded by Japanese airplanes, all members went to their quarters. Tucker was stationed at the machine gun he used occasionally. All letters received from home had been censored by officers. Any information regarding location was marked out for the soldiers' and coast guard's protection.

Familiar with the routine, soldiers began their invasions, starting at Marshall Islands-Roi and Numur on Jan. 31, 1944. "Our first invasion, the commander met with all the coxswains. He scared the heck out of us saying it's better to kill your own crew than to be captured by the Japanese. He also told us to go to sick bay and collect cotton balls for the crew's ears," said Tucker. "During an invasion a soldier was trying to talk to me from the beach. When I took the cotton balls out of my ears to hear him, all I could hear were bullets flying around me."

(USS *Aquarius*-Photo courtesy of Frank Tucker)

During the invasions, Tucker remembered trying to get soldiers safely to shore. It's a challenge. When you are backing off a beach it's a heck of a challenge. You have to have waves and if you don't do it fast enough your boat will tip over. I enjoyed being in the service. It was a little scary at times," said Tucker. On Oct. 20, 1944, Tucker was a part of the invasion to Leyte in the Philippines. Boats came in rows of eight and covered the waters as they approached the beach. As soldiers stayed low, Tucker steered to shore as the Japanese targeted his boat. I knew we were going to get hit. You couldn't turn left or right, you had to keep going. This Japanese mortar hit the boat and knocked a hole you could drive a jeep through. We quickly sank and many soldiers were wounded. I saved several men, bringing them to the beaches and was wounded as well, said Tucker. "I ducked down when we were hit. The bomb landed right in front of me, two or three feet away. Metal was flying everywhere and my chest and back began to ache." Tucker quickly began to carry soldiers out of the water and to the beach and saved the lives of five men.

I got letters from those guys for a long time and I still talk to the guys who were on the ship with me,' said Tucker. Tucker was awarded the bronze star in 1944 and then the Purple Heart later that year. He also qualified for 11 Theatre of Operation medals from each invasion.' In December 2005, Tucker along with 14 other veterans from the Coast Guard who fought in World War II, were honored in Washington, DC.

Frank took his boot camp at Manhattan Beach on Long Island, N.Y. He had two months training to operate the Higgins boat at Camp Lejeune, N.C. The first time he experienced combat was in the *Marshall Islands*. The main assault started January 30, 1944. Prior to the invasion, the US Air Force conducted air attacks on Kwajalein which was located in the Marshall Islands. This was a giant operation that would spell either defeat or victory. Admiral Nimitz had committed his Pacific fleet and Marines. The American marines and infantry took to their landing crafts (Higgins), piloted by navy and coast guard. They reached the beach islands adjacent to Roi and Kwajalein.

On July 21, 1944 another battle took place that Tucker landed troops. This was the battle of *Guam*. The 1st US Marine Division along with the 77th Infantry Division landed on this island occupied by some 18,000 Japanese. Three days later the 4th Marine Division landed on Tinian, with 9,000 enemy soldiers waiting for them. The battle on Tinian ended eight days later but it wasn't until August 10th that the Guam battle ended. Tucker received the Bronze Star for bravery in this battle.

Third Amphibious Force

United States Pacific Fleet

Flagship of the Commander

In the name of the President of the United States and by direction of the Commander-in-Chief, United States Pacific Fleet; the Commander Third Amphibious Force, United States Pacific Fleet,

Takes pleasure in presenting the *BRONZE STAR MEDAL* to

FRANK ALLAN TUCKER, COXSWAIN

UNITED STATES COAST GUARD RESERVE

For service as set forth in the following

CITATION: *"For distinguishing himself by meritorious service as coxswain of a landing boat in connection with operations against the enemy at Kwajalein Atol, Marshall Islands, Guam, Peleliu Island, Palau, and Leyte Island, Philippine Islands; from January 31st to 20 October 1944—all of these operations were carried out against strong enemy opposition and often in the face of enemy mortar, artillery, and machine gun fire. Despite these dangers; TUCKER preformed his duties with uniform efficiency and courage. During the LEYTE assault, when his boat was hit by shell fire, he assisted in evacuating all personnel from his boat, calmly and efficiently, to a rescue boat, under continuous enemy fire, and applied first aid to Army personnel who had been stunned and wounded by the explosion. His performance of duty throughout was in keeping with the highest traditions of the naval service."*

The battle of leyte, according to records, was the largest sea battle ever because of the number of ships (282) and the number of men (190,000) who participated. The biggest mistake that the

Japanese leaders made was to challenge the US Navy at *Leyte*. They paid dearly for that decision. Tucker was wounded on the date of the Leyte invasion from a mortar on his face and on his back. He was awarded the Purple Heart. His boat stayed afloat about one minute after being hit by a five inch shell. Aboard this landing craft were 36 marines and a crew of four. Many were killed. General MacArthur promised to return to the Philippines. Frank Tucker was on the shore that day and watched that historic event.

Another major battle that Tucker was involved in was the battle of *Okinawa* which started on April 1, 1945 and lasted through June. This bloody battle followed the battle on *Iwo Jima*. The battle has been referred to as the "Typhoon of Steel" in English, and tetsu no ame ("rain of steel") or tetsu no bofu ("violent wind of steel") in Japanese. Approximately 50,000 Americans landed on Okinawa. The United States losses were the heaviest of the war. The Allied countries involved were, United States, United Kingdom, Canada, Australia, and New Zealand. Allied casualties were 12,513 dead or missing; 38,916 wounded; 79 ships sunk and 763 aircraft destroyed. The Japanese had 66,000 dead or missing; 17,000 wounded; 7,455 captured; 16 ships sunk; 7,830 aircraft destroyed and 140,000 civilians dead or missing. Neither side expected Okinawa to be the last major battle of the war but it was. The Allies were planning the invasion of Kyushu and Honshu on the Japanese mainland. After the two atomic bombs were dropped on two Japanese cities, the Japanese surrendered.

Tucker served on the USS *Aquarius* (AKA-16). The *Aquarius* was laid down under a Maritime Commission contract on 28 April 1943 at Kearny, New Jersey by the Federal Shipbuilding and Dry Dock Company; launched on July 23, 1943, acquired by the Navy on August 20, 1943, and commissioned on August 21, 1943, Captain R.V. Marron, USCG, in command.

Manned by a coast guard crew, the attack cargo ship conducted brief shake down training in Chesapeake Bay and sailed on September 15 via the Panama Canal to the west coast. Reaching San Francisco October 19, the ship loaded cargo and embarked passengers for transportation to Hawaii. On January 4, 1944, the attack transport sailed for Hawaii. She sortied on January 22nd for the invasion of the Marshall Islands. *Aquarius* stood into the transport area off ROI and Namur Islands, Kwajalein Atoll, on January 31 until February 6th, unloaded her cargo and disembarked troops. She joined the 3rd fleet on February 10.

Tucker receiving Purple Heart

On March 21 she moved to Noumea, New Caledonia, loaded Army personnel and equipment; and took them to Emirau Island to serve as a garrison force. She embarked troops of the 4th Marine Regiment and took them back to Guadalcanal. She needed repairs.

Following repairs, she returned to Guadalcanal for the 3rd Marine Division rehearsals for the assault on the Marianas.

Then directed to invade *Guam*, the invasion of Guam was postponed because of the Battle of the Philippine Sea and fierce resistance of the Japanese garrison on Saipan. The *Aquarius* and other ships sorted on July 17th reached Guam on the 21st. *Aquarius* headed for Hollandia, New Guinea, arriving on the 25th. She sortied on Oct. 13th with TG78.1 to support the landings on Lingayen Gulf. On the 27th, she sorted with Division 36 for the assault on Okinawa. The *Aquarius* returned to Seattle, Washington, Jan 26, 1945 to be overhauled. While Frank was on the west coast, Japan surrendered. *Aquarius* departed San Diego on August18, arrived at Guam on September 4th, and moved to Saipan three days later to load cargo and troops for use in the occupation of Japan. The *Aquarius* shuttled Chinese troops between Hong Kong, Chinwangtao and Tsingtao and returned to Seattle on December 13th. The *Aquarius* was placed out of commission on May 23, 1945. She was stuck from the Navy list on November 13, 1946.

On June 22, 1946, this hero of World War II, Frank Tucker, convinced Joyce Wheaton Watson to marry him. Joyce and Frank have four children, one is deceased.

TOMMY L. HARBOUR

US COAST GUARD

"I participated in the assault of the Cherbourg Peninsula, Southern France (Normandy), Iwo Jima, and Okinawa and didn't get a scratch. I was lucky." **Tommy Harbour**

My interview with Tommy Harbor began with breakfast at Granny's K restaurant in Milton, West Virginia at 8:30 a.m. on September 7, 2007. We were served fluffy hot cakes, country ham with an individual cup of warm maple syrup. Tommy and I renewed our acquaintances. I had lived in Milton for eight years after returning from the Korean War. My brother and I bought and operated the taxi-bus company in that quaint city.

After breakfast, we drove two miles east of Milton to Lees Creek where Harbour has 141 acre farm in a quite secluded spot. There are plenty of deer and turkey on the property for close friends to hunt. After a couple of hours of taping Harbour's wartime experiences, we jumped on his 4-wheeler. I hopped on the back, crossed a narrow bridge and rode up to his lake to feed the fish. Because of the drought this year the level of the lake was down two or three feet—with no water from the creek or spring to replenish it. The fish were anticipating feeding time. The fish had gathered in the shallow area next to the bank with their mouths open, ready to be fed.

Driving back from the lake, Tommy pointed out an old working well. The walls were made out of beautiful stone with steps on the inside to allow a person to climb to the bottom. The top was covered to prevent animals from getting into the well. I noticed a salt lick and further down a hunters' shed. You can figure out this situation. He has a nice picnic shelter, which is used for his wife Betty's class reunions and political functions. When the present governor, Joe Manchin, was running for that office, Tommy held a rally for him. Tommy Harbour was the mayor of Milton for 17years. [An interesting side note about this shelter. While it was under construction Betty asked Tommy what it was going to cost. He said no more than $1,500. But he quit counting when the cost hit $7,500.]

The area is well manicured—a result of Tommy's mowing regularly even though he is nearly blind. During the interview Harbour would occasionally go outside to spit out tobacco juice. I asked him what he was chewing only to discover it was Havana Blossom. He offered me a chew saying it was sugar-free. I refused remembering the one and only time I had tried chewing tobacco. [During my high school days my dear friend Charles Elkins always had a package of Mail Pouch or Beech Nut chewing tobacco in his pocket when we played baseball. Charles, a gifted athlete, was the pitcher, I was the catcher. I thought I would take a big chew during one of our games. That day a huge Johnson boy from West Hamlin, WV tried to steal home base. He knocked me over about two flips at which time I swallowed my chew. I can't tell you how many colors that I turned but it was the last time I took a chew of tobacco. I couldn't care if it's sugar-free or not Tommy, no thanks!] I told him that tobacco would give him cancer. He laughed as he answered me, "If I don't chew, I might become an alcoholic." He was just kidding. I felt honored spending most of the day with this local hero. He is a very funny person who has many interesting experiences to share. This is his story as he freely shared it with me.

Tommy L. Harbour served on the US *Bayfield* for two years. The *Bayfield* was commissioned on November 20, 1944. He was a crew member on an LCVP (PA 33-4 boat). The *Bayfield* would hold 19 landing crafts, a landing craft tank and two LCTs. PA stands for Personnel Assault, the number 33 was the number of the *Bayfield*; number 4 was the number of Tommy's boat

THE NORMANDY LANDING: It was eight miles to the beach and the water was rough. There was not a life jacket in the boat. Tommy told the soldiers aboard, "You don't have a life jacket and three teenagers in a plywood boat taking you to the beach. When you hit the beach and we let you out, you were lucky to get to the battlefield." Harbour was asked if when he was taking the troops into Omaha Beach if there a lot of laughing, smoking etc. His reply was, "There wasn't any of it. They were all sitting around thinking about home and what tomorrow brings. There was no smoking, no nothing. They were quiet and hunkered down. I never did, from Slapton Sands on, when I let that ramp down [that was Tommy's job]; if you let it down to soon you swamp the boat. Those boys went out of there and didn't know what they were going in to. I never had to wait on them to get out. Some of them caught a bullet just as they went out of the boat. That's the story straight from the horse's mouth about the American troops."

"The boys had one thing on their minds—to kill a German. We did too but we couldn't find one, you know. That's why you wonder about the war over there (Iraq). If Bush could have just looked down the edge of Omaha Beach or at Iwo Jima things might be different. Bob, the dead soldiers were stacked like cord wood.

NORMANDY

"I was glad I didn't have to take a rifle and go over on the beach. But I'm going to tell you right now, the Germans were good with the 88's. One day I met an old boy on crutches with both arms hanging over. I opened the door for him and during our visit I told him where I had been. He said 'Harbour, if you hadn't dumped me out on that beach and didn't even look back, I wouldn't be in this shape.' Harbour laughed and said the guy blamed him." "On D-Day about four o'clock in the evening we picked up an officer to take him to the beach. He said, 'We ran a taxi just like you ran the Milton Taxi Company.' After my boat was sunk at Normandy, we went back to our ship waiting for orders."

Troops landing in Normandy. (Photo courtesy of Tommy Harbour)

Tommy Harbour was told that his number 4 boat that had been sunk at Normandy was located there in their museum. He and Betty spent $6,000 to make the trip to France during the 60th Anniversary of the invasion to check it out. He told the folks in the museum that he was Tommy Harbour from Milton, West Virginia and that this was the Higgins boat that he made the landing in. They said that they had been looking for someone who had been in that boat. They asked how he could prove it. Tommy told them that there was a large hole shot through the side of the craft that you could stick your fist through.

Tommy said that a piece of plywood about two feet square was nailed over that hole. The plywood had a crack in it. He said the Higgins boats were well built-but they did a poor job repairing number 4. During his inspection process, Tommy found that a star had been painted along the side where the hole was made by a German shell. He told them that there wasn't a star on his boat because it would have been a real target for the Germans. This was a very emotional time for this man who had five Battle stars and had been through so much. Number 4 was indeed Harbour's boat.

Tommy Harbour inspecting Higgins Boat #4 at Normandy

RESPECT

Harbour continues, "The Higgins boat has a wooden shield to keep the engine's blade from hitting anything. The wooden shield has a piece of steel, a quarter of an inch thick that runs all the way to the bow past the screws on the back. When you go in to the beach, the Keel hits into the sand; and that keeps the boat from wavering. A lot of thought went into building the Higgins boat.

Another thing, the way the screw is built in so it can't touch anything. The boat can land on coral and the screw can't touch it. The screw is encased inside the wood and steel. The more boats the Higgins plant made, the better they got."

The boom on the ship would lower the boat. Only the three crew members were in it at the time. The soldiers or marines would climb down rope ladders on the side of the ship to load into the landing crafts. A ring about two feet in diameter with a cable in front raises the boat is a big steel hook-an open hook. It is dangerous so the crew have to be careful especially in rough weather.

The sunken landing craft had been salvaged and Tommy had overhauled the engine in time for the invasion of Southern France in August. The crew was told to pick up a lieutenant and take him to the beach. This was on D-Day. *Utah Beach* was a lot quieter than it was on *Omaha Beach.* He said, "So I told Jones (Jones was the coxswain on the boat), you know we can't make it to the beach and back to our ship before dark." Jones said, "Well, we gotta go." So they took the officer to the beach and let him off. It was now dark. They couldn't see their hands in front of them, so they wondered which direction their ship was. They could see a lot of shelling going on at the horizon. They took their boat toward the shelling to take a look.

Jones pulled their boat beside a ship but they were unable to see the number on it. Someone on the deck hollered down and asked, "What are you S.O.B's doing down there?" Tommy replied, "We are from the USS *Bayfield,* we are lost and don't know where our ship is." The voice from the deck said, "If you don't get that damn boat out of here, we'll blow it out of the water." Tommy thinks the ship was the *Nevada*, a battle wagon. Jones backed up and turned around sideways. As they turned the USS *Nevada* fired all its guns and their boat almost capsized from the blast. Their boat was on its side before it came back down. They finally found the *Bayfield*. One of the crew members, Chaucy, went to sick bay for a few days. Harbour's ears rang so bad that he lost 65% hearing in one ear and 68% from the other.

(Habour's #4 boat landing on Normandy-Courtesy of Harbour)

The USS *Bayfield* was a Coast Guard ship and all the crew on the ship and the Higgins LCVC boats were members of the Coast Guard. Harbor had to take his discharge to prove to some veteran buddies that the coast guard served during combat. Harbour had graduated from Milton High School in May 1942, and had attended Marshall College (now University) for one semester before joining the coast guard. He was born March 6, 1925. He

was the son of Emsley W. Harbour and Lucy Hudgins Harbour of
Milton, West Virginia. Tommy and Betty Lou Morris were
married July 27, 1949. They have two children and two
grandchildren.

Harbour's #4 landing troops in Normandy

Bob: Tommy, how many trips did you make to the Normandy
Beaches on D-Day?

Tommy: I don't really know. The first day my #4 boat was sunk.
Then four or five days later we went back and salvaged it. Look at
this picture, the soldiers didn't even get their feet wet. You can see
how far on the beach our boat is. See this cable? Jones put the boat
in reverse. We were going back and I was cranking on the ramp
and another boat came in on the other side and let their ramp down
too quick and got hung in that cable. Two waves came back, the
water came into the boat and we were in water up to our waist.
That's when I got three rides back to my ship. Everyone was going
in. I had been in and didn't want to go back in any more. He
laughed.

Bob: Have you been to the D-Day Museum located in New
Orleans? Doesn't the Higgins Boat have two machines mounted on
them?

Tommy: Yes, but that was a mistake. The machine guns were in the back and had to shoot over the troops. What happened, there were too many of our troops getting shot. They tried to get too much on the Higgins. They probably would have worked well in Vietnam, shooting out the side. Just remember, when the boat goes in there with 36 men with their equipment, they will average 200-225 pounds each. Now when you unload them, the front of the boat comes up. They (Higgins) didn't think of that. When the men were transferred to the coast guard, they didn't think they would go through all this, laughing.

Bob: Some probably thought they would be patrolling up and down the Potomac.

Tommy: Yea, [with a laugh] many people don't realize that the coast guard was ever in combat.

Bob: Tommy, that's the reason that I am excited about your experiences to go along with Frank Tucker's and Don Gibson to show people the importance of the US Coast Guard.

Tommy: We never have had that respect. I told a man at the *Herald Dispatch*, Tom Massey, a good friend of mine (I let him kill his first Turkey here on the farm), when you put this article in the paper, put in there that the coast guard never did get credit for what they did during World War II. And he did. The *Charleston Gazette* wrote an article, when they were trying to get rid of the Coast Guard, that the USCG sank more German U-Boats than the US Navy. The *Campbell* sank six U-Boats off the coast of Florida. They were made out of cutters that were used to cut the ice at the great lakes and converted them. They were loaded with depth charges and torpedoes. The *Campbell* actually sank five and rammed the sixth.

Tommy continued, "The USS *Bayfield* from the tip of the bow was 60 feet to the water. We had a few guys who would dive off the bow. We went swimming in Southern France. It was too much for me, he said. It was 26 feet to the deck, Laughing, Tommy said, "You don't dive like that in Mud River, I tell you."

Tommy said that they went on the *Bayfield* in the winter, picked up a bunch of troops at Chesapeake Bay and crossed over to Scotland. "We had nothing to do during the trip but to shoot craps and things. It was so cold. I will tell you how cold it was. When the spray off the front of the boat came up and hit, it froze right then. Old Chuncy was crying because his hands were frozen." Tommy took off the top of the engine hatch and got him pair of brown gloves, then put Chaucy's hands into them and the steam just rolled. 'Years and years later during a reunion at New Orleans, Betty and me got out of the car and here came old Chuncy and he said, 'There's the guy who saved my hands.' We were real good buddies." Tommy said, 'I'm trying to talk him into going to Normandy with me in 2009. He's got the money but is too tight to spend it."

[Bob told Tommy a story of how cold it was when he moved from Nebraska. It was so cold when I went outside there were two beagle hounds with a jumper cable trying to get a rabbit to start running]. This reminded Tommy of an experience that he had on a hunting trip to Nebraska in 1961 or 1962. They were in a station wagon with a trailer pulling two hunting dogs. This was the time that Jack Kennedy was campaigning for president in West Virginia. The people knew Tommy was a Democrat and Nebraska being a republican state, threw tomatoes all over his car during the night while it was parked in front of the motel. His car had West Virginia license plates.

Tommy was asked what his main job was on the boat. His position on the boat was across from the coxswain. On the right side were two filters. On the left side were his gauges, water and oil pressure and all that. A hole came out so he could peep around to see if the water was going out of the bilges. "My job then was to keep the fuel tanks full. We kept 180 gallons diesel fuel in the tanks. Let me think a minute. I always carried a jumper cable for our battery to make sure it started. You had a primer on it—push it down a few times. We had one spark plug. The coxswain would push the primer four or five times. It would spray the diesel fuel around the cylinder and when you push the button, fire flew in there caught on fire and burned for a while—then the engine would start up like it was the Fourth of July."

Tommy kept a bunch of C-rations in the back of the craft plus candy bars, a box of cigars and stuff. When they got started and were going to make a long trip somewhere, old Jones got breakfast on. "I got the C-rations out, got out eggs and bacon, laid them on the manifold and boy in about ten minutes talk about hot eggs; we had them. Jones was the coxswain; I could have been if I wanted to. Here's what I thought. I attended diesel training school at Camp Lejeune and when I got out of the service there would be a lot of diesel engines; and I would repair them. When I got back home there weren't any diesel engines in West Virginia. All my training was for nothing. I worked at Blenko Glass Factory for a while. My dad bought a service station and my brother Paul and I ran it."

Tommy Harbour entered the US Coast Guard on July 5, 1943 and was discharged May 27, 1946. From his discharge: He was a Motor Machinist's Mate. Harbour is entitled to the American Area, European-African-Middle Eastern, Asiatic-Pacific Area Campaign Medals, World War II victory Medals. Harbour participated in the assaults of the Cherbourg Peninsula, Southern France and Iwo Jima, Okinawa.

DONNIE GIBSON
Seaman First Class

US Coast Guard   A few years ago, Vera Thompson Treadway wrote a book about Don Gibson called *One of a Kind*. [Gibson's book was published by the *Central Printing Company* Beckley,

West Virginia in 1996.] *I* was given permission to use some of the material from that book. Don is a patriotic American who joined the United States Coast Guard to serve his country during World War II. The duties and responsibilities of the USCG are many and at times overlooked. In this chapter you have read about two other members of the coast guard, Frank Tucker and Tommy Harbour, each having different roles. Gibson's story will provide another look as just how important this branch of the service was during World War II. Gibson served on a troop carrier that transported troops to the war zone and back to the states.

Don Gibson and I are long-time friends. I first met him on the practice field at Marshall College (now University) in 1947. He was a star football player, I was proud just to make the team as a freshman and only 17 years old. My interview was with Don at a teammate's house in Huntington, West Virginia on October 26, 2007. We were in town to attend the Hall of Fame Banquet and Marshall's Home Coming football game.

Don was born in Van, WV on May 5, 1924 to Benjamin Harrison Gibson and Pearl Lacy Gibson. Don had a humble beginning which was a struggle for him and his family. However, with determination and with God-given athletic ability, he has had a very successful and rewarding life. His life has had a positive influence on hundreds of people throughout the years.

As a football player, Don was average in size but far from average in ability. As a freshman at Marshall, he was named as the Most Outstanding Player and Honorable Mention to the West Virginia All Conference Team. He prides himself on the fact that from when he was a sophomore in high school, through college, he missed starting only one game and that was when his mother died.

During his time at Marshall, Pearl Harbor was bombed and by 1942 America was deeply involved in a world war. On February 3, 1943, Don received his notice to report for military duty. The induction center in Huntington was overcrowded with young men. The lines were long. Don observed that the coast guard line was much shorter than the army's. One of the recruiters, realizing that Don was an athlete, asked if he would like to play football for the Coast Guard. This is the reason that Don didn't join the army. Boot Camp was at Curtis Bay, Maryland. He made the coast guard football team although because of his size, he had to prove himself. One person using Don's name indicated that the "G" in Gibson stood for "GUTS." Guts and desire, he had plenty of both.

Football season ended. Don began to serve as first loader aboard the buoy tender, USS *Firebush*. They serviced light houses and marked all channels. Don was transferred to the USS *Monticello,* a troop transport taking soldiers to and from the United States and Naples, Italy and Marseille, France. The *Monticello* was also used to transport enemy prisoners of war home.

With time on their hands as they were crossing the ocean, Don decided to try gambling with hopes of earning some easy money. He played five-card stud and tried his luck at throwing the dice and with any luck a six and one would appear. The first night he was successful and won several dollars. With full confidence in his ability, he tried his luck the next night. His luck ran out and he lost everything. This ended Don's gambling.

The crew on the USS *Monticello* picked up troops from the Red Ball Division that were in Europe and Japan and brought them back to the United States. This was a large transport hauling as many as 7,000 troops at a time. The chow line was open all the time. One day Don and some buddies were climbing down the ladder outside the cafeteria and saw some apple pies the cooks had made. They took two pies, only to be caught. They didn't get to eat the pies but found a duty they were not expecting. With tooth brushes, Don and his pie-taking friend had to scrub down the ladder.

Gibson served two years, ten months and thirteen days in the coast guard and had enough points to be discharged. He was looking for a way to earn some easy money. He said, "I was told that people were unable to purchase liquor so I bought a case of Cutty Shark. I was going to sell it for a profit. When I got home I found out that the rules had been lifted on liquor, so I got stuck with it. Not being an alcohol man myself, I passed it on to an aunt who had rheumatism." He was discharged on December 4, 1945, when he was earning $66.00 a month. Three of Don's brothers also served their country during World War II. Orville served on the USS *Roberts*, a destroyer escort. Lou served on the USS *Nashville* that carried General MacArthur back to the Philippines; and Ray served in the army. Ray played football at Fort Knox, Kentucky.

Don said "I went back to Winding Gulf, West Virginia. My mom had rented a cabin at Farley Hill so Lou and I would have a place to come back to. My dad was gone. My brother, Ray, had been discharged and was looking after her for us. That's when Cam Henderson and Roy Straight came to visit us (Don and Lou) to play football at Marshall College." Don and Lou were worried about their mother if they accepted the coaches' offer to attend Marshall. Coach Henderson solved that problem for them. He told the Gibson's that he would take care of her too. He provided an apartment for the three on Eight Street in Huntington. It was probably the only time that two freshmen brought their invalid mother to college with them. Pearl Gibson was proud of her sons and their accomplishments. Her life had been hard.

(Don and Wertie Gibson. Photo courtesy of the Gibson's)

Don was sitting on the steps of Marshall's Student Union when he saw a Marshall cheerleader approaching. Usually Don was very shy around girls. Don said *"When I saw her, I knew instantly that I wanted her to be the mother of my children. She was tall and slender. Her long brunette hair fell past her shoulders in soft waves. She was wearing a summer cotton dress that was covered with yellow flowers."* Her name was Wertie Bowe. Wertie was born in *Charleston, West Virginia. A local newspaper later* wrote the following: *"Wertie Bowe, cheerleader for the Big Green last year and Don Gibson, versatile footballer, are contemplating marriage at the end of the coming football season. Wertie will teach at Ironton, O. this coming year and at present is switchboard operator for Montgomery Ward."*

The Ironton school board policy did not allow female teachers to be married. Don and Wertie eloped and kept their marriage a secret because Don had two more years of college. They were married on July 24, 1948. After graduation, Don's coaching career began when Herb Royer asked him to join him as line coach and scout for West Virginia Tech to success as the head football/basketball coach and athletic director at Highlands University located in Las Vegas, New Mexico.

Their first child, Donald, was born on December 23, 1950. Donald graduated from Yale University School of Law with a Juris Doctor degree. He is a partner in Driscoll and Gibson Law firm in Marshfield, Massachusetts. Their second child, Ann, attended Baylor University, Albertus Magnus College (where she graduated with a Bachelor of Science Degree in Biology) and has her Masters Degree in Business Administration and her PhD in Exercise Physiology. Ann is currently Assistant Professor in Exercise Physiology at Barry University, Miami, Florida. Don and Wertie's third child is Pamela Gibson Buchanan. She has her B.A. Degree from Florida Atlantic University; Masters Degree from Stetson University; and Doctor of Education from Nova Southeastern University. Pamela is currently an Elementary School Principal in Sarasota County, Florida.

From a humble beginning from Winding Gulf, West Virginia, Don Gibson has found the American Dream for himself and his family. It took hard work, a lot of sacrifice and determination. He served his country when called. Yes, Don Gibson is "One of a Kind."

Picture of Don Gibson that appears in the Marshall University Hall of Fame.   (Photo courtesy of Don Gibson)

CHAPTER NINE

BATTLE OF IWO JIMA

FEBRUARY 19, 1945-MARCH 16, 1945

SEMPER FIDELIS—ALWAYS FAITHFUL

**PRESIDENT HARRY TRUMAN PRESENTING THE MEDAL
OF HONOR TO HERSHEL W. WILLIAMS (IWO JIMA)**
August 5, 1945
(Photo courtesy of Hershel Williams)

Iwo Jima was the first island of the Japanese homeland to be attacked. This was a volcanic island 1,118 miles south of Tokyo, a small island, just seven and one half square miles. On February 14, 1945 some 30,000 US Marines, members of the 4th and 5th Marine Division, landed on the beachhead. The battle for Iwo Jima was one of the most savage battles fought during World War II. The losses both for the Americans and Japanese were heavy.

The Japs motto was "to kill ten of the enemy before dying." Twenty out of 22 Japanese soldiers would die in the battle of Iwo Jima. One out of every three US Marines would either be killed or wounded. Only four survived the battle from E Company, 2nd Battalion 5th Marine Division. The Congressional Medal of Honor (CMH) was awarded to 27 Americans, 13 posthumously; the most CMH ever awarded for any battle. One of the stories is about **Corporal Hershel "Woody" Williams**, the only living Medal of Honor recipient in West Virginia. He received this honor for action on Iwo Jima on February 23, 1945. "Just a pleasure cruise" was the words spoken over loudspeakers aboard the troopship, which used to describe the impending mission of the Third Marine Division. Corporal Hershel Woodrow Williams who had grown up on a farm in Marion County, West Virginia, was one of more than 10,000 Leathernecks in the Third Division who felt reassured by those words and by the vast armada of ships and planes that had been softening up Iwo Jima since December 1944. Now it was the morning of February 19, and from the deck of the troopship, the 21 year-old, dark-haired nom-com could see hundreds of landing crafts circling about on the ocean as they waited for the last thunderous bombardment to lift.

My personal interview with Hershel William's, began on Thursday September 13, 2007 at the Williams home on Wirebranch Rd., Ona, West Virginia, about two o'clock in the afternoon. I found this American hero of Iwo Jima to be very cooperative, a nice humble, highly intelligent man. "Woody" as he prefers to be called, was born in a small village called Quiet Dell, West Virginia on October 2, 1923. His family made their living on a small dairy farm with 30 to 35 cows to milk twice each-day-and by hand. They sold the milk from house to house.

When Woody enlisted in the marines, they were only accepting two men each month. While waiting to go to boot camp, Woody was driving a taxi in Fairmont, West Virginia. After work one day, an attractive young lady needed a taxi to go home. Woody asked her to ride up front with him. There were other times that Ruby needed a taxi cab and Woody was there to drive her home. Ruby could not fail to like Woody. He was a personable young man, good-looking, clean-cut in appearance but not very tall. Before leaving for the Marine Corps, Ruby and Woody decided to become engaged. Their devotion to each other held them together for the 28 months that Woody was away. On May 27, 1943, Williams left for San Diego to attend boot camp.

The fate of nations often hangs in the balance during great battles, which in turn hinge upon minor events—as the action of a single towering and heroic individual. During the Civil War in Abraham Lincoln's administration, it was decided to establish an award to the man who distinguishes himself in conflict at the risk of his own life above and beyond the call of duty, and in Lincoln's own words (on another occasion), "It is altogether fitting and proper that we should do this." The individual, who renders himself conspicuous by gallantry in action, by right, deserves to be set apart from the rest of his comrades and to be remembered by some badge or mark of distinction. [For this purpose, the *Congressional Medal of Honor* was instituted in 1861. It is the oldest military decoration, next to the *Purple Heart,* which was established by George Washington in 1782.]

Nobody has ever succeeded especially well in defining the qualities that makes a hero. Even the marines have their special heroes and Hershel "Woody" Williams fits that mold. Woody only weighed three and one-half pounds at birth. His mother, Lurenna, named him Hershel after his doctor, Dr. Hershel Yost, and Woodrow after our World War I president. The tiny boy grew up into a sturdy little fellow who each day trudged three miles to a small country school and three miles back-through rain and snow. His friends cut the Woodrow to Woody.

His was an envious childhood—the kind city children dream of baseball on the sandlot team, swimming in the "Ole Swimming Hole" near the farm with the rest of the gang. His pet collie, Ruddy, had been trained to bring in the cows from the pasture on a command from Woody. And he enjoyed rabbit hunting where he became a good shot with a rifle. Then there were hay rides, horseback riding and square dances. He learned to plink a guitar. All of Woody's time was not spent in amusements, however, for there were the long hard hours on the farm. This was especially true after his father passed away. Woody and his two brothers, Lloyd and Gerald, did all the chores and ran the dairy establishment. Woody attended a little red schoolhouse and East Fairmont High School where he made good grades. He left high school to become a truck driver in the CCC (Civilian Conservation Camp).

Woody's baptism of fire came swiftly and suddenly in the invasion of Guam as soon as he and his buddies of the 1st Battalion piled out of their landing craft in the first wave of the landing party. Woody reflected later, that after they had established their beachhead, it was a good thing the Japs were such bad shots. The Marines' orders were to grab a hunk of beach and dig in and keep moving ahead. That's the way it was for eight straight days....duck in a foxhole, crouch and hope and then move ahead to another hole. Woody was asked how did he feel when he saw a yellow face looking down and one slant eye squinted along a Jap rifle? How did he feel during their "Banzai" suicide charges? He said, "You wondered how and why they kept coming and if they would ever be any end to them. We just had to keep firing and killing them until we had killed enough of them to break their main resistance."

Was he scared? Sure, he was scared –at first. After that he said you don't care anymore. You don't give a darn whether you get hit or not. Following the victory on Guam, plans were being made for their next mission which was Iwo Jima, and the men were given a rest period. Instead of the enchanted South Sea Island pictured in the movies with its balmy breezes and glistening white sandy beaches and Tahitian maidens, there were only heat and rain and aggravating humidity, plus sharp jagged coral rock in the water. There was "jungle rot" like athlete's feet, only ten times more infectious. There were dysentery, insects and flies that came in droves. Another problem was the mosquitoes that brought malaria.

Now the beach of Iwo Jima was five miles away, but even at that distance Woody could see fiery columns of flame and smoke as 8 and 16-inch shells from cruisers and battleships blasted the volcanic Island. Then the barrage lifted and the landing craft moved slowly and inexorably toward Iwo Jima.

The following story was furnished by Woody Williams, much in own words. "We got off the ship in the wee-hours of the morning to go ashore in a Higgins Boat. There were a great number of Higgins Boats running around. Once we hit the assembly area, we started circling until we got the signal to go to the beach. We circled all day. I had never been seasick going overseas but I along with everyone else got seasick. The waves were very high and we were bouncing around like a cork all day long. I don't know if I got seasick because of that or because somebody vomited on me.

"The problem being on that 'thing' that long was that mother-nature had to be taken care of. There was water on the floor although there were wooden racks on the floor. The bilge pump couldn't keep all the water out. They took us back to the ship and when I got to the top deck, I just collapsed. I stayed there all night.

The next morning after chow, we couldn't eat so we got back on the Higgins Boat to go to our designated area. The 4th Division had gone around Mt. Suribachi which gave us enough room to land on the beach about 11 o'clock. There were so many marines on the beach that they couldn't make any gain."

The Japanese opened fire from hundreds of concealed positions. Artillery shells screamed toward the long, green lines of marines. Mortar rounds thumped into their midst. Automatic small-arms weapons unleashed a murderous volume of lead. Scores of marines slipped silently beneath the waves, their blood staining the blue water. Others reached the shore only to fall mortally wounded. Those who made it unscathed burrowed into the sand, scooping out the black volcanic ash with their hands to find some shelter from the enemy guns. They were pinned down, unable to advance up the gently-rising beaches toward the two airstrips or the highest elevation, which was Mt. Suribachi—556 feet high.

Soon Woody Williams, the 155-pound marine was assembling his special weapons section on deck and strapping on a 72-pound flamethrower. The weather had worsened during the night and the landing craft were bobbing on the heavy swells. Woody watched, chilled by the sign of violent death; but the demands of combat left little time to think and to be afraid. Company C, unable to dent Japanese positions only 150 yards away, had to advance. But how? Captain Beck, crouching behind the shelter on a dune, listened to the other platoon leaders. No suggestions. He looked at Corporal Williams with a note of desperation in his voice as he said, "What about the flamethrower? Can you do anything with it?" Woody said, "I'll see what I can do." These words had committed him, and he knew the odds against his survival were great. His fluttering stomach told him this. Yet outwardly he remained calm. "I'd like to have four men who can provide some protective fire with rifles and BARs, "(Browning automatic rifle) he said. "One of them should be armed with a bazooka. I'll also need the demolitions. It was a little more than 100 yards from Company C's furthermost penetration to a complex of three self-protecting Jap pillboxes. "We could see them as we left our front lines and began to crawl forward. The center pillbox was my main objective because it was the one really giving us fits." Williams and Tripp, the latter armed with M-1 rifles and some pole charges, moved past the last American foxhole. They were crawling with feet digging in for traction against the sandy ash. A stream of bullets whipped over Woody's helmet and he pressed his face hard against the grit. He said a silent prayer. Woody reached the lip of a shell crater and slid into it headfirst. A mortar round thumped into the porous soil not far away, and he could see sand trickling down the sides of the crater.

Corporal Tripp followed Woody into the hole and they lay there under the glare of the morning sun trying to catch their breath. Williams said, "Stay close to me. If any Japs come out of one of those pillboxes, I may need you in a hurry." "I'll be with you," the corporal replied. As they came out of the crater and were inching forward, machine-gun bullets were slitting the air just above their helmets. The muted explosion of another mortar round went off to their left.

On Woody's back were three tanks—the uppermost one filled with compressed air, and the bottom two filled with mixtures of high-octane gasoline and diesel fuel oil. With the tank of his flame thrower strapped firmly to his back, the nozzle grasped in his right hand, and charges of TNT in his left, Woody went forward alone in the face of withering fire from an enemy determined that he would never reach his objectives. But Woody had a couple of extra weapons that the Nips didn't see—Luck and Courage. He inched his way up to the first box and skirted around behind it, and heaved the stick of TNT through the opening—smoke and dust billowed out. Just to make sure the job was complete, Woody mounted the pillbox and sent a stream of intense fire from the flame thrower searing into the Japs inside, whose bodies flared up like pieces of celluloid as soon as it touched them. Woody was covered by four riflemen. His flame throwers had a life of only from eight to ten seconds. His demolition charges could only be used once. Four times during those four hours, he returned to the command post to renew his flamethrowers and to obtain fresh TNT charges and struggled back to the Jap lines.

The machine gunner inside that Jap stronghold was frantically trying to bring the gun to bear on the man with the flamethrower, but Woody was able to keep out of the line of fire by remaining in shallow trenches. Bullets began slapping into the sand in front of Woody and he pressed his face against the ground. When he looked up he saw a chilling sight. Three Japanese soldiers, dressed alike in light-brown uniforms, wrap-around leggings, and dark helmets, were charging out from behind the pillbox toward him. Woody squeezed and the flame leaped forward. When the flame hit, it just went right on through. There was one great big "puff" that paralyzed them and petrified them. They stopped dead in their tracks and just fell over.

(Photo courtesy of Woody Williams)

Using six flamethrowers and dynamite, Woody Williams, 21, a five-foot, five-inch marine corporal, wiped out seven Jap pillboxes, killing an uncounted number of Japs, to help clear the way for a Third Division company halted in its advance to the central airfield. Four times Woody threw pole charges through narrow openings of emplacements. When two faulty charges failed to explode, he worked his way back and squirted flame into the pillboxes. Woody's flamethrower stopped Japs who tried to get him with rifles, bayonets, and grenades. "I counted 21 of them" he said, "and I killed them all with flames." Jap cross-fire had stopped the advance and Jap riflemen popped out of bypassed spider traps to shoot at the backs of the well and wounded marines. The area was one of the most bitterly defended and best fortified sectors of the island.

During this time Woody's buddies killed 20 or 35 Japs who made a break for the Jap lines from their bypassed trenches. After four grueling hours, Woody-with seven pillboxes to his credit, rested. "Darned if I know why I didn't get bumped off that day," Woody said. "I didn't even get a scratch. Then a mortar shell fragment bounced off my leg while I was in a foxhole one night. Didn't hurt much and I stayed in action."

This was on the 13th day of the Iwo Campaign when Woody's luck ran out. He was slightly wounded in the knee by shrapnel but continued to fight because his outfit was low of replacements. He said, "I can't leave. The new men in my section got their first training with a flamethrower just last night. I couldn't possibly leave those guys." His heroic accomplishment made possible an advance that materially aided in the final hard won victory on Iwo Jima and the planting Stars and Stripes atop Suribachi.

On March 15, 1945, two days before the fighting on Iwo Jima ended, a captured Japanese major, one of 1,250 POWs taken before the fall of Iwo Jima, told an interrogator that 300 of his soldiers were hiding in a large cave close to the beach. Company C was only 400 yards from the cave so Woody with some BAR men to protect him moved down there with four satchel charges of C-2 explosives. He set off two charges near the entrance and tons of sand and earth cascaded down to seal the entrance and the fate of whoever might have been in there. The battle was over. The marines had paid a heavy price for this Pacific base that could be used by planes making bomb runs over Japan.

Woody went back to Guam in April. Not until August did he get any inkling that he was being considered for a medal of some kind. It happened one afternoon when he was abruptly called to the sergeant major's office. "Are you ready to go home? You are to pack your sea bag and be ready to leave at 6:00 a.m. hours tomorrow morning." "What for?" "I can't tell you. Be happy that you are going." He couldn't believe he was returning home, not until he heard it from Maj. Gen. G.B. Erskine the next morning. "I was scared to death when I went into see the general," Woody recalls. "He congratulated me and said I was returning to the States under sealed orders. "I can't tell you why," he said, "but it's something that will make you proud the rest of your life." Woody was flown to Guam, to the Hawaiian Islands, where by mistake his orders were opened. He was to receive the Congressional Medal of Honor.

On October 5th, Sgt. Hershel Woodrow Williams stood stiffly at attention on the lawn of the White House. At least it looked that way to his mother and fiancée, who were proudly watching. Actually, he had had to walk forward on his toes to keep his legs from shaking so much. President Harry S. Truman stepped toward him and hung the Medal of Honor around Woody's neck.

Woody had found the going tough on Iwo Jima but he found it even harder to face the battery of cameras on the White House lawn on October 5, 1945 when the Commander-in-chief, President Harry Truman placed the pale blue Star-spangled ribbon of the

Medal of Honor around his neck and said to him, "I'd rather have this medal than to be president."

Bob: As I understand if what I have read, you are the only Medal of Honor survivor in West Virginia. Is that right?

Woody: Yes, we didn't have any in World War I. I am the last survivor of all branches of service. There are no other MOH recipients living in West Virginia right now. It keeps me busy.

(Author VandeLinde with Woody Williams)

Bob: In previous interviews have you described knocking out the 7 pillboxes and you were attributed to killing 21 Japs?

Woody: I don't know. I have done so many of these things.

Bob: I want to get a picture of you with your CMH on. You don't have it in a case where you can't get it do you?

Woody: No. You see, Congress finally passed a law authorizing an extra medal because the original—my original is over there on the sewing machine. Previously we had to take our original with us but there was a chance of losing it or getting it stolen—or whatever. Finally Congress passed a law saying we could have one to use while speaking, leaving the original at home. The words on the back of the original is not the same they put on the substitute—

different wording. They say they could not repeat the words on the sub. In 2002 Congress passed a law providing us a MOH flag. The way they made it, I have no idea. But last year—August of last year (2006), the Commandant authorized all living MOH recipients and their widows of those who died since 2002 to come to Washington to present us with that flag. There were 19 Marines able to get there, some couldn't travel. There were four widows there. The flag itself—all it had on it was 13 stars representing the 13 colonies. There were eight World War II guys there. We went to see the Green Bay Packers play. It was a close game. The Packers kicked a field goal with six seconds remaining to win the game.

Bob: Anything else that you would like to share with me?

Woody: I do want to say and I would like for you to print this. There are many individuals who did extraordinary things and would have warranted the Medal of Honor, but circumstances were not such that the commanding officer made the necessary records or not enough survivors to make it possible for the recommendation which certainly does not take away what the individual did. On the day of February 23, 1945, two marines were assigned to protect me—they gave their lives. So when I wear the medal or somebody says something to me about receiving it, I always say that I received the medal because of what others did as much as I did. So when I wear the medal, I always wear it in their honor, not mine. This really belongs to them. If they were not there to protect me, I would not be here to talk about it. The Commandant of the Marine Corps the day after I received the medal called us into his office to interview the 11 marines who had received the medal the day before. We had to go in his office individually. Of course in the military, you go by alphabet and there was only one guy behind me. His name was Zimmer. By the time they got to me, I was absolutely a nervous wreck. But when I went into his office, I still remembered that I had never stepped on a soft rug. His office had a red rug and was soft. I had been told as the others were that when you go in you walk up to his desk with your cover under your arm-stand at attention until he tells you what to do. The sergeant said not to look him in the eye.

Bob: Where was this?

Woody: At Marine Corps Headquarters in Washington, D.C. He said the second time "At ease" which gave me an opportunity to relax and spread my legs apart. He started talking to me, most things that I do not remember. I'm sure it was fear that was taking this away. I'm just a country boy and clear out of my realm. Finally he did say something that got my attention. 'That medal does not belong to you.' That caught my attention. I hadn't done anything. We had a party the night before but I hadn't done anything bad. It really got my attention. He finished up by saying 'Don't ever do anything that would tarnish that medal.' He too was a MOH recipient. I didn't know that. He wasn't wearing the medal or even the ribbon. Everything I ever did, I did it with those words in mind—honoring what that medal stands for.

But it changed my life. I would come back home, I had two other brothers in service. One was in the Battle of the Bulge and he got beat up pretty badly; the other brother was stationed in Germany in the supply depot. My thoughts were of course to come back home and go back to farming again because that was all I knew. But my mother didn't give me all the facts when she wrote to me. When I got home, I realized she had sold everything off to get along, so I didn't have a farm to go back to. Having the medal put me in the public eye which I never dreamed of being there. For the first two or three years it was very difficult to fit myself into that society. It is customary that wherever you go, receptions or whatever, you almost have to drink or you don't belong. I had never, oh I drank cider—lots of cider and had two swallows of West Virginia moonshine, but I didn't like that stuff. It burned all the way down.

If I had a tendency, I could have become an alcoholic. Every time you walk in the door someone would hand you a drink. I was able to control it and being married to a Christian lady helped me. I was not a Christian when I was in the Marine Corps. I didn't know if there was a God or not. I just know there was some power that I asked every once in a while to get me out of this mess. My whole life changed when I became a public figure, in the limelight constantly. I hadn't planned to be there. It has been a good life and I've had experiences that no way under the sun could I have had. I have attended every inauguration since President Kennedy. I've taken all my children and grandchildren to the inaugurations. I hope someday to take my two great-grandchildren. To me that's the epitome of America. When that takes place, we can't fight each other and we don't shoot each other because we go about it pretty sensibly. The whole system changes with one man. To me that's miraculous. It's an experience that you cannot imagine.

Bob: So as a Medal of Honor recipient, you are automatically invited?

Woody: Yes, They arrange our travel by air, our hotel reservations, where, when and what you are going to eat. Our seats are up front in the President's box.

Bob, I don't know anything else to tell you. Ruby and I have been married for 62 years as of October 17, 2007. We have had a wonderful life. If we ever had a quarrel, it was probably my fault, not hers. She is a very patient person. We never had a real serious disagreement. I feel very fortunate.

Bob, when I was going into the Marine Corps, as I said my wife and I were engaged. I didn't have enough money to buy an engagement ring, so she had a little five and dime ruby ring which she gave me to wear. It turned my finger green and I had to clean it from time to time. I wore it all the time I was in service. The fellow who was assigned as my assistant, when we got to Guadalcanal, going to Guam, they took us out of the rifle unit and our job was in flamethrower demolition. I was designated the guy in charge when we left Guadalcanal. I was a Pfc. at the time. I was 5'6" and 150 pounds at the time. You add a 70 pound flame thrower on my back. My assistant carried my food, boxes, back pact, everything. All I carried was a .45 Cal pistol on my hip. I couldn't hit the side of a barn with that pistol. I always kept an M-1 that he carried for me. I would use my M-1 if I couldn't get the people with my flamethrower.

I mentioned that when I went into service that Ruby gave me a ring. My assistant, Vernon Waters, had a ring that his daddy had given him. It was a large ring—a ¾ square ring. His hands were twice the size of mine. He was a big man. His ring had the image of a lake on it. I don't know what kind of stone it was but certainly a beautiful ring. So when we went through Guam, neither one of us got into too much danger but not sure we were going to make it after Guam. We decided that we would make a pact although we knew it would be a court-martial offense if we were caught. I guess we were willing to take that chance. I was 20 years old at the time. We agreed that if anything happened to him, I would take the ring off his finger and make sure it got back to his dad. This agreement was if anything happened to me, he would take the ring off my finger and make sure it got back to Ruby.

When we went into Iwo Jima on March 7th, we were selected to be in the attack that morning. The Japanese were throwing a number of grenades and mortars at us. They had a little thing they called a knee mortar. It wasn't really a knee mortar. Some of our guys tried it and it didn't work. But we were advancing forward. I'd been hit—we were moving out, of course I wasn't moving very rapidly. We had weapons, not my flamethrower because we were in the attack. If we needed a flamethrower, we would go back to headquarters where it was kept. I got out of a hole to move forward and my buddy, Vernon was about 30 or 40 yards in front me and a Japanese mortar came in and hit him in the center of his helmet. Of course it killed him instantly. I ran to him. He was lying out on the ground. I checked to see if he had any breath and couldn't find any. I couldn't get him to move. I looked at his hand and there was that ring. He wore the ring on his index finger of his right hand. The reason being, the middle fingers on his left hand (a family trait), were grown together. I saw the ring and thought about the pact we made. I knew if I was caught taking the ring off his finger I could be court-martialed. We had not had a bath for days. We had worn the same clothes for two weeks. I tried to pull the ring off without being too obvious. It wouldn't come off. So I spit on it figuring the saliva would help work the ring off. I worked the ring off and put it in my pocket. The ring hadn't been off for months and that part of his finger was shinny. It was like a bright light. Somebody looking would have known there had been a ring on his finger. So I took some sand and tried to rub the brightness off and that didn't work. I spit in my hand and rubbed some more sand to make kind of messy glue and put that on his finger. That helped. A corpsman came along, tagged him and put him on a stretcher.

I got out of the marines in November and after I got home, I wrote to my friend's father sometime in December. I told him that I had his son's ring. I told him that I didn't want to mail it to him but I was going to bring it to them in person. They lived in Floyd, Montana next to the Canadian border. I had no idea where it was. My wife and I didn't have a car, so in January we borrowed a car from a dealer who had been supportive of me when I got home. He would haul me in his car in parades. He owned a dealership but didn't have any cars because in 1942 the last years new cars were produced. He had a 1942 Dodge convertible, as red as it could be. The top was really stretched out because it had been patched so much. When the wind blew and it rained, the top would cause the wind and rain to blow in on Ruby and me.

We finally got to Montana. It was wheat country, acres and acres of wheat. There were no markers so we had trouble finding the family house because it was way back in the country. We finally found it and his dad and two brothers were home and his mother was still living. We pulled in and introduced ourselves and I gave him his son's ring. You would have thought I was giving them Fort Knox. We spent a couple of days with them. It is kind of ironic that the father and two sons had the same finger situation he did. The folks were huge Swedish people all were over six feet and weighed between 180 and 200 pounds. The kindest people you would ever want to meet.

Bob: I'll bet they appreciated not only you coming, but also sharing with the family how their son was killed.

Woody: Absolutely. They would have never known otherwise.

Hershel W. Williams and Ruby Meredith Williams were married On October 17, 1945 by Reverend Meredith, an uncle of the bride. They have two girls, five grandsons and two great grandsons. Ruby said that "Woody was really good to write. I have all his love letters in a box but haven't read them for years." Woody trained in Fairmont for a position with the Veterans Administration. He is retired a Veterans Administration official in Huntington, West Virginia. He will never forget the homecoming the people of Fairmont and Marion Country gave him on his return from Washington, DC—the parade of welcome, with the state guard mustered to a man, and the American Legion of Fairmont Post 17 marching in review. The welcoming address by Senator Hardesty of West Virginia, the speechlessness of the townsfolk before the courthouse when he was presented to them, the police ball in his honor, the Chamber of Commerce dinner, the special meeting of the Lions Club and the stirring words of praise his old friend of the *Fairmont times*, Ned Smith. (The bridge located at Barboursville, West Virginia was named for this local HERO.)

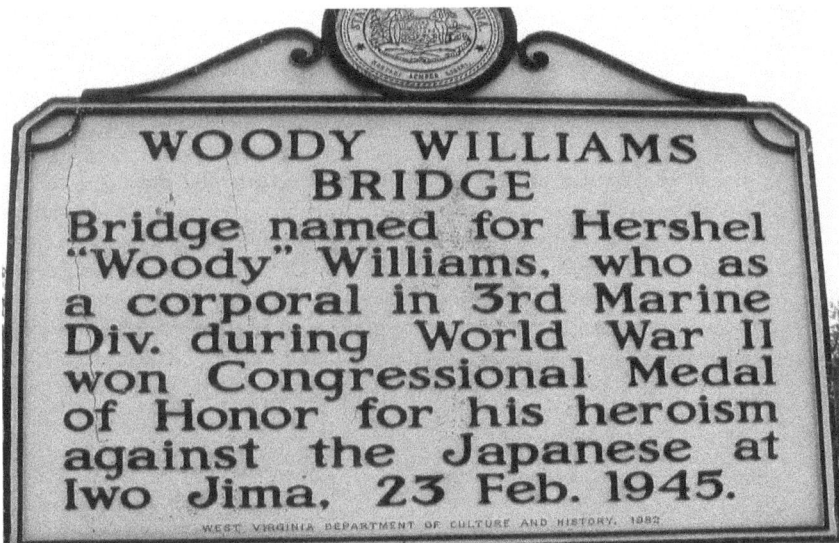

WOODY WILLIAMS
BRIDGE
Bridge named for Hershel "Woody" Williams, who as a corporal in 3rd Marine Div. during World War II won Congressional Medal of Honor for his heroism against the Japanese at Iwo Jima, 23 Feb. 1945.

WEST VIRGINIA DEPARTMENT OF CULTURE AND HISTORY, 1982

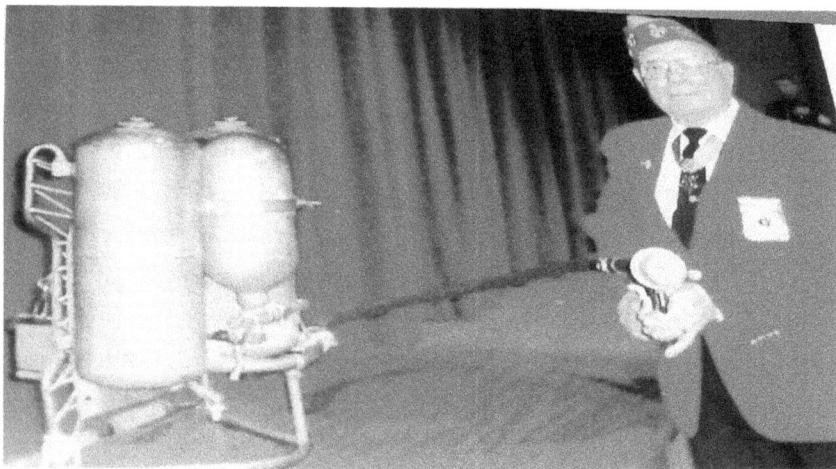

Williams viewing a flame thrower like the one he used on Iwo Jima.   (Photo courtesy of Hershel Williams)

FOR CONSPICUOUS GALLANTRY and intrepidity at the risk of his life above and beyond the call of duty as Demolition Sergeant serving with the First Battalion, Twenty-First Marines, Third Marine Division, in action against Japanese forces on Iwo Jima, Volcano Islands on 23 February 1945. Quick to volunteer his services when our tanks were maneuvering vainly to open a lane for the infantry though the network of reinforced concrete pillboxes, buried mines, and black, volcanic sands, Corporal Williams daringly went forward alone to attempt the reduction of devastating machine-gun fire from the unyielding positions. Covered only by four riflemen, he fought desperately for four hours under terrific enemy small arms fire and repeatedly returned to his own lines to prepare demolition charges and obtain serviced flamethrowers, struggling back, frequently to the rear of hostile emplacements, to wipe out one position after another. On one occasion he daringly mounted a pillbox to insert the nozzle of his flamethrower through the air vent, kill the occupants, and silence the guns; on another, he grimly charged enemy riflemen who attempted to stop him with bayonets and destroyed them with a burst of flame from his weapon. His unyielding determination and extraordinary heroism in the face of ruthless enemy resistance were directly instrumental in neutralizing one of the most fanatically defended Japanese strong points encountered by his regiment, and aided in enabling his company to reach its objective. Corporal Williams aggressive fighting spirit and valiant devotion to duty throughout this fiercely contested action sustain and enhanced the highest traditions of the United States Naval Service.

Harry S. Truman
PRESIDENT OF THE UNITED STATES

FLAME-THROWING MARINE WHO WON THE MEDAL OF HONOR

by BILL FRANCOIS

NOW! Fire flew from the nozzle of his weapon, found the slit of the pillbox, squished through the opening and enveloped the interior. Thirty seconds of hell and it was over.

(Photo courtesy of Hershel Williams)

Dixon, Mundy, Rigney, Tuck, Fowler, and Ondo
(Photography by Ray Reynolds)

Six men, who live in Virginia, meet on a regular basis to visit and have a cup of coffee and give support to each other. In

RESPECT

November 2006, a new museum opened at the Quantico Marine
Base in Northern Virginia. Accompanied by Don Temple and Dick
Beatty, five of these local heroes visited the museum in February
2007. Julia LeDous, editor for *The Patriot* newspaper, published
the following story of their visit. "They were young men in 1945
who answered the nation's call to fight the Japanese in the Pacific
during World War II. For 36 days in February and March of that
year, they participated in one of the war's epic battles, at Iwo Jima
where they drew a line in the island's volcanic soil and became
heroes. Today, they are grandfathers and great-grandfathers,
members of the Combat Veterans of Iwo Jima, Inc., who on
Sunday toured the National Museum of the United States Marine
Corps as part of their annual reunion and historical symposium."

Iwo veteran **WILLIAM ONDO** was an 18 year old marine
corporal who spent six days on the island in
1945. Ondo's time on Iwo got off to an
inauspicious start when the door to his landing
craft wouldn't open as he and his fellow
marines prepared to storm the beach. "The
door didn't go
down," he said
with a laugh.
"They couldn't
figure out why.
The sarge pushed the guys over."

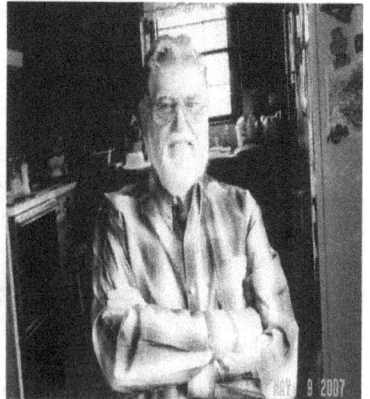

Ondo lost his left eye in that
battle, something that he didn't tell
his daughter until 15 years ago.
The soft-spoken Virginia resident
who joined the corps three days after his 18th birthday brushed
aside any talk that he and his comrades-in-arms were heroes.
"Other people did just as much," he stressed, turning the
conversation back to some of his more light-hearted memories on

the island. "We couldn't build foxholes because of the volcanic soil," he recalled. "Things happened fast there."

Ondo was born on May 23, 1926 in Passic, New Jersey. His father's name was Steve; his mother's name was Julia. He was a good athlete in school, running track and a weightlifter. Entering the Marine Corps, he thought boot camp would be a snap but soon found out that he wasn't in as good shape that he thought he was. When ask how the Marine Corps changed him, he replied, "The Corps gave me pride in myself." Ondo and wife Rose were married on June 17, 1950.

Ondo entered the US Marine Corps on June 7, 1944 and was discharged on October 5, 1945. After boot camp at Paris Island, South Carolina, he received three weeks training at Camp Pendleton, California. From Pendleton he shipped out to Hawaii receiving additional training on Maui on the BAR (Browning automatic rifle). This specialized training was preparing Ondo for the battle on Iwo Jima. The USS *Missouri* along with other ships had bombed Iwo trying to make the Marines landing somewhat easier. The trip to Iwo on the USS *New Jersey* was a long ride with many getting sea sick. Ondo said that they were not aware of the caves that the Japanese had dug, so the bombing and constant shelling didn't help very much. They were advised by their officers that this would be a two or week job to clear the island, actually "a piece of cake."

The marines who had experience combat seemed to have a worried or sad look on their faces. The others were more curious at first than scared. When asked what combat was like, Ondo said, "it was unpredictable. I didn't know what was going to happen. We were well trained to listen to our sergeant and officers."

Ondo was wounded on February 26, 1945 when he and his squad were advancing on the front line. The picture was when he received his Purple Heart Medal from the captain. He is the 7th man from the left. His sergeant told his men to get their shovels and dig in. When Ondo turned sideways to pick up his shovel, a Japanese bullet hit him across the bridge of his nose causing him to lose his left eye from the wound. He said that if he hadn't turned, the bullet would have hit him between the eyes.

Ondo was a member of C Company, 3rd Battalion. When they landed on the beach, there was little or no opposition from the Japs. With the beaches having been mined, each marine would step in steps of the man in front of him. Ondo jumped into a crater only to see something moving. He saw the largest crab, with multiple colors, crawling toward him. Without thinking, he jumped out of the crater, becoming exposed to enemy fire. At night, the island was lit up by flares from the Allied ships.

The American invasion of the island, known as *"Operation Detachment,"* was aimed at capturing the airfields on Iwo Jima. Located about halfway between Saipan and Tokyo directly under the flight paths of American bombers headed to Japan, Iwo was a Japanese stronghold of crucial strategic importance. American military commanders believed that it would make an excellent base for the Allied fighters escorting B-29s making bombing raids. And they wanted to use Iwo to protect the flank of the forces who would ultimately invade Okinawa.

"We were just a bunch of farm kids," recalled **JAHUE MUNDY** who was a 19-year-old acting marine sergeant when he spent three days on Iwo; landing on Iwo, February 19, 1945. Jahue was born in Lawrence County, Indiana on April 25, 1921. His father, Ellis Mundy, died when Jahue was in high school and he worked on the railroad to help the family to survive. He said, "We got in there and built fortifications." Three Marine Divisions composed of 80,000 men were assigned the task of wresting Iwo Jima—barely 10 square miles in area and dominated by Mount Suribachi—from Japanese control. Japanese Commander Lt. Gen. Tadamichi Kuribayashi had ordered miles of tunnels to be built underground that would be used to hide his forces.

The marines captured Suribachi in the first week of fighting. Fighting during the battle, which began on Feb. 19, was intense. Of the 22,000 Japanese troops entrenched on the island, only 1,083 survived. The United States lost a total of 6,825 personnel in the battle for the island. Admiral Chester W. Nimitz said, *"Among the Americans who served on Iwo Jima, uncommon valor was a common virtue."*

JOHN FOWLER was a 21-year-old Gunnery Sergeant who served on board a navy ship off the coast of the island during the campaign. "We protected the area throughout the whole battle," he explained. Fowler retired from the Marine Corps on May 1, 1967 after 26 years of service. He was a Master Gunnery Sergeant, the highest Marine NCO rank.

Fowler was born in Maine to Andrus and Edna Fowler. He joined the marines on August 4, 1941. His brother, Andrus served with the US Army in Korea. The one thing that he remembers about boot camp at Paris Island, South Carolina was the sand flees.

Fowler was serving on the USS *Missouri* during the battle of Iwo Jima. He can remember 100 Japanese planes coming in at the same time, attacking the American ships. They were busy fighting off the Kamikaze pilots who were willing to give their lives to sink a ship. After the battle of Iwo ended, their next mission was Japan. There were no planes flying at the time because of a typhoon had hit. The USS *Missouri* went back to Okinawa where fighting was still going on. The marines were busy patrolling the caves where the Jap soldiers were still hiding and continued to fight. After the war, Fowler came back to the states.

Fowler also served in Korea. He was in the second wave that landed at Inchon. The Inchon landing was on September 15, 1950. This was called *"Operation Chomite."* The 1st Marine Division and the 7th Infantry Division made this historic landing which completely surprised the North Koreans. This landing turned out to be a brilliant strategy by General MacArthur.

One of the most remembered battles of the Korean War was at the *Chosin Reservoir.* On November 27, 1950, the Chinese sent over 300,000 "volunteers" across the Yalu, catching the Americans and their allies by complete surprise. The 1st Marine Division and a combat team from the Army's 7th Infantry Division fought fiercely. Both sides suffered heavy casualties; Americans had 3,000 killed in action and 6,000 wounded. The Chinese had 25,000 killed and 12,500 wounded. Historians have described the campaign as the most savage battle in modern warfare, surpassing, in percentage of casualties, the battle of Tarawa. Fowler is a member of *"The Chosin Few."* His right foot suffered from frost bite which requires him to exercise regularly. Fowler said, "The

Chinese cut us right in two, they were all around us; we needed to hold that place and we held it."

John Fowler was highly decorated. He was awarded the following medals and ribbons: Presidential Unit Citation w/Ribbon bar and two Bronze Stars, Good Conduct Medal w/4 bronze stars, American Defense Service Medal, American Campaign Medal, Asiatic-Pacific Campaign Medal w/3 Bronze Stars, Victory Medal-World War II, National Defense Service Medal, Korean Service Medal, United Nations Service Medal, and the Korean Presidential Unit Citation, Navy-Marine Commendation. Fowler coached the 3rd Division rifle team at Quantico for five years. He received the "Leatherneck Trophy" for shooting 242 out of a possible 250.

The US Marine Corps Museum at Quantico, which opened in November, features an Iwo Jima immersion experience that briefs visitors on the assault before they board a Higgins Boat for the "trip" to the island. Motion, sound, and video make the boat ride a realistic experience, said the real-life Iwo vets.

Jahue Mundy said, "I like it all." Close to the boat is the flag raised above Mount Suribachi that was photographed by Associated Press photographer Joe Rosenthal. In another display 6,000 small marine and US Navy insignias represent the cost in human lives to take the island. Many hands that had held rifles 62 years on that island reached out to softly tough those insignias on Sunday.

1st Lt. Ron Yaeger of Camp Lejeune, N.C. spent more than 30 minutes talking with these Iwo Jima veterans. He wanted to know about their experiences while they wanted to know about his. "As a young marine, I'm taking away something from them," Yaeger said. "They lived history."

JAMES SWANSON RIGNEY

On the minds of many, who attended the trip to Quantico, was an Iwo veteran who couldn't take the journey due to a recent surgery, said Donald Temple, who accompanied the group. Swanson Rigney was a member of the platoon whose members raised the flag above Suribachi. "He got badly wounded, he lost his eye after the flag went up," explained Temple. "He wanted to be here in the worse way." Shown on the cover of the book is the picture of two buddies carrying Rigney off the battle-field after a mortar shell landed near his fox hole on March 22, 1945.

Rigney lost his right eye, hearing in his ear and other injuries. Swanson, as he prefers to be called, enlisted in the US Navy on March 31, 1944 but soon volunteered for the Marine Corps. The recruiting office needed one more Marine. Swanson said the other men in line stepped back and because he didn't move, he became a marine. He was born in Franklin County Virginia, and as a kid, played in the Roanoke River. The area is covered today by Smith Mountain Lake. He quit school after the fifth grade to work on the family farm.

After boot camp at Paris Island, South Carolina, Swanson was assigned to the 31st Replacement Battalion of the 5th Marine Division. On D-Day at Iwo Jima, he stormed ashore in the initial assault and later was assigned to Easy Company, 3rd Platoon as a rifleman. His job was to set T & T charges and throw them into the caves. If they saw a Jap, "we shot them" he said.

Now, 61 years later, Rigney, along with some of his buddies had breakfast with President and Mrs. George Bush at the White House. He was impressed with the White House, especially with

Laura Bush. He said, "The President has got a pretty wife," adding that she is more attractive in person than on television.

(Rigney with President and Mrs. George Bush after breakfast)

The ships had been shelling the Island of Iwo Jima for about three days before Rigney landed. He said the Japanese were under ground in holes and caves. As did the other marines who landed, he believed the action would be a "pushover." Rigney landed on Iwo on February 19th about 10 a.m. on beach number two. He was on the Island for 33 days. The men landed on a Higgins Landing Craft which carries 33 combat men plus three or four crewmembers from the navy or coast guard. He said, "As we were approaching the beach, I thought of home and thought I would never get back." He found himself praying and scared to death. The objective of his unit was to take Mount Suribachi.

After the American flag was raised on Mount Suribachi, he said "Everyone felt real good and thought we were winning." Rigney's unit, the 2nd Battalion E Company, 3rd Platoon, were the men who raised the flag. When asked how he felt about the Japanese, Rigney responded, "I hated them but I don't feel that way now."

(Swanson Rigney in the center after being wounded on Iwo)

After Rigney was brought to the hospital on March 23rd the doctor who examined him said, "You look like someone who had been in a watermelon patch and was hit by a lot of buckshot." When asked about his most memorable experience he said, "Being wounded and knowing the war was over for him." He said, "I can't tell you how it was on Iwo Jima. I didn't talk about it for a long time. But young people need to know. Kids live in a free world. Someone pays for that freedom. When asked if at the same age and his country called him to serve, he said, "Yes. I would go now if needed. I thought it was my duty to serve. All the boys around home had gone in."

The combat veterans of Iwo Jima, Inc. were founded 20 years ago, said Deputy Director Patrick J. Mooney. "Following the 60th anniversary of the battle, the organization's founder and president, retired Marine Maj. Gen. Fred Haynes, decided to start holding reunions annually. "That helped to get the families involved, to get the grandkids interested," explained Mooney. "Our motto is 'Lest we forget.' We seek to preserve and perpetuate the service and sacrifice of all Iwo veterans and to foster study of the battle."

The reunions also include a full-day historical symposium. This year's symposium was led by Col. John Ripley, former director of the Marine Corps History and Museums Division, and Dr. Malcolm Muir, Center for Military History and Strategic Analysis at the Virginia Military Institute. Family members, students and historians joined the Iwo veterans to commemorate and examine the epic battle."

WESLEY CLAYTON DIXON, a 28 day survivor of the Iwo Jima battle was asked why he joined the navy. His response was, "To keep out of the Infantry." Wes served as a corpsman, one of the most dangerous assignments anyone can have. He said that everywhere a group of marines were it seemed the Japs would drop a shell. Maps were found later revealing the plans of the Japanese. They had moved their defense from the beach to caves. Their mortars and artillery were zeroed in to certain spots on the beach. It was the Corpsman's job to care for the wounded. This required them to throw caution to the

wind and face enemy fire to get to the wounded. His supplies included morphine, pressure bandages, and blankets to try to help those who were in shock. His weapon was a 45 cal pistol. He said that they removed their Red Cross bands from their arms because the Japanese were trained to "take out the corpsmen." The Red Cross remained on their helmets because they were covered by camouflage.

Wes was born in Beverly Hills, California on May 7, 1925, but raised in Connecticut. His parents were Arthur Ray and Edith Virginia Dixon. When Wes was ten years old, he decided to raise tomatoes to sell. His mother bought a flat, which contained 144 plants, had a space plowed for Wes to plant to start making his fortune. At first business was booming. He began selling his tomatoes to a local grocery store. Having a bumper crop, he got the idea to sell his tomatoes from door to door. He thinks that he sold them for a nickel each. This idea backfired somewhat because the owner of the grocery store said Wes was undercutting him and discontinued buying from him.

Wes didn't graduate from high school before joining the navy. However, after his discharge on August 30, 1946, he completed high school and graduated from college with a mathematical degree. As a civilian he worked in computers.

Wes landed on the beach at Iwo Jima at 8 a.m. on D-Day, February 19, 1945 and said the Japs started shelling them a short time later. He was about 100 yards off the beach when wounded by a mortar shell as well as a "blast concussion." He was sent to an APA troop transport which had been converted to a hospital ship. On D-Day + 6, Wes returned to his unit and began taking care of the wounded marines. Wes was on Iwo Jima for a total of 28 days. He was a member of the 4th Marine Division, 1st Battalion 25th Marines. Wes was awarded the Purple Heart.

The personal interview with Wes Dixon by the author took place in his beautiful apartment in Roanoke, Virginia along with his wife Sue whom he married on September 24, 1983. Wes had five children and seven grandchildren by his first wife.

Wes joined the US Navy on November 18, 1943 at age 18 and a weight of 140 pounds. After completing boot camp at San Diego, California, he learned that there were three openings to attend school. Wes chose to become a corpsman. The first school was a three-month course; followed by the "field medical school" and Marine boot camp. He learned to deal with wounded men regardless how serious their injuries were. This training was put to good use on Iwo Jima.

Wes shared the several types of wounds of the marines whom

he treated on this volcanic island. He said that someone losing an arm or leg was usually easier to treat. First you apply a tourniquet and give him a shot of morphine. The easiest wound to treat was what he called a "clean wound"- when a rifle or machine gun bullet goes through some part of the body, not doing much damage. The most difficult was a chest wound or when wounded in the stomach from mortars or hand grenades. Many times the man's guts would have to be put back or laid on the top of his chest. In most cases, the corpsman would administer morphine and blood plasma. For shock, he would elevate their feet to allow the blood to flow to the heart.

As has been related by the marines in this chapter, when they landed at first there was light resistance. Wes was also under the impression from his platoon leader that this operation would last only three days. The landing craft was a new type; they troops unloaded from the rear not the front. Because of the tracks on the craft, it was very noisy. When asked his feelings when approaching Iwo Jima, Wes said, "I was excited and worried if I would do my job well." The 20 marines on the landing craft were quiet and many seemed to be praying. Everyone was ordered to keep their heads down but a couple curious marines continued to try to see what was ahead of them.

Wesley Clayton Dixon, Pharmacist Mate 3/c was awarded the Purple Heart, Bronze Star w/v device; American Theater Ribbon, Asiatic-Pacific Campaign Ribbon w/1 battle star; and the World War II Victory Medal.

WARREN J. TUCK was born in Bedford County, Virginia on September 2, 1920; and passed away on January 5, 2008. He went to work in a CCC Camp at age 15 in 1935. Tuck enlisted in the US Marine Corps December 4, 1942 because he had some friends who joined. He took his boot camp at Paris Island, South Carolina. He said that the training didn't hurt him because he was tough and could take anything.

Tuck's first combat experience was on the island of Guam. This battle started on July 21, 1944 when the 1st US Marine Division along with the 77th Infantry Division landed on this island occupied by some 18,000 Japanese. The battle of Guam ended on August 10th. Tuck along with 3,000 men were loaded on the USS *Russell* and transported to Guam. He was a squad leader. They killed several Japanese soldiers while on patrol.

Tuck had a temperature of 104 degrees and was taken to a field hospital. He thought he had been poisoned after drinking some of the Japanese Saki. It was reported that 29 Americans died from poisoned Saki. A direct order was given that anyone who was caught drinking Saki would receive a court-martial. Tuck thought it was "pretty good drinking." While on patrol one night, his squad was caught in a banana grove and experienced some hand–to-hand combat with the enemy. He said one Jap whom they killed had a leather suitcase that they found the next day. The case was full of new money. The squad split the money between them, Tuck got two packs. He also got a pearl handle gun for a souvenir that night.

Tuck's next battle was Iwo Jima. Hearing the name Iwo Jima didn't mean anything to this "boy" from Bedford County. He didn't know where it was or where they were going after loading onto a ship. He doesn't even remember a briefing prior to the landing. Tuck was in a reserve battalion. He said they could see Mount Suribachi when they landed. He was advised that this would be a "picnic." When ask what combat was like he said, "A lot of excitement. It's hard to explain. In one way I was scared and didn't sleep very much." In 2007, Japan decided to restore Iwo Jima's prewar name to "Iwo To" pronounced "ee-who-toh." There were some 1,000 people who lived there before the war.

Tuck was asked about his opinion of the Japanese soldiers. He said, "They were good fighters. They didn't think much about their lives." He said that some Japs would take their own lives instead of being captured. He did not see the flag being raised because he was on the other side of the island. He left Iwo Jima, and was glad to get away from there alive.

Warren Tuck married Ruth Tuck on April 21, 1946. Ruth passed away in July 2007. He had four brothers who served in the military. They were A.B., Jackie, Pete and Olin Tuck.

Warren and Ruth had four children; Betty, Barbara, Bonnie and Benny. They had 12 grandchildren and 32 great grandchildren.

THE TWO FLAGS OF IWO JIMA, by Col. Dave E Severance, USMC-RET. Col. Severance was one of the original US Marine Corps paratroopers when the Marines formed three battalions during World War II.

(This story appeared in the *Airborne Quarterly*).

(*Ed. Col Bill Weber' Fore note: "I am always amazed at how events are recorded! The raising of the flag at Iwo Jima, as photographed by Joe Rosenthal, is embedded in history. That it will be remembered in perpetuity is a* *given, as the USMC Memorial in Washington, DC (actually Arlington County, VA), replicates the action. But, true history should record that there was an earlier flag raising, also captured on film but doomed to obscurity because of happenstance! So, for the record, and as written by one who 'was there and did that', what follows is the story of "**The Two flags of Iwo Jima.**" The valor was equal-the recognition is not!)*

FIRST FLAG ON IWO JIMA

In December 1944 at their camp in Hawaii, the staff and unit commanders of the 2nd Battalion, 28th Marine Regiment, Fifth Marine Division was called to the War Room to receive their initial briefing on the up-coming operation, the assault on Iwo Jima Island. The three infantry company commanders were startled when they saw the sand table mockup of the Island with a 555 foot volcano on the southern end. They were even more shocked when they noticed a small flag with the 28th Marines symbol placed on Green Beach, the landing site closest to the volcano, Mount Suribachi.

Several less-than-serious suggestions were made concerning the first unit to reach the top. One proposed a case of champagne for that unit. Eventually the Battalion Adjutant, 2nd Lieutenant G. Greeley Wells stated that one of his tasks was to have an American flag with him when he landed. He suggested that the first unit to the top plant that American flag. The Adjutant did obtain a small flag from the troop transport ship he was on, the USS *Missouri*.

The initial landing on Iwo Jima was February 19, 1945. By February 22, Mount Suribachi was no longer the fortress it had been during the landings. Most of the caves were empty. Pillboxes and blockhouses had been neutralized by infantry assault teams with demolitions and flamethrowers, and by tanks.

During his briefing on the evening of February 22, the commanding officer of the 28th Marines stated to his staff and battalion commanders, "**Tomorrow we climb!**" On the morning of February 23rd, Lt. Colonel Johnson sent a four man patrol to reconnoiter the slopes of Suribachi. The group from Company F, led by Sgt. Sherman Watson, reached the top with no resistance and immediately started back down the volcano.

Seeing Watson had encountered no Japanese, Col. Johnson called the Commanding Officer of Company E (Ed. Note: Col (then Capt) Dave Severance) and ordered him to provide a 40 man patrol , to be led by the Company E Executive Officer, 1stLt H. George Schrier. The patrol formed was formed with men from Company E's 3rd Platoon, Machine Gun Platoon, and Mortar Section. Lt Schrier was briefed by the Battalion Commander, who handed him a small American flag and said, **"If you reach the top, plant this flag."**

The patrol of 40 men scrambled up the north face of Mt. Suribachi. They noticed a strange silence as they climbed closer and closer to the top. This was their fifth day on Iwo and they knew that the Japanese could jump out at them any minute. They finally reached the crest which was known to have been heavily fortified. As the men looked down into the volcano's crater, they saw dead Japanese and their wrecked guns. They still had encountered absolutely no opposition.

The patrol, their rifles ready, scouted the crater and found a piece of pipe about 20 feet long. The flag was lashed to one end and the other end was pushed into the soft ground near the north rim of the crater. The wind was brisk and the flag snapped. Sgt Louis Lowery of Leatherneck Magazine took a picture of the flag after it was raised.

Suddenly two Japanese ran from a cave. One, an officer, waved his sword and was shot. The other threw a grenade toward Lowery before he was shot. Lowery leaped and slid down the face of the volcano. The fall broke his camera but did not damage the film he had taken as the patrol climbed the volcano and raised the flag.

The names of the men who raised the first flag (at 10:20 a.m. on February 23, 1945) on Mt. Suribachi were: **Private Louis Charlo** (Company F) who was later killed in action on Iwo Jima; **Sergeant Henry O. Hansen**, from Somerville, MA, who was later killed in action on Iwo Jima; **Corporal Charles W. Lindberg**, a flame thrower operator, who was later wounded in action on Iwo Jima, and who received a Silver Star; (**Lindberg,** the last member of the flag raising team died in July 2007),**Private First Class James R. Michels** who received a minor wound in action on Iwo, February 23rd; **First Lieutenant Harold George Schrier**, the lucky one, who escaped the battle unscathed. He received both the Navy Cross and the Silver Star; **Platoon Sergeant Ernest I. Thomas, Jr.,** who was killed in action on Iwo Jima, March 3rd on his 20th birthday. These men who raised the **first flag** were every bit as much heroes as were those who raised the second flag. A strange bit of fate left them mostly in obscurity. (Ed. Note: *Hard not to acknowledge they were more heroic. After all, they went into an unknown-those that followed had every reason to believe the area was clear of enemy! In any event there was glory enough for all-why were they forgotten?*)

SECOND FLAG ON IWO JIMA

In the early morning of February 23, 1945, word filtered throughout the units and ships that an attempt would be made to scale the slopes of Mt. Suribachi. Binoculars were at a premium, and all were trained on the island fortress. With binoculars it was possible to see the Marine patrol as it climbed up the side of the mountain. At 1020 hours the first flag was raised. The ships immediately started blowing their horns and sirens. It was truly an inspiring sight and a famous moment in American history.

As the small flag was raised, Secretary of the Navy James Forrestal and General Holland M. Smith were approaching the beach in a landing craft. Forrestal indicated to the general that he would like to have the small flag as a souvenir of his trip. This word rapidly filtered down to Lt Colonel Johnson at the 2nd Battalion, 28th Marines. He had planned to keep the flag as a Battalion memento, and set about a plan to ensure the flag would be his.

He called 2nd Lieutenant Albert T. Tuttle, his Assistant Battalion Operations Officer, and sent him to the beach to find another flag. Tuttle claimed he was also told by Col Johnson, almost as an afterthought, to get a **"larger"** flag. When he arrived at LST #779, the communications Officer, Ensign Alan S. Wood, USNR gave him a large ceremonial flag he had acquired in a salvage yard at Pearl Harbor.

When Tuttle returned to the battalion, Col Johnson took the flag and handed it to Private first Class Gagnon who was about to climb the volcano with fresh radio batteries for Lt Schrier. Leaving the command post at the same time was Sergeant Strank and his detail of three men, Hayes, Sousley, and Block, who were to string telephone wire to the patrol on the mountain.

Col Johnson told Strank to have Lt Schrier put up the large flag, and return the small flag to the Colonel. When Schrier received the large flag, he ordered his men to find another pipe to which Sgt Strank and his men tied the flag. Schrier then instructed those involved that as the large flag was raised, the small flag would be lowered.

As the five men who brought the large flag to the volcano top were struggling to lift the heavy pipe, Corpsman John Bradley jumped forward to give them a hand. This flag was raised a few feet from where the first flag pole had been placed.

The men who raised the second flag on Iwo Jima were: **Corporal Harlon H. Brock** of Weslaco, Texas, who was later killed in action on Iwo Jima on March 1, 1945, when an artillery or mortar shell exploded near him as he fought between Hill 362A and Nishi Village on the western side of the island; **Pharmacist's Mate Second Class John H. Bradley** of Antigo, Wisconsin, a Corpsman with the 3rd Platoon of Company E, 28th Marines. He saved the lives of a number of Marines before he was wounded on Iwo Jima on March 12, 1945, and was evacuated from the island by plane. Although awarded the NAVY CROSS for bravery, Bradley did not disclose this fact to his family or the press. Even the Marine Corps was not aware of his award until after his death when his former company commander wrote to both the Commandant of the Marine Corps and Corpsman Bradley's family. He was reluctant to talk to the press because he did not believe he should be praised as a hero for just raising a flag. For this reason, it is believed Bradley gave no more than three interviews to the media from the end of the war until his death; **Private First Class Rene A. Gagnon** from Manchester, New Hampshire; **Ira Hayes** from Gila River Indian Reservation in Arizona; **Mike Strank**- killed on Iwo Jima; **Franklin Sousley** from Hilltop, Kentucky—killed by a Japanese sniper.") The unsung film maker was Sergeant Bill Genaust. He used a 16mm movie camera, taking pictures of the American flag being raised on Mount Suribachi but did not receive any credit. He died on Iwo Jima nine days later. His name was kept anonymous. After 40 years the Marine brass issued a letter of appreciation and finally recognized Sgt. Genaust. (End of Col Dave E. Severance's article).

G.W. "BILL" GOODWIN
MARINE MEDIC

Bill Goodwin, now 88 years old, lives in Rockingham, North Carolina. Goodwin was 25 years old when he went ashore at the beginning of the Battle of Iwo Jima on February 20, 1945. He was one of 13 marine medics with only three still standing when his unit was pulled out at the end of the battle. The other ten medics

were killed or wounded. Goodwin was awarded the Silver Star for gallantry.

Goodwin said he had given little thought to Iwo Jima until the 60th anniversary arrived. He said when he was discharged after the war, "I had a wife and baby boy waiting for me at home. I put it behind me. I never had any thought about the war until a few years ago." As he began looking through some old photos and papers from his World War II service, he found a diary he had written that covered his time in service. "If I have ever read it before a few months ago, I don't remember it. Goodwin said, "There are a few things I wrote in there that I wouldn't say today."

His diary entries during the Battle of Iwo Jima begin the day his ship arrived offshore, one day after the Marines first went ashore on February 19, 1945.

Iwo Jima dairy:

Feb. 20, 1945: "Sighted Iwo Jima. Oh but does this look bad. Hundreds of ships are shelling it and we can see tanks ashore. We heard they are having a tough time ashore."

Feb. 24, 1945: "Hit the beach at 3 p.m. and saw my first dead Nip. Drew mortar fire at the first air strip. We dug in for the night. My first night in a foxhole."

Feb. 25, 1945: Crossed the first air strip and drew heavy enemy fire. Four men were hit. Set up aid station. There I treated my first wounded Marines."

Feb. 27, 1945: *"We are getting lots of mortar and sniper fire. Casualties coming in fast. Tonight they gave me a Jeep ambulance to drive back to the beach."*

Feb. 28, 1945: *"Have been crossing second air strip in ambulance. If the mortars fall any nearer they would be in my pocket."*

Feb. 29, 1945: *"Got rid of the ambulance and I am glad. I had some very close calls in it."* (There was no Feb. 29 in 1945, with it being a leap year. Obviously Goodwin wrote the wrong date in his diary. He said he didn't have a calendar during the battle.)

March 1, 1945: *"Today we moved across the second air strip and set up. We were pinned down by sniper fire. Darling I was afraid I would never see you again. (*Referring to his first wife Margaret, now deceased.)

March 2, 1945: *"Tonight Palock (one of the medics) was hit. I took him to the beach. This is Hell."*

March 3, 1945: *"Thompson and I were sent up with the stretcher teams. He was on his first trip when he got it. He was a swell kid. This PM we were pinned down for two hours. We got a casualty from in front of the lines. My luck is still good."*

March 4, 1945: *"I know I will come through now, after last night."* (Goodwin said he was referring to surviving a particularly bad night attack launched by the Japanese. "The Japanese would charge our lines at night, screaming 'Banzai! Banzai!' We just mowed them down.")

March 5, 1945: *"Today we drew straws to see who went up (to the front line). Little Joe Ewing won. Tonight he was brought in with only one leg. Yeah war is Hell."*

March 6, 1945: *"Today I saw my best friend go up. Good luck Flynn."*

March 7, 1945: *"I worked all last night (treating wounded). I got to get some rest soon or crack up. Flynn is missing."*

March 8, 1945: *"We drew straws for line duty. Gee but that is nerve breaking. Hopkins 'Tex' won. Good luck Tex."*

March 10, 1945: *"Today we got some rest and some mail from my darling wife and mom."*

March 12, 1945: *"Today we moved up. From here we can see the ocean on the north side of the island. The end is in sight, but how so very far away. Today they found Flynn's body. What a shame. He had so much to live for."*

March 15, 1945: *Drew straws again. Hood won. I can't go through that again."*

March 16, 1945: *"This AM Fitzgerald drew the short straw and went up. Tonight they brought him back. He was hit by grenade."*

March 17, 1945: *"Today the island was secured (officially)."*

March 27, 1945: *"Today we pulled out. I hear the doggies (Army troops) are taking over. Yeah I have been lucky or maybe my prayers were answered."*

Goodwin said he didn't see the most famous incident of the Battle of Iwo Jima, the marines raising the US flag on the top of

Mount Suribachi. "I didn't know about it at the time. I never heard it mentioned until the battle was over." Goodwin was discharged from the US Navy in 1946 and came home to his wife and baby son. He retired after working 30 years for Jefferson Pilot Insurance Co. "I just thank the Lord that I got back home."

Monuments have been erected, movies have been made and heroes died trying to reach the top of Mount Suribachi. However after 27,909 American casualties and 20,703 Japanese dead, this was considered a great American victory. Many of the Japanese soldiers would kill themselves instead of bringing dishonor to their families by being captured. Yet some 216 Japanese were captured, preferred not to die.

Although costly in lives, winning the battle of Iwo Jima was of great importance. The Japanese had radar on the island to notify their air force of incoming B-29's. The US wanted to establish a base for our planes needing to make emergency landings. In the months ahead, this base saved many lives.

The American forces were moving toward Japan. After conquering the Marshall Islands, the battle of Kwajalein and Eniwetok in February, the Japanese started reinforcing strategically important Iwo Jima. It provided an airbase for the Japanese aircraft to intercept long-range US B-29 bombers. An American occupation of Iwo Jima would provide an important base for a US invasion of the Japanese mainland, a plan that seemed inevitable at the time. It was estimated that the invasion of the Japanese mainland would have cost one million American lives, killed or wounded. The Japanese were fully prepared to defend their homeland to the bitter end.

President Harry Truman succeeded President Franklin Roosevelt after Roosevelt's death in Warm Springs, Georgia on April 12, 1945, becoming the 32nd President of the United States. He learned after assuming the presidency that the United States had developed an atomic bomb. Before Roosevelt's death, Truman had been kept out of the loop and was not aware of this top secret.

[The atomic bomb was developed in Los Alamos, located in the mountains of northern New Mexico. Truman agonized and weighed all options before deciding to drop the bomb. He knew it would be a decision that he would live with the rest of his life. It was a way to end the war. Many American lives would be spared. He was informed of the damage and countless lives that would be taken. What would people think? Public opinion didn't concern the President. On his desk was a sign that read, "The Buck Stops Here," and it did. The decision was made. The Japanese had ignored the requirements outlined in the Potsdam Conference. The United States had no alternative other than to use the bomb on Japan.]

On August 6, 1945, a B-29 bomber named *"The Enola Gay"* took off from Tinian with Colonel Paul Tibbets as the plane commander. The bomb Tibbets had on board, named "Little Boy," was dropped on the city of *Hiroshima,* destroying the city. Japan still would not surrender. Three days later, on August 9th, *Nagasaki* was the target. The bomb named "Fat Boy," would kill approximately 35,000 Japanese. From the destruction and cost of lives, Emperor Hirohito finally got the message. A Washington, D.C. newspaper, dated August 15, 1945 read: "AUG 14 (AP) ***Japan surrendered unconditionally tonight. History's most destructive was is over.***"

Lieutenant General Tadamichi Kuribayashi was informed that he had been chosen to defend Iwo Jima. This was an important assignment. The general accepted. When he arrived in June 1944, there were about 80 fighter planes on the island. The United States Navy bombarded the island for two days and destroyed all the buildings and all but four Japanese aircraft in July. The general evacuated all civilians from the island. Pillboxes were built by mixing cement with the volcanic ash. Artillery units and anti-tank battalions arrived on Iwo Jima. The defense of the island was crucial. Artillery, rocket launchers, mortars and infantry were emplaced on Suribachi to the south and the high ground to the north.

A Memorial has been built on the top of Mt. Suribachi with an American flag flying beside it. Veterans from the United States and Japan made a trip to this hallowed place on the 40th anniversary of the beginning of the battle, February 19, 1945. This special event was called the "Reunion of Honor." On one side the carving is in Japanese and the other side is in English. The Japanese soldiers stood on one side, while the US Marines stood on the English engraving side. After the unveiling, the Americans and Japanese who had fought each other for many years embraced each other with tears rolling down their cheeks.

The commissioning of the USS *Iwo Jima* was held at Pensacola, Florida on June 30, 2001. One officer said, "The amphibious assault ship honors the courage and self-sacrifice of the Marines and sailors who fought on Iwo Jima." Thousands of Iwo Jima veterans and other well-wishers cheered when an amphibious assault ship named for one of World War II's bloodiest battles was commissioned as the Navy's newest warship. General Michael Williams, assistant commandant of the Marine Corps, said during the commissioning, No name is more fitting for a ship that will carry marines and sailors into combat than *Iwo Jima*. The courage and self-sacrifice of the marines and sailors who fought on Iwo Jima set a standard for valor and a standard for courage that has never been excelled."

Like its predecessor, the new *Iwo Jima* is designed to carry troops. It has a crew of about 1,000 and can accommodate 2,000 marines, including their artillery, tanks and other vehicles. A hanger bay will house up to 33 helicopters and jump jets that can take off and land from its 844-foot-long flight deck.

President Lyndon Johnson said, *"I never think of a Marine but what I think of a man who wants to do more, not less; a man you have to hold back, not shove."*

USS *IWO JIMA*
(Photo courtesy of David Laird-member US Navy-2008)

TOMMY L. HARBOUR
US COAST GUARD

The experiences of and involving Tommy Harbour during World War II are given in chapters titled *Normandy Invasion* and the *Higgins Landing Craft*. Tommy is one of many Americans who served in both theaters during the war. His unique stories exemplify the importance and value of the Coast guard in war as well as peacetime. Tommy kept a daily diary of his involvement during the battle at *Iwo Jima*. He has allowed the author to make a copy of this diary for this book.

Tommy was a crew member on an LCVP (Landing craft-vehicle-personnel). He served on the USS *Bayfield* (APA-33) for two years. This was reported in the "BAY-VIEWS 7 NEWS" dated Friday, March 2, 1945; *"American Marines advanced several hundred yards on bitterly contested Iwo Jima, overran Motoyama Village beyond the captured Central Airfield yesterday and secured most of the Islands vital Central Plateau."*

Major General Erskine, Third Division Commander, said that with the Plateau in American hands it will be a downhill fight to the North End of Iwo. An incomplete count of Jap dead as of 6 p.m. Monday was 4,784. Destruction of the Jap Garrison on Corregidor Fortress at the entrance to Manila Bay was termed virtually complete by General MacArthur today."

Tommy Harbour had been transferred to boat #5 after boat #4 had been sunk. Other men were transferred to other boats so the coast guard could have one seasoned veteran one each craft. Tommy's unit picked up 1,800 marines at Maui to transport them to Iwo Jima. After the marines landed, the *Bayfield* was taking on casualties. The *Bayfield* had a doctor and a well-trained pharmacist's mate on the ship.

Tommy said, "It took 28 days to take that island. We would make trips back and forth to the beach picking up the wounded. Two of us would grab a stretcher. We picked up this young boy and he looked up at me and I looked down at him." He said, 'you know our officers told us not to take any casualties (Japanese) and we didn't take a one.' He said that they estimated there were 13,000 Japs on Iwo Jima but they killed 26,000."

Tommy continues with his remarks: "Here's another thing, we went out to bury the dead at night. We got a call for a boat to come over to the cruiser *Indianapolis*. That was the most beautiful ship I ever looked at. It was anchored over from the *Bayfield*. We pulled alongside and there were seven Jap prisoners on there; one was on a stretcher, the other six were walking. We watched as they came down the gangplank. Those were the first ones we had seen. You don't see them like the army or marines."

He goes on, "After the initial invasion, we would get orders to go to a certain beach. An example was *Yellow Beach*. They would give us the directions. We would go over to the location we were ordered to go, pick up supplies and head for *Yellow Beach*. The army was good to help us unload—the marines were not too good to help. We would go back to the ship and wait for new orders. That's how it worked. Slick wasn't it? A call would come from the battle front to the ship to the LCVP to another ship—to the beach. The Army knew we were coming to a certain beach because a colored flag would mark where we were to land with supplies. You had better not go where there is no flag because there would not be anyone to unload it. Our problem was getting in and getting out." He laughed.

The Japanese had one of their destroyers sunk close to the beachhead, so Tommy said: "While going in we could hear 'ping-ping.' This was from the sound of a rifle bullet but there was so much noise I thought 'my goodness' I wondered what that pinging was. There was so much going on with doing my job I just passed it on. In a day or two, I told Horton that the Jap destroyer stack is gone off of it. He said that he forgot to tell me that in that stack was a Japanese sniper and the marines blew the stack off the ship. There was a sniper in that stack shooting the coxswain," Laughing, Harbour added, "The stack was gone and the Jap was gone too."

Tommy said, "When my boat sank at Iwo Jima, we had a load of 5 gallon cans of flamethrower fluid, a lot of mortar shells and a bunch of hand grenades." He continued, "Instead of the marines coming down to help unload the boat, they hit for fox holes and that left me with the ramp down and no one to unload the boat except the two seamen there. With all that stuff in that boat, one bullet would have blown us up. My good friend Woody Williams [Williams was awarded the Medal of Honor on Iwo Jima], asked me one time if I knew what flamethrower fluid was made out of and I said 'no.' He said it was diesel fluid. Williams said, 'Sometimes it got to clogging up on me and was too heavy and began jelling. So he put some gasoline in and mixed it and boy that made it powerful didn't it. Harbour was laughing.

Tommy Harbour kept his diary from December 2, 1944 to July 29, 1945. [I chose to copy and scan the days starting with the Battle of Iwo Jima. Following are ten pages from February 18, 1945 through March 23, 1945. I found this to be interesting reading, a diary that now is 63 years old. In the front of his diary, on the first page, listed a number of girls with whom he was corresponding. The last page listed his buddies who borrowed money from him. His best friend still owes Tommy $1.25.]

On Sunday 18 March 1945, the *Bay-View News* reported: US PACIFIC FLEET HEADQUARTERS, *"Three Marine Divisions sustained 19,938 casualties including 4,198 dead in capturing Iwo Jima for an advanced Air Base, 750 miles from Tokyo. Fleet Admiral Nimitz announced Saturday. Iwo was the bloodiest, toughest and costliest battle in the 168 year history of the United States Marines. Defending a piece of Japan, part of Tokyo prefecture, the Japanese on Iwo fought and died almost to a man."*

The invasion beach was a scene of indescribable wreckage-all of it ours. This was the effect of blistering Jap artillery, mortar and rocket fire on the beach heads of Iwo Jima. Wrecked landing craft littered the water's edge. Amphibian tractors were flopped upside down like pancakes on a griddle. Further inland were some of the hundreds of combat packs, clothing and gas masks, many of them ripped off by shrapnel that covered the shore for five miles.

Tommy and Betty Lou Morris were married on July 27, 1949. They have two children: a son, a daughter (their son deceased). When Tommy was discharged from the US Coast Guard at Detroit, Michigan on May 27, 1946, his pay for a Motor Machinist Mate 2nd Class was $96.00 a month. In a conversation with Betty she said, "I know why the good Lord put me on earth now. It was to take care of Tommy. [Tommy Harbour is nearly blind.]

Tommy Harbour, against regulations, kept this personal diary. He said that there hasn't been anyone who has read the diary, including his wife. However, he allowed the author to copy and use in his book notes kept during the battle of Iwo Jima. The several diary pages that follow reveal his thoughts and his involvement during the battle of Iwo Jima.

I WA J I MA

18 Feb. 45. 16

destroyer & P.D. along side. two P.R's in
water. mounted 30 Cal on boats, 10 boxes
amm. 2 springfields. and cots.

D—DAY   (19) Feb. 45. 16

Arrived in Transport area 418
Set condition 1 able. Boats 24 – 7 were lowered
Boat nos 4 – 3 – 5 were lowered at 8:30 P.M.
made trip to P.a. 206 stood by all
day until 5.00 P.M. we were loaded then
with 2 cargo nets of mortar amm. 1 cargo
net of Flame Thrower Fluid. 1 cargo nets
of Hand grenades. 1 net of Barb wire, we left
206 at 5:30 P.M. twards beach got to
P.C. 1081 at 6:30 P.M. Beach was to hot to
go in. we followed the P.C. in and out
to sea all night. at 6:00 A.M. we were
told to hit beach. Boat 21 sank. 20. Feb. 45. 6:00
we started in to Blue Beach no 2. The
mortar fire was scattering, some hit
about 50 yds off our stern. we were
only boat. about 15 yds off beach, mpw
fire almost hit boat. we hit beach
at 645 A.M. Marines started unloading
they unloaded about ½ cargo. boat
began to sink no salt water in Engine
on the fore bilge pump wouldn't pump.
(Saw 3 planes shot down on 19, 20.)

Page 17

I changed sand traps. still wouldn't work. so I took plug off primer and poured water in pump. A amphibious tractor hit our stern and knocked hole in it. water was about knee deep in stern I pulled up ramp and we broached. Boat #24 Beach master pulled us off. we pulled out about 100 yds from beach and stopped, water was over floor boards and Engine water temp. was 210° They said Cargo was more important than boat so hit beach again and unload. So we hit again. I lowered ramp to unload cargo and down went no. 5. Truman Charlton got out, Barron left. I got out and then came Horton. Barron had an MI. and ammo. we went down Blue 2 then to Blue 1. Marines were all over the beaches 4 & 5 together dead. I saw 5 japs which flame thrower had hit. one looked like a rifle butt went thru his head. I saw one of our pharmacist mates in fox hole so Charlton and me got in with him. Horton and

Barron went to look for beachmaster.
we stayed in fox hole about 1½ hr.
Horten came back about ½ hr ofter
he left us at that time no boat
were hitting Blue 1 or 2 or yellow 2
fire along the beach was lightly a
mortor now and then would hit
edge of water. Wee caught a ride back
to ship at 11:30 A.M. on LCM KA Q-2
they hit yellow 2 and unloaded and
we got on. came back to ship hit
the sack. Slept until 6:30 in morning.

21 Feb. 1945

Horten, Barron, charlton & me went over
the side in no. 2. Went to Cruiser Indin
apolis. at 9:00 Brought back 7 Jap
prisoners. at 4:00 we got a load of radio
equipment to take to Blue 2, we got
to yellow 1 at 8:00 Big Surf. Engine
died, had a time. Finally got beat
off at 9:00 3 of our ammunition dumps
blew up. we had mortor fire in
air. 125 Jap planes came over, layed
smoke screen. Shot 1 down at Battle
wagon. Came back to ship loaded
with ammunition at 10:30.

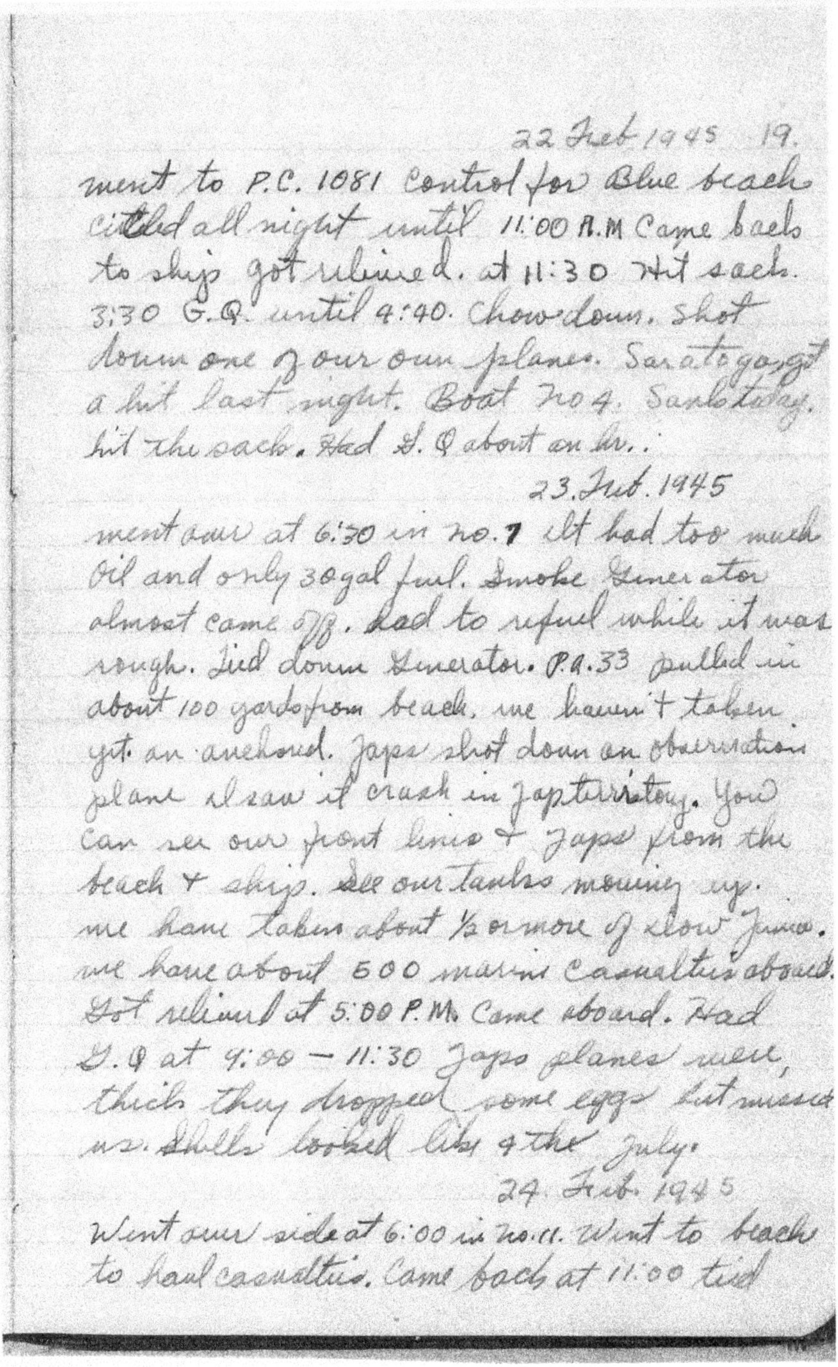

22 Feb 1945   19.

ment to P.C. 1081 control for Blue beach circled all night until 11:00 A.M Came back to ship got relieved. at 11:30 Hit sack. 3:30 G.Q. until 4:40. Chow-down. shot down one of our own planes. Saratoga got a hit last night. Boat no 4. Sank today. hit the sack. Had G.Q about an hr..

23. Feb. 1945

went over at 6:30 in no. 7 It had too much Oil and only 30 gal fuel. Smoke Generator almost came off. had to refuel while it was rough. Tied down Generator. P.A.33 pulled in about 100 yards from beach. we haven't taken yet an anchored. Japs shot down an observation plane I saw it crash in Jap territory. You can see our front lines & Japs from the beach & ships. See our tanks moving up. we have taken about ½ or more of Iwow Jima. we have about 500 marine casualties aboard. Got relieved at 5:00 P.M. Came aboard. Had G.Q at 9:00 — 11:30 Japs planes were thick they dropped some eggs but missed us. Shells looked like 4th July.

24. Feb. 1945

Went over side at 6:00 in no.11. Went to beach to haul casualties. Came back at 11:00 tied

up astern. A marine leg and part of bod
floated by the boat. Hauled 300 blankets t
Bayfield for casualties. Had a time comm
upon david. 8:00 had air raid. 3 boys in 1304
hit. 2 in my division. Bomb hit at stern. 25 Feb. 4—
    Out in boat 1 all day hauled caus
to PA.118 also mail to beach to 4th
division. Tanks are fighting not 4000 yd
here. Boys hit last night are ok Tyndall
in stomach. Madinas or am. American
is upon hot rocks. Diggs left two da
ago on island, haven't heard or seen
him since. So far over 12000 wounde
over 4000 dead on this island. We b
3 marines 1 jap our stern.

                            26 Feb. 194
Out in boat no.1 had a time with wate
in stern. Hauled 2 bt loads of casualti
to F.H. no. 2. The Ship Bubby is on is
about 1000 yds from us P.A. 44
I'm going to try to see him tomorrow.
1 american plane shot down today. M.t.
marine from Bluefield W.Va. Still haven
heard from Diggs yt. We have been an
about 500 yds from beach last few days.

27, Feb 1945 21.

Was on smoke pot detail all night.
a few jap shells landed off our stern.
So far 3,368 japs have been killed,
10 taken prisoners, The prisoners
are on this ship. 6 in brig and
3 in Hospital. 1 buried over the side
I took a nervous spell this morning. and had trouble with my back.
Went over to P.A.44 told a guy to
tell Bubby I am around close.

28, Feb. 1945

Smoke pot duty until 7:30 A.M.
came aboard, ate chow, Hit the
sack. Still have same detail tonight.
(We bring aboard, on average a marine
casualty every few minutes. 50 at one
time last night.) G.Q at 8:00 some guns
fired no damage.

at sea   ① March, 1945

1 letter from Home, Mailed Jan. 12. One,
American plane shot down at 9:30 this
morning. on Condition 3 I have 4 - 8 watch
still anchored 50 yds off Iwa Jima.
pulled out to sea. Buried 2 marines over
the sides Deep Six. Pulled out for Sypan
at 8:30. Just missed big airraid.

at sea.   2 March 45. 21
Been under way all day to Sipan. They
secured my gun watch at 8:00, Worked in
A & B Compartments. Inspection this afternoon.
Sea pretty rough. We now have 19 boats.
3 Ka's with us 4 destroyers as escort.
    at sea   3, March 45
Worked from 8:00 to 11:30 longing down
the forward troop quarters. Worked the
same place this afternoon. cleaned
the compartment. Be in Sipan tomorrow.
Scuttle butt. another invasion 6 wks from
now, 250 miles from Tokyo.
                          4 March 45
pulled in Saipan at 7:45 AM. anchored.
Had 12-4 Bt watch. at 2:00 went in to
dock C-4 still in. Unloaded casualties and
are refueling. Received 6 letters, wrote 3.
                    5, March. 45
Still tied up at docks. Pay day. I let
my pay ride. I wrote 7 letters and
received 2. Went to ships canteen.
worked on no 7 boat. Loaded on
the 2nd marine division about
1300 men, most all of them have
been through 3-4 Campaigns.

⑥ March 1945

Today is my 20th Birthday. went on a working party. loading supplies. Saw the Statue of Toyjo. went to camp Calhoun. we took on part of the 2nd marine division today. Loaded jeeps, trucks, and all other supplies. met a marine from Beckley. wrote 3 letters. Saw some Jap prisoners at work.

7, March. 1945
went on working party, out to B.29 base, large airport, several hundred B29's also P.61's. Looked for charles. Ship pulled out from docks at 6.00. anchored out in Bay.

8. March. 1945
1 letter today from mo N. C. Babe. out in boat all day. made liberty landing. ate Chow on P.A.154. wrote one letter, saw movie. all 2nd mariners are aboard, cargo loaded.

9. March. 1945.
went to rest camp. played horse shoes, went swimming. had a good rest. came back had 2 letters. wrote 2 myself.

10, March 1945 23.

went over to P.S. 44 saw Buddy he was well & o.k. had been thru 6 invasions. and going with us to Onkonewo thats the next invasion. He pulled out tonight for Guam, had watch on P.C. N.

11. March 45.

Got Fruit Cake from mom, had a run at 12:30 last night. Had maneuvers in the harbor all afternoon, no letters. wrote 1

12. March. 45

Rained all day. Went over the side 3 times. Worked back in Machine shop recieved 2 letters. Saw movie,

13, March. 45

worked on my boat all day. we now have a new Higgins Boat. #5. was rough, windy and rained all, went to movie, Escape from Hongkong

14. March, 45

went to Y.S. 652 got radio Batteries ate good chow on board. was very rough, got wet. Busted rudder when haisted. Recieved a letter from Charles Connor. Answered it.

15. March 45. 2
went over side at 7, hoisted at 12:
rudder is fixed. Saw movie "Are
Husbands necessary" wrote 1 letter.
invasion is near. Had trouble with
my chest. Utala violet Ray treatment and
some pills but still hurts me.
at sea   (16) March. 45
worked on boat, went to sick bay
had chest under heat lamp. no mail.
at 4:30. pulled anchor came out of
nets to convoy. are now underway.
Manoures tomorrow, Reville at 4:15
at sea IWO JIMA BATTLE WON. 17. March 45
pulled in at Tinnian at 7:15. lowered
all boats at 8:16. my boat no. 5 is
6 boat in 1st wave. we are toking
the 2nd marine division assault troops
in this next invasion. We circled and
came back at 1:30. was hoisted
aboard, got underway at 4:00 and
still are.
at sea   18. March. 45
Off Tinnian, on Manoures. Went over side
at 7:00. over to P.a. 206. Loaded marines
2nd boat in 1st wave. Came aboard
Bayfield at 1:00, layed smoke screen.
ship makes run to sea each night.

COLONEL J.SHELTON SCALES (RET)

Shelton Scales won his first battle on Iwo Jima in 1945, and he was not about to lose his second one. That one began in 1995 when, as a tourist on the island, he learned he might not get to the top of Mount Suribachi.

Scales was born in the small town of Sandy Ridge, N.C. on April 28, 1917. He graduated from the University of North Carolina, Chapel Hill, in 1940. With draft registration approaching in October, he applied for Marine Officer training. He joined the infantry, not the air arm, reasoning that if he were shot, he preferred falling six feet rather than 6,000. In November 1940, he entered an officer's candidate class at Quantico, Virginia. After receiving his commission in February 1941, he attended Reserve Officers Course training for new lieutenants. His first assignment was to return to candidate's class as a staff member. He was with the school at the start of the war and remained at Quantico until 1943.

In July of that year, Scales reported to the 4th Marine Division and became commander of Company A 1st Battalion, 23rd Marines. He found service in the 4th Division quite different from Quantico's artificial atmosphere. "It woke me up rather rudely," Scales recalled. Although he was in the Marines before the war started, it was not until February 1944 that he first saw combat. He was in the 4th Division's combat debut on *Rio-Namur* in the Marshall Islands. During the struggle for Roi, Scales led Company A. At one point in the fighting for the Japanese airfield that dominated the island, while crawling on his belly through a ditch, he saw his first dead Japanese soldier. Suddenly, war was no longer theoretical.

The author's interview began with Colonel Scales at his home near Martinsville, Virginia on September 4, 2007. The colonel is 90 years old now. He is a very distinguished gentleman, with a keen mind and an interesting story to share. I appreciate his willingness to provide his experiences for this book.

Following the struggle for Rio, the 4th Division was sent to Maui, Hawaii, to rest and recuperate, and to assimilate badly needed replacements. Scales was promoted to major in April. He then became battalion executive officer under Lt. Col. Ralph Haas and served in that capacity during the division's bloody encounter on *Saipan* and *Tinian*. Although he contracted dengue fever, Scales remained on duty throughout the fighting on Tinian. From Tinian, the division returned to Maui to prepare for its next operation where Scales took charge of the 3rd Battalion to shape it up.

Scales believed in giving a man a second chance if he had fouled up in some way. When a marine who had deserted on Saipan was transferred to his Battalion, Scales gave him an opportunity to redeem himself, which he would do on Iwo Jima. Scales had been in charge of some 200 men. He found himself the battalion commander at the age of 27 in charge of approximately 900 men. And it was these men whom he would lead into what would be remembered as perhaps the Marine Corps' most brutal battle of World War II.

The 4th Marine Division was to be part of the V Amphibious Corps' three-division assault on Iwo Jima, known as "Sulfur Island." One member of the Japanese garrison described Iwo Jima as "an island of sulfur, no water, no sparrow, and no swallow." What made the small eight-square mile island so important in early 1945 was its location.

Scales division would be one of two that landed on D-Day, February 19, 1945. Finally, at 6:45 a.m. hours, anxious marines in the invasion fleet heard the order passed down from the amphibious forces commander Admiral Richmond Kelly Turner: "Land the landing force." The boats were soon away and by 9:00 a.m. the marines were making their way inland from the landing beaches. By the time Scales' battalion landed, Yellow Beach was an abattoir that he remembered as "wall-to-wall, coast-to-coast dead men."

Scales' men passed through their pinned-down colleagues from the 1st Battalion and by 6:00 p.m. had reached the edge of the airfield. Although there was no massive Japanese attack that first night, Marines continued to die. Among those killed on the first evening was Scales' old commander, Colonel Haas.

At dawn the next morning, Scales' battalion and the other marines continued on toward their objectives. While the 5th Division moved on Suribachi, the 4th advanced northeast toward the remaining airfields. Among the immediate objectives facing Scales was seizing the rest of Airfield 1. For the rest of D+1, the 23rd Regiment fought to capture the airstrip and paid dearly for an advance of less than 100 yards. After a short break, Scales and his men plunged back into action and his battalion, along with the remainder of the 4th Marine Division, advanced northward to seize the rest of Airfield 2. The marines particularly suffered from superior Japanese artillery.

Much of the Japanese fire that the 23rd Marines were receiving was directed by spotters atop Mount Suribachi. The flag-raising forever immortalized in Associated Press photographer Joe Rosenthal's famous photograph, is one of the most well-known moments of the battle. Although he was busy with the action to his front, Scales was fortunate to be looking through binoculars in the direction of Suribachi when he caught a glimpse of "Old Glory." He described it as "the second prettiest sight I ever saw in my life." [The first was his wife on their wedding day.]

Combat evokes man's best and worst, and on Iwo Scales saw it all. Scales, who himself received a Legion of Merit, recommended one of his privates for the Navy Cross thinking it would be down-graded to a Silver Star. Division, however, told him to recommend Douglas Jacobson for two Navy Crosses. Then Fleet Marine Force told him to recommend the Marine for the Medal of Honor, which he ultimately received for destroying 16 enemy positions and killing more than 70 Japanese soldiers on the advance to Hill 382.

While courage could keep the men going, humor was important too. When Japanese machine gun fire came perilously close to Scales' command post, a nearby marine attached a bandana to the bayonet on his rifle and waved it overhead as "Maggie's drawers," the sign of a miss on the rifle range.

Bob: Tell me about loading on the ships, the experiences.
Scales: We trained at Camp Pendleton, California leaving there on January 13, 1944. We were the only marine unit that went directly into combat from the states. We had no staging areas. We first landed at Atol, on February 1, 1944 which was 65 miles from one end to the other. There were two small islands—one had a Jap airfield that we really wanted. Our regiment was to take that island which we did the first day. It was an easy operation which was the first after Tarawa—Gilbert Islands. This is where the 2nd Marine Division got chewed up badly. This was a terrible battle. So we went back to Maui and trained until the end of May. We landed on Saipan on June 15th. It took a month to take Saipan which was an island about 12 miles long and 8 miles wide. There were 30,000 Japanese defending that island.

The Second Marine Division along with my 4th, landed there on D-Day, the 15th of June. Then the Army's 27th Division who was in reserve was brought in. We made an amphibious landing at Tinnier, then returned to our base came on Maui. We trained until late August and I was given command of the 3rd Battalion, 23rd, 4th Division. We went aboard ship on New Year's Eve, December 31, 1944 to Pearl Harbor. This was a new troop ship. We went through a lot of exercises, mainly for the crew. We then headed west 3700 miles from Pearl Harbor to Iwo Jima.

We landed first at Saipan then had a big rehearsal off the coast of Tinnier. We went through the motions up and down the cargo nets into the crafts. We then headed north to Iwo Jima. We got there early and could hear the bombardment form the Navy battle-ships, cruisers and airplanes. My battalion was in reserve, the 1st and 2nd battalions of our regiment were going to land at H hour, that's the time the first wave was supposed to land. We missed it by two minutes—which was very good considering that you had to go 2 ¼ miles from the ship to the beach. At first it was scattered opposition. Not all that bad and you began to think this was going to be an easy one—like the first one was.

But after the beaches got crowded with marines, that's when the Japanese gave the order to start shelling artillery up and down the crowded beach with every shell hitting 7 or 8 marines. This was about 10 o'clock on D-Day, February 19, 1945. The regimental commander motioned me over. I was on the control vessel with him. The waves were coordinated and sent in at intervals. He told me that he wanted me to go in, go through the 1st Battalion and continue the attack. That was my orders. I got on the radio and alerted my men to get ready on the LCVP landing craft.

My executive officer went in the third wave; I went in on the sixth which was standard procedure. It was the biggest shock of my life without any question when that landing craft ground up in the sand and lowered its ramp. We were to rush off and scatter and spread out. The whole beach was crowded. I thought, 'My Lord, this is a wall to wall dead man.' Many of them were dead and they had not had a chance to get them off the beach. I spent the first hour going up and down my sector, Yellow #1 landing beach kicking butts, getting the men to spread out and move inland. You would see bodies flying through the air. It was a nightmare magnified. Why I wasn't hit during that time, I never to this day have figured it out. It wasn't my time. The shells were hitting where I walked. That night we got to the airfield which was the center of the island. There were actually two operational airfields on Iwo Jima. There was a third on the northern sector under construction by the Japanese. That first night, we –all of us, I think the commanding general all the way down to the lowest private were expecting the Japs to come balling out of their defensive positions with a charge and overrun us. But that didn't happen. I don't think we would have stopped them that first night.

We had heavy casualties getting to the beach and at night under those circumstances. We had very little help from the naval gun fire. The heavy battleship fire can't hit over 500 yards from the troops because it's so powerful—dangerous. At any rate we managed to get through that first night. The next day our battalion went across that airfield and then we were heading north with Suribachi behind us. I was up on a block house, a Japanese fortification with a roof, looking at my troops out about 150 yards or so and had fire coming several times from Suribachi hitting on our lines. So when they took Suribachi, the 5th Marines relieved us.

Our only concern was the Japs in front of us because for a time, we were in the middle.

This was the bloodiest battle the Marine Corps had ever been engaged in—Iwo Jima. The 36 days, there were 6,821 killed or dead of wounds or later declared missing. There were 19,000 wounded of our forces. That's the only battle in the Pacific that the Japanese inflected more casualties on us than we did on them. I had 40 officers in my battalion and six were killed on the island and one died on the hospital ship. I don't think there were but two or three that didn't get wounded. Years later I was told by a good friend in Washington, who was in position to do research, that out of 24 battalion commanders who landed on Iwo, five were killed, 14 wounded and five, me and four others came off without a purple heart. I'm told there are only three of us battalion commanders still living and I happen to be one of them. That's the way Satan dealt with it.

For the first three landings I carried a carbine. Before we started to Iwo Jima, I wanted a 45 cal. pistol with a shoulder holster. I told the quartermaster if I make it through this battle, I'm going to take the pistol home with me. He said he would mark my record now, lost in combat. I brought it home with me and sold it a few years ago for $325.00.

After the battle, we went back to Hawaii to the same base camp. The natives gave us a big welcome, knowing we had been in a terrible battle. They had the hula dancers and the works. I think it was the middle of July that we were told that we were going to retake *Wake Island*. We were to land there on the 1st day of October, 1945. I thought what in the world were we going to mess with little old Wake Island in the Northern Pacific. Then I realized that we were getting ready to invade the home islands of Japan. We needed the airfield at Wake for emergency landings and refueling. We started training, the 23rd and 24th Regiment of the 4th Division. We were assigned to take Wake Island. On the other four landings that I had been in, Marshall's, Marianna, Iwo Jima, I never had the feeling that I was going to get killed-probably get wounded—not killed. But when they assigned us to land on Wake, I knew I was going to get killed period. No if and buts, maybe or anything. It was so real when the Japs surrendered I knew how a prisoner on death row felt; he's going to live now. If we would have gone to those home islands, there is a chance I wouldn't be here today.

The two atomic bombs finally convinced the Japanese that the war was lost. It amazed me that they stopped fighting. They were good fighters, the Japanese were.

Bob: If we had invaded Japan I believe it was estimated that the allies would have had 1,000.000 casualties. Is that right?

Col. Scales: Yes. No one knows of course but it was estimated by some knowledgeable people. Look what it would have cost the Japanese. We had command of the air. We had them in a corner but everybody was fighting us, old people, children, everyone.

Scales continues: Bob Davidson was commanding the 2nd Battalion, I had the 3rd. The Adjutants tent was a couple of feet from mine and he had a field telephone next to his bunk. He would receive calls from time to time. About three days after the Nagasaki bomb, I heard his telephone ring and I was listening. He said Captain Talbert the next thing—I will never forget what he said; 'What do you mean the war is over?' God almighty, I came ripping out of my bunk, got tangled up in my mosquito net and I had on my skivvy drawers. Someone had heard on the radio that the Japs had surrendered. We broke out the champagne that we had been saving. It was about 2 a.m. in the morning and we celebrated up and down the company streets. The next morning we found out it was a false alarm. It was about three days later that the surrender took place. (August 14, 1945). There was no champagne left. We were out in the field training when the news came. We came back to camp for memorial services conducted by our chaplain. I think everyone in the regiment was there to remember their buddies who had not made it. We had to do something to keep the 20,000 marines from sitting around doing nothing. We tried close order drill competition etc. We drew straws to see who would go home first. Our 23rd got the long straw. The 24th and 25th would go back before we did. We had a point system. The magic number was 85.

We appointed a sentry with binoculars to watch for a ship to come in the harbor. The first day he was reporting fishing boats, canoes and anything that moved. We told him to knock it off. We want a big ship to take a bunch of marines back to San Diego. Finally a medium size carrier, the *Casablanca,* came in. I sent a captain down to see how many marines they wanted to come aboard. He came back with a big smile with a message from their captain. The captain said, 'Is it true that you marines have been over here for two years and been in four landings?' When asked how many men he could take aboard, the captain said 'As many marines that you can get aboard and I will take them to San Diego.' We ended up with about 1,600 on board. I was in command.

I think it was October 19, 1945 that we docked at San Diego. A lot of wives, parents and children were there to meet their loved ones. Marines were walking down the gangplank hugging and kissing and greeting everyone. I was improperly dressed, standing on the deck when a message came over the PA system. 'Major Scales, report to the after gangplank.' I said, 'What the hell is going on?' I had to run back to my room and get my tie and shoes on and overseas cap. A young marine corporal said that General Shelton wanted to see me on the dock right away. He said 'Scales, I want you to go back with the troops up to Camp Pendleton. We are going to march in the Navy Day Parade on Saturday in Los Angeles.' This was Thursday. The general said there would be no liberty until after the parade. The marines were on base and their families were in a motel across the street from the main gate. I changed the general's orders and gave the men liberty but told them they had better be back on Saturday at 4:30 for the parade. No one got in trouble and the general never knew about it.

I got up at 4:30 a.m. to call my wife to avoid the long lines. After all it would be 7:30 on the east coast. My wife said, 'When are you coming home?' I said 'Honey, I don't know. I have to wait until the other LTC comes in so I can be processed.' She told me that she was coming out and I said 'come on.' I had received $202 dollars and some odd cents travel money to get home. A buddy and his wife teamed up with me and Stacy and we celebrated at the Coconut Grove—dancing. We spent all of the $202 and I called my mother to wire me some money to come home on. That's another story.

My wife died on November 6, 2006 with Parkinson Disease. We lacked two months celebrating our 65th Anniversary. She was a healthy person, never had a headache—so steady—never down or depressed—on cloud nine. Our children gave us a big party on our 50th Anniversary. On my 90th birthday, April 28, 2006, I was surprised with a special birthday party. The invitations that were sent by a young lady said 'I hereby order you to attend.' Seven or eight marines came from Quantico. There were about 150 people who attended my party.

Bob: Colonel, how did you feel about the Japanese in battle and how do you feel about the Japanese today?

Col. Scales: I have given that a lot of thought. The Japanese were good tenacious fighters. They were trained not to surrender. One of my grandson's who graduated from Harvard spent a year in Japan on an exchange scholarship. His field is in Computer Science. He married a Japanese girl. We now have two great granddaughters 4

½ and 6 months old at the time of this interview. My attitude has naturally changed. The Japanese people are honorable. Look what they have done since the war. They lead in manufacturing automobiles in the world now. Can't argue with success like that. The young lady my grandson married had a Buddhist ceremony in Japan and an Episcopal wedding in Titusville, Florida where his parents live. Stacy and I went. I don't think my grandson has taken on any of the Oriental religion."

Sixty-two years later, the battle is still with Scales. He wonders about surviving the war and enjoying a postwar life missed by those who were killed. The dead miss holidays, anniversaries, and children. "That was taken from them," he says. "And you don't give your life for your country. You don't give it. It's taken from you, in many cases brutally." He added, "Iwo was a graveyard for the dead and hell for the living,"

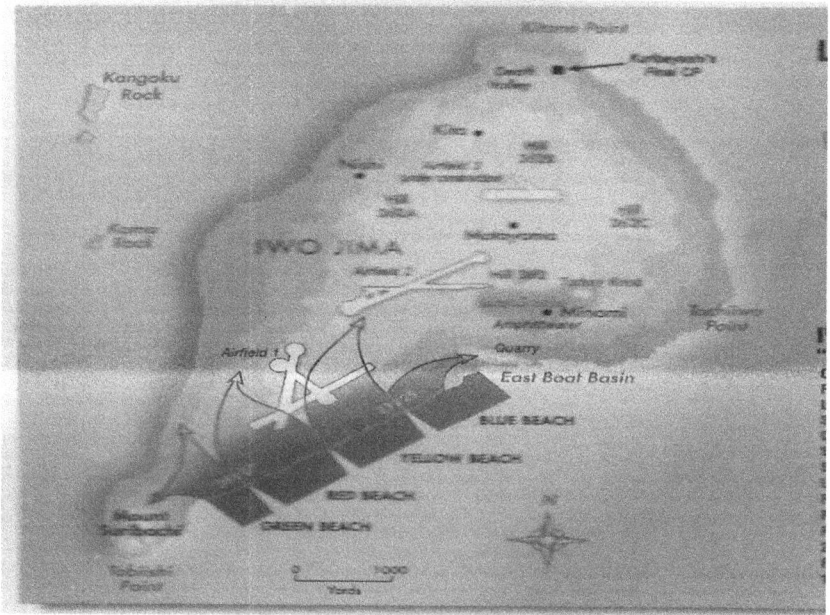

After the war, Scales left the marines but remained in the active reserve, from which he retired as a colonel. He retired from business and has been active in his community. He has attended marine reunions and enjoys the lifelong bonds he made during the war. For those with whom he served, he wishes a "long and happy life; they've earned it."

This small volcanic island of Iwo Jima, is only seven and one half square miles. On February 14, 1945, some 30,000 US Marines, members of the 4th and 5th Marine Divisions, landed on the beachhead. The battle for Iwo Jima was one of the most savage battles fought during World War II. Twenty out of 22 Japanese soldiers would die; one out of every three Marines would either be killed or wounded. Iwo Jima is located 1,118 miles from Tokyo.

CHAPTER TEN

WORLD WAR II STORIES

RAYMOND G. HAYMAKER

"On 28 August 1944, Lt. Haymaker flew in an attack on enemy motor transports near Viennes, France. After his P-47D Thunderbolt was crippled by anti-aircraft fire, he repeatedly strafed the objective destroying four large transports."

The author's personal interview began with this World War II hero about one o'clock on Monday, July 30, 2007 in Ray's living room on Smith Mountain Lake, Virginia. Haymaker is a small man in stature but had the will and heart of a giant. He is a remarkable individual. The author found this highly decorated World War II fighter pilot suffering with both shoulders from rotator cuff damage. This damage was caused from caring for his wife, Dell, for twelve years following her stroke. His wife passed away in 2002 after 54 years of marriage. This story is about a man we call a hero, but Ray in his modest manner refused to accept the hero title. He said "The real heroes are those who didn't come home."

Ray Haymaker was born on April 9, 1920 at Jordan Mines, Virginia. His parents were Albert M. and Minnie Apritt Haymaker. He graduated from Covington High School in 1938. In 1942, Ray entered the US Army Air Force with a dream of becoming a pilot. He was first sent to Maxwell Field, Alabama. After his training at Maxwell, Ray started aviation training at Clarksdale, Mississippi. His dream came true. Ray became a pilot on a P-47D Thunderbolt bomber, flying 44 missions over Europe.

The P-47D was equipped with eight M2 Browning 50 cal. machine guns and carried up to 2,000 pounds of bombs. Rockets would be added later for additional fire power. The plane had a crew of one, the pilot. Its maximum speed was 426 mph at 30,000 feet. Ray said that the range on a combat mission was about 800 miles. The Thunderbolt was manufactured by Republic Aviation Company, Farmingdale Plant, in Long Island, New York. Because of the demand for this fighter-bomber and the number of losses, a new plant in Evansville, Indiana started building the plane. The Thunderbolt was designed by two Georgian immigrants. The cost in 1945 was $83,000. Previous models of the P-47 were built and used in

combat prior to the P-47D. The fuel capacity was increased to 375 gallons, with "drop tanks" added to the wings later.

The picture above is of Ray holding a model of his P-47. In combat the Thunderbolt distinguished itself because it had dual power, fighter-bomber plane capabilities. By 1944, it had served in combat in all of its operational theaters, except the battle of the Aleutian Islands. The P-47D had a total of 3,752 air-to-air kills, losing 3,499 to all causes in combat.

Haymaker's job was blasting enemy communications, motor transports and gun positions in support of Allied ground troops in the Mediterranean theater. Before he was assigned to the 12th Air Force, this unit had participated in campaigns such as *El Alemein, Sicily, Salerno and Anzio.* Between April 1 and June 5, 1944, Allied planes were carrying out daily missions to bomb potential targets to make the landings on beaches less dangerous for the Army. During this period the Allies lost an estimated 2,000 aircraft and 12,000 air crew members killed before D-Day-Normandy. By August 25th when operation *"Overlord"* ended, 28,000 crew members were lost over France.

Weeks before Normandy, Ray's unit, with help from the US Navy, pounded Southern France day after day. Their mission was to knock out big gun emplacements and German troop movements. Hitler and his generals were not certain now exactly where the main invasion of Europe would take place. Could it come from the South now? Haymaker was among the first Thunderbolt pilots to pound Southern France D-Day targets and his squadron was the first Twelfth AAF tactical unit to hit enemy targets in Germany and Austria from the south.

The fighters roared from their bases in flights of 8-12 or 20 to bomb and strafe communications behind the German lines. Other pilots circled over Allied lines awaiting calls from the ground commander for them to dive bomb and strafe enemy artillery, mortar and machine gun positions. Ray commented that to make a dive into all the enemy fire was just like looking down their barrel. This took guts. These P-47 pilots had what it takes to complete a mission regardless of the danger. They would dive, strafe, drop bombs, and climb up into the atmosphere only to dive toward their assigned targets again and again.

The operation by American pilots over southern France was called *"Uppercut."* Thunderbolt pilots also proved the planes precision accuracy in *"Operation Strange,"* which shut off rail and road supply arteries to the Germans prior to the drive on Rome. During May 1944, the fighter-bombers destroyed almost 2,600 German motor vehicles and damaged an estimated 2,200 more. In addition, many locomotives, rail cars, tanks, half-tracks and other equipment were destroyed or damaged.

Attacking an enemy convoy in the *Uppercut* operation along the Rhone Valley in France, Haymaker's Thunderbolt was heavily damaged by fierce anti-aircraft fire. Courageously maintaining his crippled plane in formation despite the continued barrage, Haymaker repeatedly strafed the enemy area in low-level thrusts which destroyed four large transports and damaged nine other vehicles. Ray said, "When you fire your 50 cal. machine guns, a camera records any damage caused. You don't get credit unless there is an explosion or fire." The normal air speed for landing a P-47 was 100 mph. Ray said due to the damage, he was required to land at a speed of 150 mph, another anxious moment.

For this action Haymaker was awarded the **Distinguished Flying Cross**. The CITATION reads as follows: Headquarters 12th Air Force: *"The Distinguished Flying Cross is awarded, Raymond G. Haymaker, 2nd Lt. Air Corps, 87th fighter Squadron, 79th Fighter Group. 'For extraordinary achievement while participating in aerial flight as pilot of a P-47 type aircraft on 28 August 1944, Lieutenant Haymaker flew in an attack upon a concentration of enemy motor transports near Viennes, France. Upon the approach to the target, direct hits from intense anti-aircraft fire heavily damaged Lieutenant Haymaker's airplane and holed all other planes in the formation. Courageously maintaining his crippled aircraft in formation in the* *face of continued heavy ground fire, Lieutenant Haymaker repeatedly strafed the objective, destroying four large transports and damaging nine other vehicles. His outstanding proficiency and steadfast devotion to duty reflect great credit upon himself and the Armed forces of the United States. Signed by: John K. Cannon, Major General USA Commanding. G.O. No 168, 12 September 1944"*

Haymaker's 79th fighter group had moved into southern France from Corsica, Italy. They were flying out of a strip near St. Raphael. In one way the squadron had it made. They were quartered on the Riviera, living in Villas on the beach. For the first time in many months, they had hot showers, better food, and a bed.

It was a beautiful day. All pilots had left the flight line except three when a special mission was called. These three P-47 pilots were ready and willing to meet the challenge. Later, Haymaker became involved in this mission. The German 19th Army had begun to withdraw their troops and equipment. It seems that the Germans were unable to defend themselves from the 79th fighter group. There was only one major highway out of southern France for the Germans to plan their retreat. This gave Ray's squadron an advantage.

As usual, the targets were trucks, cars, motorcycles all moving north. The pilots had flown several missions in the vicinity of the Rhone valley which had two mountain ranges. Below the main highway was located a rail line. The Germans, anxious to move their equipment to avoid an attack, had the road completely covered with various vehicles moving as fast as possible. The convoy didn't slow down or stop even when the P-47s began their dives. One of the pilots estimated that the German trucks etc. were approximately 33 miles long.

The lead pilot gave the order to attack some distance from the head of the column, hoping to cause a road block. It was only natural for the Germans to achieve their goal of retreating, required a lot of fuel for their vehicles. If the American P-47 pilots could only have a bit of luck and hit the trucks carrying their fuel, this would bring their movement to a complete halt. When the attack began on the column, the Americans were met with heavy ground fire. Several planes were damaged. The planes continued strafing with the flak becoming more intense. Haymaker, who flew a total of 44 missions, had faced this type of danger many times before. He said that because of the training they had received, fear at the time of attack was not an option. But after the mission had ended, thoughts crossed his mind of what could have happened to him. He said that he thanks his "maker" every day for allowing him to survive.

Ray Haymaker survived the many combat missions as a P-47 pilot. He is a proud man who served his country in the "Big War." In addition to being awarded the Distinguished Flying Cross, Ray also was awarded the Air Medal, the European theater ribbon w/5 battle stars. He married Dell Jordan on April 17, 1948. They had a son Kenneth, two grandchildren, Michael and Christopher; four great grandchildren, Robby, Heather, Alexia and Patrick. Ray was promoted to First Lieutenant on August 25, 1944. He had a brother, Kenneth, who ran away from home at the age 18, joined the army and achieved the rank of Colonel before retiring. The Air Medal Citation reads as follows: *"The Air Medal is awarded to: Raymond G. Haymaker, Second Lieutenant, Air Corps by direction of the President, under the provisions of Army regulations 600-45 as amended, and pursuant to authority vested in me by the commanding General, Mediterranean Theater of operations.*

CITATION

For meritorious achievement while participating in aerial flight as pilot of a P-47 type aircraft during an attack upon enemy communication lines near Ferrara, Italy on 7 July 1944. Lieutenant Haymaker's proficiency in combat reflects great credit upon himself and the Military service of the United States. Signed by: John K Cannon, Major General, USA, Commanding G.O. No. 127, 11 August 1944

CHARLES W. BOSS
US NAVY

After the USS Cushing received between 20 and 25 hits from the Japanese attack, the Captain ordered "Abandon Ship." **Boss**

Charles Boss was born in Bradford, PA on January 20, 1922. On October 8, 1940, at age 18, he joined the Navy and served his country in battle after battle until the end of World War II. He was discharged from the navy in October 1946. After six weeks of boot camp at the Naval Training Station at Newport, Rhode Island, he was assigned to the USS *Cushing* (DD3760) at Pearl Harbor on February 8, 1941. Boss served on the *Cushing* until November 13, 1942. The *Cushing* operated during peacetime until September 15, 1941 when she returned to the Destroyer Base in San Diego, California for an overhaul. While in San Diego Boss attended Fleet School for training as a fire control man and returned on board of the *Cushing* on November 15, 1941.

This aerial view of the *Cushing* on the next page shows the two 50-cal. water-cooled machine guns mounted for AA protection atop the gun-crew shelters forward of the bridge and on the after deckhouse. Her main battery consisted of five 5-inch-38 dual-purpose guns and twelve torpedo tubes in three quadruple mounts. Boss's station was on one of the 5-inch guns.

The destroyer, USS *Cushing*, was christened on December 31, 1935, at the Puget Sound Navy Yard, Bremerton, Washington, by Miss Katherine A. Cushing, the daughter of the ship's namesake. With her, is Admiral Thomas T. Craven, USN, commandant of the Navy Yard. After a shakedown cruise in Hawaiian and West Coast waters, the *Cushing* reported to the Pacific Fleet. The headlines recording the commissioning were,

"NAVY MEN TAKE OVER NEW SHIP." Under a cloudless sky and with an audience of several hundred Bremerton people, the USS *Cushing* this morning became a part of the United States

Navy. In a brief ceremony, Rear Admiral T.T Craven, commandant of the yard, turned the vessel over to her first captain, Comdr. E.Y. Short, saying that he was sure the vessel would be operated efficiently and would have a creditable career.

(Official Navy Photograph-courtesy Charles Boss)

(Miss Katherine A. Cushing and Admiral Thomas T. Craven)
(Official US Navy photograph—courtesy of Al McCloud)

Addressing officers of the ship, Admiral Craven said, 'It is up to you whether this ship becomes the kind of machine which the Navy intends her to be. She is equipped with all the latest devices for ships of her class. She has more horsepower than the USS *Colorado,* a battleship. If you slouch down, and consider her merely a place where you have a job, she can easily become a dungaree ship; take pride in her, and run her as I know you will, she will become a brilliant unit of the fleet.' The 1,500-ton vessel, second of her kind to be built at the navy yard, is rapidly being made ready for a shakedown cruise, the itinerary of which will be announced within the next few weeks. Her sister ship, the USS *Perkins,* will be commissioned with similar ceremonies on September 11."

On December 7, 1941, the day of the Japanese attack on Pearl Harbor, the *Cushing* was on Mare Island being loaded with provisions and ammunition. Their first duty was patrolling for Jap submarines. Then on December 15th, they convoyed to Pearl Harbor. The Cushing on January 10th with the USS *William Ward Borroughs* convoyed to Midway Island. It was on Midway that Boss's ship was under the first shell fire from the Japanese submarines. Boss said, "No hits, no runs, no errors." Charles Boss served in *Battle of the Coral Sea, Midway, Santa Cruz, Guadalcanal, Baker Island, Wake Island, Marshall and Gilbert.* After returning to Pearl Harbor, the *Cushing* then returned to San Francisco and was attached to a task force that included three battle ships; *Pennsylvania, Idaho* and *Mississippi.* This duty was for training new personnel on gunnery doctrines and naval procedures aboard the battlewagons.

BATTLE OF CORAL SEA   May 7-9, 1942

Charles Boss was aboard the USS *Cushing* during the battle of the Coral Sea, southwest of the Solomon Islands. This was the first battle in the Pacific with Japanese aircraft carriers. The Japanese goal was to capture Port Moresby by an amphibious landing and establish an airbase there. Port Moresby was located on the southeastern coast of Australia. The other Japanese minor invasion was at Tulagi, in the Southern Solomon's. Two aircraft carriers, the *Shokaky,* and the *Zuikaku,* would provide support while providing escort service for the cruisers and destroyers.

The US Navy countered this attack with two aircraft carriers, the USS *Lexington* and USS *Yorktown,* destroyers, submarines and bombers. The US had help from two carriers from the Australian Navy. The United States lost one carrier-the *Lexington* which went on her side following a big explosion, probably caused by the detonation of torpedo warheads; and had another carrier damaged, and lost a destroyer. The naval units from Japan suffered losses as well. Damaged from bombs was their aircraft carrier, *Shokaky* by planes from the USS *Yorktown* (CV-5). The *Yorktown* was damaged from Japanese dive bombers. The *Zuikaku's* air group was badly damaged as well. Both these Japanese carriers were not able to participate in the Battle of Midway, because of the damage caused in this battle. The Japanese carrier *Shoho* was torpedoed.

BATTLE OF MIDWAY   June 4-7 1942

Charles Boss said that their task force intercepted a Japanese fleet headed from Australia. Due to the size and overwhelming number of ships in the US force, no contact made with the enemy. The enemy fleet turned tail and was met by a US Naval force from the North and reported destroyed.

The Battle of Midway was one of the most important sea battles during World War II. Until Midway, and following their attack on Pearl Harbor, the Japanese had superiority on the seas. Following this battle, however, the US Navy force was rated as equal to its enemy. The USS *Yorktown* was hit by three Japanese bombs on the first day of this battle. The USS *Hammann* was sunk.

The Japanese fleet commander was Admiral Isoroku Yamamoto. It was his intention to destroy the US carriers because of having been embarrassed by the Doolittle raid on the Japan home islands in April and also by the Battle of Coral Sea. Again America's intelligence reports helped to eliminate Yamamoto's surprise attack. Japan lost four carriers, and much damage was caused by the dive bombers from the USS *Hornet* and USS *Enterprise*.

The following month, August 1942, the USS *Cushing* convoyed the USS *North Carolina* on its maiden trip to Pearl Harbor from San Francisco. The *Cushing* was then attached to the USS *Enterprise* striking force.

BATTLE OF SANTA CRUZ   October 25-30, 1942

Boss said, "I saw the most inspiring sight by watching destruction of the enemy aircraft. I also witnessed the great loss of the USS *Hornet* and the damaging of the USS *Enterprise*. We escorted the *Enterprise* to Esperito Santos, New Caledonia."

Vice Admiral Edward N. Parker, USN (Ret) (Commanding Officer), gave this account. "On the morning of 26 October the *Hornet* and *Enterprise* launched searches to the N.W., and later launched air strikes against the enemy. I believe the first strike fell short. They were refueled and re-launched. But the aborted first strike aircraft returned, one of the torpedo planes (presumably out of gas) landed on the water on the starboard side of the D/L *Porter* (the flagship of Comderson 5). Very shortly thereafter the *Porter* was struck on her starboard side by a torpedo, which immobilized her. Other destroyers went alongside and removed her people and fired another torpedo into her and sank her.

The *Cushing* was in the circular screen around the *Enterprise* which at this time was launching the second strike. About this time we saw that the *Hornet* was under air attack. Then the Japanese dive bombers, followed by torpedo planes, attacked the *Enterprise* force. This was the first time any of the destroyer crews of our Squadron had been subjected to a massive air attack.

An amusing but sad event during the attack was that a Japanese torpedo plane, having launched his torpedo, flew across the *Cushing's* bow at about the height of the bridge. Our forward 20mm, in perfect position to get him JAMMED! One of our signalmen was firing his 45 cal automatic at the Jap, who we plainly saw thumbed his nose at us. A bomb landed on the top of Turret #2 of the *South Dakota*, wounding Captain Gatch who was on the bridge.

As the attack ended we saw smoke from the *Hornet*, and received word that the *Enterprise* had a bomb hit on the flight deck in the vicinity of the forward elevator. The damage of the *Hornet* was quite severe, the planes from both groups tried to land on the *Enterprise*. Many planes ended up landing in the water as they ran out of fuel.

The destroyers, including the *Cushing,* followed along after the carrier picking up the aviators from fighters, dive bombers and torpedo planes. The fighters (one man) sank as soon as the plane was in the water; the dive bombers floated a little while (30 to 90 seconds); the torpedo planes (three men) floated long enough for the men to launch the rubber boat and the crew to get into it. The *Cushing* picked up about 20 aviators, cleaned them up, fed them and let them get a good night's sleep. The way these rescues worked, the planes would approach from astern, passing up our starboard side and put her down in the water about 300 yards ahead of us. We would slow down and try to stop alongside to pick up the men, then charge ahead, trying to catch up with the *Enterprise*.

We sent the aviators over to the *Enterprise* the next morning by highline. [Later, while on Guadalcanal I met several of the ones who had been aboard the *Cushing*.] I did not see the end of the *Hornet* but knew she was so badly damaged that she had to be sunk by torpedoes from our own destroyers when the Jap fast battleships came into view against the setting sun. But later information was that the *Hornet* was struck by two torpedoes which caused her to lose power, and by three bombs and two Jap Kamikaze planes which crashed into her.

The Japanese carriers in this battle were the *Shokaky* and *Zuikaku* (which had participated in the raid on Pearl Harbor and were in the Battle of the Coral Sea) and a smaller carrier the *Junyo*. All three were damaged by our attacks that they had to return to Japan for repairs, and, were therefore unable to support their surface Navy in the final efforts to drive the US out of Guadalcanal. The cruisers and destroyers of the *Hornet* Group joined the *Enterprise* Task Force and we headed for Noumea, New Caledonia."

Next was the battle of **Guadalcanal.** On November 1, 1942, Boss was on the *Cushing* as they escorted a convoy with US Marines and Army troops with freighters to Guadalcanal.

THE FIRST NAVAL BATTLE OF GUADALCANAL
November 12-13, 1942

The US Marines landed on Guadalcanal on August 7, 1942. The Japanese wanted to take the island back. The Japanese Army underestimated the number of marines and soldiers on the island and their scheduled attacks at different times caused them failure in trying to overrun Henderson Field. For months the Japanese made an effort to take Henderson Field, but the marines held their positions.

The American convoys had departed their anchorages on the 8th and 9th, respectively, under the overall command of Rear Admiral Richmond Kelly Turner. After unloading their cargo, Turner received a report from Australian coast watcher further up in the Solomon's that a Japanese force consisting of two battleships (or heavy cruisers), one light cruiser, and eight or ten destroyers was heading south. Turner, believing the Japanese were planning to deal with his transports, decided that his ships should leave. The majority of the escort, five cruisers and eight destroyers would be left behind under the command of Rear Admiral Daniel Callaghan to engage the Japanese. Aboard Callaghan's ships, notice had been received from *Helena* regarding the presence of enemy vessels bearing roughly 315 degrees from *Cushing*, the lead destroyer. *Cushing* made contact with *Yudachi* and *Harusame*, broke left to unmask her batteries, and queried Callaghan to open fire, a request Callaghan ultimately denied. *Cushing* corrected her turn, now behind the leading Japanese destroyers, and sighted *Nagara*. Her moves had put the American formation on a collision course with the huge Japanese battleships.

On Friday, November 13, 1942 at 2:10 a.m., the USS *Cushing* received its first enemy hit. *Cushing* began a losing dual with *Nagara* and *Yukikaze* after releasing six torpedoes at *Hiei* (the Japanese Flagship) that missed. Hiei's reply hit *Cushing's* engine space, rendering her unfit for her dual; she could only fire her hand moved 20mm guns, for power was lost completely. Her service was over. The task force consisting of 13 ships met and engaged in ship-to-ship combat with a Japanese convoy. After the *Cushing* received between 20 or 25 hits from the Japanese attack, the Captain ordered "Abandon Ship." Boss said, "About 1,030 of our crew were picked up by a marine landing barge. We spent 13 days on Guadalcanal learning about the true conditions of modern warfare." Boss added, "The second night I was on the island, a marine tapped me on the shoulder and said, 'You're a marine now,' and handed me a machine gun. After he was wounded, I had full charge of the gun. I was very lucky not to have been wounded or killed. The marines shared what little clothing and food they had with us. The hardships that we endured were many, but the hardships of the marines who took and held Guadalcanal were far greater than the civilian population shall ever know."

On December 1, 1942, all survivors were on their way to the States, arriving at San Diego on December 20th for some R & R (rest and recuperation). They received thirty days delayed orders to report to Puget Sound Navy Yard, Bremerton, Washington for new construction.

On February 14, Boss was transferred to a receiving station, San Pedro for duty aboard the USS *Boyd*. The USS *Boyd* was launched on October 29, 1942 by Bethlehem Steel Co., San Pedro, California and commissioned on May 8, 1943 with Lieutenant Commander Sharp, Jr. in command. *Boyd* departed for Pearl Harbor on July 14, 1943. After additional training she departed as part of screen of Task Force II, which had been formed for the purpose of taking part in the occupation of **Baker Island** (September 1, 1943). On September 23rd until the 29th, the USS *Boyd* acted as an escort for the *Essex, Yorktown and Cowpens* during the training of air groups and crews. On that day *Boyd* departed with Fast Carrier Group to hit **Wake Island** raid on October 5th and 6th. The Wake Island battle began simultaneously with the attack on Pearl Harbor and ended on December 23, 1941 with the surrender of the American forces to the Japanese. The Japanese held the island until September 4, 1945 when the remaining Japanese garrison surrendered to a detachment of the United States Marines.

The USS *Boyd* left Pearl Harbor on October 10th with *task group* for the *Gilbert Island* operation. Charles Boss also made the **Gilbert Islands** landings November 19 to December 8 and a heavy night air attack off **Tarawa**. On the 25th enemy torpedo planes attacked the formation, dropping flares but inflicting no damage. The following night enemy torpedo planes attacked again. *Boyd* fired on one group of ten to twelve planes. Again no ships were damaged. An hour after the attack, *Boyd* made surface radar contact and closed target. On approach, the radar pip disappeared from the screen and a sound search was conducted. *Boyd* dropped two depth charge patterns. Fifteen minutes after the second drop, a loud underwater explosion was heard. The following morning planes from the *Enterprise* reported large oil slick in the vicinity. During the bombardment of **Nauru** Island on December 8th, the *Boyd* was damaged by a Japanese shore battery while on a rescue mission.

The *Boyd* was directed to pick up survivors of a plane crash. Three planes were directed to assist in the search. At 11:35 a.m., the lookout reported an object in the water which looked like a man waving his hand. At 11:42 a.m., two shells hit the ship, one exploding in forward engine room, shearing or puncturing all steam lines and a main power distribution board. *Boyd* immediately commenced maneuvering radically and began counter battery fire, using manual control. In this attack all personnel of the forward engine room, with the exception of one who was seriously burned, were killed. The total casualties were one officer and 11 enlisted men killed and eight wounded. Burial of ten of these men was held on December 9th. Two died later after transferred to the *Alabama*. The USS *Boyd* had to return to Espiritu Santo, New Hebrides for repairs and overhaul for trip back to the States.

On December 20, 1943, the USS *Boyd* entered Pago, Samoa for refueling along with the USS *Denver,* which was damaged also. They entered Pearl Harbor on December 29th for refueling and

BOSS, CHARLES, BETTY

additional repairs before returning to San

Francisco on January 2nd. On January 5, 1944, Boss was granted a 21 day leave. The USS *Boyd* received 11 battle stars for World War II and five for her Service in the Korean War. After serving in the battles of the *Coral Sea*, *Midway*, *Santa Cruz*, *Guadalcanal*, *Wake Island*, *Marshall*, *Gilbert Islands* and *Tarawa*, and the USS *Cushing* being sunk, requiring the crew to abandon ship, Charles Boss, the First Class Storekeeper, received his discharge in October 1946 after six long years serving in the US Navy.

Charles married Betty C. Boss on February 22, 1944. They live in Richmond, Virginia. (Charles Boss, age 85, passed away on December 12, 2007 in Richmond, Virginia).

JOHN EDWARD SINGLETON, III

"During the attack on the Essex on November 25, I reached my station safely and reached the flight deck just as the ship was struck by a Kamikaze."
John Singleton

John Singleton, served on the USS *ESSEX*, an aircraft carrier during World War II, and carries eight battle stars on his chest to prove it. He was born in Richmond, Virginia on April 25, 1925 to John E. and Edna Coleman Singleton. John's father served aboard a destroyer during World War I; and several relatives served in the Navy. His great-great grandfather served in Co. F, 38th regiment, Virginia Infantry during the Civil war. (John was awarded "the Cross of Military Service" from the United

Daughters of the Confederacy). John was approaching eighteen years old and had a very important decision to make. The war was in full swing. John Wayne, everyone's hero, and William Bendix, were making movies that encouraged young men to join the military to fight for their country. Soon he would have to register for the draft. The US Navy was John's logical choice. It appeared that most of the daily news and newsreels were reporting predominantly naval battles.

John was a typical seventeen-year old. His hobby, like that of his friends was collecting 78 rpm records, something today's generation have never heard about. John's favorite artist was Harry James who played a trumpet and had his own band. Among John's collections was "When the Lights go on Again," "Paradise Isle," and "Down Where the Trade Winds Blow." Harry James was married to the sailor's favorite pinup girl, Betty Grable. WOW! What a gal! Her legs were insured for a million bucks.

With time running out, John had to make a decision. If he waited to be drafted he would probably become a marine or serve in the army infantry. On the other hand, if he enlisted, he could choose the navy. This presented two other problems. First, he would be required to obtain his parents' permission; secondly, he must pass the physical. John was not the Charles Atlas (a body builder) type. He weighed only 127 pounds soaking wet and had a health problem. John said, "Extreme exertion or overheating sometimes brought about a noisy wheezing in my chest, residual from two childhood occurrences of pneumonia."

During the first week of April, just days before his 18th birthday, John rode his bicycle for five miles, walked into the Post Office Building on Main Street (Richmond, VA) to locate a navy recruiter. After completing all the paperwork, he stated, "I left the recruiting office with undiminished enthusiasm and with an appointment for a medical examination at the induction center the following week." The induction center was in the Belgium

Building located on the Virginia Union University campus. This structure had been part of the 1937 World's Fair in New York and had been donated to the University after the fair closed. It had been moved to Richmond, reassembled and appropriated by the federal government for military use. This must have been a very traumatic experience for a 17-year old Richmond native with health issues. John entered the massive doors of the awesome blue-grey building, trembling and with cold sweat which he had never experienced before. He said, "There I was directed to join a group of several dozen men in a required state of complete nudity." One doctor thumped on his chest and proceeded with a stethoscope exam. He even broke out in a rash, which one corpsman made a joke about.

John took the oath on April 12, 1943. The next morning' with his satchel filled with various articles, he said goodbye to his parents and left for boot camp at the United States Naval Training Station at Bainbridge, Maryland. Recalling the incident, John said, "As the bus pulled away I could see my mother standing at the window with handkerchief to her face in the eternal contrast of older hearts sinking with despair as younger hearts soar with their pursuit of independence and adventure."

The bus, then train, trip to Bainbridge was not uneventful. Delays were caused by a train derailment, with the train to arrive only too late, for the bus scheduled to transport the 31 recruits had already returned to the base. With about four hours sleep, John and the other Navy recruits heard the bugle at dawn. It was their first time to hear reveille. Next, each man was issued his clothing, bedding and other necessities and a sea bag to put everything in. Now they were ready for the 13 weeks of intense training. John said, "Bible students among us would have a better appreciation for the trials of Job, for our drill instructor's power was as Satan's was being addressed by the Lord in Job 2:6, 'Behold, he is in thine hand; but save his life.' The chief in charge of John's training said, "They would remember him with pain for the rest of their lives, but some may have longer lives because of him."

Next, they were marched to the base barbers. Their beautiful, neatly combed hair was all removed, down to the scalp. The pay scale for the new seamen was $50.00 a month. The Navy advanced each man $5.00, and then directed everyone to sign up for a $10,000 life insurance policy. The first month's premium was $3.40, which took most of John's advance.

The following 13 weeks were the most physically and demanding of John's life. John describes it this way, "The greater part of everyday involved close-order drill with rifles shouldered, rifle drill in the manual of arms, running in formation and out of formation, and calisthenics. Interspersed were classes in seamanship, knot tying, semaphore, Morse code, navigation, marksmanship, wrestling, boxing, jujitsu, swimming and abandon ship drill." Of course inspection after inspection kept everyone alert.

The moment had arrived. The 13 weeks had ended with a parade. John and the other recruits had become a part of a team and ready for their next assignment. With twin white strips of a seaman second class on his cuffs, three months' pay a ten-day leave and a rail ticket to Richmond he said, "My cup was filled with joy." Anyone who has experienced this same situation can easily identify with John's excitement.

Following John's leave, he reported to Lakewood, New Jersey, to train for meteorology. He said, "I was pleasantly surprised to arrive at Lakewood and find a campus setting of impressive stone buildings in a park like forest of tall pines, bordered by golf greens and fairways." Although the schooling demanded most of John's time, he was able to visit Atlantic City beaches with beautiful girls at the beach getting a tan. A dance pavilion with mellow music and pretty girls presented "the irresistible appeal to which young men have responded through the ages." John met and danced with a petite secretary who was on vacation, walked along the beach, and then caught a bus back to camp.

John graduated 19th in the class of 98 from the meteorological school. In October 1943, John passed over the seaman first class rating and became a petty officer. His pay was increased to $78.00 a month. Following graduation, John was assigned to the Western Sea Frontier Weather Central in San Francisco.

John had joined the navy to serve on a ship, not shore duty.

After a year in the navy, he applied for a transfer to the USS *Casco*. To be transferred, he had to convince the commander, which he did. He met the *Casco* at the Bremerton Navy Yards on

USS *Essex* (Photo courtesy of John Singleton)

Puget Sound. When John arrived at Bremerton, the *Casco* had put out to sea. He returned to California and said, "I was banished to Camp Shoemaker, a muddy retreat in the shallow hills near Stockton, California." He was there for five weeks.

During April 1944 the fleet aircraft carrier, USS *Essex* came into port. John and a friend, Pete Oyie, went to the yard to get their first look at a battle carrier. The carrier's flight deck was approximately 60 feet above the water. "We walked up the gangway to the cavernous hanger deck which extended unbroken the full length of the ship, almost 1,000 feet. We explained to the officer of the deck that we wanted to visit the aeronautical office," John reported. After meeting the staff, John found two men who were interested in being assigned to duty in San Francisco rather than on the ship.

John and Pete applied for a transfer to the *Essex*. They actually were allowed to trade duty with the two men whom they had met on board the *Essex*. They left port on April 16, 1944 with a crew of 3,000 men and 1,000 marines. The marines would leave the ship at Hawaii to be replaced with 100 airplanes and their personnel.

John's reflection was, "I stood on the flight deck as we passed beneath the Oakland Bridge and marveled that the ship was as rigid and solid beneath me as had been the city streets. After passing the well-known landmarks of Coit Tower, the Cliff House, Seal Rocks, Golden Gate Park and its equally renowned bridge, it was with some surprise that I found the ship, regardless of its tremendous bulk, beginning to respond to the ocean waves as do all seagoing vessels." The *Essex* weighted 28,000 tons; the top speed was 33 knots (38 MPH).

The *Essex* was capable of traveling the 2,100 mile trip from San Francisco to Hawaii in three days. However, because of enemy submarines, the *Essex* was required to maintain a zigzag course. The ship docked during that night. The next morning the view of Oahu was breathtaking with Diamond Head to the city of Honolulu. "Having been reared within easy driving distance of Virginia's Blue Ridge Mountains, I have an appreciation for the ever changing beauty of living mountains," John replied.

John celebrated his 19th birthday in Honolulu. He described the event this way, "Waikiki beach was my first destination and the Royal Hawaiian Hotel my specific point of interest. Its stately luxuriousness was timeless and as yet untouched by the claustrophobic building surge which could not then be envisioned. The Royal Hawaiian reigned supreme on Waikiki midst regal palms inclined as though in supplication. Crimson Poinciana and Bougainvillea flowered in profusion and added their fragrance over all. Nature's perfection was so complete that even barbed wire interwoven along the beach could be accepted as a temporary encroachment. Though time would eliminate this, all else must surely remain."

April 1944: The *Essex* and crew were back at sea and heading

toward Japan with her marine passengers having been replaced by a full air group and planes with folded wings. John described it this way, "The intricately organized movements of aircraft handling crews were executed with the perfection of ballet performers. Each specialist was jacketed and hooded in brilliant color to separately identify fueling, arming, arresting gear, plane handling and crash crews. As each craft landed the colors would separate, combine and then part again as the groups came on stage for their individual and collective performances."

The days were full of activity beginning with the bugle call to general quarters one half hour before sunrise and ending following a repeat of that summons before sunset. During these hours the *Essex* was subject to both air and submarine attacks. John said,

"The flight personnel aboard these craft must have had unshakable nerves or blind faith, for even with the long towing cable between plane and target sleeve the tremendous power of exploding five-inch shells must have been painfully apparent to them. They certainly were to me." John said their task force usually consisted of three large carriers of the CV class, one or two excort or CVE carriers, a battleship, four cruisers and as many as 20 screening destroyers.

May 19 & 20, 1944 was the date of their first attack against the enemy. *MARCUS* was a lone Japanese held island 2,700 miles west of Pearl Harbor and 1,000 miles from Toyko. The *Essex* launched air strikes all day. A similar launch was made on May 23 against *Wake Island*. John describes this action, "I remember this as my last time of complacency in the Pacific. Several days after departing the Wake Island area our radar began picking up flights of enemy planes. Late in the evening one of their task forces came under attack as John stood on the flight deck to witness a sight then unique in his experience. He said, "All the ships of that force were firing into the darkened skies to effect an unequaled display of pyrotechnics. The dazzling steams of color were punctuated aloft as the larger shells exploded at preset altitudes. A flight of planes had slipped through our defenses. On the gun platform I could see nothing but the bursts from our five inch mounts as their ominously pointing barrels elevated towards the vertical."

Following the Wake Island battle, the *Essex* moved to *Majuro* in the *Marshall Islands* for provisioning and grouping with other forces to form the Fifth Fleet. John describes crossing the Equator, "Traditionally, all seafarers crossing the equator for the first time undergo certain imaginative, and sometimes moderately painful, initiation rites necessary to the transition from pollywog to shellback. The shellbacks were those who had previously crossed the Equator. It was their responsibility to induct the newcomer in such a manner as to asssure lasting memories of the occasion. No one was exempt. Everyone was herded before two personages dressed in the regalia of King Neptune and his queen. The bearded king was royally bedecked with crown, robe and trident. The queen was suitably attired and sported long blonde locks which, upon closer inspection, could be identified as the base end of a clean white mop We were ranked before the king for his decision as to whether we should be treated to distasteful dishes with discouraging suggestions as to content, to be coated with grease and plunged into a water filled canvas reservoir. Some were subjected to multiple indignities and such was our most famed crew member, Wayne Morris.

Morris was a star of many action movies in the late thirties and early forties, was a much-liked pilot in our fighter squadron. It was surprising to see Morris, a husky man, fit into the cockpit of a F6F. He was brought bodily before the throne for the full weight of the court's decision. Lieutenant Morris' plane had five miniature rising suns painted on the side, one for each Japanese plane that he shot down. Morris survived the combat."

June 12, 1944: the *Essex* with John Singleton aboard, began air strikes against the *Marianas* preliminary to landings on the island of *Saipan*. The Marianas were rich with shipping, and their skies were vigorously protected by enemy aircraft. John said, "As we were at battle stations all day and far into the night, I learned how extreme could be the order to secure all necessary water lines and blowers. Hours of sporadic firing went by with the Pacific sun penetrating metal helmets and flash protective clothing until, one after another, we began shedding first the elbow length cotton gauntlets and then the head and neck hood." The Marianas stay was active one, John added. "Our fighter sweep destroyed 147 planes the first day and the *Essex* alone located a 20 ship convoy attempting to run from Saipan and sank or damaged 15 of them."

June 14: The force that included the *Essex*, traveled 700 miles north to the Bonin and Volcano Islands, only 600 miles from

Tokyo. John related this, "As much as the success of such attacks depended on surprise, we left the Marianas during the night when the radar screen was clear, steering in an oblique direction in order not to disclose our intended target. Our first strike was airborne well before dawn and on its way to downing the first of 85 enemy planes which would fall before their guns during June 16 and 17."

John indicated that none of these raids was without loss to our forces. Survival would depend on parachuting or water landing near the destroyer screen, or coming aboard along the flight deck and crashing into the upraised barrier amidship. John said that the hardest tragedies to accept were the unexpected ones.

The *Saipan* landings, scheduled for June 18, 1944 presented a dilemma. The complication occurred when submarines spotted large concentrations of the Japanese fleet moving towards the area. The Japanese planes were launched about 400 miles from the Allied fleet with the purpose of attacking and returning to Guam for refueling and rearming. Only a few penetrated the screening ships to find targets among the carriers, most of the Japanese planes were picked off by the F6F fighters. The dive bombers which had taken off from the *Essex* to keep out of the way, decided to bomb the airfield at Guam. After the attack, they learned that the enemy had lost almost 400 planes, with some of the American ships damaged. Many of the American pilots were downed by enemy planes and antiaircraft fire.

June 20, 1944: The Japanese fleet of 64 ships was located, including nine carriers. John said, "This was the first time I had seen planes armed for attack against warships. The bombs and torpedoes were awesome and deadly in appearance, even at rest." The planes from the *Essex* took off at 4:30 p.m. for the Japanese fleet which were located 275 miles away. The planes located their targets about two hours after take off. Twenty American planes were shot down by Japanese vessels. The enemy lost one aircraft carrier, two fleet oilers, plus four carriers and three other vessels were damaged.

On return, many American F6F planes were riddled with holes, some with communication and navigation equipment shot away. They were also low on fuel. Admiral Mitscher took one of the grandest gambles of the war and ordered the entire fleet to turn on their lights for the pilots to land. Of the 216 aircraft which sortied that afternoon, 100 failed to return. Some planes who did return did so because of Admiral Mitscher's decision.

While cruising the Marianas seas until early August, assault forces continued their landings on *Saipan, Guam* and *Tinian.* Refueling was accomplished from fleet tankers. This would allow a patrol to be stretched for several months. After resupplying, the *Essex* was directed to *Ulithi,* a deep-water atoll anchorage in the Western Coralines, east of the Philippines and north of New Guinea.

John describes Ulithi in this manner, "Ulithi basked in tropic beauty and gave the appearance of having been untouched by the war. The waters were aglow with colors and the wide, sheltered lagoon ringed with coconut palms and lush, flowering growth. After months at sea, I was eager to go ashore; however, loading and cleaning details were first on the agenda. I went swimming and found the 30 foot dive from the hangar deck wasn't so bad as it looked. During our stay at Ulithi nearly everyone who so desired had opportunity to go ashore. The island seemed to be moving under me as I walked upon it. I realized the ever-moving ship had become firm to my senses and now that which was firm was perceived as in motion." During September, 1944, John sailed south to the *Palau Islands.* They launched against the target island of *Pelelieu* until the marines stormed ashore on September 6. An estimated 10,000 Japanese troops were on the island of *Babelthaup,* the largest of the Palaus.

John's new quarters were with the flight personnel, and were more comfortable. However, his effort to enjoy his bunk came to a halt one night when a violent end landing operation which he had seen many times before went wrong. One plane came in too fast and floated along the deck with its down-groping hook missing cable after cable. The whirling propeller blades chewed through the steel curtain followed by exploding motor and ammunition. John followed the foam crew to find the shack a charred wreckage of bunks, bedding and gear. John received a new issue of clothing and bedding but never again would close his eyes to sleep in that shack.

(Photo courtesy of John Singleton-John is 4th from the right)

September 9, 1944: The *Essex* began strikes against *Mindanao* and on September 21 against *Luzon*- the two largest of the Philippine Islands. The planes from the *Essex* went directly into Manila Bay and had orders to avoid damage to the "Pearl of the Orient" city of *Manila*. John said, "I had long before found the difference between firing my 20 millimeter cannon at a target sleeve and firing at a plane plunging at hundreds of miles an hour.

I think every gunner shared the illusion that the diving planes were pointed exclusively at his position. Bombs were dropped so close along our starboard side that the erupting geysers had drenched our position. During one such day of attacks I acted as loader and trunnion operator. C.P. Cumerford, a lanky youth from Pueblo, Colorado, was my alternating gunner." Though the ship was almost 1,000 feet long, that footage seemed to reduce to one in relation to the speed of the attacker. John continued, "We both knew that short bursts were prescribed, but it took superhuman effort to release the firing bar when you saw a plane screaming downward, bent on your destruction. They (the Japanese) had attempted to carry out their assigned task and had failed. We had attempted ours and had succeeded."

October 1944: This was a traumatic month for those in Admiral Halsey's Third Fleet. They ranged throughout the Western Pacific launching strikes against *Okinawa, Formosa* and *Northern Luzon.* The Formosa campaign with its proximity to land bases on that island, in China and the Philippines began a harrowing period of constant air opposition. On October 13, the enemy sent 1,000 planes against Halsey's fleet in waves which were impossible to evade. The *Franklin* was the victim of a Japanese plane which had been badly hit by the ship's gunners but still managed to crash just abaft the island structure. John said, "As I stood on the *Essex,* I could see the plane plunging in a steep dive to explode with flames flaring to the topmost mast. As our ships were identical, I seemed to be watching our image as though in a mirrow with each tortured and burned position on that ship being a reflection of my own." The *Franklin* seemed to be picked on with additional enemy bombs and Kamikazes finding her as a target. Finally, one such attack would leave her with a staggering loss of over 700 men.

John reflects on somewhat of a relaxing moment when their ship was moving toward another target or refueling. He said, "I would often spend the late evenings on such occasions walking about the deserted flight deck or sitting on its edge to enjoy the cooling breeze and the impressiveness of those tropic nights. Pete Oyie often sat with me while we talked of home or just looked about us at all there was to absorb." Pete Oyie was a young man who stood out in a quiet manner which seemed from no conscious intent. He was married, wrote frequently and had a way of speech which was clear and concise, and with none of the coarseness which was akin to verbal punctuation in the speech of many. He was friendly and easy to talk with. He was a man of faith and principles. John said he never saw Pete sit at meals without bowing his head in silent grace. He could often be found during off-duty hours reading from a pocket Bible.

(Official government photograph of the *USS Essex*)

As the night provided no absolute protection from the enemy so the weather could be a threat as well as a refuge. A typhoon is a phenomenon of nature which, once experienced, is unfortgetable.

On October 17, 1944, John experienced his first typhoon which he called "nature on rampage." He had plotted such storms before and marveled at the violent conflict of readings on the weather charts which traced their progress. Messages came from submarines from the Aleutians to Australia, but those most to be wondered at came from the Sea of Japan and the inland China Seas. The typhoon could not be avoided without being pressed to the China coast. The *Essex* was a sturdy ship, but when the wind velocity mounted to 135 knots, "the waves tossed and twisted us like a canoe in a rock-strewn rapids," John related. He continued, "A catwalk extended under the overhanging flight deck and normally almost 60 feet above the water. Its steel rails provided a steadying support as we made our way forward to stand at the foremost part of the ship. The rise and fall was like riding a roller coaster." With his curosity, John had to go forward because of his interest in the effects of weather.

October 20-24, 1944, the second battle of the *Philippine Sea*. The Philippine island of Leyte was the site of landings on October 20, with coverage from the *Essex* and fleet until October 24. On the 24th, the fleet turned north. As the American fleet approached the enemy, land-and-carrier based planes began attacking. Several of the Japanese ships were sunk or damaged to the point they were out of commission.

John recounted the experience, "We had fended attacking planes since dawn and were straining to spot others as we stood at battle stations. The light carrier, *Princeton*, was running close beside us and just off our starboard stern. We were landing planes and rearming constantly for launch against the nearby fleet. As I scanned the sky a plane dove from above the *Princeton* to penetrate her crowded flight deck. The initial explosion was followed by one eruption after another as her bomb and torpedo-laden planes ignited on the flight and hanger decks. My breath was halted as towering mushrooms of flames burst from the ship's every extreme and I envisioned over 2,000 men being subjected to the violence which was tearing her apart. A destroyer drew near to snatch men from the water and to direct fire hoses on the flaming mass. The cruiser *Birmingham* also pulled alongside and men could be seen leaping onto her decks from the carrier. The rails of the *Birmingham* were lined with sailors attempting to save those fleeing the stricken ship and the tons of lifted debris snuffed out the lives of both rescuer and rescued.

"I think the sinking of the *Princeton* marked a point of psychological change for me. Until that moment I had been more exhilarated than frightened by much that had occurred. A physical trembling possessed me as though from exposure of a chilling wind, and I knew fear." On October 28, 1944, the *Essex* reversed her course towards Leyte. After days of sandwiches and occasional water served at battle stations, the mess halls were reopened to permit service on a revolving-shift basis. John relates another experience, "I joined those of my gun crew to go below, but had hardly begun to eat when the bugle began anew its racing call to return to the guns. The speaker system followed with the summons to stand by to repel torpedo attack. I wondered what would happen if a torpedo struck the crowded mess hall before we got above the decks. As I pulled my way up the almost vertical ladder leading to the hanger deck the guns began hammering and I knew the attack was underway. I fell prone on the deck and arose to the smell of cordite and a dense screen of smoke over all. At first I wondered that many of those rushing with me to their stations remained where they had fallen. Then I saw the blood spreading about them and knew they would never rise. We had been bracketed by three torpedoes, one across the bow, one astern and one to race along the starboard side. The Japanese planes flew over and strafed the ship with bullets which penetrated the steel curtains of the hangar deck to explode and create the havoc about me. I reached the flight deck on the port side and ran its full width to the island structure and to my gun on the far starboard extreme."

During the attack on the *Essex* on November 25, John reached his station safely and reached the flight deck just as the ship was struck by a Kamikaze. The Japanese sucide plane plunged into the 20 millimeter battery located off the flight deck gallery directly across from John's station. Its bomb load exploded, killing the crews of the entire battery. John said, "Our flight and hangar decks were spotted with planes armed and fueled for takeoff, and as these flared it appeared we were due to duplicate the tragedy of the *Princeton.* Thanks largely to Carpenter Hutcheson and his damage control party, the fires were contained and we were able to effect temporary repairs and launch again before the day was over. The 59 casualties could have been multiplied many times if not for the reliableness of that cautious but able sailor.

The targets of the *Essex* during December ranged from *Luzon* to *Formosa* and northward to *Okinawa.* During this voyage, John had this experience, "Another Xerographer, Mac McCormick, who was from the Bronx in New York, was with me making readings. The overcast, moonless night was black as we threaded our way past the gun mounts we could hear nothing but the rush of water as the ship sped on its silent course. We mounted the steps to the confined area and Mac opened the door. In the darkness and with the sound of wind and water rushing by, I sensed rather than saw that Mac was no longer beside me. There was no place for him to go except over the side. I dropped to my knees to find that he had slipped through the protecting chain and was hanging by his hands, 80 feet above the water. Stretching out flat, I was able to grasp his wrists and, between the two of us, get him back to the platform." After the war was over, on Mac's invitation, John visited him and his family in the Bronx.

December 13, 1944: John was standing watch alone when the barometer fell steadily. He woke the assistant Aerological Officer,

Lieutenant Schofield, to inform him of his findings. The lieutenant discounted John's findings and went back to sleep. By morning the *Essex* was locked into a position and unable to get out of it. By the time the storm had run its course, three destroyers had capsized with a loss of 790 men; 28 ships were damaged and 146 planes had washed overboard or destroyed. Schofield was relieved of his position and transferred to the carrier *Franklin*, a ship which had been hit by the enemy several times. True to form, on March 19,1945, the *Franklin* took two bombs off the Japanese island of Shikoku. Flames covered the entire ship before it was taken in tow.

There seemed no end or limit to the violence which continued as horrible routine during the months of January through March, 1945. Even though the war appeared to be near the end, there was no safe place for the fleet. While at Ulithi to load supplies, the crew were watching a movie, "The Virginian," during which time two enemy planes attacked the carrier *Randolph*. They launched against Formosa and the Pescadores islands to sink 51 ships on January 9, 1945.

On January 12, they sneaked through the Bashi Channel, south of Formosa, risking attack from the Japanese air base just 80 miles from the coastal torpedo boats. Slipping into the South China Sea, John said that they struck 400 miles of Indochina coast from Saigon and Hainan to Hong Kong. The fleet were credited with sinking 41 more ships; then it attacked Okinawa on January 21st.

February 16-17, 1945: They were now off the main islands of Japan to launch against *Nakajima, Koijima* and *Tokyo*. John said, "Our destroyers coursed ahead as we thrust northerly through the only snow storm I experienced in the Pacific. The destroyers elimated the small patrol crafts and pulled numbers of Japanese sailors from the waters. These near-naked men, who were brought to the carriers for confinement, were the first living Japanese I had encountered in the Pacific. Regardless of the violence I knew them to be capable of, I found it impossible to feel animosity for those dwarf-like beings as they were led aboard with only strips of cloth about their loins."

John said that his last participation aboard the *Essex* alternated between Japan and Iwo Jima prior to and during the occupation of that volcanic island.

(John with his parents. Photo courtesy of John Singleton)

Earlier John had taken an examination for admission to the Navy's V-12 Officer Training Program. Being selected, he had just two hours to leave the *Essex* ,which provided him a life time of memories from the many battles he participated in and the friends that he lost. A tanker transported him to the island of Eniwetok, in the Marshalls. The ship which took John to Hawaii and then San Francisco had also taken a Kamikaze attack but wasn't sunk. He reached the mainland on April 25, 1945, his 20th birthday. For John, World War II had come to an end. He crossed the Pacific, then the 48 states to Princeton University to take a refresher course. John was discharged on his 21st birthday; April 27, 1946.

John Edward Singleton returned to his home town, Richmond, Virginia. Wearing his dress uniform with a chest full of ribbons , he now weighed 145 pounds and was ready for a new challenge. Probably one of the first things that he did was to become active in a local Baptist Church where he encountered the most beautiful and vivacious young girl that he had ever seen. When asking a friend who she was, the friend said, "Forget her, you don't stand a chance." A year later on April 9, 1947, John married Eileen. They have three children and six grandchildren and John adds, " all of whom are, of course, perfect."

John's medals and ribbons are: Philippine Liberation Ribbon w/2 Battle Stars; Pacific Theatre Ribbon w/6 Battle Stars; Good Conduct Ribbon, American Theater Ribbon, Victory Medal, Presidential Unit Citation (USS *Essex* crew), and the Philippine.

John followed the *Essex* for many years. After he left the ship, the *Essex* continued on to Tokyo Bay for the Japanese surrender. This was followed by Korea, VietNam, Grenada and the Far east. After the *Essex* was dismantled, she was replaced in 1991 by a new *Essex*. John attended the launching in Pascagoula, Mississippi He met Vice President and Mrs. Dick Chaney at the ceremonies.

To conclude this remarkable story, John remarked, *"I am grateful and conscious of God's presence in my life during those precarious times of the forties. I have been blessed far beyond my due for the 81 years that have been granted me and I am thankful for each of those years. But, particularly, for having been led to that small Baptist Church and the most beautiful and vivacious young girl I*

SINGLETON, JOHN, EILEEN

*have ever seen. During 59 years of marriage she has been my love,
my joy, my companion and my best friend."*
LUTHER S. REAMS   (B-17 Navigator)

*On Reams 16th mission, his B-17 bomber and its 11-man crew
were rocked by anti-aircraft fire. Reams fell to the floor, his right
leg half blown off, yet as the plane's navagator, he brought them
safely back to their base in Foggia, Italy.*

Reams reported for service on September 12, 1941 at Fort
Eustis, Virginia. Following basic training, he was assigned to the

coast artillery. Reams
had, at one point in his
life, become interested
in becoming a pilot.
When his son David
was a small boy, he
remembers his dad
telling him that his
reflexes were not good
enough to become a
pilot. Reams entered
Officer Candidate
School on April 20,
1942 at Camp Davis,
North Coralina, and was
commissioned as a 2nd
Lieutenant in July of that year. Since he didn't qualify to become
a pilot but had a desire to fly, Reams decided to train as an Army
Air Corps navigator, graduating on July 1, 1944 from the
Advanced Navigation School at Ellington Field, Texas. He
shipped out from Newport News, Virginia in October 1944 to
Foggia, Italy with his Bomber Group.

Luther Reams was born in Richmond, Virginia on March 20, 1918 to Richard and Virgie Reams. After his discharge in June 1946, he met Dollie Early who became his wife on June 19, 1948. Luther and Dollie had two sons. After various stops along the way and transport aboard the hospital ship, *Seminole*, he was admitted to McGuire Hospital in Richmond, Virginia on May 6, 1945. The following year Reams entered Virginia Polytechnic Institute under the G.I. Bill. He graduated in 1950 with a degree in electrical engineering. After graduating from Virginia Tech, he accepted a position with the Dupont Spruance Fibers Plant in Richmond. He retired from Dupont in 1985.

(Photo courtesy of Luther Reams)

Lt. Luther S. Reams, with his right leg half blown off by a direct flak hit, refused morphine so that he could direct his plane which had become lost from its formation, back to its base in Italy. This was his 16th combat mission. He recounts this event, "We were going down the bomb run when something hit me and knocked me across the plane. The bombardier, Sgt. Alvin T. Hoffman, Delmar, Delaware seeing what happened, rushed to my aid. He was wonderful. With one eye on me, he kept track of the lead plane so that he could drop his bombs at the right time. When the bombs dropped, Sgt. Hoffman gave his full attention to me. He applied a tourniquet to my leg, and bundled me up as warmly as possible. He then huddled over me to keep the wind that was rushing through the nose section from making me too uncomfortable. I called up the pilot to advise him of what had happened and told him to follow the other planes home. There were no other planes to follow. Because of the damage to our plane, we had been forced to leave the formation and were alone. The rest wasn't anything heroic, it was just a case of necessity.

My leg wasn't giving me any pain. I guess it was frozen. I refused morphine because my life depended on getting that plane back to its base. I asked the pilot what direction he had taken in coming off the target, and then gave him a heading toward home. Occasionally, I'd ask for landmarks. I was flat on my back and couldn't see out, when the pilot told me what he saw, I checked him on his headings. In that way we got back to the field with no further aid." Reams was a 1st Lieutenant with the 15th flying Fortess Squadron. He had been drafted into military service which he said came as a surprise. He said, "They called me, so I went. Whether or not I would have volunteered, I can't say." " In a way the service did me a favor. I was a pipe fitter before I was drafted. I probably would have stayed a pipe fitter."After his 16th mission, he had no doubt he would lose his leg. He said, "Doctors didn't even have to ask. They might have asked me in a conversational manner

REAMS, LUTHER S., DOLLIE

'we're going to have to amputate your leg,' and I may have said, 'OK. Let's get it done with it and move on.' He added, " I enjoyed every minute of the military except getting hit. I had a ball." Reams was promoted to captain when discharged.

Reams lived in Richmond with his wife Dollie where they were active in Bon Air Baptist Church. Luther fell in

January 2003 and sustained a serious head injury; had been a resident of the Nursing Home Unit at McGuire VA medical Center in Richmond. Author's note: (I received word from Luther's son, David, that his father passed away on Sunday, September 16, 2007 and was buried at Maury Cemetery in Richmond on Thursday, September 20th). Dollie passed away on November 13, 2006. Captain Reams received the *"Congressional Veteran Commendation."* The Commendation reads in part *"On behalf of a greatful nation and the citizens of the 7th District of Virginia, the Congressional Veteran Commendation is awarded to **Luther S. Reams** for honorable service performed while a member of the Armed Forces of the United States. For his gallant service to our county, Captain Reams received the Purple Heart and the Air Medal with one Oak Leaf Cluster and has been authorized to wear the European, African and Middle Eastern Theater of Operations Campaign ribbon with one Campaign star."* This honor concluded with these words, *" His actions are consistent with the finest traditions of military service and reflect great credit upon himself, the Commonwealth of Virginia, and the United states of America. Signed under my hand this eleventh day of November, 2002."* Eric Cantor, Member of Congress. The name, Luther S. Reams was added to the war heroes at the Virginia War Memorial, Richmond, Virginia. (Incidentally, in this Commendation, it was mentioned that Reams lost his left leg. His left leg is OK—he lost his right leg above the knee).

WARREN A. LEONARD
MARINE CORPS

The US Marine Corps has a history second to none when it comes to fighting as illustrated by the Sixth Marine Division. This is the only Marine Division that, as an entire unit, never spent as much as one day in the continental United States. It was composed of three infantry regiments on Guadalcanal in the Solomon Islands in September 1944.

One of those Marines was **WARREN LEONARD** who now lives in Midlothian, Virginia. Leonard completed his 12 weeks of boot camp at Paris Island, South Coralina and joined a fighting unit in the Pacific.

After the fighting on Guam, this unit moved to Guadalcanal where they were joined by the 1st Battalion of the 29th Marines who had fought on Saipan in The Marianas. After training on the Island of Guadalcanal, the division traveled 6,000 miles and landed on Okinawa on April 1, 1945; capturing the northern half of the island. In April the division moved south to join in the assault of a strong Japanese defense line across the southern part of Okinawa.

The Battle of Okinawa lasted 82 days. During this furious battle, the Sixth Marine Division had nearly 1,700 Marines and Navy Medical Corpsmen killed in action or died of wounds, plus over 7,400 wounded. The highest casualties were from the rifle companies. The Island was assaulted by 180,000 American troops. The Japanese death toll was nearly 93,000 troops and 94,000 civilians, many of whom committed suicide.

LEONARD, WARREN, THELMA

It was on May 14, 1945, during the Battle of *"Sugarloaf Hill"* on Okinawa, that Leonard was wounded. [Sugarloaf Hill changed hands 14 times in the hand-to-hand combat].

Leonard was born at Shores, Virginia on March 24, 1923. He was a corporal in the marines. He married Thelma on February 12, 1943.

Okinawa was the last battle of World War II. Allied vessels assembled totaled 1,457. One sourse lists the navy lost 400 ships, either sunk or damaged. The fierce fighting would be at places called Sugar Loaf, Strawberry Hill, Chocolate Drop and other hills that those who survived will always remember. More marines would be killed or missing than on Iwo Jima and Guadalcanal combined.

All marines believe that their unit is the best, and this is as it should be. But the Sixth Marine Division was at least the equal of any Marine division that fought in the Pacific. For their heroism on Okinawa, the division was decorated with the Presidental Unit Citation. Okinawa remains as important base in the event war was to break out in East Asia. The United States has some 19,000 Marines with 10,000 troops from other services stationed on this Pacific Ocean Island.

An article appeared in *Parade* on Sunday, March 11, 2001 entitled, "Should We Leave Okinawa?" The bottom line is, if the United States should pull out of this Pacific Island, the Chinese would want to extend their influence over Okinawa. Not a good idea.

LIFE ABOARD AIRCRAFT CARRIER-USS *WASP*
CLAUDE DEMONT GRINSLADE

"The memory of that day in 1942 when the Air-Craft Carrier USS Wasp became a flaming torch burns brightly still today in the hearts of the men who were there". **Claude Grinslade**

This is one survivor's, Claude Grinslade's, account of his narrow escape from six decks below. September 15, 1942, a day that will never be forgotten by Claude Grinslade and the other survivors of the USS *Wasp*. It was noontime on this fateful day when Grinslade was hurrying down six decks below to pull a four-hour watch in Central Station. On the way he passed Talmadge May, a good friend, and said, "See you later." Central station was one room in this compartment six decks below shared by Inter-Communication Room on one side and Plotting Room on the other. Grinslade's responsibility during his watch was to record the ship's position on the hour as the *Wasp* zig-zagged through the Coral Sea. Between times he recorded the ship's location, Grinslade would read and memorize scripture from the New Testament. Because of his relationship with God, he was able to remain calm, helping others while his ship was sinking.

Ships enroute to their destination would zig-zag to avoid an attack from enemy submarines. However, the *Wasp* on this day at 2:45 p.m., without warning (except from a lookout who called out, "Three torpedoes...three points forward of the starboard beam!)," took three Japanese torpedoes, that slammed into the starboard side just forward of the bridge and Central Station. Seven other men were in the compartment with Grinslade when they were hit. Four of these men immediately left to man their battle stations, leaving Grinslade and three others.

The torpedoes stopped the *Wasp* dead in the water. Grinslade's battle station was on the third deck, where he proceeded to go. He needed to keep the electrical power supply to the bomb elevator in working order. Just as he reached the top of the ladder of the fifth deck, there was another explosion, which threw him back to the deck below. Sea water flooded this area and chased him back inside Central. Acting on instinct, Grinslade closed the water-tight door which kept them safe from the rush of the water.

(USS Wasp-Photo courtesy of Claude Grinslade)

For the moment, the men located in the Central Station were safe. The question was, "How do they get out of there?" The entire compartment was filled with smoke and the electric power and lights were out and the main telephone system had quit working. These trapped men had received permission to secure that area and leave, but how? One of the men, Wolfford, had knowledge of an overhead hatch that the other three men were not aware of. This was a possible escape route through the Fire Control Tube. This was a heavy-armored, 36"-diameter tube that protected electrical cables and a ladder reaching all the way up 120 feet to the bridge.

After considering their options, the men concluded that this was the only way out even though some decks were raging with fire and others with exploding ammunition. Wolfford led the way in complete darkness. Grinslade said, "I could not see the man ahead of me, nor even my own hands in front of my face as I continued climbing." Suddenly, through the blackness, came a flash of brightness which pierced his eyes. The light came through the hatch in the bridge. Grinslade continued, "Wolfford was not in sight, in fact no one remained in the fire-gutted bridge. I didn't see the other two men. I found myself all alone. Yet, I felt not alone, as the peace of God's presence and love covered me like the beautiful blue canopy of that South Pacific sky." Fires had broken out simultaneously in the hanger and below decks. The water mains in the forward part of the ship proved useless."

Down on the hanger deck, littered with broken and burning aircraft, men were preparing to abandon ship after all effort ,to save her had failed. Billowing smoke from raging fires towered into the sky and signaled her doom. Without adequate water pressure, fire hoses had failed to control the destructive inferno. Reluctantly, Captain Sherman, after consulting with rear Admiral Noyes, gave the order came to "Abandon Ship" at 3:20 p.m.

The men operated in a remarkablly orderly manner. The only delays were caused by the men who did not want to leave the ship before all the wounded had been taken off. The badly wounded were lowered into rafts or rubber boats. Almost 40-minutes later at 4:00 p.m., Captain Sherman himself left the ship.

Grinslade said less than one hour after the first torpedo hit, which interruped his daily devotional reading, he was climbing down the cargo net to get into the water and away from the ship. After swimming from the ship and through oil on the water, he inflated his life belt which allowed him a period of rest.

Looking around, he could see his ship, his home, sinking in the Coral Sea. He said, "That was the moment when my emotions overwhelmed my being and sealed forever the scene before me, never to be forgoten." The "Lansdowne (DD-486) was ordered to fire five torpedoes into the dying ship. The USS Wasp finally sunk at 9:00 p.m. Grinslade continued, " I was grateful to be alive but I was grieved to realize that many other shipmates were still trapped and dying aboard ship, or even being attacked by sharks. Then my thoughts turned to their loved ones back home expecting to hear from them, or perhaps, even now, reading that letter joyfully, not knowing the hand that wrote it is closed in death."

Grinslade said that he "wept." Then he cried out one question to God, Why? "Why am I spared? What purpose do you have in me for the rest of my life? If it is to serve you and my fellow man, I do here in the presence of this burning altar dedicate all to You!" The splashing waves of the Coral Sea was a reminder that he wasn't home yet. Suddenly a sister ship, the USS *Duncan* came on the scene, throwing a lifeline to pull the men who survived safely aboard. When Grinslade got aboard the *Duncan*, he saw a good friend, Roy Reedy, who had led the Bible study aboard the *Wasp*.

Grinslade gave this account of what happened after they abandon ship. "After clearing the ship, I tried to gather as many swimmers as possible into a close group. We all managed to swim to the *Duncan* slowly. I saw one shark eight-feet long, but apparently he bothered no one. (This is corroborated by Stone, near whom the shark passed.) Stone and I said nothing of this until aboard Duncan, fearing panic if its presence was known." "I cautioned the Captain of gasoline on the water, and informed him of what I knew to be happening on *Wasp*."

The USS *Wasp* (CV-7), was launched on April 4, 1939, and commissioned on April 25, 1940. Its overall length was 688 feet; speed at 29.5 knots, with a range of 12,000 nautical miles. During peacetime 1,800 officers and men served on the *Wasp*. The *Wasp* had an almost complete lack of protection from torpedoes due to major inherent design flaws. These flaws proved to be fatal.

The *Wasp* departed on April 14, 1942 to take 47 Supermarine Spitfire Mk.V fighter planes for the British who were faced with the possibility of losing their superiority in the air over the island. Her mission was an important one—one upon which the fate of the island bastion of Malta hung. The ships tried to pass through the Straits of Gibraltar to avoid being discovered by Spanish or Axis agents. The *Wasp* then retired toward England. The Spitfires were followed by the Axis intelligence and many were destroyed while on the ground by German air raids.

More planes were needed to provide support for Malta. A direct request from Prime Mnister Winston Churchill to President Roosevelt was to allow the *Wasp* to ferry more Spitfires. Permission was granted by the President, so the *Wasp* loaded up again and sailed for the Mediterranean on May 3.

Following the battles of *"The Coral Sea,"* and the *"Battle of Midway,"* the United States only had two carriers left in the Pacific. The *Wasp* was to be transferred but first needed repairs, which required them to return to the Norfolk Navy Yard in Virginia. On July 1, the *Wasp* sailed for the Tonga Islands. She was en route to the South Pacific when the Japanese landed on Guadalcanal. The *Wasp, Saratoga* (CV-3) and *Enterprise* (CV-6) were ordered to be in support for the Marines from the Second Regiment who landed on Guadalcanal. At 5:30 a.m. on August 7, 1942, the first planes took off from the *Wasp's* deck.

The *"Guadalcanal"* battle was fought between August 7, 1942 and February 7, 1943. The Allied forces who were involved in this campaign were the United States, Australia, New Zealand, and the British Solomon Islands. The Allied casualties were 1,768 dead (ground), 4,911 dead (naval), and 420 dead (aircrew). The Japanese reported 24,600-25,600 dead (ground), and 3,543 dead (naval). This battle was fought by ground troops, the navy and the air force against the Empire of Japan.

Later Grinslade was transferred to the heavy cruiser, USS *Helena* for a few days before returning to San Diego on a troop ship. SAN DIEGO, HERE WE COME! However, there were 193 names which were posted on the bulletin boards. A sad day. The names of their friends listed brought more pain. Finally the name of Talmage G. May, Grinslade's "spiritual brother" was found listed on the bulletin board. Earlier in the day, Grinslade had passed May and said, "See you later." More tears, more pain. May could be heard while preforming his duties singing his favorite hymn, "If I Could Only Hear My Mother Pray Again."

Claude S. Grinslade was born on November 16, 1922 at Wewahitchka, Florida to Herman and Lillie Grinslade. He joined the US Navy on January 31, 1941 after his 18th birthday, and was discharged on January 24, 1947. After reaching San Diego, he was stationed at Bainbridge, Maryland. He married Wilda York of Medway, Maine on November 10, 1942. After a child, the first of eight, was born in 1944, he returned to duty in the Pacific to complete his six year hitch. In November 2007, Claude and Wilda celebrated their 65th year together. Grinslade quoted Proverbs 17:6a "Children's children are the crown of old men." He and Wilda have two sons, eight daughters, 24 grandchildren, 32 great grand children and one great-great grandchild.

Grinslade talks of two contrasting scenes from the decks of the aircraft carrier, the USS *Wasp*, that changed his life forever. First, when anchored in Casco Bay, Portland, Maine, the first scene was "white mounds of snow covering her flight and upper decks." The second, "flames and smoke billowing from her flight and lower decks while sinking in the Coral Sea. Both were far away from the small country town of Wewahithcka, Florida, his birthplace.

After completing boot camp at Norfolk, Virginia, in March 1941, he was assigned to the *Wasp* on April 25th. [April 25th just happened to be the first anniversary after the *Wasp* had been commissioned]. As many young men from small towns, Grinslade was in awe while traveling the romantic Caribbean Sea, Iceland, and Newfoundland. But as is true for more than 16,000,000 men and women who served in the armed forces of the United States during World War II, his life would change forever on December 7, 1941. He was on the boxing team who fought in "smokers" for entertainment. He fought lightweight class and had several victories under his belt. He felt like a champion, enjoying pats on the back from his friends, until he met an "old" army sergeant. After several rounds, his lieutenant, threw in the towel. His left eye had been cut and would not stop bleeding. Claude said, " The army guys were cheering for me, because they didn't like the sergeant." Now for the real enemies, the Germans and Japanese.

The *Wasp* sailed north to waters off New England. There, during January-March, the *Wasp* conducted flight training. Grinslade said, "Yes, this Florida boy wanted to serve his country and God, but sin had robbed his peace from pleasing the Lord. He knew God was displeased with my taking His name in vain. Making excuses didn't help. Making resolutions didn't work. Finally, in desperation this contrite lost sailor and 'ex-boxer' threw in the towel. The game was over! Guilt and despair had driven me to my knees in repentance. Immediately mercy, peace and forgiveness came by Grace, through faith in Jesus Christ our Lord." Discovering other shipmates who were concerned about their relationship with God, they started a Bible study group aboard ship. These men became like family over the three months while docked in Maine.

On March 26, the *Wasp* pulled up anchor and along with Task Force 39 departed Casco bay for Scapa Flow in the Orkney Islands. The next day Admiral Wilcox was swept overboard and lost at sea. On April 10, 1942, *Wasp* entered the Clyde River on its way to King George Dock, Glasgow, Scotland. There it loaded 47 supermarine Spitfires for the island of Malta on April 20. The Germans issued a false report that the "American air-craft carrier, USS *Wasp* was on fire in the Mediterranean Sea." It is interesting that Claude Grinslade and two friends had escaped the grip of Maine's cold winter but not the winsome ways of her women. They became engaged to three lonely young ladies left behind at the church.

The *Wasp* passed through the Panama Canal on June 10, to join the USS *Saratoga* and USS *Enterprise* in the Pacific to cover the landing of Marines on Guadalcanal, August 7, 1942. This was the first offensive by the Armed forces in the Pacific after Pearl Harbor. When the marines landed on Guadalcanal, they caught the Japanese by surprise. There was little resistance as the marines secured the airstrip. However, the six-weeks' planned objective turned into a six months' bloody ordeal for the courageous and victorious marines. After the USS *Saratoga* had been damaged by a Japanese torpedo, the USS *Hornet* joined the *Wasp* and Task Force 18 in lauching planes late on September 14 in search of Japanese forces.

Claude D. Grinslade served on the *Wasp* for one and one half years; two years in Guam. He wears the European-African (Defense of Malta Medal), Guadalcanal (Invasion Air cover Medal); American Defense w/Bronze "A", American Area, Asiatic Pacific w/2 stars, Good Conduct Medal, Victory Medal World War II. His rank: Electrician's Mate First Class.

This then, was a story about a man, his ship, his friends, and his relationship with God. His memories are sad when he thinks of his buddies who were lost as the USS *Wasp* sank, a picture that will never be erased from his mind. However, he has truly been blessed with his wonderful wife and family. Our nation is indebted to men like Grinslade who served their country when there were needed to preserve freedom for future generations.

"The Casco Crew" (LtoR: Roman O'Mary, Russell Obenchain, Roy Reedy and Claude Grinslade-photo courtesy of Grinslade)

CHAPTER ELEVEN

SOLDIERS OF THE LAW

JUDGE ADVOCATES IN WORLD WAR II

The material for this chapter was taken from writings by a former JAG officer, Colonel Robert F. Gonzales. Colonel Gonzales graduated from Texas A& M University with a Bachelor of Arts degree in government and received a ROTC commission in May 1968. He completed his law studies at the University of Texas School Of Law with a Juris Doctor degree in May 1971; he became a member of the Texas Bar in September 1971.

Colonel Gonzales immediately entered the United States Army as a first lieutenant in the Adjutant General's Corps and attended the AGC Officer Basic Course at Fort Benjamin Harrison, Indiana. His first assignment was in Tam Ky, South Vietnam. After completing his Vietnam tour, he was reassigned as the legal officer of Headquarters Command, Fort Carson, Colorado. After completing JAGC Officer Basic course in Charlottesville, Virginia, he served as a defense counsel and then as a trial counsel in the 2nd Infantry Division, Camp Casey, Korea. In May 1975, he attended airborne school at Fort Benning, Georgia, and reported to the 82nd Airborne Division, Fort Bragg, North Carolina.

After serving his country for 36 years as a JAG officer in different assignments and in many parts of the world, Colonel Gonzales retired on October 1, 2001. We are grateful for his service and for his compilation of all the information in this chapter to share information about this important branch of our military. What follows are verbatim excerpts of Colonel Gonzales' story as he wrote it.

"Between 1939 and 1945, the world was engulfed by six years of violence that we call World War II. In terms of geography, level of destruction, and human suffering, the Second World War dwarfs all other aggression in history. Although described as a global conflict, it was primarily fought on fields and towns of Europe, in the jungles of Asia, and in the deserts of North Africa. When it was over, hundreds of cities lay in ruins, and millions of people were dead, injured, displaced or impoverished.

"As in my life, I have lived in the shadow of World War II. I never expected to write about it. Beginning with the desperate British evacuation of Dunkirk in early June 1940, and France's shocking surrender to Germany later that same month, the American political and military landscape was shocked into the sobering realization that the time had come for the United States to prepare earnestly for war. Not only were there concerns about Germany's expansion across the European Continent, there also were troubling signs of further Japanese incursions into China, Indochina, and the East Indies. With the British, French, and Dutch preoccupied at home against Germany, a European power vacuum in Southeast Asia and the Southwest Pacific presented Japan with a golden opportunity to spread its empire.

"Arguably, only the United States stood in the way of Germany's and Japan's drives for global territorial dominance. If Western democracies were to survive World War II and, perhaps, even prevail, the United States was going to have to assemble an Army that could challenge Germany's and Japan's ground forces in open combat.

"Unlike today, the Judge Advocate General's Department's (JAGD) perspective was quite different during the days leading to World War II 60 years ago; the JAGD did not view the integration of the judge advocates into a unit's plans and operations as part of its mission. In the months preceding Pearl Harbor and even after the Japanese attack on US forces in the Pacific, the JAGD viewed its mission as providing the best possible lawyers to handle purely legal issues that commanders and their staffs faced at division level and higher headquarters. A judge advocate had to be a mature person, at least twenty-eight years of age with at least four years of demonstrated excellence in the practice of law.

"The Army needed every judge advocate, not just a few, to be prepared to follow the examples of Maj. Gen. Blanton Winship and Maj. Patrick J. Hurley. General Winship distinguished himself during World War I by commanding the 110th and 118th Infantry Regiments in the 28th Infantry Division as a judge advocate colonel. He was awarded the Distinguished Service Cross. Major Hurley was the judge advocate of the Army artillery, First Army, and was awarded the Silver Star for gallantry." **Major General Myron C. Cramer (above),** served as The Judge Advocate General of the Army, December 1, 1941 to November 30, 1945.

Colonel Gonzales has written about oral histories and personal experiences of twenty judge advocates covering a period of nearly ten years. Books have been written, movies have been made, television shows have portrayed the many battles, on land, sea, and air that occurred during World War II, such as Pearl Harbor, Corregidor, the Battle of Midway, Guadalcanal, D-Day, the Battle of the Bulge, and Iwo Jima. These are familiar stories, but they are not the whole story.

"In this war, characterized by the largest Army in US history, operating in all parts of the world, the administration of military justice under the Articles of War of 1920 was .... difficult and time consuming. This required the services of more dedicated judge advocates than ever before. Personal property would be lost and damaged, and innocent victims would suffer injuries or even death, giving rise to claims against the United States government. In this war, violations of the accepted rules of warfare and the provisions of the Geneva Conventions were committed by the enemy with unprecedented recklessness and brutality. The evidence had to be evaluated, indictments had to be prepared, and the offenders in trials in Germany, Japan, China, and the Philippine Islands had to be prosecuted. Most of the World War II judge advocates entered the Army directly from the civilian practice of law.

"There were 103 Judge Advocates on active duty on July 1, 1940. During this week, President Franklin D. Roosevelt nominated Henry L. Stimson as Secretary of War with the Army's maximum strength of 16,719 commissioned officers and 280,000 enlisted men. By June 30, 1945, the Army of the United States would reach 8,112,657 commissioned officers and enlisted soldiers. The President of the United States, by law and regulation, selected one senior officer of the JAGD to lead this department with the title of The Judge Advocate General of the Army and the rank of major general.

"By March 31, 1945, there were 2,296 judge advocates on duty, the vast majority of who were graduates of the JAG school. Regardless of the source of commission, these men came from the benches and bars of every State, from law offices and courtrooms, from law school staff and faculties, from the corporate and financial world, from state and federal public agencies, and from local, state, and national elected bodies. At all times, however, they were expected to be an officer."

The assignments of the new Judge Advocates began on March 21, 1942. Some newspaper headlines on that date were:

MOSCOW, Saturday, 21 March 1942—*The Russians put more pressure on the German Sixteenth army trapped at Staraya, Russia today.*

MELBOURNE, AUSTRALIA- *General Douglas MacArthur arrived here early today and was enthusiastically greeted by a large crowd.*

WASHINGTON, DC- *Of 15 million workers to be employed in American war industries by next January, about one-third will be women.*

WASHINGTON, DC—*The Military Personnel and Training Division in the Office of The Judge Advocate General (OTJAG) will handle the assignment of all officers in the JAGD department.*

"As a result of the global nature of the war and the widespread distribution of American forces, judge advocates were needed in all parts of the world. By direction of the President under the authority of Article of War 50 ½, staffing each BOTJAG overseas was established. The first BOTJAG was established on March 11, 1942, in the Far East on Corregidor, Philippine Islands, and four judge advocates were assigned to it. This office ceased to exist on May 6, 1942 when Lt. Gen. Jonathan M. Wainwright surrendered all US forces in the Philippines to the Japanese.

"Seven Judge Advocates were captured at Corregidor on May 6, 1942 and they would spend the next 42 months in Japanese Prison camp. One source stated the following:

CORREGIDOR, *Philippine Islands, Wednesday, 6 May 1942— Major Samuel L. Heisinger and Lt. Col. Albert Svihra, both judge advocates became prisoners of war (POW) today when the US Army Forces in the Philippines on this island surrendered to the*

Japanese Imperial Army. LTC Svihra wa0s a 1922 graduate of the United States Military Academy at West Point, New York.

"A little over three months after the Allies surrendered at Corregidor, Lieutenant Colonel Svihra began recording his recollection of that event in his personal diary to his wife. On August 21, 1942, he wrote: *"How shall I describe the days immediately preceding the surrender, and the surrender itself? It is like a nightmare to me now, and I can't believe it happened at all. It would have been impossible to write about it at the time. I recall now that I wrote you last about the 28th or 29th of April and gave the letter to "E" who was about to depart by plane for Mindinao, from whence the plane was to proceed to Australia. I little suspected then that Corregidor would fall so soon afterwards, although I should have known better. Even then artillery fire and air bombing were increasing in intensity. Our outdoor toilets and shower batch, about 100 feet to the south of the east entrance [of Malinta Tunnel], had been demolished. The shells and bombs shook the very tunnel itself, often landing just over or near the entrance, filling the tunnel with smoke, dust and the acrid fumes of puric acid, and making it so dark inside that, despite lights, one could scarcely see 10 feet and causing apprehension that the entrance had been blocked. The power plant was off for days, and the tunnel lighted by means of an auxiliary diesel engine, which on occasions went out of commission, throwing everything into total darkness. Meals were often delayed and sleep often became impossible. Those were unbearable days."* [Colonel Svihra buried his diary at the prisoner of war camp before the Japanese placed him aboard the *Arisan Maru* for evacuation from the Philippines. Surviving prisoners later retrieved it and gave it to the Svihra family.]

At about 11:00 p.m. on May 5 1942, Colonel Svihra and the entire staff were told to report immediately under arms to the headquarters located in lateral #3 of the tunnel. At 11:00 a.m., May 6, 1942, General Wainwright entered the headquarters lateral and read a radio message from President Roosevelt. The substance was that the entire nation appreciated the heroic defense that had been made in the Philippines, under trying conditions and on reduced rations.

"After the surrender, the Japanese officer, followed by armed soldiers, conducted his inspection and took watches, rings, and fountain pens as suited his fancy. Svihra had placed his watch, rings and pen in his musette bag. The Japanese took all the food, leaving the Americans to find food on their own. Fortunately, someone discovered a cache of canned and boxed food. That night, Colonel Svihra had crackers and sardine sandwiches and some canned fruit for dinner. In the prison camp, their meals consisted of rice and onion soup.

"Colonel Svihra died October 24, 1944, when the POW ship he was on, the *Arisan Maru*, was torpedoed by an American submarine and sunk in the Bashi Straits off the coast of China. Of the 1,778 POWs on board, fewer than a dozen survived. Most of the POW's managed to get into the water, but no attempt was made by the Japanese to take them aboard nearby ships. Most perished from exposure in their weaken condition. Colonel Svihra was survived by his wife, Ila, and their three daughters, Anne, Elizabeth, and Betsy.

An entry in Col. Svihra's dairy, August 31, 1943 read: *"Our anniversary dear. Do you recall 15 years ago---little did we think about war in those days! And even if we did have some pretty good "spats" together—they were mostly, if not always, my fault,--they were followed by worse misery for me. When I think of the food that I've had to get along on these past two years, it makes me ill to remember how fussy I was about food at home. Well, I don't believe you will have much trouble with me on that score again. If I just get enough to keep the body fit to carry on my duties, I'll be happy....Well, I only hope I can be given the chance and can be spared to show you what I'm really like, and how different I can be—the kindness, the appreciation, the devotion of which you are deserving. I took no vows when we were married that can't be fulfilled the rest of my days and my vow on this anniversary is simply this, that henceforth, God willing, I'll be what a husband and father should be."*

OMAHA BEACH, *Wednesday, 6 Sep 1944. After a short stay in Birmingham, England, Captain Calvin L. Rampton crossed the English Channel and landed here today.*

"Rampton was working in the Utah State Attorney General's Office when Pearl Harbor was bombed. He was a second lieutenant in the Field Artillery reserve. A week later he reported for active duty. During his medical exam, the electrocardiogram test indicated that he had a heart problem and was released from duty. Later, after a civilian doctor indicated that his heart was in excellent condition, Rampton received orders to report to Camp Roberts, California in January 1943. Since he was a lawyer, he was assigned temporarily to the camp's judge advocate's office."

Later by recommendation from the Camp Officer, Rampton was transferred to JAG. He reported for school at Ann Arbor, Michigan on May 1, 1943. Two days after his class started, Lieutenant Rampton wrote in his diary: *"I'm in doubt whether this is an Infantry school or a JAG school. We must march in formation to all classes and have an hour and a half of close order drill and exercises in the afternoon. The discipline is very strict, the point being to make officers out of civilians in the shortest time possible. We arise at 6:30, breakfast at 7:15 and then attend class from 8:00 until 12:00. After lunch, we again have class from 1:00 to 3:00 and then drill and exercises until 4:30. Between 4:30 and 6:00 we have a retreat parade. After dinner, we are free until 7:30. From 7:30 to 11:00 we are restricted to our rooms for the purpose of studying."*

"Rampton graduated as the top officer in his class and was promoted to first lieutenant. Six months later he was promoted to captain. One week into his rigorous claims course, Captain Rampton wrote in his diary, May 20, 1944: *"We finished the first week of the school today. This afternoon we went to Camp Forrest where we all went through the infiltration course. This is an area of rough land about 70 yards long, which is covered with barbed wire and other obstacles. All the men must crawl across this area on their stomachs in a given time while machine guns fire live ammunition over their heads at a height of 30 inches."*

"After reporting to Camp Reynolds, Pennsylvania in August 1944, Captain Rampton drew his equipment, participated in daily gas chamber drills, and qualified with both carbine, caliber .30 MI and the Colt 45. He boarded the *Ile de France* luxury liner transport ship. His team landed on Omaha Beach on 6 September 1944, they drove inland spending their first night near Bayeux, France. He set up a claims office in Le Havre. Claims were considered under the general rule that no payment could be made for combat damage that US forces caused, but if the damage occurred for reasons other than combat, then compensation was approved.

"The claims commissioner had jurisdiction to settle and pay claims up to $500.00. Claims in excess of $500.00 were forwarded to a three-member regional claims commission that had payment authority up to $2,500.00 or to a three-member senior claims commission in Versailles, France, that had payment authority up to $5,000.00. Any claim in excess of $5,000.00 was forwarded to Congress through OTJAG with a recommendation as to its disposition.

"In early December 1944, Captain Rampton moved his claims detachment to Beauvais, France. This office was closed at the end of January 1945 and moved to Eindhoven, Holland, about thirty-five miles from the Rhine River where the principal fighting was going on. They were nearly hit by a German V-1 missile bomb. Captain Rampton next moved to Veghel which was located about halfway between Eindhoven and Nijmegen, Holland.

"Airborne soldiers from the 101st Airborne Division had landed south of Veghel five months before during *Operation Market Garden* and requisitioned what they needed from the land and local residents. Consequently, the claims in Veghel fell into the same pattern and were settled very quickly. Veghel continued to be bombarded by planes or shelled by artillery. The Germans were only fifteen miles away.

"Colonel Gonzales' note: There are many memorable experiences that the JAG claim officers had. Here, I want to share some of them.

The residents of Maarstricht had very little meat during the German occupation. The 29th Attack Aviation Group had strength of about 1,000. They moved out but the quartermaster continued sending a full supply of rations. Major Tompkins and Captain Rampton asked what to do with the extra rations. They were told to ship back the staples and keep the perishables. They interpreted the frozen sides of beef as perishables and took them to a cold food locker in a local hotel. They contacted the mayor, had the town to bake bread and served 10,000 barbecue sandwiches.

[On April 12, 1945, President Roosevelt died. The Dutch people were more saddened by this tragedy than the soldiers. The Dutch people brought bouquets of flowers to the claims office. They thought the President's death would change the course of the war.]

"During the ten months he was with Claims Team #14, and although the team moved a number of times, its officers were always in demand to participate in courts-martial. Captain Rampton personally served in about twenty trials. Rampton was promoted to major with additional responsibilities.

"His new office was in a chateau located in Rheims, France. The chateau had been the property of Baron Mumms, the producer of Mumms champagne. Mumms was arrested as a German collaborator. While there, Major Rampton learned about the dropping of the atomic bomb on Hiroshima, Japan on August 6, 1945. Then the second bomb dropped on Nagasaki, Japan on August 9, 1945, forced Japan to surrender five days later.

"In September 1945, Rampton was reassigned as a one-man commissioner in Nancy, France, and then to the senior claims commission in Versailles, France. The claims office was just outside the front gate of King Louis XIV's Palace of Versailles.

"Another interesting claims story about Major Rampton occurred when he investigated a claim for $2.5 million damages to a crystal factory in Baccarat. In January 1945, American soldiers passed through the town, deliberately pushing priceless pieces of crystal onto the floor with their bayonets. Major Rampton was convinced that the incident occurred. The claim was approved by Congress and paid.

"*Lt Lawrence W. Lougee was serving with Major Rampton during the summer of 1944. One day there was a knock on his door. A stylishly dressed French woman entered. She explained that she was Madam Tholet and that she operated a bordello in St. Brieux called Maison de Joie (House of Joy). During the German occupation, it was frequented often by German officers who told her it was the best little establishment in France. The Americans filled her place the first night. An infantry captain told her, "Madam Cherie, you have a wonderful place here. But what you really should do is build an addition and get more patrons. Expand your business and all the Americans will come." She added eight rooms. A jeep came by with MP's and put a "off limits" sign on her place. She came with a fist full of bills from the carpenter, the plumber, the mason, and others. She wanted reimbursed 124,000 francs ($2,400) to cover the cost of the addition. Lieutenant Lougee went to her establishment as any good claims officer would do, to inspect the premises. He denied her claim. About a month later she was convicted by a Free French Court for collaborating with the Germans. She was paraded through the streets in a farm wagon as the citizens jeered and booed. Her head had been shaved.*

"Major Rampton received orders on January 20, 1946 to return to the United States. He had been overseas for fifteen months but had not accumulated enough points to rotate. Eighteen years later in the fall of 1964, Calvin L. Rampton was elected Governor of Utah and served twelve years as the chief executive of his State.

"One of the most celebrated general courts-martial during World War II was the desertion case of the *United States* v. *Private*

Eddie D. Slovik, Company G, 109th Infantry regiment, 28th Infantry Division. He was convicted of "two specifications of desertion with the intent to avoid hazardous duty and to shirk important service, for a total of forty-three days, in violation of the 58th article of War" and sentenced to be executed by musketry. A review was ordered and the theater judge advocate presented it personally to General Eisenhower. The sentence was upheld and Private Slovik was executed at 86 Rue du General Bourgeois, Ste. Marie-Aux-Mines, France on January 31, 1945.

"In April 1945, The Judge Advocate General assumed the responsibility for sending 60 legal officers to Germany to assist in investigating and prosecuting war criminals. The 60 officers were sent in groups of twenty after they received three days of training in OTJAG.

"In the Moscow Declaration of November 1, 1943, the foreign ministers of the governments of the United States, Great Britain, and the Soviet Union, took note of the atrocities perpetrated by the Germans and laid down the following policy:

"That at the time of the granting of any armistice to any government which may be set up in Germany, those German officers and members of the National Socialist German workers' (Nazi) Party who have been responsible for, or have taken a consenting part in, those atrocious acts will be charged, tried, and punished.

"That lists will be complied in all possible detail from the countries in which the atrocious acts were committed; and that the collection of such lists, the recording of the available supporting evidence, and the making of recommendations as to the tribunals to try and the procedure for trying war criminals, will be a function of the United Nations Commission for the Investigation of War Crimes."

"President Franklin D. Roosevelt appointed The Honorable Herbert Claiborne Pell as the United States Commissioner on the

UNCIWC. Three judge advocates were assigned to assist Mr. Pell, the most junior being Lieutenant Wolff. With his active and skillful participation on the commission, one of Adolph Hitler's worst possible nightmares had come true. Lieutenant Wolff was a displaced German Jew. Wolff was born in Montreal, Canada. Both of his Jewish parents were German citizens.

"Wolff's family had moved back to Germany when he was three-years old. He was happy living in Germany. He had just completed his doctor of laws (LLD) degree, with a dissertation on comparing the German and American laws on the warranty of title in the law of sales, from the University of Heidelberg. He first went to the United States in 1929 to visit his younger brother, Frank.

"While in New York, Wolff attended Columbia Law School and earned a general master of laws degree in 1931. He served on the faculty at Columbia for one year. He returned to Germany in 1931, passing the national bar exam in 1932.

"Adolph Hitler and the Nazis came to power on January 30, 1933. Wolff received an official government letter dismissing him from the state-sponsored apprenticeship program on the grounds that he was *"non-Aryan."* He sensed Hitler would turn on the Jews, take away their citizenship, and pass laws taking away their property. He decided he had no choice but to leave his home and family in Germany. He boarded a train in Berlin for Rotterdam, Holland. The train stopped at the border and was boarded by members of the Gestapo. His passport indicated that his religion was Jewish. They removed him from the train for additional scrutiny and interrogation. He was later released.

"Wolff remained in Holland for six months before he received permission to immigrate to the United States in September 1933. He returned to Columbia University and continued his research and writing in comparative law. Wolff became a United States citizen on June 12, 1939. This qualified him to take the New York

RESPECT

bar exam, which he passed. On December 11, 1942, at the age of thirty-six, he was drafted into the United States Army. He took his basic training at Camp Croft, South Carolina. "Wolff decided to apply for a transfer to the JAGD. Colonel Archibald King assisted Private Wolff with his application for the Officer Candidate School (OCS) at the JAG School. He was approved to attend the 4th JAGD OCS class at Ann Arbor, Michigan in December 1943, graduated and was commissioned as a second lieutenant on March 14, 1944. His first assignment was to work for Colonel King, two months before D-Day at Normandy, France. First Lieutenant Wolff was sent to London to serve on the UNCIWC staff on August 18, 1944, where he remained for two years. The commission name was changed to UNWCC or the United Nations War Crimes Commission which Wolff was elected the presiding officer.

(Photo courtesy of Col. Robert Gonzales)

(Wolff is 5th person from the left with members of the 4th OCS at Judge Advocate School-University Michigan)

"In August 1944, Supreme Headquarters, Allied Expeditionary Force (SHAFE) directed all army group commanders to report all incidents involving war crimes irrespective of the status or nationality of the victim. Some members of Committee One advocated placing on the list the names of all individuals who were known to be members of the Schutzstaffel (SS) or the Gestapo. The US policy was that membership alone in the SS or Gestapo was not sufficient of a basis to be branded a suspected war criminal. A substantial controversy occurred whether UNWCC should recommend the use of the so-called "conspiracy theory" for prosecution of the top Nazi arch-criminals.

"This involved an effort to create *ex post facto* law by charging the launching of aggression as a war crime. Aggressive war was declared an international crime and, in this trial, it was based on the idea that Nazism was a twenty-six-year long criminal conspiracy. Its aim was to build a war machine, satisfy Hitler's psychopathic hatred of the Jews, and turn Europe into a German empire known as the Third Reich.

"Although his efforts supported them, Lieutenant Wolff did not personally participate in the war crimes trial for twenty-four high ranking Nazis before the international tribunal at Nuremberg held between November 20, 1945 and October 1, 1946. Nor did he take part in the nearly 500 exclusive American military tribunal trials that tried 1,672 war crimes defendants between July 1945 and July 1948. Now a major, Wolff returned to the United States in June 1946 and was discharged at Fort Myer, Virginia. Wolff said *'As a 1933 refugee from Germany, to serve in the Judge Advocate General's Department and to represent the United States on the United Nations War Commission was the highlight of my legal career. I remain in active reserves out of a deep sense of gratitude for the incredible experiences the Army had given me.'*

"Upon his discharge in 1946, Wolff returned to the Department of Justice where he worked for fourteen years where he worked in the Alien Property Office of the Civil Division. After the war, Congress enacted legislation that allowed for the return of the property in the United States owned by German and Japanese persons who were living in Germany and Japan, was seized by the United States. He remained in the Criminal Division until he retired in 1971 after thirty years of federal service.

Judge Advocates in the 11th Airborne Division

"ANN ARBOR, MI, Monday, 9 Sep 1944—First Lieutenant Richard R. Hunter from Waukesha, Wisconsin, graduated today from the 7th Judge Advocate General's Department (JAGD) Officer Candidate School (OCS) Class. He eventually will be assigned to the 11th Airborne Division in the Philippines. Lieutenant Hunter began his military service as a private. Private Hunter was sent to armor basic training at Fort Knox, Kentucky. There, he qualified as a driver in the Sherman M4 tank.

"Private Hunter graduated from Northwestern Law School in 1933. He was working in the law firm of Lockney and Lowry in Waukesha, Wisconsin, when he heard the distressing news over the radio that the Japanese had bombed Pearl Harbor. He decided to join the FBI in February 1942, rather than a branch of the armed forces, because he was married with one daughter. He spent nineteen months with the Federal Bureau of Investigation.

"Lt. Col. John E. Blackstone, who was an officer in JAGD working in OTJAG wanted to know if Private Hunter was interested in becoming a commissioned officer in the JAGD. Private Hunter indicated that he was very interested. He graduated on September 9, 1944, was commissioned as a first lieutenant. Although he requested an overseas assignment with combat troops, Lieutenant Hunter's first assignment was to the 5th Service command in Chicago, Illinois, for six months of applicatory training.

"In 1945, he received reassignment orders to Eighth Army in the Philippine Islands. He arrived in Manila April 24, 1945; almost two months after that city had been liberated from the Japanese. Shortly after his arrival, an opening in the 11th Airborne Division occurred and Lieutenant Hunter volunteered to fill this vacancy. Maj. Gen. Joseph M. Swing, the division commander, complained, "I don't want a lieutenant for my JA." General Swing quickly resolved the rank problem by promoting Lieutenant Hunter to captain.

"Captain Hunter could not remain in the Division as a non-airborne "dirty leg" soldier. He had to make a choice between attending jump school or glider school. He chose glider school.

"The 11th Airborne Division, nicknamed *The Angels,* had been activated at Camp Mackall, North Carolina, on February 25, 1943, under the command of General Swing. After 14 months of training in ground and airborne tactics at Camp Mackall and at Camp Polk, Louisiana, the 11th was sent to New Guinea in May 1944 for five additional months of jungle training. On November 8, 1944, the 11th landed at Bito Beach, Leyte, and was engaged in three months of bitter fighting, clearing the treacherous mountain passes from Burauen to Ormoc.

"Once it reached the southern outskirts of Manila, the 11th broke off from the main assault of the city for a land, sea, and airborne raid on Los Banos Internment Camp located fifty miles behind the Japanese lines. It successfully rescued over 2,000 internees and prisoners of war on February 23, 1945. Captain Hunter worked closely with the chief of staff, and provided legal advice to commanders, legal assistance to soldiers, and military justice classes to officers.

"Japan's surrender on August 14, 1945 cancelled all invasion plans of its mainland. The 11th moved to Okinawa by air and by ship to the Atsugi Airfield outside of Yokohama, Japan, August 30, 1945 to spearhead the occupation of Japan by US forces.

"After completing sixteen months overseas, Captain Hunter left the 11th Airborne Division and returned to the United States

August 17, 1946. He was discharged at Fort Sheridan, Illinois October 24, 1946 at the rank of captain. He resumed practice of law with the same law firm in Waukesha that he was associated with before the war.

"By the time the 11th Airborne Division was relieved of its occupation role in northern Japan and moved to Camp Campbell, Kentucky, in February 1949, Maj. Marion H. Smoak had been the Division's staff judge advocate for eight months. The chief of staff for the 11th was Col. Harvey J. Jablonski who was an All-American football player from the United States Military Academy at West Point, Class of 1934. "He was the most two-fisted paratrooper I have ever seen in my entire life." Colonel Jablonski called Major Smoak and asked him if he was interested in being the Division's staff judge advocate....and that he would get him ready to attend jump school. Major Smoak told Colonel Jablonski, "I was born ready, sir."

"The biggest part of Major Smoak's legal business was military justice. When he arrived at the 11th, he found a backlog of twenty-nine general court-martial cases. Some involved situations where Japanese citizens were the victims. Major Smoak retired as a lieutenant colonel in 1961. He had earned his master parachute badge while with the 82nd Airborne Division at Fort Bragg, North Carolina.

"There were 20 judge advocates mentioned by Colonel Gonzales. They brought with them a wealth of legal knowledge, a high degree of maturity, and a sense of justice and fairness that had been fashioned in courtrooms across the country. They were graduates of the best law schools such as Boston, Chicago, Columbia, Georgetown, Harvard, Hastings, Oklahoma, Michigan, New York, Northwestern, Virginia and Washington to name a few.

"As these civilian lawyers came onboard, they found that the JAGD was reflective of the civilian profession of law. There were no women and no black lawyers among its officer ranks when

World War II started. Of course, this was not unusual for most branches of the armed forces at the time. But the times were about to change.

"The generation that would fight World War II had its beginning during the years that bracketed World War I. They had been shaped by the Great Depression. They had learned deep values about family and country, but above all, they had learned to have supreme confidence in and responsibility for oneself. Although some may not have been treated perfectly before the war, they used the war to take a giant step towards being treated equally. The JAGD was one place where this eventually occurred.

"The United States participated in World War II for forty-five months. For nearly two-thirds of that period, the JAGD remained comprised of only white men. It was not until May 4, 1944, that a persistent Captain Phyllis L. Propp became the first female judge advocate. That same month, thanks to the intervention of some influential people, Privates William A. McClain and William R. Ming, became the first two black lawyers to attend the JAG School at the University of Michigan Upon their graduation from the Officers Candidate Course on September 9, 1944, they were both commissioned as lieutenants in the JAGD.

"The number of JAG officers never came close to meeting all of the legal needs in an Army that quickly expanded to over 8 million soldiers. Of course, part of the JAGD reaction to meeting the manpower requirements was to establish a school that would convert civilian lawyers into officers and judge advocates that could fill variety of legal positions.

"The cases overseas that took the most time and effort, not surprisingly, came under the heading of domestic relations. History has shown that the marriage ties are strained, in many cases beyond the breaking point, by the protracted separation of soldiers from their wives. World War II was no different. Long periods of military service overseas contributed to yet another tragedy of this war, the breakup of many marriages.

"In addition to their outstanding contributions described in four legal fields, out of this war, many judge advocates came away with the satisfaction of having served, as needed, in non-traditional roles to support the war fighter in accomplishing the unit's mission. Whether it was Major Samuel L. Heisinger supervising communications links on Corregidor; or LTC Albert Svihra taking charge of work details as a prisoner of war in the Philippines; or Major Carlos E. McAfee serving as the senior officer of the prisoner of war camp in Tanagawa, Japan; or Major Pelham St. George Bissell, III leading the Security group onto Omaha Beach on D-Day; or LTC James O. Bass guiding a truck convoy from Holland to Belgium; or Captain Lenahan O'Connell's commanding troops on the trips to and from the Pacific Theater; they each demonstrated courage, commitment, and competence in performing their duties. They did not demand to be remembered, but their service as *soldiers of the law* would never be forgotten."

[This ends the piece by Colonel Robert F. Gonzales]

CHAPTER TWELVE

BATTLE OF THE CHOSIN RESERVOIR, KOREA 1950

Historians have described the *Chosin Reservoir* campaign as the most savage battle in modern warfare, surpassing in percentage of casualties the battle of Tarawa, where some 15,000 Americans took 3,400 casualties as they all but annihilated the 5,000 Japanese defenders. Facing numerical odds of 8 to 1, elements of the 1st Marine Division, and 300 men of 41 Independent Commando Royal Marines who were attached to the 1st Marine Division (under Commander Lt. Col. Douglas B. Drysdale) and a combat team from the Army's 7th Infantry Division fought fiercely. Major General O.P. Smith was commander of the 1st Marine Division. Smith was ordered by MacArthur and Major General Ned Almond, US Army, to fight his way out of this trap. When asked if the Marines were retreating, Smith said, "Retreat? Hell, we're attacking in a different direction!" Sixty percent of the American and allies became casualties, but the Chinese suffered more. The total UN losses were 2,500 killed, 192 missing and 5,000 wounded with another 7,500 victims of frostbite and other cold-related injuries.

The stories in this chapter are furnished by some of the brave men who survived and are members of *"The Chosin Few,"* several of whom would become prisoners of the Chinese. [I have had the privilege of meeting all of these heroes.] Even though the Korean

RESPECT

508

War is often called "The Forgotten War," the heroism exemplified by the Americans produced 13 Medals of Honor and 70 Navy Crosses, the most ever awarded for a single battle in American military history.

Author's note: [In August 1948, I was taking basic training at Ft. Bragg, NC. My training was under the famed 82ndAirborne. I was fortunate in that I was the only person in my company who had an automobile. During World War II, the automobile makers turned their plants into producing tanks, trucks and war material for the military. The making of automobiles ceased in 1942, therefore, it was difficult to obtain a new car. My father had some influence with the automobile dealer in Hamlin, West Virginia and was able to obtain a brand new 1947 green Pontiac convertible. He and my mother brought the car to Ft. Bragg. My having a car allowed me to go off post to a town other than one near the post such as Fayetteville.

One of my favorite places was McColl, South Carolina. One weekend two of my friends and I stayed in a home where they rented rooms since there were only a few motels in that day. When we checked in, I saw trophies, blankets and other paraphernalia belonging to an All American-football player. I was impressed, being a football nut. When I saw that the items belonged to Doc Blanchard who played at West Point, I said "Wow! Blanchard is my hero." During our visit with the owner of the house, I naturally asked him about Blanchard. He said, "I am Doc's uncle. He and his wife are at church. Would you like to meet him?" What a question. I of course answered "Yes."

Blanchard had just graduated from training in Texas to become a pilot. The dinner (lunch) table was set southern style. I had never seen such a beautiful table setting. We waited until Blanchard came home. He was kind and thoughtful, taking time to visit with us even though the family was waiting to eat. He allowed us to take pictures too. Doc was called "Mr. Inside" while his sidekick,

Glen Davis, was called "Mr. Outside" on Army's football team. Both were All-Americans at West Point and both were Heisman Trophy holders. I asked Doc, "where is Glen Davis?" He replied, "Glen is serving the army in Korea." I said to myself "Where is Korea?" Many others, including the men about whom I am writing about in this chapter, had no idea where Korea was. I soon found out by landing in Korea in September 25, 1950 with the 187th Airborne Infantry Regimental Combat Team.]

"But first, a bit of history." General Douglas MacArthur, the United Nations Commander, assured President Truman that the Chinese would not enter the Korean War. The general also promised the troops that he would bring them home by Christmas. He made this statement as early as September 1950 when my unit was aboard the USS *General Anderson*, heading for Korea. But MacArthur didn't say which Christmas. On November 27, 1950, this changed. Disaster struck when the Chinese sent some 300,000 troops, whom they called, "volunteers," across their border at the Yalu River.

Korea was originally spelled "Corea" in our geography books. Korea is a 600-mile peninsula that protrudes into the Yellow Sea, the Sea of Japan and the Korean Strait like a small fat thumb. At one time or another, China, Japan and Russia each have tried to annex Korea's territory into its own. Although it is the same latitude as Kentucky, temperature's can reach 50 below zero. Our soldiers experienced deep snow's, viscous mud, heavy summer rains and bitter biting dust, but the beauty of the rice fields can take your breath away. One thing that we will never forget is the foul smell-the use of human excrement to fertilize the fields.

In 1833, Americans wanted to trade with Korea. In 1866, French and American missionaries were put to death in Korea. And in 1882, America's first treaty was drawn up, establishing commercial relations with Korea. On March 1, 1919, thirty-three Korean leaders including Syngman Rhee met at the Moon

Restaurant in Seoul for a meal and to read the declaration of independence aloud. They signed their names to this document and called in the police. Those who marched were unharmed, but in the next few weeks, thousands were put to death by the Japanese. America did not interfere.

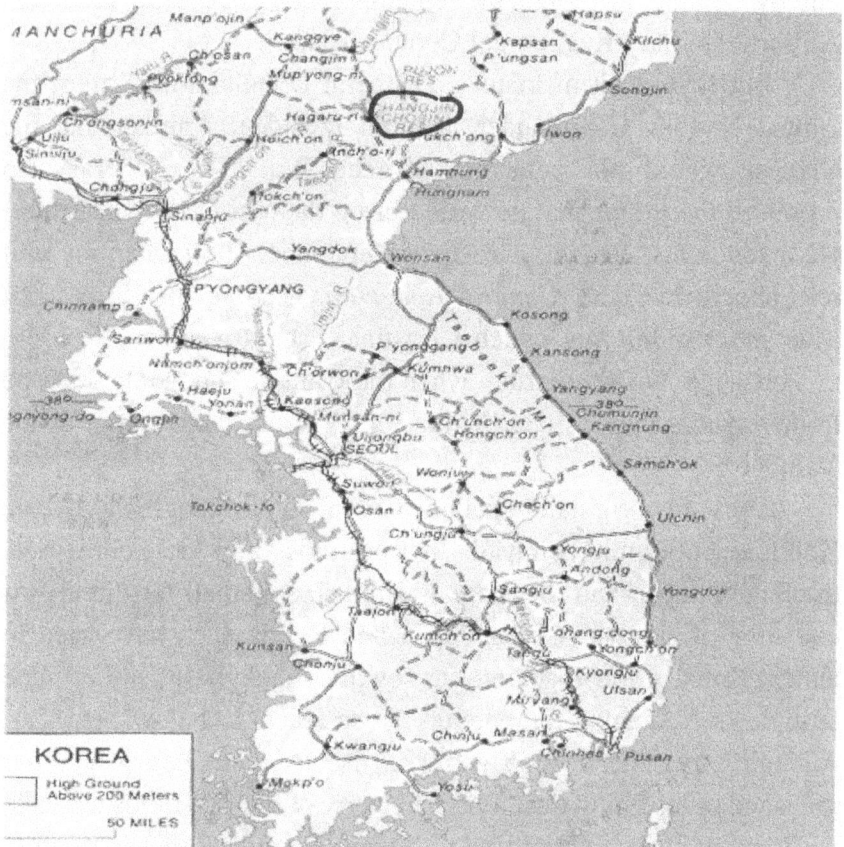

After World War II, which ended in 1945, Korea was divided into Soviet and United States zones in 1948. During the Potsdam meeting, just before the Japanese surrendered, Truman and Stalin had approved a statement giving Korea its independence after five years. Following the 1948 Korean elections, Syngman Rhee became the president of "The *Republic of Korea*" with the capital in Seoul. Russia moved to create the *"Democratic People's Republic of Korea"* with its capital at Pyongyang. America began withdrawing its troops from Korea. It is well known that the Russians withdrew in 1948 but left their weapons, which included tanks, heavy artillery and automatic weapons and about 180 new airplanes.

Four different battles were fought during the Chosin Campaign in freezing weather. The Chinese commanding general was Sung Shi-lun. Under this general's command were 12 divisions; it is believed that only eight divisions were committed. The 8 to 1 odds amounted to an estimated 120,000 Chinese soldiers who tried to annihilate some 15,000 Allied ground troops. Some estimates place the number of the Chinese at 80,000 because their divisions were not up to strength.

This was a ten-day battle between November 27 and December 6th. Some 3,000 troops from the US Army 7th Infantry Division, RCT 31 were isolated by the Chinese on the eastern side of the Reservoir.

The RCT 31 was almost wiped out. The few survivors joined the marines at Hagaru-Ri on December 2, 1950. Major General Smith ordered Colonel Chesty Puller (1st Marine Regiment), to send a task force comprised of about 900 men to open up the road between Koto-Ri and Hagaru-Ri. The Chinese ambushed the task force and cut it to pieces. Nearly 300 got through to Hagaru-Ri, 300 were killed or wounded and nearly 135 were taken prisoner.

The area between Koto-Ri and Hagaru-Ri, a distance of 11 miles, was later named *"Hell fire Valley."* Lt. Col. Douglas B. Drysdale, the commander of the Royal Marines Battalion, was told by Smith to "Press on at all costs." Drysdale, being a typical British officer responded, "Very well then, we'll give them a show." Drysdale had been wounded. Roughly 400 of his task force were surrounded by the Chinese without radio contact with anyone. Most of the 60 Royal Marines were killed, wounded or taken prisoner. Only a few slipped through the Chinese lines to Koto-Ri.

The UN troops were forced to evacuate and withdraw from North Korea to the port of Hungnam, where a major evacuation was carried out. The UN troops were in constant battles with the Chinese during the retreat. The marines and soldiers were able to destroy or effectively disable all seven Chinese divisions that tried to block their escape. The evacuation of about 105,000 soldiers, 98,000 civilians, 17,500 vehicles and 350,000 tons of supplies were shipped to Pusan in December 1950.

This battle at the Chosin Reservoir was a Chinese victory but due to the odds, the battle had to be a "moral" victory for the UN forces. The US Marines to this day consider the Battle of the Chosin Reservoir to be one of the proudest parts of their own history despite their heavy losses. Nine members of RCT 31 were awarded the Distinguished Service Cross. The Chinese invasion was eventually stopped and the UN forces advanced into the North before the truce was called. The truce was signed on July 25, 1953.

The Chinese Peoples Army had 25,000 killed, 12,500 wounded and 30,000 frostbite casualties. The UN forces, including American and British Marines, had 2,500 killed, 192 missing, 5,000 wounded, and 7,500 cold- related injuries.

JAMES C. VICKERS

"Chinese troops fired at the soldiers from all sides, and with great intensity. They used human- wave attacks. They would send these guys toward us, and we would shoot them, then ten more would pop up. Their commanders didn't care a bit for these soldiers." **James Vickers**

James Vickers was awarded the Silver Star for bravery at the Chosin Reservoir, 48 years after the Korean War ended.

JAMES C. VICKERS—SILVER STAR AWARDED FOR BRAVERY

James C. Vickers was awarded the Silver Star for bravery at the Chosin Reservoir, forty-eight years after the Korean War ended James was the son of Watt and Desta Vickers and at one time lived on Nine Mile in Lincoln County. He entered the U.S. Army at Beckley WV on April 12, 1950, took his basic at Ft. Knox, KY and was discharged from Knox in November 1957. He had five brothers to serve in the military: **WANDELL VICKERS, HAROLD VICKERS AUDDIE VICKERS, BILL VICKERS,** and **JIMME LEE VICKERS**. James was wounded at Koto-Ri, North Korea on November 29, 1950, and awarded the Purple Heart.

The following is James' story as written in the Coal Valley News on Wednesday, March 21, 2001:

"James Vickers of Barrett waited 48 years to receive a silver Star, awarded for his service in the Korean War and he honestly felt he would never receive it, but the remembrances of his comrades-in arms will finally allow the 69 year-old Barrett resident to be thanked by a grateful nation. Last Thursday, he received the coveted military medal while nearly 100 of his friends, neighbors, military friends and national guardsmen looked on. The medal is currently awarded by all branches of the service to any soldier who, 'while serving in any capacity, is cited for gallantry in action against an enemy of the United States, while engaged in military operations involving conflict with an opposing foreign force, or while serving with friendly forces against an opposing armed force in which the United States is not a belligerent party."

Vickers was from a patriotic family who believed in serving their country when needed. James had five brothers who served in the military as listed in the previous material. Vickers entered the US Army at Beckley, West Virginia on April 12, 1950 and was discharged at Ft. Knox, Kentucky in November 1957. Vickers said, "I was trained as a gunner on a 57mm recoilless rifle. It was a crew-served weapon that you fired from over your shoulder. The rifle fired a pretty powerful round." He was assigned to the 7th Infantry Division and made two amphibious landings in Korea, the first in September 1950 in Inchon, South Korea, the second in November of that same year in Iwon, North Korea. His military career was soon to become harrowing later that same month. His company was attached Task Force Drysdale, which included

RESPECT

514

elements of the 1st Marine Division and troops from South Korea as well as British Royal Marines.

"Our mission was to clear several roadblocks set up by the Chinese army between Koto-Ri and Hagaru-Ri, two towns in North Korea. This was a distance of about eleven miles," Vickers said. "We had advanced about five miles when just before dark, B Company was surrounded by Chinese troops and cut off from the main body," Vickers said, describing the road as quite similar to ones in Boone County, West Virginia, with similar territory.

Chinese troops fired at the soldiers from all sides, and with great intensity. "They used human wave-attacks. They would send these guys toward us, and we would shoot them, then ten more would pop up. Their commanders didn't care a bit for these soldiers." An officer later made the observation that after the battle for Hell Fire Valley a soldier could walk on Chinese bodies for half a mile without his feet ever touching the ground. During one engagement, Vickers' company was pinned down under intense fire from a machine gun emplacement. According to statements given by Vickers platoon leader, retired Major William Meanor, Vickers showed great courage while trying to save his comrades. "I observed the firefight in which Vickers, after considerable exposure to enemy fire, was able to knock out a Chinese machine gun nest that endangered his entire company, Major Meanor said.

"The mountains along the river valley through which we were proceeding were thick with Chinese troops and our task force's troops were constantly sent to clear the hills of Chinese firing on the convoy," Meanor said. Meanor continued, "My platoon was immediately in front of Vickers' platoon and on to my rear." He reported that Vickers' unit was pinned down by 50-caliber machine gun fire from nearly 1,000 yards away. The emplacement could not be reached by the small arms that the soldiers carried, so Vickers and his recoilless rifle were called to knock it out. Vickers fired two rounds with no success, and then his assistant gunner was killed. He then fired his last round, a white phosphorous shell, which knocked out the enemy machine gun.

Vickers sustained two separate wounds, one from shrapnel and a second from a bullet fired from a submachine gun carried by a Chinese soldier. "We formed a perimeter on a nearby riverbank and started for the mountains," Vickers remembered. "Then we went South as fast as we could, which wasn't too fast because it was so cold." After a march that lasted 3 or 4 days, Vickers and his group of men came upon the marine lines. "I remember climbing onto a marine tank, and that's all I remembered until I woke up in a first aid station a few days later." Vickers was airlifted to Ham Hung, North Korea, where he was treated for his wounds and frostbitten feet. There he first learned of the military medal that was promised, but would elude him for nearly 50 years. "One of my officers, Lt. Anderson, came into the hospital and told me, 'Vickers, I am going to recommend you for a Silver Star.' Some two weeks later he was transferred to a military hospital in Osaka, Japan.

James is happily married to his childhood sweetheart, Janet. They have two sons, Mark and Russell, and five grandchildren. James Vickers is shown being comforted by his buddy, Frank Kaiser of Charleston, WV during their 2007 convention. This article was written by Rusty Marks of the *Charleston Gazette*, Charleston, West Virginia. *"Kaiser served with Vickers, both corporals in an Army heavy weapons platoon thrown into heavy fighting along the Chosin Reservoir in North Korea. General Douglas MacArthur, commander of UN forces, had pushed his armies deep into North Korea, and by November 1950 many people thought the Korean War was over. MacArthur had not counted on tens of thousands of Chinese soldiers who swarmed across the border to help their North Korean allies, trapping 30,000 UN troops at the Chosin Reservoir. Nor had he counted on temperatures that plunged to 40 degrees below zero, the coldest winter in Korea in 100 years.*

(Kaiser and Vickers) (Photo courtesy of the Charleston Gazette)

"Vickers and Kaiser were part of Company B of the 7th Infantry Division's 31st Infantry Regiment. 'We were kind of the bastard company," Kaiser recalled. The mixed unit of about 900 men set out the morning of November 29th, but by noon had made it only about a mile up the road when they were stopped cold by a Chinese heavy machine gun dug into a hole in a mountain.

"It is still hard for Vickers to talk about what happened next. Vickers sneaked in through a culvert under the road to try to get a better shot at the Chinese machine gun. Armed with a 57-mm recoilless rifle—a type of light artillery piece—he tried to spot the enemy gun "I had three rounds of ammunition," Vickers said. Vickers was looking for the machine gun nest when a young

private held up a can of spaghetti and asked if anyone wanted a bite. Apparently spotting the glint of the metal can, the machine gunner opened up again, blasting the can from the soldier's hands.

"Vickers now knew where the machine nest was located. He got the machine gun nest with his last round. "We fought them all night long, Vickers said. But with the unit surrounded and out of ammunition, their commander decided to surrender. "There were some of us who decided not to surrender," Vickers said. He and a few others headed south, eventually making it back to the village of Koto-Ri, where they had started. A few days later, an Army observation pilot named Moseley made about 20 trips to fly Vickers and other wounded soldiers to safety. Nobody told Kaiser about the surrender. When the firing died down, he and some others came walking back down the road, and ran right into the entire Chinese Army. Kaiser and dozens of other prisoners were marched about 120 miles in about 20 days before ending up in a prison camp, where he remained until August 1953."

SEDRIC ALLEN WIRT

Wounded and left for dead with no food, in temperatures that hit 30 below, all Sedric Wirt could think about was staying alive long enough to be rescued so that his family would know what had happened to him.

Sedric Wirt was born in Little Rock, Arkansas on September 21, 1932. He is a member of the *"Chosin Few,"* having survived what can only be described as a nightmare at the Chosin Reservoir in North Korea. He joined the US Army just nine days after his seventeenth birthday. He was a handsome lad with blonde hair and blue eyes, weighing 140 pounds. The Korean War didn't start until June 25, 1950, so to become a soldier was an adventure for him as it was for many other young men. However, as you will learn, at age 18, Sedric defied all odds and miraculously survived.

This is Sedric Wirts story in his own words: "I went in the army at age 17 and took my basic training at Ft. Riley, Kansas. After basic, I received advanced infantry training at Camp Carson, Colorado. We were putting on a fire-power demonstration for the National Guard and ROTC when the Korean War broke out. I was ordered to Korea. They gave me a ten-day delay in route which allowed me to go home then report to Seattle, Washington. I reported in at gate 291. The guard told me if I had any time left on my pass, I could use it because it would be the last time I saw the USA for quite some time.

"They kept us overnight and asked us to send our personal belongings home. We left for Anchorage, Alaska where we stayed for one night before flying to Japan. We stopped at Wake Island on the way. When we landed in Japan, we were sent to a camp outside Tokyo. We stayed in Japan for a few days before boarding a ship, the USS *Butler*, for Korea. I remember seeing Mt. Fuji in the distance. We were on board ship for several days before arriving in Pusan. My company was to go to Pusan to relieve the men there, to help them out of the trap they were in. I understand the Marines were sent to Seoul.

"We stayed at Pusan a week or so and went through a bad storm in September 1950. After we landed, I had my 18th birthday. I was a runner at first. I don't think they had a place for me in the company at that time, so I was made a runner. Later on I became a radio man and rode a jeep along with the company gunner, and machine gunner. Some took a train.

"At that time, I remember them saying that we would be home by Christmas. I'm sure somebody knew better but we didn't. Everybody was really looking forward to that. On the way down to Pusan, most of our enemy fire came from snipers along the road. They would fire at us and we would take care of them.

"Next they loaded us aboard a ship and took us back up to North Korea. We went ashore in North Korea in a place called

Iwon in the Sea of Japan, and unloaded the trucks, jeeps and all. We traveled in a convoy to a place called Koto-Ri. It was about eight miles from Hagaru-Ri where a lot of marines and army soldiers were trapped. We stayed the night in Koto-Ri. Our jobs were to break through to the men who were trapped in Hagaru-Ri. We started out early one morning in the midst of a blizzard and were ambushed. I guess we fought all day off and on. It was just about the time the Chinese came into the war. This valley later would be dubbed '*Hell Fire Valley.*'

"The next day we would travel about four miles. We were ambushed along the road. We would see some of our troops coming back who had been wounded. They would be walking back from Koto-Ri. It took us all day because I know it was getting late in the evening when we stopped for no reason that I could see but found out it was a roadblock that stopped us. They would holler for us to unload. It got later and later and there was still a lot of firing going on. I was riding in a truck near the end of the convoy so I didn't know exactly what stopped us up front.

"Sergeant Posey was my communications chief. We were in the same truck with all of our equipment. Sgt. Posey ordered me and another boy to go to a railroad track. He told us to go out there and stop. We could hear Chinese soldiers on the other side of an embankment talking. We didn't know what to do. We waited for a few minutes and couple of Chinese started coming over the top of the railroad embankment. We fired into them—they ducked. I think they were surprised that we were that close to them. So we decided we had better get back. About that time the Chinese began firing at us and we could hear the bullets whizzing by our head. They didn't hit us. We got back to the convoy behind the trucks a few minutes later.

"There were bonfires set by the Chinese. Evidently they had piled up a bunch of brush and not having flares, lit the bonfires which worked pretty good for them. And all heck broke loose and from then on it was a lot of Chinese soldiers. A lot of our guys were getting wounded and killed. Nobody really seemed to know what to do. We had a few officers that were trying to tell us to guard this way and guard that way. I got back to the truck where Sgt. Posey was. There was another truck behind us that was evidently from another convoy. The Chinese started firing on that truck. Someone said our radio man had been hit or killed so I was trying to go from one truck to the other. It looked like a kid's sparkler lit up with bullets.

"They started up the convoy, one truck after the other still receiving heavy fire. I made it to almost where they finally stopped me. I had gotten shot through the calf of my left leg. It felt then like a hot piece of iron that is all that I can remember. It didn't keep us from moving. The next I heard a grenade or a mortar shell exploded. I got a piece of shrapnel in my right leg so a few minutes later I heard a thump behind me. A grenade had been thrown and went off and blew me down and forward. My rifle fell a few feet in front of me. I was trying to get hold of it and along came a Chinese soldier and picked up my rifle. I had my bayonet fixed. He pointed the rifle at me; I thought he was going to kill me. He just kind of grinned, left and took my rifle with him.

"There was a jeep there, so I was able to get under the jeep. They (the Chinese) were shooting back and forth and they shot the tires, the radiator and the battery out. The battery acid and radiator anti-freeze all came down on me and later I discovered the battery acid had gotten on the back part of my coat and ate it out. There was a road ditch, so I decided it would be better place than on the road. I crawled to the side of the jeep and later into the ditch and stayed there. Later, I heard a moaning GI who had been wounded on the road. I looked up and got hold of him and dragged him into the ditch with me. We stayed there all the rest of the night. Most of the firing had stopped, but now more shooting going on. We stayed in the ditch and during the night this GI died. I don't know his name. I didn't get his dog tags. He died with his arms around my legs. During the night he froze solid and I had to pry his arms from around my legs. That's how cold it was. The next morning when I came to or woke up, I heard men talking and was coming over toward a creek which was frozen. There was a fire over there.

"One of our officers was there and had some men trying to get together to get back to Koto-Ri. All we had were field jackets and liners (not a parka), this was our uniform. We had what they called snow packs-boots. They were rubber up part of the way, the top was leather. We were supposed to change socks real often. We keep one pair inside our shirt to dry out; then put the wet pair in there. Well, you know if you are busy, you don't have time to set down and take your shoes off. So during the night my feet had frozen. I heard these men talking so I got up on my feet. I remember walking. It was like trying to walk on stilts when I was a kid. My feet were frozen so that there wasn't much balance what so ever.

"I got to where the fellows were and they told me what they were going to do and asked me if I could walk with them. I told them "no" I couldn't walk that far. It was probably 20-25 feet to where they were going. There were some other GIs there. The Chinese soldiers came where we were and told us they were going to take us back up North. They were trying to get all of us to walk and nobody could walk. Some did try to get up and go with them. Later on I found out they went up the railroad and one of our officers that I talked to later, was shot through the foot. He had to go up the railroad pushing a little side car on the rails with a wounded GI on it. I guess that was probably his punishment because he was an officer. The Chinese soldiers came by and got by the fire. They told us if we didn't get up and come with them they were going to throw a grenade in the fire. It was hopeless for us to walk the way we were. We thought that would be the end. A couple of soldiers and the Chinese soldiers picked us up and carried us to an old hut-farm house at the edge of the road. They put us in there.

"There were ten of us. The Chinese had guards who would come in so often to search us to find out what we had on us. They weren't too smart. I had two pair of pants on and a billfold in the inside pair. They could feel my billfold but couldn't find it. We went through that search several times and they would go out and stay out for a while and try to get us to walk. They wouldn't give us anything to eat. The whole ten days we were there, the only thing we had was found in the corner of this old building was some little bitty potatoes. We ate those. They might have made two meals, maybe. Water wasn't a real problem. There was so much snow we got all the water we needed that way.

"I remember one day we had an old well out back of this old farm house. I was going to go out there and get some water. I used a couple of belts we fixed together and a steel helmet. All this time the Chinese Communist had not found my watch. I bought a new watch just before I went to Korea. I was real proud of it. I thought it was real pretty. When I got to the well I threw the watch in the well. I threw it in there. I figured they weren't going to get it anyway. I got the water and trying to get back to the house and looked up and there was an airplane flying overhead. He dove down at us and came right by us so loud it would almost shake your insides. One of the British soldiers that were with us had a little green beret. He waved that thing. Evidently the pilot recognizes we were prisoners, so they never fired through that hut while we were there, but fired all around the valley we were in.

"They dropped a lot of [napalm] bombs. A lot of our trucks were still on the road not far from the hut we were in. One day one of the Chinese soldiers came in and said if we could get one of the trucks or jeeps started that we could leave. There were only five or six still alive there. What they were doing was trying to get us to walk. One or two of the men tried to get out to one of the trucks or jeep. We never heard from them again. We figured that wasn't a very good idea.

"We also had the Chinese come by and say if we could get out there and get some of the C rations, we could have those. Nobody tried that either. So after several days there were only three of us left, me, Robert Smith, who was the first quadruple amputee? He lay in a snow bank for quite a while and finally crawled to the old hut and we got him inside. His hands were frozen solid. He couldn't hold anything. We stayed here for a few more days. The Chinese soldiers....I could hear them digging at night. I guess I don't know how they dug in the frozen ground. I don't know if they were burying our guys of if they were digging foxholes, because the planes would come by to strafe and dropped bombs. The Chinese would take off when they heard our planes.

"So Robert with his hands frozen; we had found in the back of one of these covers that went over the field jacket, some roll your own tobacco. We would roll our own cigarettes and try to smoke one ever now and then. I remembered that Robert couldn't hold anything, so we had to hold the cigarette for him. There was also a marine with us whose name I can't remember. He was from California. The three of us were the only ones to get out of there alive when the marines and army broke out of Taegu. One night we were laying there and kept hearing a bulldozer. We thought it was a tank. When he got to our convoy, we learned he was plowing the trucks and jeeps off the road to allow the other vehicles get down the road.

["Robert Smith was the first US soldier to lose four extremities in Korea. He was from Middleburg, PA. Robert came home to Walter Reed Hospital in Washington. He was wounded at Chosin Reservoir were he suffered frostbite in both hands and legs. Amputation was necessary. Smith's morale was called 'excellent.' He may even be walking on artificial limbs in two months."]

"One of the GIs came to the door of the hut. They didn't come in at first thinking it was a booby trap. They asked some questions then came in and got us. They took us out, put me on a jeep and I hung over the back. I don't know what they did with Robert and the Marine. I was lying on the back of a jeep. We had to go back to Koto-Ri. At that time most of the Chinese soldiers had pulled back from the road to the edge of the hills. When we went down the road they would fire at us and thank goodness they didn't hit me anymore while on the litter. I don't know how they kept from it but they didn't shoot me anymore.

"I got back to Koto-Ri to the aid station. It was the first medical treatment that any of us had had since we got wounded. I had taken an old towel that I had around my neck and loosened my belt and strapped it to my back over my wound where the grenade had hit me. When we got back to the aid station of course a lot of wounded soldiers were coming in all the time.

"I was a little unlucky. They put me in the back of the tent. The people they were bringing in that were wounded, were put in front of me. The aides would come and pick up a GI and leave me on the stretcher which was closest to the door. I lay there all day. Finally, a priest or chaplain came in and I told him that I had been there all day without any medical treatment, no food or water. I asked him could he help me and he said "Yes, you will be the next." So they came and got me and took me out to a little air strip and loaded me on a Piper Cub or some small airplane. Later we found the pilot that flew me out of Koto-Ri to a hospital ship where they loaded me aboard and started treating my wounds. They tried to get me to eat. I hadn't eaten anything to speak of for ten days so I really wasn't hungry. They tried to get me to eat and would bring me stuff that I might like. I got a little stronger and they operated on my feet. Later I discovered the doctors report said when they operated on my feet there were still ice crystals in them. So they were pretty well gone."

Sedric's parents were notified by the Defense Department *"that their son had returned to the Korean fighting, when he was at the Brooke General Hospital, Ft. Sam Houston, Texas."* Fact, the 18 year old Wirt had both his feet amputated as a result of frostbite. Sedric wrote to his parents, "Everything has been pretty tough over here. I got it in the back and legs pretty bad and was a prisoner for 10 days. I am on board ship now and will be home before long." Lt. Victor J. Lustig, a Navy Chaplain, wrote to Cedric's parents explaining and that he was on his way home. Sedric was awarded a Purple Heart at the 155th Station Hospital at Yokohama, Japan for wounds received in action in Korea. He was also awarded the Korean Service Medal w/2 bronze stars and the Combat Infantry Badge.

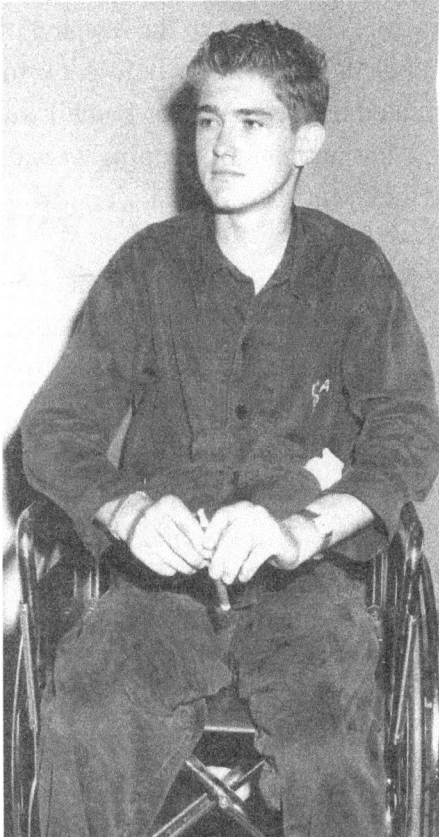

Sedric continues his story: "They put me on a hospital ship to Japan and unloaded me there. I stayed there...not long...then they put me on an airplane to San Antonio, Texas at the Brooke Army hospital. I stayed there and my mother, father and uncle came to visit me. They had done the amputation on both feet below my knees. Now back to my other wounds. They had operated several times but I didn't heal. The shrapnel had gone through my fatigues and drove a piece into my leg. The doctor said it wouldn't heal because of that. They were nice to the GIs in the hospital at San Antonio. I really did appreciate that. The wards had other GIs similar to my wounds which made it a little easier than to be by myself. My legs…after they had thawed out had gotten black up to 4-5 inches above the ankle. Before they amputated them they were black and hard. They wrapped gauze straps on each side of the leg to a pulley that was on the end of the bed. These weights pulled down on the skin. I had healed mostly, not completely but a lot better shape. They sent me to Letterman Army Hospital in San Francisco, California. They loaded me and a bunch of other fellows on an airplane. There they finished the healing process and also made some prosthetics for us and gave us walking classes on how to walk and how to balance and all of that. The people in San Francisco were really nice to us also. They came to the hospital on weekends and invited us out to their house. They would cook for us and really good people who treated us great. Nice to know I was home in MY AMERICA. After a few months of learning to walk again and do things on my own they sent me home. I weighed 97 pounds when I arrived in the US.

"I had met my wife–to–be earlier. She was from Minnesota. So I thought I would go back to Minnesota and find my wife Phyllis, to be. I lucked out. Found her and proposed and we got married on June 7, 1952. It is probably an ordinary story from this on.

"We had two children. I went to school under the GI Bill and learned watch and jewelry repair. I worked for ten years at US Pines Corp. I left there to open a business of our own. My previous employer told me if I ever needed a job to come to them first. It was an incentive for me to do well. Phyllis and I have been married for fifty-four years (at this writing). We have two children and four grandchildren. I AM PROUD TO BE AN AMERICAN FROM A COUNTRY LIKE WE HAVE."

Sedric was 18 years old when this experience took place. He still considers himself blessed that he made it home. He said two-thirds of his troop lost their lives in that battle. Fitted with prosthetic legs, he has never considered the loss of his legs a handicap. His wife Phyllis believes because her husband was so young when it happened, he learned to adjust. He gets around as well as anyone, surprising most people who learn that he actually walks on artificial limbs. Sedric met Phyllis before he left for Korea. They corresponded with each other.

Sedric said "When you are 18 years old, what are you going to do?" "You're an amputee. Are you going to sit there and let the world pass you by or are you going to get up and go on?" His wife, Phyllis, looking at his picture in the wheelchair said, "He still is handsome, but he was handsome with that beautiful curly hair." Sedric laughed and said, "It's all gone now." The Wirts visited South Korea on the 50th anniversary of the end of the war. The North Korean borders remain closed. He feels strongly that if the borders were opened and he was able to go back to those places, he could find the burial sites of some of those soldiers on the MIA (missing in action) list. He added, "Missing, yes, but never forgotten."

Cpl. Sedric Wirt was honored in different ways after returning home. An annual event was slated for the Coliseum in Little Rock, AR. He was selected to cut the ribbon officially opening the Coliseum doors for the third annual San Antonio Home show.

JAMES C. DeLONG

"When they captured me they took my watch, my rings and wallet. They took everything valuable. Except I had a .45 shoulder holster with a 45 caliber revolver and they never found it. It was under my armpit. I carried that for 10 days after I was a prisoner. Finally decided I better get rid of this thing because if they find it they're going to kill me. So I threw it away over one of the mountain passes when we were marching one night."

James DeLong's parents, Thomas and Clara, received the following telegram from Washington, DC. *The Secretary of the Army has asked me to express his deep regret that your son Sgt. Delong James C has been missing in action in Korea since 12 Dec 50 upon receipt of further information in this office you will be advised immediately.* This is the type of telegram that a family dreads to receive but there is still hope. James did live but was a POW (prisoner of war) for 33 months. This is his story. [James was awarded the Prisoner of War Medal.]

James was born August 10, 1931, on Cotton Street in Reading, Pennsylvania and the family later moved to Morgantown, where he briefly attended Caernarvon high School. He quit school in the tenth grade to go to work. On December 28, 1948 at the age of 17 he enlisted in the US Army. "It was the thing to do in those days," he said. "We were coming right out of the Second World War, and we were all keyed up for the Army. It was the patriotic thing to do in those days. All my friends joined too."

Over 55 years have passed since James lay in a ditch fighting for his life. He was almost 7,000 miles from home, cold and tired after the third day in temperatures that had dropped past 40 below. He was surrounded by an enemy that kept coming in waves, intent to take away his final breath. If you can really understand the hell that is war, then DeLong passed through the very center of it. And the thought chills him to this day.

DeLong's memories of his days in Korea and his nearly three years as a prisoner of war during the Korean War are not pleasant ones, although the nightmares of what has come to be known as the "forgotten war" have long since ceased. He said that he was over them now but there is not a day in his life that he hasn't thought of Korea since he came home.

DeLong took his basic training at Ft. Pickett, Virginia. He was then shipped to Yokohama, Japan where he was assigned to a machine-gun squad and eventually became squad leader. He learned to ski at Camp Crawford. This training was very important because they trained the men to survive in cold weather. This type training later saved his life.

When the North Koreans crossed the 38th parallel to attack South Korea, DeLong was 18 years old and still in Japan. He was part of the 7th Infantry Division, 3rd Battalion, K Company. His unit was put on alert. He said, "I was so young, it didn't bother me, I never dreamed that I'd get captured or killed. I could conquer the world at that point in my life." DeLong's squad was part of General MacArthur's invasion at Inchon, which trapped the North Korean army between the 38th Parallel and the Pusan perimeter. By the time he reached the Chosin Reservoir, the North Koreans had been joined in the conflict by the Chinese. DeLong said, "They hit us on the November 27, 1950. There were about 3,000 of us, and there had to be it seemed like 100,000 Chinese came in on us. His squad was in a U out into the flat and they (the Chinese) were on the mountain. The only heavy weapons that DeLong's group had were two 40 mm guns on half tracks and 105 mm howitzers—no tanks. But they held the Chinese for five days.

"Every night the Chinese would try to overrun us." DeLong said that he lost his machine gunner and that his assistant machine gunner was gut shot. Both were good friends of his. They almost lost half of the company the first night. DeLong was wounded on the third night when a mortar round landed in front of him and blew two of them and their machine gun out of the hole. But they got back in and started firing again. It was for survival.

DeLong was hit across his back and shoulders but didn't bleed much because it was so cold. The worst was yet to come. One of his friends, Sgt. Fontaine, was killed at the Reservoir. Fontaine was in Burma during World War II and fought with Merrill's Marauders. He told DeLong the first night, "Jim, we're not going to stop them. They're going to keep coming until they either overrun us or they kill us all." Fontaine had the third squad, DeLong the fourth.

When DeLong was wounded he said, *"I was firing a machine gun. They zeroed in on some mortar rounds, and they finally got their mark and a mortar round came down. We had dug a big rock out of the hole that day and put it up alongside of the hole. The mortar round landed on the other side of the rock and it protected us from getting really the full shock of the shrapnel. I got it across my back and shoulders. The other guy got it in his right arm. It blew us both out of the hole. Fortunately we just crawled back into the hole and set the machine gun back up and kept firing. It didn't hurt the machine gun; it just knocked it over. I went to the aid station. They were so busy, and I just sat there for a while and I decided, hell, I wasn't hurt as bad as the rest so I just went back to my gun and never did get any first aid for it. I didn't bleed that much because it was so cold. Your blood didn't flow. It was so cold, it would just freeze. I didn't have any problems with it till I came back home from Korea. In 1957 they had to take it out." [**DeLong was awarded the Purple Heart.**]*

The third night DeLong was in the hole next to Fontaine. The Chinese were breaking through so his machine gun was busy firing all night. The next morning, he looked over and Fontaine was sitting in his hole. DeLong hollered at him, but he never answered. When checking his friend out, he discovered that he had been shot between the eyes. In front of Fontaine's hole were 21 dead

Chinese whom Fontaine had killed. DeLong said, "The last one that dropped, dropped right down in front of him and must have pulled the trigger and shot him right between the eyes. He (the Chinese) had his rifle pointed right at his eyes. That was a rough night."

DeLong continued, "On a machine gun, you're firing 600 rounds a minute. You ain't worrying about where they're going you're just worrying about what they're stopping. They're out there and you're just shooting. You're raking the whole area and people are dropping. You don't see their face; you don't see anything. You just keep firing till they stop coming and then you stop firing. But I know in the morning after a night battle we'd have to go out and move bodies so we could get our field of fire for the next night, and they'd be stacked up."

After five days of continuous fighting, the Allies were ordered to break out. The wounded were loaded on trucks. DeLong said, "We had at least 500 wounded that we had to try to take out with us, which we found out later was impossible. We got about a mile and a half down the road, and they blew the bridge on us." It was dark. The trucks went down into a ravine and had to go up Hill 1221—which the Chinese had taken. Delong continues, "The last three trucks were sitting on the curve with wounded in them. I stopped at the last truck to see if I could help any of the wounded. And that's when the Chinese came in force and just surrounded us."

They took DeLong and the others, lined them up on the road. They got all the wounded who could walk, off the trucks that could walk. The ones who couldn't walk, the Chinese soldiers got in the truck and machine-gunned them. There was nothing anyone could do to help them. DeLong said, "They killed them all. It's hard. It's hard. I know some of the guys from my company were on that truck. Maybe some guys from my squad. It's hard to even think about it."

If at that moment DeLong thought it couldn't get any worse, the road down which they started to march down, took them even deeper into hell. He said "They're running us down the road, and this little chink runs up in front of the kid in front of me. He was running with a limp. And he just puts his rifle up aside of his head and just blows his head right off. I had to run over that kid and I never even knew who he was. That's hard. I had nightmares about that for years, wondering who the kid was." The Chinese tied their hands behind their backs and took them down the road and put them in a big ravine. They stood around them with their Thompson submachine guns. The POWs were kneeling in this ravine. DeLong saw "this little chink run up the road and he hands this one a piece of paper, and he got us up out on the ditch and started marching us back." The Chinese marched the prisoners around North Korea for 18 straight days in temperatures that reached 40 to 60 below. The prisoners only had a frozen potato or sorghum ball each day. Of the 500 Allied soldiers who started the march, only 258 were alive when they reached Kanggye on December 21st. They stayed at Kanggye the rest of the winter. Many more died in that camp.

With all the hardships of being a prisoner of war, the guys would still find something humorous to do. For example, the Chinese would hold a bed check at 11:00 and every hour during the night. A guard would come into their compound, shine the flashlight and count to make sure everyone was there. There were 45 guys in the old schoolhouse where DeLong was. Clarence Young would get down two boxes. He had a high box and a low box. He would throw a rope up over the rafters and put the rope around his neck. When the guard came in, he's hung. You have to understand these guards are squeamish. The guard comes in, shines his light and he hollers 'Raaah" and he runs out and he hollers for the other guards. While he's out getting the other guards, Young gets down and puts everything away. He hides the rope and boxes. The guards come back in and there's nobody there. Everyone is in bed. They were snickering because they thought this was funny.

The guards were walking around counting everyone, and they swear there was someone there. So they get everyone out of bed. They make everyone stand by their bunks. At first it was funny but after six hours of standing, it wasn't funny anymore.

When the soldiers died, the men would take rocks or whatever they could find—pack snow over them to bury them. The ground was frozen solid so they were unable to dig a grave. But DeLong said they were so weak that they didn't have enough strength to dig a hole anyway. He was weak with dysentery and malnutrition. When captured, he weighed 160 pounds. Twenty-five days later he only weighed 95 pounds. A marine sergeant named Hayden mixed a glass of warm Epson salts and it took care of his problem. Hayden saved a lot of lives doing this procedure. DeLong said that he talked to Sgt. Hayden 30 years later during a reunion in Norfolk, Virginia. He said, "When I saw him (Hayden), I knew who he was. It was an emotional reunion. God I hugged that guy. He saved my life, that man,"

"While we were in the prison camp at Kanggye, we were questioned and "indoctrinated" for about four hours each day. The Chinese would tell us "how rotten we were, that we were fighting for the capitalists-the Americans." DeLong said that the Chinese told us that they were being lenient on them but in fact were starving them to death.

I asked James to share with me what an average day was like in the Chinese prisoner of war camp. He said, "You get up around 6:00 a.m. in the summer; and 7:00 a.m. in the winter. First, you fall out for a head count and do some exercise. Breakfast follows. Around 8:00 a.m. we do some P.T. (Physical Training) and in the summer the indoctrination program for approximately four hours, which we didn't find at all good. We would then have some free time. In the summertime we would lay in the sunshine and try to tan; in the winter we would try to sleep and keep warm. Sometimes we had to go on a work detail around the camp or a wood detail to

RESPECT

gather wood for the fire to keep us warm. Because of the extreme cold, we keep the fire going 24/7. Around 5:00 p.m. we would eat dinner. In the summer we would sit around and tell stories or play games such as basketball. Mostly, we would sit around and talk about food. In the summer, we would go to bed around 8:00 p. m. or 9:00 p. m. In the winter we went to bed immediately after dinner. And that was the life of a POW in North Korea in 1950-1951-1952 and 1953. Thirty-three months."

This telegram, dated March 15, 1951 was received by Thomas and Clara, DeLong's parents: *"The name of James Calvin DeLong has been mentioned in an enemy propaganda broadcast at P D Prisoner of war status is not officially established by this report. P D further information will be forwarded when received."*

On March 20, 1951, the Chinese took 64 prisoners, which included DeLong, and started marching them all over North Korea for the next seven months. The prisoners were marched from village to village for propaganda purposes. The Korean people would spit on them, kick them, and throw rocks at them. Three months earlier when the American troops were going toward the Chosin Reservoir, the Koreans were waving South Korean flags.

The purpose of this exercise was obvious. The North Koreans wanted their people to know the Americans had been captured. They would march them into a POW camp where they would have young kids who were captured and they were to tell them not to be afraid. "Bull. You had to always be afraid. You never knew when they were going to kill you," DeLong said. DeLong estimates that they walked between 1,500 and 2,000 miles during that time. He was barefooted most of the time. His feet had become "as tough as shoe leather."

Washington, DC, December 19, 1951, a new telegram was received by his parents that gave the family some hope. *"The secretary of the Army has asked me to inform you that the name DeLong James C. believed to be that of your son is included in a list of prisoners supposed to be held by enemy forces. This list was provided by the enemy forces. It is not yet verified and no assurance as to its accuracy can be given at this time. When it is certain this is a true list you will be notified as soon as possible and without request on your part."*

By the winter of 1951, they had marched north to Camp 1, near the Yalu River in the northwest corner of the country. They stayed there until August 1952 when they were moved to Camp 4. At this time, the Chinese brought all the sergeants from all the camps in North Korea. Their reason was that they said the sergeants were influencing the privates and corporals not to listen to their captors. DeLong was staying in an old schoolhouse. They built bunks and because of the peace talks between the North Koreans and the UN, the food improved. The prisoners started getting rice three times each day and meat on occasions. At times, they even received some packages from the Red Cross. And they even started receiving letters from home.

DeLong was asked if he considered trying to escape. He said *"Hell yes, but the odds were against you to start with because your skin wasn't dark, you didn't have slanted eyes and everybody was your enemy. You had no friends. Once you're out in those mountains there was nobody who would help you. Not even the North Korean civilians because if they were caught helping you, they would be shot. I don't know of anybody escaping. We had guys try it. They'd be gone two weeks; they they'd be coming marching down the road with a big grin on their face, spending six months in the hole."*

In July of 1953, the Chinese called the prisoners to the playground to announce that the war was over. The Chinese were all smiles and began to make speeches. The prisoners stood in silence and didn't move. Nobody shouted hooray or anything. After the captors dismissed them, the POWs marched back to their compound and then they celebrated. They didn't want the Chinese to see their joy and happiness.

September 1, 1953, Washington, DC telegram reads: *"The secretary of the army has asked me to inform you that your son*

PFC. DeLong, James C. was returned to Military control in Korea and will be returned to the United States by surface transportation at an early date. You will be advised of arrival date. Signed: Wm. E. Bergin, Major General USA."(The Adj. General of the Army)

On September 3, 1953, James DeLong was finally released after 33 months a prisoner of war. He said *"When I crossed that line to freedom, they gave me another stripe. I became a sergeant first class. They gave us anything you wanted to eat. I wanted ice cream. I ate ice cream. Well, I got sick on ice cream. They put us in helicopters then and they started flying us to Inchon. We all got sick. Everybody's throwing up in this helicopter. Well this pilot is having a heart attack. He's gotta clean this plane and we're all sick. They shouldn't have given us so much. They could have killed us."*

Usually a prisoner is asked what food he wants the most after being freed. For DeLong it was ice cream, as he has just related. On September 20th, DeLong was on the USNT *Brewster* (the same ship he had traveled on to Japan four years earlier), on his way to San Francisco and then home.

DeLong said, *"Life is very precious when you get right down to it. It's something you don't give up easily. Your freedom—when you don't have freedom you don't have anything. You can't think for yourself or do what you want. It's something that's hard to describe—when you don't have it. But it's the most valuable thing in the world—your freedom."*

James DeLong was discharged on October 28, 1953 at Camp Kilmer, New Jersey. He attended night school and earned his G.E.D. and a diploma from Twin Valley High School; and a two year degree in production control from Penn State. He retired in 1992 after 35 years with Brush Wellman.

DeLong and his wife Audrey were guests of the Korean Disabled Veterans Association and returned to Korea on the 50th Anniversary of the Korean War Commemoration Committee. James met Audrey Elizabeth Kerper during a Sunday school picnic after he returned home. They were married on May 7, 1955. He said, "I'm a little apprehensive." He had made his home in Leesport for the past 40 years. "It's certainly not going to be like when I went over here." There's not going to be the death and destruction when we visit Korea, but they won't let us go to North Korea. If I could visit North Korea, I'd like to go back to the battlefield where we were. That would be the Chosin reservoir in the central part of North Korea. For years after DeLong returned home, he didn't talk about that experience. He said, I think it helps me now to talk about it, but it's not a pretty story.

On May 7, 2005, the DeLong's celebrated their 50th wedding anniversary. They are a special couple indeed.

MSG JEAN F. McCRADY

"I was checking the rear when I was captured by two chinks. They took me North and then East across the road and mining track to a house and stood guard over me. Later I caught my guards asleep and escaped." **Jean McCrady**

Jean McCrady, like Wirt and DeLong, joined the army in 1948 at age 18. He is currently serving as the 1st Vice President of *"The Chosin Few"* organization. He entered the army from Virginia, taking his basic training at Fort Jackson, SC. The following year, January 1949, he was shipped to the Japan. He was assigned to the 17th Infantry Regiment in Camp Schimmelphennig, Sendi, Japan. His job was an auto mechanic.

McCrady was in a field hospital with a case of yellow jaundice when the Korean War broke out. After being released from the hospital he received light duty for six months. Wanting to be reunited with his old outfit, he decided to go AWOL (absent without leave), but found that his unit had shipped out. McCrady was then assigned to B Company 31st Infantry Regiment as a sniper. Now in the infantry with the rank of corporal, he was ready to enter into the fighting.

[Author's note: A soldier wants to be with his original outfit because of his buddies and the relationships that have made. I was first wounded on October 22, 1950 in a small village, Yongyu, about 40 miles north of Pyongyang. I heard rumors in the hospital that they were sending us (paratroopers) to a regular ground outfit. Nothing wrong with a ground outfit but I was Airborne all the way. I had three open wounds at the time. I borrowed a cane, walked out of the hospital and talked a pilot into taking me to go to Pyongyang with him where my unit was located. So I understand Jean McCrady's feeling to go AWOL too.]

As he mentioned, McCrady had just been released from the hospital. The march from Inchon to the Suwon Airfield because of his tender feet caused some damage. When he removed his boots, he found his feet bloody. The medic wanted to evacuate him but was told to put some sulfur medicine on his feet, wrap them up, because McCrady wanted to remain with his unit.

McCrady landed at Inchon, Korea on September 15, 1950. The first mission of his unit was to secure the airport at Suwon. While they were securing the Suwon Airport, the platoon was split up and dispatched to separate areas for security details. Jean and a Katusa soldier were taken by jeep to an area to guard a cache of rifles and medical supplies. They were located in two wooden buildings across from each other in an old farm area. There were no other people around.

McCrady looked over the situation and found various medical supplies, including vials of medicine used for shots. All the weapons were new and covered in Cosmoline. The weapons were S.K.S. carbines along with Thompson submachine guns with ammo by the case. When dropped off to protect this area, they only had rations for the day. The trucks were supposed to return that evening to pick up the two men and the equipment.

McCrady began to be concerned about 4:00 p.m. because the trucks had not arrived. About that time he spotted a man coming down from the hills and told his buddy to take cover. When the man approached him, McCrady challenged him, searched him, and learned that he was a captain in the North Korean Army. The captain advised McCrady to surrender and let him have the weapons and other supplies. The North Korean captain said that he had 40 men in the hills and at sundown, they would come down and kill them and take the equipment. An important decision had to be made. During the conversation with the Korean soldier, McCrady asked him, "Why does his people tie the hands of the American prisoners then shoot them?" The captain said that some units did this and some did not. This had happened to some of our soldiers down South a couple of months before.

He tied the captain up across the road from the weapons building so he could watch him. If the Korean soldiers tried to free their captain, McCrady could open fire on them. McCrady said, "I knew if I took the wrong action, I would be in trouble as not only as a corporal but I knew we wouldn't have a chance with 40 men attacking the two of us. I told Katusa to take the captain down the road toward the North, hoping that he would find our unit. Then I proceeded to destroy all the medical supplies with my rifle butt. I then took some rifles out of the cases and laid them end to end from the weapons building to the medical area. I wanted to burn them completely but only had one W.P (white phosphorus) grenade to set the fires. It worked fine; leaving both buildings burning and all hell took place."

As they headed north, they ran into an American major in a jeep. McCrady explained the predicament that they had been in and the decision he made to destroy everything. The major said that he had done the right thing and congratulated him. The major took the Korean captain with him then had another jeep take them back to their unit.

In October McCrady was sent to Iwon, North Korea. His unit was sent to the Fusen Reservoir to conduct motorized patrols. On November 20th, he was promoted to Sergeant E-5 and celebrated with a hot turkey dinner later that week. His unit was called to move from Iwon to join the rest of their regiment which was located east of the Chosin Reservoir. It was snowing when they reached Koto-Ri on November 28th.

An attack was scheduled for the next day. McCrady was sent to secure supplies of ammunition from the ammo dump to distribute them to the squad. After he returned, he met a British Royal Marine who invited him for a cup of hot tea. McCrady said, "His demeanor was quite different from mine. He was laid back and I was chomping at the bit." The attack was set on November 29, 1950 at 9:30 a.m. to break through nine road blocks in order to get to Hagaru-Ri. This action was known as *"Taskforce Drysdale,"* named after the British Commander of the 41st Regimental Combat Team which consisted of about 900 men.

The convoy, in which McCrady rode, was moving. Suddenly, they were attacked by an overwhelming number of fanatical enemy troops. McCrady was now a squad leader because his squad leader had been killed in action that afternoon. Without regard to his safety, McCrady manned a 50 cal heavy machine gun mounted on a truck. Although he had no training on this particular weapon, he began firing on the enemy allowing his fellow soldiers to get into a defensive position. He was able to cut down the first wave, annihilating a great number of them. The gun jammed, so he removed the back plate and got rid of it in the snow. He fell to the ground, which knocked the air out of him. Pfc. Claude Eads, a member of his squad, was the only person still in the area. Eads thought McCrady had been wounded, and helped him to his feet. The two soldiers went about ten feet, a mortar shell exploded and knocked them to the ground. Eads was wounded pretty badly. Now it was time for McCrady to carry him. For this action, Jean McCrady was recommended for the Distinguished Service Cross.

Sometime later, McCrady was firing his sniper rifle, killing "the chinks" on the trucks when he was hit with another mortar, which knocked him unconscious and destroyed his weapon. When he came to, he found that his M-1D sniper rifle had been destroyed. Unable to find another sniper rifle, he found a 45 cal Thompson submachine gun. He was collecting ammo, redistributing it to the men to continue firing at the enemy and taking care of some of the wounded.

About this time, Marine Major Mclaughn called to McCrady, "Hey Lt., get some men and put them in the rear of the position." McCrady replied, "I am not a Lieutenant I'm a sergeant but he carried out his order. The only automatic weapon in the area was a BAR (Browning automatic rifle) manned by Corporal Roy Bradford an Ex-Marine 1st Lt. It was later that evening that McCrady was captured. However, he escaped. He believed that the best time to escape was A.S.A.P. after being captured. The Chinese had made him take off his shoe packs. Catching the guards asleep, he retrieved his shoe packs which were almost covered with snow, and returned the same route that his captors had taken him. When approaching friendly lines, he was not intercepted by our own soldiers or even challenged. When he got inside the area he cursed the soldiers for not staying awake and firing at the enemy. He told them that he had just escaped and if they didn't stay alert, they would be captured too.

Since the Chinese at the time of his capture had taken his Thompson submachine gun, so he now didn't have a weapon. He found an M-1 rifle with eight rounds in the clip. There were short periods from time to time when there wasn't any firing from either side. But the Chinese were getting close so close in fact that McCrady was hit by a hand grenade. He thought he had lost his leg. He said, "I pulled off my trigger mitten glove and felt for my leg to find it was still there but completely numb. There was no bleeding so I just kept rubbing my leg and hitting it on the ground to get circulation going to keep it from freezing."

A short time later, Major McLaughn called to a "chink" officer, giving him 15 minutes to surrender. The Chinese officer said, "You got it wrong. It is us that give you ten minutes to surrender or I will send a fresh regiment through here and kill all of you. Major McLaughn advised his men of the offer. The Chinese officer asked, "How do I know that you will come back?" The American gave his word that he would return and become a POW. Instead of surrendering, McCrady took off for Koto-Ri when the 68 men of B Company became prisoners of war.

McCrady, heading for Koto-Ri, crossed the river and traveled along the low hills. There were a few other soldiers who had made the same decision not to surrender. On the way they met some Chinese soldiers who did not for some reason fire on them. The Americans did not fire on the Chinese either because they were outnumbered. A Korean interrupter came up front to talk with the Chinese. The "chink" yelled at him and he took off for the rear again, leaving the men not knowing what to expect. Without any hesitation, they headed south again. Believing these men to be the enemy, friendly tanks began firing on them. Finally they recognized them as their own troops and ceased firing.

When they finally reached Koto-Ri, they saw a black marine standing by an ambulance with a fire. The marine said, "You men look like hell." He offered McCrady a can of frozen sausage patties and even

opened the can for him. McCrady said, "I cried like a baby." "I just felt like I was in New York City; I just felt like I was secure at last."

McCrady immediately reported to the aid station to have his right leg examined. They told him that his leg would gradually get better and "that he would live." The medics also treated his frostbitten feet by soaking them in some kind of purple water.

Needing all the men who could fight, McCrady was again assigned to a 50 cal machine gun on a truck. Things were as well as could be expected when you are completely surrounded. He said, "We stacked the enemy up by fire at night and at daybreak we went out and spread them out so the next attacking enemy could not hide behind them. I can't stress too many times that this all took place with the weather 30 to 40 degrees below zero. This battle continued for nine days from November 30th until December 10, 1950. At this time, they pulled the troops out and marched back to the Funchilin Pass to Ori-ri. The 3rd Infantry picked these troops up, put them on flatbed trucks and transported them to Hungnam. From Hungnam, they boarded ships and were transported to Pusan.

For the next seven months they conducted attacks and patrols up the Korean Peninsula. Finally for Jean McCrady, the fighting, the cold, the suffering caused by the enemy and the unbelievable Korean winter were over. He rotated back to the States. Around April 1951 he was promoted to Sergeant First Class (SFC) and offered a battlefield commission. He turned down the offer. Col. McCraffery told him that he could keep him in Korea as "essential." McCrady's reply to the Colonel was, "They just relieved a five-star general named MacArthur, and they do not need me." [General MacArthur was replaced on March 24, 1951 by General Matthew B. Ridgway]. The Colonel told McCrady to have a good trip home.

Twelve years after the Korean War ended (July 25, 1953), Jean McCrady found himself in the jungle of Viet Nam, in the ID

Rang Valley Battle, which took place in November the same month that the battle of the "Chosin Reservoir" had begun. This battle was covered in the book *We Were Soldiers Once and Young.* This battle started on November 14, 1965. McCrady's unit got into the battle on the 18th when they were attacked by a reinforced battalion. By this time, he had been promoted to a master sergeant, E-8, assigned as combat operations and intelligence specialist.

President Ronald Reagan cited CHOSIN as among the epics of military history in his first Inaugural Address. *Time Magazine* described it as "unparalleled in US military history...an epic of great valor." The Chosin Fighters by decimating and checkmating the Chinese forces in the mountains, enabled the evacuation of nearly 100,000 North Korean men, women and children by sea, the last on Christmas Eve. The US Government formally described the humanitarian feat as "the greatest rescue operation in the history of mankind." Never in recorded history, have combatants rescued so many civilians in the midst of battle.

FRANK J. KAISER

"After I was captured on November 29, 1950 we were taken from Hells Fire Alley to a place called Kangyee. We walked from November 30 to December 20th." **Frank Kaiser.**

Frank J. Kaiser was born in Columbus, Ohio on December 3, 1932. He entered the US Army at age 17 on April 12, 1950 only to find himself a prisoner of war in Korea a few days before his 18th birthday. This is Frank's story about his life for 33 months in a Chinese prison camp, as told to the author in Charleston, West Virginia on Saturday, October 20, 2007.

Frank said that they marched all night after they were captured, for 20 days at least. "On Christmas Day they took us to a barn—a big barn—I remember that. When the Chinese were marching us from Koto Re, of course Bob you know what the terrain is like in Korea, if a guy fell down and you went back to help him, you would catch a rifle butt in the back. It was like, ok, here's the deal; I'm going to look straight ahead if I fall down nobody is going to be able to help me and if I can help someone else....but I can't take any more rifle butts in my back."

Wheeling POW greeted by new nieces on homecoming. Left: Ellen

Jean and Susan Villee, right give Uncle Frank a big hug.
(Photo by Wheeling News Register 1953)

Q. Would they kill the men who fell?

A. I don't know. We never knew if they killed them or took them someplace else. We just don't know.

Q. You couldn't look back and find out, could you?

A. There was no way. When we're walking at night and a guy falls down in the snow, you know we were together in Japan for a month maybe, and then we made the Inchon landing. You see we were a bastard company attached to the Regiment. They sent us out there to do recons to find out what we could and if we got in a fire fight, we got out of it the best way that we could. We didn't have time to get close to anyone. I knew the guys in my squad but I can't remember my squad leader's name to save my soul. We cannot get a morning report because all of us would like to learn about the others.

Frank said, "Here's what happened. I was captured. We went as a group to a place called *Kangyee*. I have a roster of everyone in Kangyee. They took us outside every night and gave us some political BS to brainwash us. The Chinese tell us that we were good guys but the Americans were warmongers in Korea. They would tell us that the Chinese Liberation army was friends of ours. One night I was standing out there, who knows, 20 below zero, and I passed out. They said it was probably hypothermia. They took me to a Korean house. Everyone had evacuated Kangyee and went someplace else to another camp. A Chinese patrol came by and picked me up with a group that was going down South to be released. We walked almost to the 38th Parallel to be turned loose. That's when the American force made a push North and the Chinese instead of turning us loose, turned around and took us all the way back north to the Yalu River. I remember Sheeley being in that group and he remembers me. I was separated from just about everyone in Company B."

The map on the next page shows the operation beginning November 28, 1950 when Frank and the other prisoners were attached to Col. Drysdale, to the open road, to the marines tied down at the Chosin Reservoir. They were ambushed as they started north and again at "Hellfire Valley." Frank was captured the next morning and began the walk to Kanggye. They walked all night.

Frank said, "At Kanggye my squad and I were billeted in a room that previously was a stall. Although we were prisoners of the Chinese, we were staying with a Korean family. Every night the Chinaman would show up and we were taken outside for our brainwashing session. I was left with a Korean family and sometime later I was picked up and joined a group that was being taken south to be repatriated. They released some marines but we turned back North ending in Camp 1. Conditions were very bad and we lost many of our brothers.

(Map courtesy of Frank Kaiser)

"Most of those guys ended up in Camp 3. I was in Camp 5 or Camp 1. I found a record of Camp 1 with my name on it. The Chinese would change the numbers on the camp from time to time. There are a lot of stories coming out of there that I don't remember."

This is an article that appeared in the *Wheeling New-Register* dated September 14, 1953 by Shar Southall. Here is the entire account, even though there may be some duplication in the personal interview.

"Headlines read: "Local POW Home, Tells Vivid Story of Prison Life."
Memory of Horrors Tinges PW's Fete here. Sgt. Frank Kaiser reunited with family after 33 months under Reds iron rule. It's Christmas, Easter, Fourth of July, and birthdays all rolled into one, all the holidays that are ever celebrated for a Wheeling family today. For their son, Sgt. Frank Kaiser, is home after 33 months in a Communist prison camp in North Korea. Mirth and gaiety runs high at the Kaiser home at 13 Memminger Ave., but there's a somber note, too.

Sgt. Kaiser wants his family and the people of Wheeling to know the story of life behind the Communist lines, what it's like to be indoctrinated with Red philosophy, to be able to read nothing but Communist okayed literature, to be fed food that Americans wouldn't even think of feeding to their pet dogs and cats. "You had to go along with them," he said seriously, "or else keep your mouth shut if you wanted to live through it. Some of the POW's went too far and became what we called 'progressives.' They were opportunists. There weren't very many of them. In my group only about eight out of 100 were suspected of going along with the communist line. They had to be closely guarded once they crossed the border and arrived at Freedom village."

"What was it like to see freedom Village again after 33 months in a prison camp in North Korea? Well, I couldn't even talk. Everyone was asking us how we felt to be free again and I couldn't tell them. It hardly seemed true."
"Getting back to the United States again and seeing my parents and family after so long was wonderful," he said. "But you know I never really gave up hope that I'd be released sometime. Once in a while when the going got tough I sort of doubted it, but I never gave up that glimmer of hope. I knew that I'd get out some way."

Sgt. Kaiser arrived at the Wheeling airport at 1:30 p.m. on Saturday. His parents and family greeted him and have been wonderfully understood. He hasn't talked much about his life in the prison camp but he does want people to know the truth. "We were able to write letters back to our parents, but the Chinese told us what to write in those letters. I wrote, simply to let my folks know I was still alive, but I hoped all the time that they wouldn't believe the things I said," he mused. "I think that the Chinese were running the whole show. The North Koreans were beaten early in the war. The Chinese are mobilized. They aren't just a 'few volunteers' the way some of the propaganda states."

Frank enlisted in the Army in April 1950 and went to Korea in September of that year, serving with Company B of the 31st Infantry regiment 7th Division. It was in January 1951 that his parents were notified that he was missing in action. Then, four months later, they were told that he had been captured and was a prisoner of war. It was in action near the Chosin Reservoir that Sgt. Kaiser was captured in November 1950. He and many other prisoners were marched by the Communists to their first prison camp, north. At one point during their 20-day march they crossed the Manchurian border and then re-crossed it and arrived at the Kanggye POW camp.

From the first, the steady indoctrination began as the Communists waged their battle for the possession of the prisoners' minds. "They used to come around to our mud shacks and read to us from the Shanghai newspaper which gave only their side of the war," Frank explained. "Then they would ask us questions on what they had read or told us. It was like a class in school."

"Sometimes a fellow prisoner would just disappear from camp and you would never see him again. You didn't ask questions, though," he said. "The Communists told us that they didn't capture us, they only liberated us from the capitalistic way of life. That was the big indoctrination."

Then they would let us play basketball and other sports, under supervision of course. They did it for propaganda purposes back home. They took pictures of us and sent them back to their newspapers to show how well they were taking care of POW's."

"I can't even describe the food to Americans because they won't be able to understand what it was like. We got some fatty pork with little or no lean meat on it; a kind of beef, not at all like we eat in the States; nothing but potatoes when they were in season for maybe six months; then nothing but Chinese cabbage for the next six months. Then turnips, and rice, rice, rice. They mixed the rice with a maize sorghum that made it taste terrible. I couldn't eat it at all," Sgt. Kaiser said.

In April 1951, they moved us to Camp 1, the largest POW camp in North Korea. It had about 1,600 prisoners at one time. We lived in mud shacks, slept on a mud floor, and carried our own firewood down from the mountains in the *summer months, storing it for the winter. Sometimes there were as many as 100 prisoners in a small room, 15 by 12. We finally had to build double bunks for ourselves to have some place to sleep.*

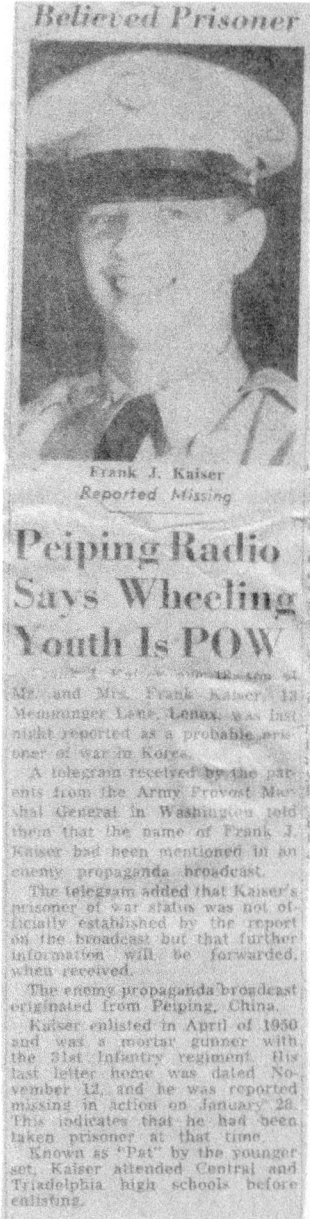

Believed Prisoner

Frank J. Kaiser
Reported Missing

Peiping Radio Says Wheeling Youth Is POW

Mr. and Mrs. Frank Kaiser, 13 Memminger Lane, Lenox, was last night reported as a probable prisoner of war in Korea.

A telegram received by the parents from the Army Provost Marshal General in Washington told them that the name of Frank J. Kaiser had been mentioned in an enemy propaganda broadcast.

The telegram added that Kaiser's prisoner of war status was not officially established by the report on the broadcast but that further information will be forwarded when received.

The enemy propaganda broadcast originated from Peiping, China.

Kaiser enlisted in April of 1950 and was a mortar gunner with the 31st Infantry regiment. His last letter home was dated November 12, and he was reported missing in action on January 28. This indicates that he had been taken prisoner at that time.

Known as "Pat" by the younger set, Kaiser attended Central and Triadelphia high schools before enlisting.

In the winter of 1950 it was cold—30 degrees below zero part of the time. All heating was from fires under the mud floor. We wore cotton padded clothes given to us by the Chinese. Health wasn't very good. A lot of men died from dysentery, where with some medical care they might have lived. We had a lot of stomach trouble too. I frankly think that the Communists aren't releasing all of the prisoners, because there were a lot more than have been brought over the border to Freedom Village so far.

Sgt. Kaiser is currently enjoying a 30-day rest and recuperation leave. The whole family is at his parents' home—his grandmother, Mrs. McBee; his sister, Mrs. George N. Villee of Johnstown, Pa., and her two young daughters. Frank will report back to Fort Meade, Md., for complete medical checkup and discharge from the Army at the completion of his leave. Plans for the future? Well, he's hardly had time to think about that with all the wonder of homecoming. He is considering enlisting in the Air Force. But the decision can wait until later. Right now it's just good enough that he's home again.

Q. How much did you weigh when you were captured?

A. I weighed about 170-175 pounds when captured. At times I was less than 100 pounds, between 85-90 pounds. I was probably 135-140 pounds when I was freed.

Frank doesn't remember the exact day that he came to what they called the Freedom Village to become a free man. He said it was either August 21 or 23, 1953, sometime in August.

Q. Do you remember how you felt when freed and came across that bridge?

A. Like "yea, we're home."

Q. While you were prisoner for 33 months, what food did you think about that you really wanted?

A. Glazed donuts.

Q. Did you get the donuts?

A. Yea. And I was able to eat them.

Frank is a family man. He has three sons, three daughters and 12 grandchildren. After his discharge from the army on November 20, 1953, he attended West Liberty State College in northern West Virginia, graduating in three years. He went into the trucking business and became manager of a motor freight company. Since 1970, Frank has owned and operated his own insurance agency. He and his wife Betty lives in Charleston, WV.

Q. Frank, when did you arrive in Korea?

A. I was in the Inchon Landing. [The Inchon Landing called "*Operation Chromite*" was on September 15, 1950. The 1st Marine Division and 7th Infantry Division made a brave and historic landing at Inchon, which completely surprised the North Koreans. The landing was similar to World War II landings at Salerno,

Anzio and Italy. This turned out to be a brilliant strategy by Gen. MacArthur].

Q. Frank, were any of the Chinese guards kind to you?

A. Most of the time the guards were just there. Bob let's face it. We could walk out of the camp anytime we wanted to. I'm 6'4", blond hair and blue eyes…and I'm going to walk out of the prison camp to an area where the people are about 5 foot tall, black hair, slanted eyes and dark skin. I'm going to stick out like a sore thumb. They really didn't care about us walking out. We were not going anywhere.

Q. What kind of food did the Chinese feed you?

A. You wouldn't eat anything because it was grown with human manure. You couldn't drink the water because it caused dysentery. Sorghum was the main diet. [Sorghum is grasses that have long stems bearing large panicles of spikelet with numerous small, glossy grains; grown for grain, syrup and fodder]. We got rice once in awhile. They would give us millet sometimes. We had bread shipped in from Russia. We may have had potatoes one time. Essentially it was sorghum. The Chinese rations were mostly soy beans. Most everything they ate was from soy beans. Soy milk, soy bean pies, soy bean cakes etc.

I do remember when I first got there, there was a creek back there and a row of huts in the upper corner was a death house. If anyone could not get up and go, they were put there to die. Right beyond there was a Chinese kitchen where they cooked for themselves. They had these big round things that were set over boiling water. They had several layers of these things where they cooked their pasta, meat and everything. If we were lucky and caught the Chinese gone, we would steal food from them.

Q. Were you ever put in the "hole?" Could you lie down in it?

A. Yes. It was just a hole with a cover over it made out of …like corn stocks. You could stretch out but you couldn't lie down. You could curl up but you couldn't stretch out at all. I was only in there to my knowledge one time. I stole a bag of sugar and someone turned me in. I was out on wood detail, stole the sugar and hid it in the kitchen in our area. The Chinaman came down to get me and took me up to this room and wanted me to sign this paper, a confession. They tried to make me confess to everything. I told them that I didn't steal the sugar. They took me into this room where they had hibachi pots in all four corners. They made me stand on my tip toes. It got hotter and hotter. When I would let my heels touch the floor, this Chinaman would whack me with his damn rifle. Finally I said B_ _ _ S_ _ _ _, I will sign anything you want me to sign. I stole the sugar and hid it. OK? I'm a terrible person for doing that and the Chinese people treat me really good and I shouldn't have done that. Whatever you want for me to sign just lay it out there for me and I'll sign it. There were other things that happened. I could have been killed over the sugar incident.

Q. Frank, can you remember any funny incidents that occurred while in the POW camp? Let me give you an example. In my first book I wrote about some guys who were in the Bataan Death March and were prisoners of war in a Japanese camp for 42 months. One man stole a tuxedo from a Japanese family. He was trying it on when they were called outside for roll call. He fell out with that tuxedo on. The guards didn't know what to do with him so they took him to their officer. When asked what he was doing wearing the tuxedo he said, "Tonight, I'm doing a minstrel show." That night he blacked his face from the stove and sang "Mammy."

A. Frank [laughing] the soldiers from Turkey called "Turks" were in a separate compound. The Chinese were afraid of the Turks. They were only allowed out at certain times when no one else was out. Bob I don't know if you know it or not but the Turks were a tough bunch of guys.

There was a Chinaman we called "Big Stoop." Big Stoop was a mule train driver. If we had anything of value and needed something, Big Stoop would trade with us. I'm not sure if it was Big Stoop's mule or not, but one night the Turks got out. The next day the Turks were selling mule meat.

Another humorous thing that happened was that one of the guys and I got into a fight. There were six of us in this hut. The only guy I remember in that hut was Earl Smith. He was a little taller than I was. We got into a fist fight. We were so weak that when we hit each other, it didn't even hurt. It's like I'm going to bust your nose. I hit him and he said, "It didn't even hurt." We didn't have enough strength to hurt each other. I don't have any idea what started the fight.

Q. Frank, can you describe what an average day was for you in the POW camp?

A. Most days were about the same. We were to keep our huts clean, sweep and maintain the outside area. We would go to the creek and clean our clothes the best we could. We would go out and gather wood for the fires to keep us warm. We slept head to toe, head to toe in a room big enough to handle all of us lying down. If you wanted to turn over, you tell the other guy to turn at the same time. They were mud huts and we slept on the floor.

Q. Did the Chinese issue you any clothes or did you wear the same clothes that you were captured in?

A. They did eventually issue us some clothes. I can't tell you exactly when it happened. We did get some kind of padded uniforms to wear in the wintertime. They issued us some simple uniforms to wear in the summer. The thing that we liked about the Chinese garments was that there were no seams for the lice to get in. Their garments were seamless. No place for lice.

Q. Frank, when were you wounded?

A. I was wounded in Hells Fire Alley on November 29, 1950, the day I was captured. I was hit by shrapnel in both legs. The Chinese didn't provide any medical treatment for these wounds. [For this, Frank was awarded the *Purple Heart Medal*]. They had a hospital up on a hill. When my real serious sickness began, there was a little grade up to the latrine and I couldn't walk up frontwards. You can walk better backwards. It's amazing. When they opened the "so called" hospital, it was in a Temple. The deal was they would treat you up here but you had to get up there under your own power. They would not help you. A guy named Delany threw me over his shoulder like a sack of potatoes… like I said, I weighed 85 pounds more or less, and he carried me up to that so called hospital. I was weak as a cat.

One morning I woke up and felt like I had something in my throat. I coughed and it would not come out. In fact, I pulled out a worm the size of a night crawler. I had these intestinal worms that were eating me alive. I was very fortunate that I had my squad sergeant who had given me advice. He told me that I couldn't smoke cigarettes at night because the Chinese would see the flame and during the day they could see the smoke. He told me that I was going have to chew the tobacco. He told me that I couldn't spit but would have to swallow the juice. The first time I swallowed the juice, it came back up. The sergeant said, "Let me tell you something son, he was a World War II guy, he said, 'If you chew the tobacco and swallow the juice, you will never have worms.' I had these worms in my body so I remembered what he had said. I bummed some cigarette tobacco from somebody, I don't have any idea who it was, chewed it, its nasty, swallowed the juice. The next morning I passed a pile of worms –I mean it was a pile this size [indicating larger than a softball]. It saved my life. So there are things like that, which really stick in my memory.

Another life-threatening experience was when my tongue was swelling and hardening to choke me. One of my guys went to the Chinamen and told them. One of the Chinese came and gave me a very small yellow pill (maybe a vitamin), and it cured me.

Another time I came close to being shot was during our march to Kanggye. One of the Chinaman wanted my snow packs and threatened me with his Thompson. I refused until he came up with something to trade. (My cellmates said "shit," give them to him or he's going to shoot you). He came up with a pig's head and neck to trade with me. We boiled the pig's head. I really thought he was going to shoot me.

Q. Frank, do you have any idea how many men were in your POW camp to start with?

A. No. I don't. When the men died, we buried them behind the billet. After that I don't know what happened to them. I must have been one of the first people to move into that camp and after a while the camp got bigger and bigger. The Chinese would move us around. I understand that they had more than one company of prisoners.

Q. In the winter time you would gather wood. What kind of heat did you have?

A. Bob you know the way they heat in Korea. It was a good heating system. There was a kitchen at the end of the house and they have ducts under the floor. Nothing is wasted. You cook out and the heat comes under the floor to heat the house. One night we were caught on fire from too much heat. We were sleeping on the floor. I poked the fire and apparently it got so hot that it separated the mud from the rock and a flame came up. It was a straw floor and the heat set the straw on fire.

Q. Frank, what do you think helped you to survive as a prisoner of war for 33 months?

A. Well, huh, I believe that I prayed a lot. I believed that I had been raised in a family where you don't give up and you'll not be beaten. My grandfather was a German immigrant. My mother was first-generation German and we were very-very strong willed people. I was really devastated when my wife died. It was the first time that I went into something like I could not beat.

Q. What was your overall health when you were set free?

A. When I was set free I had already passed those worms and it was, I was alive. I don't know how I got down to the Freedom Village.

WESTERN UNION- August 21, 1953
The telegram has faded and difficult to read if photo copied. Here are the contents: Washington, DC: To: Mr. & Mrs Frank J. Kaiser
"The secretary of the Army has asked me to inform you that yur son Sgt. Kaiser, Frank Jr. was returned to military control in Korea and will be returned to the United States by surface transportation at an early date. You will be advised of arrival date. Wm. E. Bergin Major General USA the Adjutant general of the Army."

Q. When they started the peace talks, did the Chinese start to feed you better?

A. A little bit. I think we may have received some Red Cross packages, but I wouldn't swear to that. You would have to talk to my buddy Jack Sheeley. Jack's a super guy and has a wealth of knowledge. He lives in Georgia.

Frank visited the Korean War Memorial in Washington, DC He said he would be 75 in December and that he stood there at the Memorial and cried. It seems that we are becoming more emotional with age doesn't it? Frank, as most veterans, has never talked about his experiences in Korea. He said, "You know, I never talk about it. Most of the guys have never talked about it except lately when Oliver North started doing those war stories. My kids said, 'Dad you were there.' People don't know about the Chosin Reservoir, about the Americans killed in action and those of us who were prisoners, so we just don't talk about it." He said that he

didn't make contact with anyone from Korea for 35 years. It was in 1988 during an EX-POW Reunion in West Virginia.

FREEDOM BRIDGE: This is a picture of the *Freedom Bridge* taken by the author's son Terry VandeLinde, on a revisit to Korea. This bridge is where the American prisoners of war like Frank Kaiser and James DeLong, and Dick Still either walked across or rode in some type of vehicle to their freedom. No one can imagine how these men felt.

When you visit the Korean Memorial in Washington, DC, you will find 19 men dressed in combat gear as if on a patrol as viewed in the next picture. Nineteen times two is 38 representing the 38th Parallel where the North Koreans invaded South Korea on June 25, 1950. This is a very impressive memorial. One of these statues, only one, represents a person. That individual is Col. William E. Weber, (US Army Retired). As a young 25 year-old captain, Weber was the author's company commander in Company K, 187th Airborne Infantry Regiment. While commanding Company K on Hill 342, at Wonju, Korea, on February 14, 1951, Weber was seriously wounded. Weber lost his arm from a hand grenade. 20 minutes later another grenade took off his leg. He was later hit with shrapnel in the back and face. They were unable to evacuate Captain Weber because the 450 paratroopers were surrounded by 2,000 Chinese troops in a fierce battle. Because of the 30 degrees below zero weather, Weber didn't bleed to death. He survived, remained in the army to retire as colonel.

The Korean Memorial was dedicated on July 27, 1995, exactly 42 years after the fighting stopped in Korea. Korean veterans gathered in the heat of the nation's capitol to see their memorial dedicated. Speakers included President William Clinton, Vice President Al Gore and South Korean President Kim Young Sam. Retired Marine General Davis, who was awarded the Medal of Honor in Korea, served as Chairman and the Master of Ceremonies. The war's totals for the US and UN was: 628,833 dead; 470,267 missing; 92,970 captured and 1,064,453 wounded. The wall has an inscription that reads *FREEDOM IS NOT FREE.*

The peace talks began with a meeting at Kaesong on July 10, 1951 with Turner Joy, General Mathew Ridgway's naval chief, in charge for the United Nations. True peace was never achieved, however, on July 25, 1953 the fighting finally ended.

The next building shown is at Panmunjom where the peace talks were later held. This picture was taken by Terry VandeLinde on a revisit to Korea by members of the 187th Airborne Regimental

Combat Team. The two guards shown in the picture are North Korean Soldiers...standing in North Korea. Inside was the table they used. Standing on one side, you were standing in North Korea; the other side of the table was in South Korea. We were required to sign a form before the tour relieving the government of any liability should we be killed or wounded. This is a very dangerous area which could explode at any time. We were asked to dress properly, not in shorts, sandals etc. The guards from North Korea would take pictures and show their people how poor the Americans were. While standing inside the building, one of the guards was picking his nose. Colonel Sullivan from the 8th Army advised us that he did that to insult us. In view from this location was a huge structure that they called *"Freedom Village."* This was a large building with a huge North Korean flag flying and music playing constantly. Actually no one lived there. This was strictly for propaganda. The American soldiers serving at Panmunjom are all volunteers. They are highly trained and ready to engage the enemy at a moment's notice.

Author's note: [I have indicated that I am a veteran of the Korean War, and proud to have served. From time to time, I will hear someone make statement's that really hurts, because I lost 39 friends from my company in Korea. Retired Colonel Bill Weber, [whom I referred to earlier] was one of my company commanders in Korea. He has written an article in the *Airborne Quarterly* that he has given me permission to use. I think it is very appropriate.]

STALEMATE? Forgotten War! By Colonel Bill Weber (Retired)

"Elsewhere in this issue (*Airborne Quarterly*) is a story I've written about my recent visit to Korea and the opportunity provided me by my Korean hosts to visit Hill 342. In that story I relate some of the events that made that Hill and what transpired there a signal event in my life. "Not only did Hill 342 become seared in my memory because of the brave soldiers in my company (Company K) that sacrificed their lives and limbs to take it and hold it-but also because of the way it changed what I thought my life and military career would be like. "However, that is not germane to why I'm writing this!

"Every since our 'Forgotten War,' I have been frustrated (POed is more of what I feel), by the manner in which historians, politicians and the so-called 'pundits' have characterized the war! The one constant that we are presented with is that we fought to 'die for a tie' or that after three years we ended up right where we started. Or that irrespective that we met and defeated all that was brought against us, all that we achieved was a 'stalemate'! **TO THAT I SAY….."BS!"**

"If one looks back and seeks out why we were sent there by our nation and people, you will find that it was to prevent the North Koreans to subjugate by armed force the nation of South

Korea. We were not sent there to conquer North Korea nor to unite the two Koreas! We went to restore freedom to South Korea!

"Yes, once the battle was engaged and political and military opportunism made possible the potential for unification, those who led us took advantage of that. They 'bastardized' our crusade of restoring South Korea's independence and embarked on something we were not sent there for!

"The Chinese entry checkmated that and brought on the fear of a larger war. And we were confronted with a new enemy and the goal of returning to our original mission—that of ensuring that South Korea (the ROK) REMAINED FREE!

"And after three years, and almost 35,000 KIA, 102,000+ WIA and 8,000 MIA, that was achieved and remains so today---- 54+ years later.

"One need only evaluate the ROK today to understand that! One need to only visit the ROK to view a people who are free and who have made of that freedom a form of democracy that should be (and is) envied by other less fortunate nations!

"And so I say, 'How dare they call what we did a STALEMATE---A TIE! I don't give a 'tinker's damn' what the 'pundits' say! We won our Forgotten War' because we did what we were sent to do

"We earned the right to have history record our 'Forgotten War' as a VICTORY! If I had my way we'd have a VK Day just as we have a VE Day and a VJ Day! It is long past time for history to acknowledge that, pundits "et al" notwithstanding, **WE WON OUR 'FORGOTTEN' WAR!** Thanks Colonel Weber.

[This article represents all the brave soldiers who served in Korea].

Author VandeLinde with his former Company
Commander, Col. Bill Weber during a 187th Airborne Reunion.

CHAPTER THIRTEEN

CHAPLAINS

Chaplains have always played an important role in the lives of military men and women, especially during combat. Soldiers who are deployed endure stress stemming from their fears and separation from their loved ones. When counseling is required, the chaplain is there for them. It is the intention of this chapter to provide the basic requirements needed to become a chaplain, in addition to one personal story from Chaplain Bill Leonard, who wore the cross on his collar.

To become a chaplain and serve on active duty, there is a three year enlistment requirement. Chaplain candidates must obtain ecclesiastical endorsements from their faiths. He/she must be qualified spiritually, morally, intellectually and emotionally to serve as a chaplain in the army. They need to be sensitive to religious pluralism and able to provide for the free exercise of religion by all military personnel, their family members and the civilians who work for the army.

A chaplain must be qualified by having completed the following educational requirements. They must have a baccalaureate degree of not less than 120 semester hours. In addition, a master's degree in divinity or a graduate degree in theological studies, including at least 72 hours, is required. Applicants for active duty must be US citizens. A background check will be made and they must pass a physical examination.

Chaplains are not required to go through basic training but they have to attend the Chaplain Basic Officer Leadership Course, which is a 12-week course. The school they attend (the USA

Chaplain Center and School) is located in Fort Jackson, SC. The school is taught in four phases. First is the chaplain initial military training program. If someone who is training to become a chaplain has prior military service, the four-week resident course, which covers map reading, military customs and courtesies and combat survival is optional. Phase one is a two-week course that focuses on Army writing and correspondence. The second and third phase is a two or three-week resident course of instruction in army-specific chaplain duties.

What is a chaplain? The chaplain is a person on duty 24/7. Basically he is a person who serves a person who serves. The Chaplain would be required to follow soldiers all over the world, wherever they are stationed. They are expected to observe the distinctive doctrines of their faiths while also honoring the rights of others to observe their own faiths. The army is a pluralistic environment. Rabbis, ministers, imams and priests serve our soldiers with conviction and commitment. While soldiers are at the heart of a chaplain's ministry, chaplains are also responsible for caring for the soldiers' families, and may often find themselves serving the spiritual needs of sailors, Marines, or airmen. Leading in worship, preaching, administrating the sacraments, or counseling young couples, are all an important part of their duties.

Army chaplains provide for the spiritual needs of army personnel of any denomination. Chaplain Assistants provide much-needed support to the chaplains during missions and everyday activities. A Chaplain assistant primarily provides support for the Unit Ministry Team programs and worship services.

Each Chaplain assistant is required to attend seven weeks of classroom instruction where he or she learns: English grammar, spelling and punctuation; typing and clerical skills; preparing forms and correspondence in army style; roles and responsibilities of army Chaplains and religious history and background. The duties of a Chaplain assistant includes coordinating Unit Ministry

Team activities; maintaining physical security of Unit Ministry Team; safeguarding privileged communications and offerings; arranging religious retreats and memorial ceremonies; and maintaining the chaplain vestments and religious items.

BILL LEONARD

This is an e-mail in response to my request to obtain information from someone who had served as a chaplain. This is an exact report submitted by Bill Leonard.

"Thanks Bob, for your email of 29 March. I will do my best for now...with possible further follow-up emails. You mentioned the 187th Regimental Combat Team (RCT) and behind the lines jumps in Korea. Am sure you must have known my dear friend, Bob Rayburn, chaplain with the 187th, making one of those jumps behind the lines!! Our lives touched in many ways! His daughter, Bronwyn, for example was married to my younger son, Steve Leonard, Army paratrooper, then chaplain, PCA pastor, now retired. The 187th was on our flank for a couple of operations in Korea, but Bob and I were able to get together only once...for about three hours...I hosted him for a hot meal...in one of our 'holy tents' a tent with holes from enemy fire.

"I was very interested in dear Dave Peterson's Carbondale, IL, comments "but chaplains don't serve on the front lines, and they don't carry weapons." Too bad Dave was in the army, not in navy or marines in World War II and Korea. Dave, of course, is correct for the chaplaincy as it is today, but not as it was in much of my own active duty. Years ago, when I was still making trips to Washington regularly, I was sitting with our Navy Chief of Chaplains, talking about "the old days." I mentioned that I was assigned a .45 pistol and a carbine to use in the Korean War and he said "You surely didn't carry weapons as a chaplain, did you?" I replied that I did and I knew how to use them. When the Korean War began I was pasturing Westminster Presbyterian in Newburgh, NY and teaching History, Political Science, Economics for Dr. J. Oliver Buswell in NYC three days a week.

"After my WWII experience I was immediately called back to active duty on August 4, 1950 and assigned to a Navy Transport home-ported in Seattle, taking troops into Pusan. I made one trip and was back in New Orleans picking up another load of troops when I received orders to report ASAP to the 1st Marine Division in Korea. I hitch hiked flights to Seattle where my dear wife

Helen and our three children were living. I then went across the Pacific to Japan where several of us officers were taken to the firing range to check out in the weapons and issued our own weapons. A Methodist chaplain with me at the time was a bit freaked out about this. He didn't know one end of a rifle from the other but I had hunted all my life and weapons were no problem. The two or three chaplains and I in our group were issued .45 pistols and carbines rather that the longer, heavier M-l's to us if needed in Korean combat. Chaplains, our CP's (Command Posts) are being over-run in the middle of the night so we have to be able to protect ourselves and the men around you. I never had to fire my weapon in combat, but was able and ready to do so if necessary.

"In combat as Marine chaplains, our duty station was a forward first aid station, very close to the front lines where men would walk if able, or be carried, for immediate attention, then airlifted (in the old Mash-type bubble canopy helicopters), with a couple of what we called "caskets", one above each wheel in which we strapped one Marine each, sedated, wounded, then ferried back to a rear-area field hospital or hospital ships just offshore. In those forward aid stations, usually a tent…a "holy" one at that, (one with many holes), we did what we could to stabilize the wounded and return them to safer rear areas ASAP. Only emergency surgery was performed under very difficult conditions that were absolutely needed to keep men alive. Chaplains sometimes scrubbing up to help where we could. We were always shorthanded. Of course in those early Korea days, we had no female nurses in those forward aid stations.

"Dave Peterson was right, chaplains were not usually assigned to forward combat areas but in the Marines many times my service was in just such areas in spite of efforts to protect our chaplains. The battlefield was very fluid, changing constantly. I was assigned duty with a combat engineer battalion early in the Korean War. We had one company away from the main battalion for which as chaplain, I was responsible. I remember one time taking my jeep and my chaplain assistant as a driver, and another officer, taking off to locate this company. I was told that it was 'somewhere on the ridgeline north of our position.' The dirt roads of course were open at night many times and we had thousands of refugees flooding thru our lines night and day. They were carrying all they could on their familiar "A frames." The enemy caught on and sent soldiers dressed as refugees, carrying land mines in their packs, mining the roads at night. We lost many men and vehicles until our engineers rigged long booms with iron chain flails on our tanks and vehicles. They would explode the mines before they could do much damage to the main vehicle. Most refugees cooperated gladly when we checked them. Those that did not cooperate were either taken prisoner or shot if trying to flee.

"We got to the ridgeline and found no troops at all, no company of our battalion. We continued over the ridge, dropping down into the valley beyond and continued for nearly an hour. I began to feel strange and told my driver to stop the jeep. Everything was deathly quiet with no usual muttering sounds of the battlefield with no weapons being fired, no troops in sight. We turned around and hightailed it back to the ridge we had crossed over. This time we met Marines on guard. He said "How the H_ _ _ did you get down into that valley. That's no man's land." The forward edge of the 1st Marine Division in that part of Korea at that time was the ridgeline. Things were very fluid and we hit it at a time when our perimeter was not fully set up and we slipped thru in the confusion. (I can hear Dave and my Army sons saying, "Dad that wouldn't have happened in the Army! Nuts, my guess it did.") We could have been killed or captured at any moment but at the time we saw no troops whatever, enemy or friendly. It truly was a 'No Man's Land.'

"I reported to the 1st Marine Division, 20 April 51. Our small twin-engine from Japan landing in a corn field south of the Chosin reservoir, as close as he could get to 1st Marine Division Command Post (corn had been cut, stalks about a foot high). The pilot didn't even turnoff the engines. We jumped out, he turned around, gunned it for takeoff before a mortar came in. President Truman had relieved MacArthur a week earlier and General Ridgeway had taken over. The Chinese had entered the war late in November 1950. The troops at the Chosin Reservoir evacuated in late December 1950. (Many were captured). A new Chinese offensive began April 22nd, TWO DAYS after I reported. We "advanced to the rear", moving our CP to the south. We moved 30 times in 31 days, moving at night and regrouping just north of the Pusan Perimeter, then fighting back north to the 38th Parallel. In our counterattacks (from notes made at the time), we inflicted some 70,000 casualties. I was later detached leaving Korea for Japan 1 Nov 51 then came back to Camp Pendleton, California with General Chesty Puller.

"I didn't get into World War II until May 1944. After a brief time in the states preparing troops for the landing in Europe, I was sent to the Pacific Theater where I took part in the *Leyte* landings and *Philippine* liberation. I was assigned to an attack transport (APA), with Marines and landing craft on board for beach landings."

Authors note: I volunteer as a tour guide at the National D-Day Memorial. This is a way for me to share with people who visit from all over the world, the invasion that was the turning point of World War II. I love sharing the facts to inform everyone about this great event, and about the heroes who sacrificed so much for the freedoms we enjoy. The profits from the sale of "RESPECT," will be donated to the Memorial to assist in future plans. For this reason, I decided to complete this book with an article about the Memorial for your information. This piece was written by Shannon Y. Brooks, Associate for Research for Publications for the D-Day Memorial.

Atop the highest hill in the sleepy little town of Bedford, Virginia stands a massive granite arch. Forty-four-and-a-half feet tall, the monolith frames a pair of soaring peaks-the Peaks of Otter, Bedford's claim to fame for many years. That was before

Bedford's sons and husbands marched away to war, before anyone here knew where Normandy was or what would happen there that would change this tiny town and the entire world. The arch that stands here now tells it all with the single word engraved upon its brow: *"Overlord."*

Home to the National D-Day Memorial, Bedford now knows only too well the significance of that word. Operation Overlord, the official name for the invasion of occupied France, commenced on June 6, 1944, a date known ever since simply as D-Day. Among the 150,000 soldiers transported across the English Channel to establish an Allied foothold in enemy territory were some thirty sons of Bedford belonging to Company A of the 116th Infantry Regiment, 29th Division. Assigned to land as part of the first wave of soldiers at Omaha Beach, Company A soon found itself decimated by shellfire, mines, obstacles, and deadly machinegun fire from intact enemy positions. Within half an hour of landing, the unit was down to half-strength. By day's end, only 15 from the company were capable of fighting and 19 sons of Bedford had lost their lives.

With the population of just over 3,200 citizens in 1944, Bedford's loss represented the highest per capita loss nationwide and a devastating blow to the close-knit town. Across the country communities and families everywhere received the same terrible news in the weeks just after D-Day; some 2,300 Americans lost their lives on that day alone. As time passed, many towns erected monuments of their own to memorialize their fallen, yet there remained no national testament to their collective valor, no national gathering-place to commemorate their sacrifice.

The 50th anniversary of D-Day in 1994 saw a surge of interest in creating just such a place. D-Day survivor and Roanoke native Bob Slaughter had long dreamed of a place where area veterans could gather to pay homage to their comrades and reflect on their experiences in Normandy. His plans for a small, regional memorial quickly gained support and evolved into plans for a national memorial located in the little town with the terrible record. On June 6, 2001, the National D-Day Memorial was dedicated in Bedford, Virginia. Over 24,000 people attended the ceremony, including President George W. Bush and hundreds of D-Day veterans from around the globe. The Memorial's motto: Commemorating Their Valor, Fidelity, and Sacrifice. Its mission: to educate generations about the lessons and legacy of D-Day.

The nine-acre memorial fulfills that purpose on a grand scale, guiding visitors through the D-Day experience symbolically across three plazas, reminding them of D-Day's epic quality and human dimensions simultaneously. Lush gardens and bronze portrait busts of Eisenhower's commanders depict the months of planning and training in England before D-day. From here, the sound of crashing water leads to a beach tableau with bronze soldiers struggling heroically towards shore as simulated enemy fire rips across the water. Close by, bronze plaques bearing the names of over 4,400 Allied soldiers killed in action at D-Day line the walls. Overhead, Victory Arch looms large over Final Tribute, a silent reminder of the sacrifice that accompanied Allied success.

Since the dedication, the Memorial continues to fulfill its educational and commemorative mission. Nearly 80,000 people visit the Memorial annually, approximately 10,000 of whom are students participating in the Memorial's Hands-On-History program, an interactive experience sharing the details of daily life for D-Day soldiers and citizens on the home front. The Memorial also presents most two dozen special events each year, including commemorations, lectures, family events, and concerts. Dozens of D-Day veterans' oral histories have been collected by the Memorial as part of its work with the Library of Congress Veterans History Project, and Memorial volunteers contribute over 14,000 hours of service annually.

From guided tours to community outreach, original research to public commemoration, the National D-Day has committed itself to ensuring that the legacy of what was fought for, what was gained, and what was lost so long ago on far-off shores is neither forgotten nor taken for granted. For the living who gave so much, and the fallen who gave their all, it is the least we can do.

For more information about the National D-Day Memorial, please visit our website at www.dday.org or call (800) 351-DDAY

INDEX

www.ingramcontent.com/pod-product-compliance
Lightning Source LLC
Chambersburg PA
CBHW060320100426
42812CB00003B/828